THE URBAN FACE OF
MISSION

THE URBAN FACE OF
MISSION

MINISTERING THE GOSPEL IN A
DIVERSE AND CHANGING WORLD

HARVIE M. CONN
AND OTHERS

EDITED BY
MANUEL ORTIZ AND SUSAN S. BAKER

PUBLISHING
P.O. BOX 817 • PHILLIPSBURG • NEW JERSEY 08865-0817

Page design and typesetting by Lakeside Design Plus

Printed in the United States of America

Library of Congress Cataloging-in-Publication Data

The urban face of mission : ministering the Gospel in a diverse and changing world / Harvie M. Conn and others ; edited by Manuel Ortiz and Susan S. Baker.
    p. cm.
  Includes bibliographical references and index.
  ISBN-10: 0-87552-401-X (pbk.)
  ISBN-13: 978-0-87552-401-6 (pbk.)
   1. City missions. 2. Missions—Theory. I. Conn, Harvie M. II. Ortiz, Manuel, 1938– III. Baker, Susan S., 1945–
  BV2653.U68 2002
  253'.09173'2—dc21
                                                   2002072402

Contents

103576

INTRODUCTION

MANUEL ORTIZ WITH WILLIAM S. BARKER
AND SAMUEL T. LOGAN JR.

There are so many things to recognize and celebrate about Harvie Conn's life and his contribution to the church, but one thing that was extremely important to him was God's concern for the poor. He taught, preached, and lived in such a consistent manner that it seemed to be a high calling for him. The city was not just a place where people lived; it was also a place that housed many disenfranchised people, especially here in the United States. The city was not just a place or a topic for sociological discussion; it was where many of those who were ignored lived, and Harvie was concerned that we not ignore the people dear to the heart of God. This was a priority embraced by my brother. Justice was at the forefront of his thinking. His concern for globalization was not just a matter of religious pluralism and multiethnicity; it had to do with the poor who were moving into the cities and the need for ethnic and socioeconomic reconciliation.

As a missionary in Korea, he worked with prostitutes in the red-light district because he knew that women were being oppressed, and they were usually the ones who were poor and powerless. He continued to remind the church of its treatment of women, and at times this caused him some deep heartache and conflict. As many of us know, Harvie did not like confrontation, but it seems that his calling to proclaim justice and justification brought him many uncomfortable and sleepless nights.

1

As I reviewed his papers and letters, I noticed numerous letters to the president and the dean of the seminary about raising money for minorities, particularly African-Americans and Hispanics. He wanted to provide theological education that would equip our brothers and sisters in the city to be more effective ministers. Contextualization was not just a theme to be discussed in mission circles; it had to do with reaching the unreached, especially in our urban and poor communities. Harvie realized that systemic evil existed in Christian institutions, and he wanted to bring the gospel to bear on the hearts of administrators and faculty. He knew that racism and sexism were sins against creation and the gospel, and it was no small thing to him.

Harvie found that the best way to confront injustices and instill compassion for the poor was to write books and articles on this subject, to lecture at the invitation of churches and educational institutions, and to live in community with his family. His many books and articles unreservedly promoted conviction, repentance, and transformation.

Another important aspect of Harvie's life and work was his love for the Word of God. In all his work, both writing and teaching, he pursued exegesis along the lines of Westminster Seminary's tradition. Much of his work concerning the city came out of his exegetical work in the gospel of Luke. Dr. Conn realized how important this New Testament text is to understanding the city. Here the good news flows from Galilee to Jerusalem. His thinking and writing was always in submission to the authority of Scripture.

This volume is intended to communicate some of Harvie's concerns for world evangelization. It is integrative, and therefore the themes of justice and the poor may be highlighted more in one essay than in another. As Dr. Baker and I started to assemble the authors for this volume, we looked particularly for those who were friends and colaborers in this march toward justice and mission. Matching the basic themes with the right authors was not an easy task, and we found ourselves missing a few authors who could not participate. We thought that the major themes listed in the table of contents would both bring honor to Harvie's work and provide students ministering in the city and in mission with a helpful and useful text for ministry.

I am writing this on the second anniversary of Harvie's death, and my wife and I have been thinking about him and how he loved my children and wanted to see them before his death, especially Elizabeth. Early this morning, Erik Davis, the comptroller at Westminster, was also reminded of Harvie's farewell, and he sent us a reminder through the Internet. I have included it here in order to provide another picture of this wonderful servant of God:

Friends,

Today I enjoyed some delicious fresh tomatoes, as many of us do at this time of year. Sometimes the mind is interesting when it comes to loved ones, as memories surface when one least expects them. As I savored the flavor of a tomato tonight, I remembered how every year Harvie would share his exquisite Wayne Avenue tomato harvest with the Westminster community. He would come into each office, short of breath, with armloads full of huge tomatoes in paper bags. They were the kind of tomatoes you could bite into like an apple, no need for salt or pepper. With his Harvie chuckle, he would tell us how he and Dorothy would never be able to eat all of them, so he wanted to share them with us. It was part of every August until a few years ago.

As I reflect on it, I realize that this story is symbolic of Harvie's life among us. He was a prolific harvester of souls, never content to keep his Lord to himself, eager to share the bounty of the Gospel with anyone, and always with that trademark laugh. Harvie understood the need to multiply himself, as a seed, so that future generations would carry his torch of Christ's love for the poor and the cities of this world. His zeal for the Kingdom was as infectious as his laugh. None of us who knew Harvie will be the same again. I miss him especially tonight. Wow, it'll be two years tomorrow that Harvie left us. Let's thank the Lord again for His work through our friend.

Erik[1]

In order to provide yet another window into the life of Harvie Conn, I have also included a Christmas letter from Harvie to Dr. Edmund Clowney and his wife, which Dr. Clowney forwarded to me for use in this volume. It reads as follows:

Dear Friends,

Almost two thousand years ago, John gave the world his news bulletin: "The Word became flesh and lived for a while among us" (John 1:14). And, with John, we still add our own personal amen: "We have seen his glory, the glory of the one and only Son."

The 1980s are almost gone. The Swaggarts and the Bakkers come and go. Papers herald the end of the Cold War. But the glory of the one and only Son does not fade.

Two hundred and eighty-nine million new Christians in these past ten years, with a projected figure of 308 million more to appear in the next ten years. In the past decade we have seen what the scholars predicted: there are now more Christians in Asia, Latin America, and Africa than in the Anglo-Saxon world. More Christians speak Swahili or Spanish, Hindi or Chinese, than English or French or German.

And our life continues on, far less dramatic, far more mini-textured—chronicling the history of the church around the world; sticking in a few warning pins here and there; continuing to teach and write and stir; enjoying worship in a multi-ethnic church. Children to remind us we're getting older, students at Seminary as excited as ever about what God can do in His world.

With the joys and frustrations—bodies that no longer do what they did five years ago; churches that still major in minors and minor in majors; a drug epidemic that sweeps the neighborhood in which you live. Not enough progress in sanctification, not enough time for neighbors and friends, not enough of "enough."

And in it all, God still says, "I'm not finished with you yet." The mighty Lord of Calvary who turns Europe's history upside

4

down in a month still has time to handle our washing machines that don't work and our tempers that don't cool. Old friends touch our lives with a phone call or a card at Christmas. And our lives stop for a minute for perspective. After all the sermons are preached, all the articles written, all the meals prepared, the bottom line is the same: Our God reigns.

May you know His reign in a special way this coming year.

The Conns—Dorothy, Harvie, and "the children"[2]

The first essay of this book is a lecture by Dr. Conn on the importance of integrating theology and mission. He was vehemently opposed to what he termed "academic apartheid"—separating the two disciplines into different academic departments. He reminds us that missions is the mother of theology. This selection should be helpful and insightful for those who are serving in higher education, training Christians in local communities.

Finally, William Barker, the former academic dean at Westminster, and Samuel Logan, the president of Westminster, share their thoughts about Harvie.

Harvie as a Teacher—
Words from William S. Barker

Serving as academic dean at Westminster Seminary after 1991, I was privileged to know Harvie Conn as a teacher through my meetings with him and through student feedback during his final eight years of classroom instruction. During the preceding five years, I knew him as a faculty colleague. But my memories of him and his unique manner of communicating go all the way back to when I was a university student and he was a seminarian assisting in an Orthodox Presbyterian church in New Jersey. Back then, in the 1950s, he was a lanky redhead whose smile and laugh were already unforgettable.

My impressions were renewed a decade or two later, when I heard him lecturing at Covenant College, describing his unusual experiences in Korea. Humor and seriousness were blended as he modestly used the second person in order not to call attention to himself, but rather to the Lord's work through the gospel: "You are in the red-light district in Seoul. . . ." Some years later, I played a part in having him speak at an urban missions conference at Covenant Seminary, where he emphasized the need for contextualization in cross-cultural communication. In addition to his own vivid stories, he was not afraid to use contemporary cinema to stimulate thought and discussion, as all the participants in that urban missions institute attended Martin Scorsese's film *Taxi Driver* with him.

Harvie was indefatigable in his care for his students. Even in the year after his retirement from full-time teaching, before his death from cancer, with the burdens of his own treatments, of his limited eyesight, of his wife Dorothy's failing health, and of his continued reading and writing projects, he made great efforts to meet with students, counseling them spiritually as well as guiding their research. His students' course evaluations reflected his special sensitivity to African students, Koreans, women, and ethnic minorities in the United States. As African-American pastor Wilbert Richardson said at Harvie's memorial service, his teaching manifested the joy of the Lord, humble prayer, and theological knowledge.

Often wearing bib overalls and punctuating his lectures and chapel messages with his memorable laugh, Harvie could surprise some listeners with his theological insights. His faculty colleagues recognized him as one of the most brilliant intellects in their company. This was demonstrated in his editorship of the Westminster faculty volume on *Inerrancy and Hermeneutic,* which included his introductory essay and a chapter on "Normativity, Relevance, and Relativism,"[3] and in his participation in the periodic meetings of the faculty's hermeneutics discussion group. He readily handled the difficult issues of interpreting Scripture, but uppermost in his heart was the gospel's application. He began his time on the faculty of Westminster as a professor of apologetics in 1972, but concluded it in 1999 as professor of missions, teaching a variety of subjects, including the Korean-language section of preaching. If his retirement period had been longer, he would have written on the evangelization of Muslims and on the care of Alzheimer's patients.

Harvie could become impatient with church squabbles and administrative or academic controversies, just as he was impatient with any efforts to honor him with recognition. In one of his final published pieces, he commented on the death of two outstanding students headed for the mission field who were killed in an automobile crash caused by a drunken driver. Referring to Moses' words in Psalm 90, Harvie commented: "Moses is praying for an awareness of how few are the days of human life. Psalm 39:4 comes close to his intention: 'Show me, O Lord, my life's end and the number of my days. Let me know how fleeting is my life.'" He then spoke of Henry Martyn, a nineteenth-century missionary to India, who died at age 31 after only six years of missionary work and Bible translation: "In his diary were these words written upon his arrival: 'Now let me burn out for God.'"

When he was dying, Harvie said, "Soon I shall walk by sight; now I have been walking by faith." A missionary colleague from Korea, Ted Hard, commented at Harvie's memorial service that Harvie's sight was weak, but his faith was strong. So also were his hope and love, love for his Lord and for all for whom the Lord died and rose again. I trust that Harvie Conn will be unforgettable to those of us who knew him as a teacher because he reflected in word and in deed the Master, our Lord Jesus Christ.

Harvie's Significance as a Missiologist— Words from Samuel T. Logan Jr.

What does it mean for the American church that there are now seven times as many Anglicans in Nigeria as Episcopalians in the United States? What does it mean for American Presbyterians that there are now four times as many Presbyterians in South Korea as in the United States? What does it mean for all Christians that we make up approximately 30 percent of the world's population? What does it mean for all Americans that we are 6 percent of the world's population, yet control 59 percent of the world's wealth?

These are the kinds of questions that Harvie Conn brought to the table—or, more accurately, to faculty meetings—at Westminster Theological Seminary. This institution, perhaps more than most American theological seminaries, is intensely aware of its past and its heritage. We are confessionally defined by documents written in the middle of the seventeenth century. We are institutionally defined by ecclesiastical events of the late 1920s. How do we sing the Lord's song in "the strange land" that is now the twenty-first century? How do we take appropriate account of where and when we are without compromising the "old, old story of Jesus and His love?"

Harvie Conn, more than any other individual that I have ever known, pressed these questions upon me in both personal and professional ways. He continually insisted that it is necessary, but never sufficient, for God's people to seek to understand "the unchanging Word." It is always required that we bring that Word to bear upon our "changing world," and that we start this process with ourselves. Although Harvie regularly teased me about my admiration for Jonathan Edwards, no one in my acquaintance better exemplified Edwards's famous dictum, "No light in the understanding is good which does not produce holy affection in the heart."

And no one in my acquaintance ever embodied in life more fully than Harvie the things of which he spoke and wrote. Shining the light of the gospel on dark places of all sorts was Harvie's specialty—in the classroom, on the written page, in the neighborhoods of Philadelphia, on the streets of Seoul. He was passionate about bringing *every* thought captive to Christ, including (perhaps especially) those thoughts which had become part of this or that theological tradition. And he *did* it . . . in his life, as much as in his words.

In all of this, Harvie Conn was the paradigm of what a missionary/missiologist should be. He labored tirelessly toward the goal of seeing all people everywhere bow before Jesus, rather than before any human creation—even if that creation was modified by the adjective *theological*. He went personally to the people whose knees were defiant—from Seoul prostitutes to seminary professors—and challenged them lovingly to recognize the sweet lordship of Jesus.

That is the purpose (and I believe the accomplishment) of the essays in this volume. Voices from around the world call all of us to think again about what the unchanging word of Scripture really does say about the changing world in which we live—a changing world in which the center of Christianity has shifted dramatically (10 percent of the adult population in Scotland attends church regularly, while 70 percent of the adult population in the Philippines attends church regularly) and in which white, male, American assumptions about the world (most of Harvie's colleagues at both Westminster and in the Orthodox Presbyterian Church were white American males) are increasingly being challenged by evangelical Christians who are different in one or more of those categories.

This book is, therefore, part of Harvie's legacy to the church of Jesus Christ. There is always more light to spring forth from the infallible and inerrant Word of God. We all need to become *more* like the Savior whose name we bear. The Lord used Harvie Conn in mighty ways to spread the sanctifying power of the two-edged sword of Scripture. It is my confident hope that he will do the same with these essays that are dedicated to the triune God in thanksgiving for the life and ministry of Harvie Maitland Conn.

1

MISSION, MISSIONS, THEOLOGY, AND THEOLOGICAL EDUCATION

HARVIE M. CONN

Editors' note: The following is a previously unpublished manuscript of a lecture Harvie presented at McMaster Divinity School in Ontario, Canada, on February 4, 1992. It is included in this volume in order to give the readers at least a small sense of where Harvie's heart and mind were leading him on these important issues.

Suppose with me, for a minute, that you are a missions professor at Urbana, a situation equivalent to a chocolate lover being hired as a food taster at Hershey's. You are talking to a university student who is serious about overseas ministry. He is asking about the missions program at your seminary. "Is your program theoretical or practical?" he asks. "I mean, how much time will I spend in the classroom? Do you have an internship program? I'm not interested in learning about missions. I want to do it." At this point he adds, "Can I major in missions? I'm not much interested in theology or church history or that kind of stuff. I just want to get some basics in how to do missions."

How would you answer?

Suppose with me, for another minute, that you are sitting at the lunch table in the dining hall of a large seminary. You have come to give a special lecture on missions in the classroom of one of your friends. The purpose of your presence is unknown to the others at the table.

The conversation at lunch is an animated carryover from previous class experiences of the morning. The Anglo-Saxon students at the table fill the air with magical theological words like *hermeneutic, redaction criticism,* and *narrative theology,* and big names like Gutiérrez, Fiorenza, and Gadamer.

Finally, one of the students notes your silence, introduces himself, and inquires as to your presence. You respond, "I'm a teacher of missions; I'm here to give a special lecture on the missionary challenge of the twenty-first century." The silence at the table is deafening. Students search desperately for something pleasant to say. "Are you giving a slide show?" someone asks with a chuckle. Everyone laughs and the conversation returns quickly to the "reality" of the classroom.

What has happened?

I see these conversations as suggestive epiphanies, clues, tip-offs to a kind of non–South African academic apartheid: the isolation of mission from theology, of theology from mission, of church from world. I see my task in this presentation as threefold: (1) sketch out why there is this apartheid, (2) suggest some current modifications going on now, and (3) offer some practical suggestions to encourage the process of modification. Please note my modesty in all this. I deliberately use words like *sketch, suggest, modify, encourage,* and *process.*

Academic Apartheid: The Heritage of the Past

Both table conversations I have described suffer from the same historical problems—the compartmentalization of mission and theology and a misunderstanding of both. We will now look briefly at both.

Mission Marginalized

In the pre-Constantinian centuries of the church, the dialogue between mission and theological formulation was an invigorating one. *Dialogue,* in fact, may not be the best word to describe the relationship. Even a term like *interaction* may create too many barriers. Theology's agenda was shaped by the church's mission in the world. And a mission motivation to reach the Greeks drove what we now call the church's theologians to in-depth study of Christology. Was Justin Martyr's apologetic to the Jews a missionary theology or a theological mission? Should one call the interplay of Origen and Clement of Alexandria with Greek philosophy mission or theology?[1]

The church had not yet become a world-conquering majority; it did not even possess the Empire's Good Housekeeping seal of approval. The missionizing, minority church found itself in what David Bosch calls an "emergency situation."[2] In this situation, mission was "the mother of theology."

In the years that followed, the two began to drift apart. As Europe became Christianized and Christianity became the established religion in the Roman Empire and beyond, the "regions beyond" horizon of mission began to recede and theology restricted itself to the church or, at most, Christendom. Missions increasingly looked like the religious arm of politics, the bearer of power and culture. And theology lost more and more of its "on-the-road" quality.

There were exciting interruptions to these tendencies. The springtime of missions in the thirteenth century saw the formation of the Franciscan and Dominican orders and their missionary thrusts into places like Mongolia and China. At the end of the fifteenth century, the sea routes to India and the Americas were discovered. "Gold and God" drove explorers and evangelists into an alien and larger new world.

Protestantism's response to an enlarged world was mixed also. While Calvin continued to restrict his understanding of mission largely to the church and Luther railed too often against Jew and Muslim "Turks," the Anabaptists broke through the links between church and society and sought to liberate once more the outsider orientation of missions and theology. Lutheran Pietists and Moravians followed that same direction in the seventeenth century.

I have called these directions "interruptions" in the marginalization of mission. A second historical factor diminished their significance. That second factor was the shift that took place in theology.

Theology Abstracted

Edward Farley, in his 1983 book *Theologia*, sees a massive historical change in our understanding of theology. In its earliest form, theology was seen as the reflective wisdom of the believer, a self-conscious habit or disposition, a *habitus*, of the human heart.[3]

But, he continues, with the coming of the universities in the twelfth century, that definition began to change. A new emphasis began to grow: theology as *scientia*, as a theoretical discipline. The practitioners of theology began to narrow: from believer to scholar, from lay people to clergy. And with this emerging paradigm of theology, the gap between theory and practice began to grow.

I myself suspect that the roots of this change lie deeper in time than Farley underlines. The dialogue of the early church with Greek philosophy left its mark on more than the Greeks:

Clement of Alexandria came to Christianity by way of philosophy. Could one expect such a man to see easily the Christian as anyone other than "true Gnostic"? Origen was a professional philosopher. Like a dentist who looks at faces and sees mouths, he looked at Christianity and saw the *paideia* of humanity, Greek wisdom at the bottom line of divine providence.[4]

Can we trace at least the partial beginnings of theology as a scientific discipline to these earlier days? Theology already had begun, however faintly, to search for essences untouched by the realities of the cultural and social context. The goal of theology was emerging as a rational display of the Platonic ideal. The Latin Fathers, with their legal training, reinforced this perception. The Cappadocian Fathers, Basil of Caesarea and the two Gregorys, in the second half of the fourth century, carried it on. In the language of Werner Jaeger, "They ... think of theology as a great science based on supreme scholarship and as a philosophical pursuit of the mind."[5]

True theology has begun to take on the shape of *scientia*, the liberating search of the mind for essence, core, unhindered by any kind of historical, geographical, or social qualifier. Theological pursuits are freed to become the Platonic search for abstract, rational principles.

According to Farley, the Enlightenment structuralized and modified further the two definitions of theology. And, in doing so, I would add, it reinforced further the apartheid isolation of theology from mission. Theology as cognitive *habitus*, as the individual quest for the wisdom of redemption, became the practical know-how necessary to ministerial work. Theology as disciplined *scientia* became a technical and specialized scholarly undertaking. Farley labels this "systematic theology."[6]

The institutional setting in which this occurred was the university. And the schooling model that it left was what Farley calls the "four-fold pattern" of Bible or text, church history, systematic theology, and practical theology or application.

Under the influence of Schleiermacher in the nineteenth century, this pattern triumphed in Europe and eventually North America.[7] "'Practical' theology became a mechanism to keep the church going, while the other disciplines were examples of 'pure' science." The two elements were held together by what Farley calls the "clergy paradigm."[8]

Isolationism and Redefinitions Sealed

This grossly simplistic history leaves us with our present frustrations over the identity of both theology and mission. The operative definition of theology with which I suspect most of us realistically function is that of an academic discipline that is clergy-oriented. And there are other dimensions that sound like caricatures without the nuances I cannot provide now: a church-centered theological agenda whose horizons are often limited still by a flat world—European, North American; a form of schooling whose socializing process is largely middle- and upper-class; a search for some theological bottom line of biblical Essences (with a capital E), without attention to the social and cultural dimensions that led us to that bottom line; a cognitive struggle for truth that marginalizes the missiological demands of that truth.

In the same vein, mission has been touched and even reshaped by this history. The passage of the gospel from its Western base across oceans in the nineteenth and twentieth centuries has underlined the geographical border-crossing character of the church's mission. And, in reflection on that history, mission is often called missions. In more recent history, its place as an academic discipline has been recognized with a new title, missiology. But even this term is restricted by its recent geographical history. For many, missiology remains a science of and for the foreign missionary.

Its place in theological education remains debated. For some, the study of mission is appended to one of the existing four disciplines of the school. Following the lead of Schleiermacher, this is usually practical theology. Others, following the tradition stabilized by Gustav Warneck, see it as a theological discipline in its own right and speak of missiology. A third approach, followed mainly in Britain, "was to abandon the teaching of missiology as a separate subject and expect other theological disciplines to incorporate the missionary dimension into the entire field of theology."[9]

But, in spite of all these approaches, by the 1950s mission or missions or missiology still sounded too often like some forgotten, marginalized, and peripheral "department of foreign affairs" for the seminary. In the United States in 1950, the Association of Professors of Mission came into existence. But, argues Pierce Beaver, its appearance was "not as an expression of the old missionary triumphalism but as an attempt to build a lifeboat for floundering brothers and sisters."[10] In 1956 there appeared the "Study of Theological Education in the United States and Canada." It was commissioned by the Association of Theological Schools and directed by H. Richard Niebuhr. It excluded missiology as a subject field.[11]

The second half of this century began, then, with theology and mission still appearing to function as very distant cousins in the theological encyclopedia. And mission particularly, in that relationship, was a colorful extra, still looking for its place in the theological sun. European studies may underline its theoretical side, North American research its pragmatic dimension, but it still sounds like an overnight guest shuffling around in bedroom slippers in the palace of the theological seminary.

Encouragements for a New Understanding

I am hopeful this situation may now be changing. From the missiological side, there are those like Norman Thomas describing the present moment as "a *kairos,* a critical time, for missiology."[12] David Bosch sees characteristics now coming together for the emergence of a new, postmodern paradigm in missiology.[13]

From the theological side, there are hints at reinvestigation. Edward Farley's continuing study of the nature of theology[14] appears to be stimulating a new look at theological study. And there is Max Stackhouse's 1988 book, *Apologia.*[15] The work is a summary of more than five years of ongoing theological dialogue at Andover-Newton Theological Seminary. The interaction has revolved around the themes of contextualization, globalization, and mission. The nature of theology itself and its relation to truth and justice have been opened to fascinating scrutiny by the seminary. And by us.[16]

"Outside" Realities

The partner, the discussion stimulator, in this new ferment is no longer simply metaphysics or philosophy alone, as in the past. New partners are shaping a new dialogue.

The reality of a global church is intruding on North American theologizing. A shift in the Christian axis has occurred within the last two decades. And the new center of ecclesiastical gravity has moved from the Northern to the Southern Hemisphere. To modify slightly the language of Gerald Anderson, the old centers of male, Anglo-Saxon theological influence and church growth in Europe and North America are becoming the new peripheries. And the new centers of vitality and creativity in theological construction are now coming from women, the African-American community of North America, Asia, Africa, and Latin America.[17]

Theological and missiological ferment flows from this new reality. New names bombard our curriculum—feminist theology, black theology, liberation theology, minjung theology, African theology. The world we had relegated to the missiological has spilled over into the theological.

There are the sociopolitical dimensions that also bring theology and mission closer together. Questions like power and powerlessness, the oppressor and the oppressed, are not only expanding the horizons of mission; they are shaping the theologies of Jürgen Moltmann, Rosemary Radford Ruether, and James Cone. Theology and mission are turning to one another as new questions require combined wisdom. How do we live and witness to our faith under conditions of racist oppression and sexist authoritarianism? What do we do in the face of Muslim strictures against baptism and church building? How should Christian discipleship face the suppression of human rights, the ecological crisis, secularization? Does the Bible demand we be Sandanistas or Contras? Or neither? Is liberation a neglected biblical category for interpreting the Atonement in an African-American context?

The vast scale of human poverty in traditional "mission fields" presses mission and theology alike. Can missions alone address the intolerable fact that two-thirds of our human family go to bed hungry every night? What will our theology say and do about an alleged 15,000 people who starve to death every day? Will it be theology or mission that deals with the 20 percent of the human family said to control 80 percent of the world's resources?

And what of growing apathy in the U.S. toward the homeless? Estimates of that number have ranged from 300,000 to three million.[18] The *New York Times* reports that "Americans are beginning to turn away from the outstretched hands, numbed by the severity of the problem and confused about how to respond."[19] Missionary compassion no longer demands border crossing; theological reflection can no longer be done from the balcony at a safe distance.

Another outside reality is the awesome size of the world's non-Christian population. In Jesus' time, it numbered 250 million. In 1992, out of a total world population of 5.4 billion, it is estimated that 3.6 billion are not Christians—over thirteen times as many non-Christians as when Jesus preached the Sermon on the Mount.[20]

Forty years ago, this statistic would have been quoted in a New Hampshire congregation's foreign missions conference. Now we say it in the shadow of a Sikh temple in British Columbia, in the face of a Muslim community of over two million in the U.S.

And we say it in the face of the increasing secularization of the Western world. In Canada's Protestant denominations over the past forty years, there has been a drop-off rate in church attendance of 35 percent, 40 percent in Roman Catholic parishes. In Canada, argues Glenn Smith of Montreal, "The moral consensus of a society increasingly bypasses the traditional values of the church"[21] in national debates over social policy and morality.

In response to this situation, mission statespeople like Lesslie Newbigin have returned from a lifetime in India to now ask, "Can the West be saved?"[22] They call for a new thrust in mission that will unlock the geographical "elsewhere" character of that concept and develop a domestic missiology for North America, "mission in reverse." And they are not afraid to question the role that theological education has played in hindering the development of a "hermeneutic of the gospel." Newbigin observes, "We have lived for so many centuries in the 'Christendom' situation that ministerial training is almost entirely conceived in terms of the pastoral care of existing congregations."[23] If I read it right, the book *Apologia*, by Max Stackhouse,[24] comes partly as a response to these realities. And one of the centers of its interest is the role of theology and theological education in this new situation.

"Insider" Reflections

Out of this context, the study agendas of mission and theology are converging in perhaps a new way. And the questions they ask together have a strong element of self-introspection. They give off loud whispers that the questions can and may lead to new self-understandings, to new mergers and tighter connections between mission and theology. We will now discuss two of these agenda issues.

One is *contextualization*. The topic, we note, was thrust on the church by the new realities of its truly global mission character. And, significantly, the word first appeared in studies of the Theological Education Fund of the World Council of Churches in 1972.[25] Mission and theological education were brought together by a joint issue—the emergence of local theologies spawned by the mission of the church.

In study circles associated with missiology, evangelical contextualization discussions have moved in directions that might be expected—the relation of the gospel and culture,[26] church planting appropriate to the setting,[27] and communication issues.

Within the North American, Anglo-Saxon, conservative-evangelical movement, these discussions have often been controlled by the fear of syncretism. Will the gospel core be lost? Can theology become so local that its universal element is sacrificed? The question is a legitimate one. But the danger in dealing with it is that contextualization can become a platform for an apologetical dialogue on Western issues of the past—for example, liberalism versus this or that.

Discussions then are sidetracked from creative theologizing and the impact of contextualization studies on our own self-understanding. We return, in the name of contextualization, to earlier indigenization discussions, to questions of appropriate worship patterns and styles of leadership. In those instances where the debate on hermeneutics has been reopened, sometimes one feels the answers proposed are not really touched by the implications of contextualization, and that we have moved very little.[28] One also senses that North American discussions in such circles are frequently imprimatur debates on some "foreigner's" theological proposals.

Some of this is understandable. The past isolation of mission from theology has left missionaries and missiology with little enthusiasm for theological discussions in Africa or Korea or Indonesia. The pragmatic focus of North American missiological education has kept us closer to the how-to-do-it area of church planting and administration. And the isolation of North American white churches from Hispanic and African-American communities has kept us from listening to the creative theological formulations now emerging from these minority sources.

To some degree, I am not encouraged either by the attention paid to this issue from the theological side of white North America. Feminist and liberation theologies are gaining attention in mainline circles, far less so in ours. Theological developments from the so-called Third World appear even more rarely. Academic writing that networks between Christianity and non-Christian religions is proliferating. But again it is often the object for study of a selected few on faculties. And those selected few are too frequently in the growing academic dumpster called "practical theology." Farley's response would be, "I told you so."

Again, these directions are understandable. The isolation of theology from mission has left theologians with the sense that many of these issues are missiological issues, or even ethical topics, but not "real" theology.

At the same time, contextualization is there to collapse both sides of our watertight compartments. In my judgment, it has yet to force our Western church worlds into the richer dialogue that I had hoped for in an earlier day.[29] But I remain optimistic when I hear theologians like Tite Tiénou combine both worlds and say that "a theology that communicates is always missiological."[30] Or when Raimo Harjula speaks of theology as "the critical reflection on, articulation and

20

translation of God's self-disclosure . . . in and for a given historical and cultural context."[31] In these functional definitions I hear something more than theology as the result of some missionless study. Theology begins to sound like something more than the "production of theological goods which are marketed to consumers."[32]

In the last decade especially, another discussion has intruded into North American theological circles that may impact further this isolationism of mission and theology. I speak of *globalization.*

In one sense, globalization is intimately linked with earlier contextualization discussions. Like them, its impetus has come from theological education, specifically the Association of Theological Schools (ATS). Like them, it seeks also to pay serious attention to a world context. It recognizes the interdependency of the human community in the twentieth century and the pain of that world community—the realities of hunger and homelessness, oppression and spiritual lostness.

Like them also, it would appear to recognize the failures of the Western church in the past—the dominance of Western culture over the church; the effort of the Anglo-Saxon church to occupy a center seat in the world church community.

With contextualization discussions also, it seeks to promote a holistic dimension. The ATS offers a fourfold typology for globalization:

> For some, globalization means the church's universal mission to evangelize the world, i.e., to take the message of the gospel to all people, all nations, all cultures, and all religious faiths. Second, there is the idea of globalization as ecumenical cooperation between the various manifestations of the Christian church throughout the world. This includes a growing mutuality and equality between churches in first and third world countries. It involves a new openness to and respect for the great variety of local theologies that are springing up within the church in its various concrete situations. Third, globalization sometimes refers to the dialogue between Christianity and other religions. Finally, globalization refers to the mission of the church to the world, not only to convert and to evangelize, but to improve and develop the lives of the millions of poor, starving, and politically disadvantaged persons.[33]

Can globalization contribute to a new understanding of the inter-connective roles of theology and mission? I believe it can. Having an agency as significant as the ATS place it on its accrediting criteria will not let it slip away quickly into faddism.

But there are problems it will have to overcome in the process. The ATS regulations allow a large measure of flexibility to its member institutions to incorporate one or more elements of its fourfold typology into their own self-definitions. Will the element of integrative holism that can tie mission to theology be lost in this freedom? Will we make theological education "global" by simply "adding to our curriculum courses on ethical questions around the world, questions of justice and peace, global outlook and world Christianity"? Will the totality of our curriculum be penetrated by the global dimension?[34]

Second, unlike contextualization discussions that originated in the Third World, globalization is chiefly a North American concern. There are Third World church leaders who already fear that these geographical roots will make it difficult for us to break free from any "ideological captivity" of too many of the theological undertakings here in North America. From whose perspective will mission and theology be globalized?[35]

Third, how seriously will the North American theological school link together overseas concerns with those of the minority communities of North America? David Schuller, until recently the associate director of the ATS, notes in a 1986 survey that most theological schools make no such division.[36] We are more skeptical, based on our own limited perceptions. If I am right, can globalization become another in-word for Anglo-Saxon parochialism? Will globalization find room for the missiological and theological context of North America's underrepresented constituency?

Fourth, can globalization reinforce contextualization's potential for a new look at the nature of mission and theology? Farley's warnings against the fragmentation of theological education into isolated specializations have power, no matter how we modify and correct them. Will globalization surrender again to its power? Will that possible surrender leave us once more at the starting gate?

Some Practical Suggestions

In closing, I offer a very few tentative trails to explore for change. There are many to try. Mine are unoriginal, often expensive, too simplistic, or even too radical to explore. Much depends on your own preunderstandings of the nature of theology and of mission. Even globalization is a blurred word and has multiple meanings in multiple communities of discourse.[37]

First, I suggest that we seek to diversify the student body ethnically, socially, and religiously. Enlarge the enrollment of non-Anglo-Saxon students. Especially, find ways to welcome the multicultural perspectives that are already part of North America's unique heritage.

A third of my institution's students now come from such backgrounds, with a very large segment from American minorities. And, when they participate in classroom discussions, they ask questions many of us in our narrow conservative-evangelical circles have not heard before.

"What is church?" has a different agenda when asked by a house church leader from the People's Republic of China. An African-American student suggests that our white Christologies place too much emphasis on the deity of Christ to be of functional use on the suffering streets of the black ghettos. "That kind of Jesus ain't got no feet," he argues. "He's a Gnostic Jesus, something for our trophy cases. He won't make out in my neighborhood." An Indonesian student struggles with the functional absence of the world of spirits from our discussions of the kingdom of God. In the Sudanese context, those concerns are paramount. In our theological world, they are peripheral.

Seek for ways to listen to those marginalized by poverty. Graded tuition scales, scholarships may open such doors. Better yet, joint classes with a theological institution serving the needs of the poor, your students in the minority, can promote conscientization. A book like James Cone's *A Black Theology of Liberation*[38] indicates that systematic theology will not remain untouched by such an encounter.

Dialogue with people of other faiths needs to be explored as a regular part of the regular theology classroom experience. Imagine the impact in a class on the doctrine of God with four members of Krishna

23

Consciousness sitting in the front row, interacting with the professor. Or six Muslims auditing a course on Christology, or a course on canonical studies.

Second, struggle with the composition and formation of your permanent faculty. Visiting scholars from the Third World and faculty exchanges will stimulate. But time does not always allow any visiting faculty, either from North America or not, to rethink already prepared lectures from a new context or reflect on the new context after they have returned. Visiting scholars, no matter where their base, can be theological tourists.

Other avenues may be more fruitful. How much non-Western, nonwhite experience is represented on your faculty? How "colorful" does your full-time faculty look? How much training and experience does he or she bring from outside the Anglo-Saxon world? What should be the role of such study and experience in evaluation for promotion and tenure? Do sabbaticals and faculty research projects show engagement with a world that the recipient would recognize as not one's own? Are joint writing projects with those from another socioeconomic context encouraged?

Third, encourage exposure situations for long-term faculty and student participation in other social and cultural settings. Short, intensive experiences offered outside the "ordinary" can be useful, even dramatically worldview-changing. But these opportunities are not deeply, ultimately incarnational. Nothing usually promotes long-range change and sensitivity better than living and doing and being in a cultural setting that you perceive as "foreign" to yourself. Ask any foreign missionary.

How do we find this experience? I commend to you the urban communities of the poor. In the city as resource, you will see the struggles of the world not as an observer, but as a participant. Power's temptation seems clearer to the powerless. There those marginalized by ethnicity and economics can offer a faculty member or student living there a new way of creating an agenda, not only for mission, but for theology also. In the city, the line between action and reflection will blur.

Fourth, encourage full participation by all faculty and students in joint reflection on these experiences. Reflection, after all, is the major task of the theological seminary. Avoid isolating the global dimension into one part of the school curriculum, whether Christian ethics or "practical" theology or missiology. Consciousness-raising should have an integrative purpose: theologian stimulating, even irritating, missiologist; missiologist stimulating and irritating theologian.

The totality of our curriculum must be penetrated by the questions of global solidarity, mission, and justice. To use the language of Miguez-Bonino, "The battle for global solidarity in theological education is fought and won or lost in the teaching of the Bible, in the teaching of Church History, of Systematic Theology, of Pastoral Theology. If it is not fought at that level, all that we add in terms of other more fancy things will not help very much."[39]

Conclusions

Will this change the models for theology and mission from our long past that structure our understanding? I cannot say. I began this lecture with a more easily reached goal—"to encourage the process of modification."

Should specialization disappear? I would hope not. There is too much to learn and there are too many voices to hear for everyone to listen to all the same messages. A disenchanted critic of annual church gatherings and conventions once said to me, "At such church assemblies, everything has to be said—and everyone has to say it." I do not recommend this method of operation for church assemblies—or theological seminaries.

David Bosch follows Hans-Werner Gensichen and suggests another direction that may need some expansion. He argues for a dual function of missiology within the broad framework of theology. There is a dimensional aspect to missiology and an intentional aspect.

The dimensional aspect of missiology highlights its relevance to the world. It permeates all disciplines and is not primarily one "sector" of the theological encyclopedia. It infuses the entire curriculum; it dialogues in free partnership with other disciplines. It works at retrieving the good news universality that is at the heart of biblical, theological, historical, and pastoral studies. It reminds its colleagues in the curriculum that theology must always be "theology on the road."[40]

25

At the same time, missiology has an intentional aspect. It has its own proper task as a discipline to perform. Part of that task will be to introduce the church in the Western world to the Third World and to prepare "specialists" to go and work there. Another equally important part of its task will be to introduce the wisdom and experience of the Third World to the West. Issues like evangelism, enculturation, dialogue, liberation, poverty, and absence of faith are not only problems for the Third World. They are also challenges to the Western church in its own context. The globalization theme that is at the heart of missiology cannot be limited to Third World concerns. The clientele of missiology will be found in Timbuktu and Toronto, Marakesh and Memphis.[41]

Adding to Bosch's agenda, I would suggest that theology also needs its dimensional and intentional aspects. The dimensional aspect of theology highlights the need for critical reflection on the church's self-understanding of its calling in the world. God's divine revelation has been encumbered with a history of hermeneutical concerns and trails shaped by past history and our cultural place in that history. Theology's task is to constantly reexamine that global, missiological history in the light of the Scriptures and how we have shaped it by our theology and our history from the past. Mission without this theological dimension becomes only action. Theology without the mission dimension becomes only abstraction.

Theology, like mission, also has its intentional aspect, its legitimate role as a discipline to perform. It is a critical companion of the Christian mission, not a luxury of some world-dominating church. To a church engaged in mission between the already and the not-yet, the here and the there, theology says, "Reflect, repent, renew."

In mutuality and comradeship, theology and mission say together, "The mission of God is our concern; the global mission of the church is our life."

PART 1

THE CITY'S ROLE
IN MISSION

2

Urbanization and Evangelism: A Global View[1]

Raymond J. Bakke

I want you to picture an image that comes from Psalm 107. In the psalm, people are hungering and thirsting and crying out in the desert, in parched paths of life; they cry out to the Lord, and the Lord answers their prayer. He leads them from the north, the south, the east, and the west to a city in which to dwell. Psalm 107 portrays what I see happening worldwide. We are living in the midst of the greatest migration in history.

Picture the world in motion: the Southern Hemisphere is coming north, the East is coming west, and on all six continents migrations are to the city. In 1900 about 8 percent of the world's population lived in sizable cities. Today over 50 percent of this earth—over three billion people—lives in world-class cities. We aren't prepared for that. Most of our mission industry, most of the ministries that many of us represent, are still thinking in terms of tribal world, a world where we cross oceans and deserts and jungles to get to the lost groups of people. There are, indeed, still about a billion people who are geographically distant from existing churches, so we will need traditional ministries on into the future. But far more than two billion of the world's nonchurched people are no longer geographically distant from the church; they are culturally distant. They live in the largest cities of the world.

These cities are like giant magnets attracting people. We use two definitions. By *urbanization* we refer to the city as a magnet. Urbanization pulls people in from rural areas. By *urbanism* we refer to the city as a transformer, transmitter, and magnifier of culture. Even though Detroit or many other cities are losing population in the city center as the city spreads out, urbanism will not go away. The entire planet is becoming highly urbanized. There is no place to escape anymore. These days the people are running away from Los Angeles into the people running away from places like Chicago, somewhere near Colorado Springs. There is no place to hide from what I am describing: a migration that is happening on all six continents.

A World Tour

In the epistle to Philemon, the second shortest book in the New Testament, we have a marvelous comment on an intercontinental refugee named Onesimus. Paul, in a beautiful little piece of reflection, gives us a hermeneutical window to look at global migration. Onesimus, the slave, had stolen money, had run away from Asia to get lost in the European crowd in Rome, found Christ in Rome, and was now coming back to Asia to assume some leadership and to integrate a local house church, where slaves joined nonslaves in the fellowship of the church. Paul says to Philemon, "Perhaps the reason he was separated from you for a little while was that you might have him back for good" (v. 15). As I look at the international migrant streams, we need Paul's hermeneutical window.

Imagine an urban tour of London: the East End is basically becoming Asian today; South London is by and large black—West Indian, Jamaican, Ugandan; West London, outside the theater district and outside the Westminster Palace area, is becoming largely Arab. The British Empire once included fifty-two nations, but now all fifty-two nations live in London. I call this the "empire strikes back" syndrome.

The British are still not prepared for all this. Neither are the mission realities of the United Kingdom. There are now more Muslims throughout the cities of the United Kingdom than there are Baptists and Methodists combined. In cities like Bradford, near Leeds, there are eighty Asian populations. The churches have been recycled; many of them are now mosques or Sikh temples. Mission no longer goes one way; there is a reverse mission coming back to the United Kingdom.

Move on to Paris. In the south of the city, the eighteenth arrondissement is incredibly Algerian. France once ruled forty-six countries, twenty-six African nations and another twenty countries on five continents—440 million French-speaking people in very diverse places on five continents. Now, all of those five continents are coming back to France. In France now, there are very heated debates about what to do with the coloration and pluralization of French society. The French are not ready for this; the mission of the French people is not ready for this.

Consider other cities of Europe. A hundred years ago, as part of the *Drang nach Osten*—the push to the east—the Germans built a railroad to the Bosporus. Now hundreds of thousands of Turks and many others live in the cities of Germany. About 50,000 Yugoslavs live in Sweden. Consider Norway, St. Olav's Catholic Parish in the center of Oslo: ninety-seven nations can be found in that one parish—nearly one-half of the nations of the world (197 nations came to the 2000 Olympic Games in Sydney). We could not imagine a more dramatic pluralization of what was once a homogeneous community and society. I assure you, the Norwegian church is not ready for this.

It may surprise you that one million Japanese now live in São Paulo, Brazil. You cannot get further away from North Pacific Japan than South Atlantic Brazil without starting to come back around the other way. How do a million Japanese get to São Paulo? Some eighty million Chinese live outside of China, including Hong Kong. While we have been focused all these years on how to get the mission into China—the Silkroad mission of A.D. 615 to Baghdad, the Nestorian church, the papal mission of Marco Polo, the Jesuit mission of Mateo Risi, the nineteenth-century Protestant mission—eighty million Chinese have been scattered by the Lord of history into cities all over the world.

We are living in that day of incredible global migration. In St. Paul, Minnesota, 25 percent of the public school children are Hmong. They don't even have a country of their own, but they have a big chunk of St. Paul in neighborhoods not far from Luther Seminary.

What Is God Doing?

The whole world has come to the cities. When we moved to Chicago in 1965, we discovered that there were sixty-three nations in the high school where our children would eventually attend. They were teaching eleven different languages and over 50 percent of the children were foreign-born. That's when I began to ask the theological question: "What is God doing?" I know the migration theory about push and pull factors, but the theological issue remains: "Why at this time in history are the nations coming to the cities? What is God doing in this massive migration of the world?"

I was helped by Fredrick Norwood, whose study begins with Abraham and the exiles in Babylon and shows the diaspora movement in the history of the church.[2] Other scholarly works helped me to discover that from a theological and pastoral perspective, refugees are not victims, they are missionaries. I remember reading the gospel one Christmas when I realized that this story was about an Asian-born baby, born in a borrowed barn, who became an African refugee. In that simple story, Jesus was in touch with the greatest migration in human history, because over half of the babies born in the world are born in Asia, and over half of the world's 30 million refugees are Africans.

I began to think about the martyrdom of those innocent children in Bethlehem—a whole village full of babies died for Jesus before he could die for them on the cross. In Chicago, one hospital reported two years ago that 46 percent of the babies that lived to be born were damaged: crack addicted, HIV-positive, or suffering from fetal alcohol syndrome. The damage came in some way by the sins of adults. Surely, the Jesus of the Christmas story understands the pain of crack and fetal alcohol babies. Bible stories look different in the urban context.

Moses' mother was a classic "public aid mom." She had an illegal baby and her husband was not in the picture. She makes a little boat, floats the child down the Nile River, gets him rescued, and gets paid for raising him. She beat the system!

According to Stephen in Acts 7, Moses was learned in all the wisdom of the Egyptians. He had gone to palace school to learn pharaonic culture. Then he had an internship in the desert, where he studied public health and primitive communities, sheep culture, desert language, and literature. God made him practice with sheep in a bad neighborhood before he would trust him with people in a bad neighborhood. Moses led a mud-making migrant group out into the worst neighborhood in the Middle East. They were on "food stamps" called manna for forty years. Moses did human development, leadership development, community development, and economic development. As I read the Pentateuch from my perspective, the stories come alive in a different way!

I discovered that we do have a theology as big as the city. The Hebrew word for city (*'ir*) occurs 1,090 times in the Old Testament, and the Greek word (*polis*) occurs 160 times in the New Testament. We find 142 cities in the Scriptures, some mentioned hundreds of times. One can list twenty-five kinds of urban ministry mentioned in the historical books alone. The apostle Paul only went to cities, but he never approached any city the same way twice. There was indeed a great deal of grist for theology and for the practice of ministry as I began to look at the cities of the world.

The Challenges of the City

But the cities present amazing challenges. Take, for example, the demographic challenge: the sheer pluralism of all these nations now living in a confined space. An extraordinary amount of sociology is required to exegete a community. Everybody who comes, comes with sending-culture baggage. Whether in Cairo, Paris, or London, pastors must sort out the agendas of the sending culture while trying to pastor the agendas of the host culture.

Further, cities are not neutral: they package people in certain ways. When John Kennedy was elected president in 1960, he made a deal with Lyndon Johnson to deliver the Baptist (or Bible Belt) vote to a Catholic president. My church in Seattle was in the midst of a building project at the time. The first thing that the Department of Defense did under Robert McNamara's leadership was to withdraw the biggest government contract that Boeing, in Seattle, had ever had. The contract was rescinded and given to Lockheed and General Dynamics in the South. My entire congregation was unemployed overnight.

That made me realize that cities are not neutral. A political decision to shift capital that was made 3,000 miles away in Washington, D.C., had unemployed my congregation and impacted my ministry. I knew then that I had to pay attention to things beyond the parish in order to function in the parish.

When you ask people in the city who they are, they tell you what they do. When Boeing threw away my congregation, they didn't want to come to church because they didn't know who they were. I realized then why blue-collar workers don't come to church most of the time. They can't compete with the pastor's identity. And so the world's chronic economic, unemployment, and underemployment issues are not primarily economic issues. They present an identity crisis. All of these issues, along with race and culture issues, impact pastors in urban congregations, forcing them to grapple with a whole new understanding of the nature and mission of the church in these contexts.

Consider the ecclesial challenge: churches on every corner offer their own version of the gospel. Manila presents this exaggeration. In the Philippines, there are 7,100 islands. The missionaries, back in 1918, had a comity agreement. They decided to split up the islands, and so there became Baptist islands, Lutheran islands, Anglican islands. Everyone got to be catholic on his own island. Every island had its own hymnal, its own Bible, its own liturgy, and its own practice of ministry.

But since World War II, all of those islands have been sending people to metro Manila. Now, on every corner of every neighborhood is a church with a Bible that is different from the neighboring church's Bible. The pastors, normally trained in the barrios, don't understand this. They internalize their inadequacies. They were not prepared for this in Cebu, where they went to Bible College. Now they come to metro Manila to pastor a flock that includes all the proliferation of the kingdom of God. They have no idea which Bible is correct, but they think that their own must be, and that their own hymnal is correct, which means that everyone else's must be suspect.

So the pastors adopt authoritarian modes of ministry, keeping the church busy every night of the week so that nobody can be contaminated through contact with any other Christians. The churches pass like ships in the night. The bigger the city, the less they do in evangelism. They program and overprogram so they won't leak away and be contacted by other denominations. It's a massive problem on six continents! How do we prepare pastors to move in and build bridges of hope for these kinds of places?

The theological issues are tremendously difficult. In the past, we struggled with interdenominational questions. Today, it's interfaith questions. Rev. B. Herbert Martin, pastor on Chicago's South Side and a member of my urban support group, has for ten years had a Monday night Bible study for men. About a hundred men come to a "cousins" study: for black Jews, black Christians, and black Muslims. They are all the children of Abraham, and they all live in the neighborhood. I've never heard of anybody else who calls a "cousins" Bible study. They come together and read the Old Testament, and the word is that many Muslims have decided to follow Jesus—in a cousins Bible study. When I was in seminary, nobody told us we could do that! But Martin Kähler, the German missiologist, was right when he told us back in 1908 that "mission is the mother of theology."[3]

Mission is forcing us, as it gets closer to mid-America, to reinvent the church and to rethink theology and mission practice. Having been in and around seminaries for thirty years, I can assure you that we are not ready for this. We are producing pastors who are clinicians, very often "Rogerian," which, when it comes to counseling in my neighborhood, is a little like rearranging deck chairs on the Titanic. Somebody has to patch up the leaky boat. We need missiologists, sociologists, demographers who can deal with great issues of mission and evangelization, and we are not getting those out of most of our seminaries. Our seminaries are autobiographically preparing people to move into the narrow stream of whiteness and the middle class, but while that remains a major stream of Americana, it makes up only 13 percent of God's earth. Eighty-seven percent of our world is nonwhite. We desperately need some models within the Evangelical Lutheran Church of America and other denominations to lift up as examples of people taking risks and preparing ministers for this new reality. Seminaries have done well at being the memory bank of the church, far less well at being the research and development unit for the future.

Cities present enormous pastoral challenges. How does a pastor build a sustainable spirituality in the city? How do you raise your children there? What do you do when everything you do is cross-cultural? Missionaries had furloughs and support systems that urban pastors do not.

Urban Ministry Specializations

Urban ministry has developed areas of specialization, at least five.

One is work with the *at-risk people groups.* At-risk people are children damaged before birth. They are street kids, abused kids, abandoned kids. They come from broken families; they are burdened with addictions and dysfunctionalities of all kinds. One classic study suggests we can help only 15 percent of the homeless population by the traditional "soup, soap, and salvation" methodologies of rescue missions.[4] Basically, 85 percent of the homeless population in this country are now layered with addictions, and we will need new strategies for long-term incarnational work with people. Are we ready to do this? It's much easier to move into the areas of success and upward mobility and work with the traditional people who have paid our bills and built our churches; and I'm afraid that's where we are going. But the explosion of mission is in the other direction, and I don't think we are ready for it.

A second area of specialization involves *at-risk communities.* The ministry of John Perkins and others has produced the Christian Community Development Association, a group of denominations that are targeting the last, least, and lost neighborhoods in America. Every November two to three thousand people meet to share their expertise and their struggles to plant churches in the absolute armpits of this country. Fortunately, this kind of movement is happening around the world as well. For me, the greatest sign of hope in the Middle East is in Cairo's Maquattam Mountain garbage dump, where a Willow Creek model of the Coptic Orthodox Church exists. About 10,000 people came recently to a Thursday night Bible study, the majority under 30. The people have literally carved a cave out of the mountain of Cairo's garbage that seats 10,000 people. It's a church. Hundreds and thousands of young people are coming out of the Coptic centers of Egypt and bringing their Muslim friends to hear the gospel. People are working in the biggest and worst slums in cities around the world. People are deliberately choosing to move their ministries to those places.

A third specialization is *multiethnic and multilingual ministries.* My son's church in Chicago ministers every week in twelve different languages. We need churches today that function like hospitals and supermarkets and police stations. They have to be open twenty-four hours, which means that we need day pastors and night pastors speaking all different languages. My son's church has banners on its walls in those twelve different languages, so as soon as people step in they see "Jesus Christ" in their own language—they know that the church has a ministry for them. When I went to seminary, we didn't get trained to pastor the world's nations in one parish. The church was multilingual the day it began at Pentecost, but did not become multicultural until Antioch. There were many hurdles to get over before the church could get from merely speaking the languages to building the multiethnic pastoral team that Barnabas put together in Antioch. The city-center model, which invented foreign missions in Antioch, is the model we need again in the center of our modern cities.

Another specialization involves *laity in the marketplace.* In the urban parish, it is not enough to have a busy program at the church. We need to equip people to move into the subsectors of the city: the court system, the advocacy roles. We need to send people into politics because the laws are unfair and unjust. We need Christians who will articulate the gospel in the business world. We need people to serve in convention businesses, in theaters, in the arts, in all the subcultures of the city. So pastors have to be the equippers of the laity and commission them to move into the marketplace.

And then, of course, there are those specializations that involve *adapting the functions of the true church to the places where God has placed us.* In other words, what forms do worship, discipleship, stewardship, fellowship, and service take in urban settings? My friend George has six worship services. At 6:00 Sunday morning, George is in a robe, standing behind a pulpit, and the Holy Spirit is in a pipe organ. At the second service, the Holy Spirit is in a guitar, George has no robe, and the people are all over the place. The third service is the children and family service: children and their parents do all the ushering, share in the lectionary readings, act in a drama, the "Littlest Angels" choir sings, the Holy Spirit is in the piano, and the sermon deals with a family issue; but it's the same lectionary text. The fourth service is a teenage rock service: the Holy Spirit is in the praise band, hundreds of kids are present. The fifth service is another afternoon contemporary service. The sixth service is what George calls "the Alka Seltzer service" for all the losers in the neighborhood: the ushers are just out of jail, just off drugs, or struggling with addictions; it's the church of the twelve-step groups.

I heard a young man stand up in that worship service and say, "When I came to you this past year, I was a child molester, and you knew it. And you have taken me in now, and you've become my family. And now with your help and prayers, I'm going back to California and try to find my wife and my family and ask their forgiveness." I tried to remember if I'd ever been in a church service on a Sunday anywhere in the world where somebody could stand up and say, "I was a child molester," and be hugged by everybody before he could get out the door. The good news is that there are city churches doing this kind of ministry. They are on the frontier of mission. It is not nice or pretty or comfortable. But that is where the gospel is in the city. It is about crucifixion in places that we don't like to be.

Five Theses

Let me conclude with five theses:

Thesis 1: Urban ministry is cross-cultural. The frontier of mission has shifted. It is no longer geographically distant; it is culturally distant. A hundred years ago, we sent missionaries to the nations to look for the cities. Today, you go to the cities and you find the nations. The defining nature of the city is not inner city versus outer city. Only in the United States do the poor live in the city and the rich live in the suburbs. Everywhere else in the world, the closer you get to the city center, the richer you are—especially places like Paris. The old inner-city/outer-city paradigm does not work. Nor does it work to say that

the city is black and the suburbs are white. The biggest cities are neither black nor white. Tokyo is yellow; Mexico City is brown. The
biggest cities in the world do not have race problems as we define
them. The American ways of defining city as black or white, as urban
or suburban, just don't fit. We need a missiological definition of the
city. The city is a place where the nations are gathering. Therefore,
the pastors who are put in the city must be missiologically trained.
We would never think of sending a person to a tribe without language and cultural study.

Urban neighborhoods are now infinitely more complex than
tribal cultures. They are kaleidoscopically restructuring themselves, and we have no way to prepare pastors before they enter
these neighborhoods. We grind up pastors in the city by not giving them the kinds of orientation and the tools they need to work
cross-culturally. So my first thesis is that urban ministry is cross-
cultural. The nations have come to the cities, so we have to have a
global perspective. We have to move missiology from the fringe
to the core of the curriculum, and we have to read Scripture from
that perspective. We have to study the history of the church from
a cross-cultural perspective (more like Latourette than Williston
Walker). We will study Stephen Neill and his missiology, wrestling
with the church's crossing cultures and the impact of these new
churches. We will study Benedict's Rule and the monastic movements, which were engines of economic development without outside funding. We will look at the way lay people built monaster-
ies, and how the Cluniac reform movements nurtured those
Benedictine movements. We will look at all the same things, but
we will see them from a different perspective as we prepare urban
pastors for a whole new day when the nations live in the cities. All
the nations of the world are now within the shadow of the spire
of Lutheran churches.

Thesis 2: We will have to do a dramatic gospel and culture inventory.
Consider Acts 10, Peter's confession, which I call the climax of Pentecost—the second conversion of the preacher of Pentecost. Peter,
who had followed Christ and seen all the miracles and heard all the
sermons, denied Christ under pressure three times, but was forgiven

by the risen Christ. Peter, who preached at Pentecost and was apparently filled with the Spirit, was still struggling with things like little kids bringing ham sandwiches to Sunday school picnics. The Peter of Acts 10 was still culturally chauvinistic. He was ethnocentric, still a benign racist.

We all need Peter's conversion. My oldest son brought home a boy from school; we fed him for six months, and then we adopted him. Now in my family we have two Brians, a white Brian and a black Brian. That meant we had to change everything: our vacations, our food, our discipline patterns. To incorporate another culture into Scandinavian tradition was agonizing. My wife is a concert pianist with a doctorate in worship and art. Her whole repertoire was European. It forced her to look at rag and blues and jazz in a whole new way. It will not be easy.

My favorite writing of Luther is the essay in which he exegetes the Jerusalem Council and the seven ecumenical councils of the early church.[5] Luther realizes that the church was perilously close to saying that the way to the cross is through the gate of the synagogue. You have to become culturally Jewish in order to become Christian. Peter was still struggling with that issue. Like a lot of Eurocentric Christians, we too would like to keep the threshold high to preserve our northern European culture and values. And we say, "You can come to the cross and you can come to Jesus, but you have to step over that threshold of Johann Bach and the *Augsburg Confession* and, along with that, a European cultural tradition that is extremely significant for us." Like Vatican II, we must sort out all the issues in the light of a global church. Every generation needs to do this. Luther was right. His 1539 essay is a seminal piece of literature on the homework we have to do on the culture/gospel inventory.

Thesis 3: The image of the pastor has to change. We have the image of preacher, educator, counselor. We need to add the image of missiologist. It's an integrative discipline. It's not made out of whole cloth. It's a way of looking at traditional disciplines and social courses and documents in new ways.

Thesis 4: We must identify the real barriers to effective urban ministry. I used to think that if churches and pastors all over the world had the right information and right motivation, we could reach the cities with the gospel of Jesus Christ. And so I set out to do that. By the time I ended up in Cairo in 1982 with about fifty-five pastors on a retreat, I realized that I was naïve and wrong. I started doing surveys, and I thought the barriers to mission were the big, bad cities.[6] Having mastered something of the culture of the cities, I thought that if I could just distill that and help pastors get the right motivation spiritually, we would then reach cities. But 90 percent of the barriers to reaching cities are not in the city at all; they are inside our churches—things like "Our bishop would never let us get away with that," or "They'll call us liberal if we do that," or "We can't do that, the seminary prepared me for that." The barriers are inside our structures. The heads, the knowledge base, the intimidation factors of our church are the things that keep us from reaching cities.

Thesis 5: There is a fundamental difference between Jesus Christ and Ann Landers. She offers advice; we offer news. Advice, by nature of the case, is something you must do. If it works, we say that it was good advice. Advice is patronizing—we give advice, you receive our advice.

We are not in the cities in the advice business. We are in the cities in the news business. The news is that God has in Jesus Christ done something for you on the cross, and that the risen Christ and the empty cross are reminders that God as the ascended Christ offers now to forgive all those who repent and believe. And we must not deny the poor the possibility of repenting from their sins. Raymond Fung of Hong Kong and long-time evangelist for the World Council of Churches has pointed out that the poor are not only sinners, like all of us, but, more often than not, they are also sinned against. So the doctrine of hope comes knowing forgiveness.

I believe in all these social programs that come along and open gates for people. But, if there is no gospel that says, "News, not advice! Something happened in Jesus Christ, and you have the possibility of new life," then there is no hope. If people are given only hope, but then end up locked in prisons forever, that hope eventually turns to cynicism. So we need a new partnership between the hope people and the love people, between the truth people and the grace people. We need to come alongside each other, people who are evangelists with the news and people who come with tools to set people free. We can't do one without the other.

They are two sides of a coin in the city. If we only had Colossians, we would take on all the structures of the city and reclaim the systems. If we only had Philippians, which starts with Jesus in us, we'd be Wesleyan and we'd work out of a personal evangelism model. But the truth is that we have them both, side by side in the New Testament. So we have an intensely personal faith, the Philippian option. We have a public faith, the Colossian option. The fact is, we have to put these two pieces of Christology together to make it work in the city. And if we do, we will not only see people transformed and churches transformed, but we will also see communities and cities transformed.

—3—

THE CHURCH AND THE CITY

MANUEL ORTIZ

It was predicted by Rafael Salas that by the end of the twentieth century the world would experience radical and overwhelming change, with the majority of people living in urban centers, primarily in the cities of Asia, Africa, and Latin America.[1] Harvey Cox goes further when he says, "Future historians will record the twentieth century as that century in which the whole world became one immense city."[2]

Urban growth is more than a sociological reality; it is the fulfillment of God's intentions since the beginning of time. "The cultural mandate given to Adam and Eve in the garden to fill, rule, and subdue the earth (Gen. 1:28) was nothing more than a mandate to build the city."[3] The missiological side of this coin is that the nations are coming to our cities to become new citizens and not just temporary residents. Immigrant churches from Asia, Africa, and Latin America will continue to grow at an increasingly rapid rate.

The missionary movement is exploding in these nations as they send out missionaries. Recently, in an article in *Christian Mission*, it was noted that "Spanish-speaking missionaries [are] reaching Latin immigrants in London and Paris . . . [and are] taking the gospel to Muslims in Spain. . . . It's European missions the South American way!"[4] These churches are ignited by the Holy Spirit to spread the good news of Christ throughout the world. This mission activity will continue to enter our North American cities, and it will be an ongoing factor in the new missionary era. The dominant role of Western missions in the modern mission movement is slowly disappearing. The following considerations will require shifts in our thinking: (1) the church as mission, (2) the pastor as shepherd and church planter, (3) the new relationship between sending and receiving churches, and (4) old and new models for missionary enterprise.

The Church as Mission

In this century, there must be a greater engagement between the church and the city. In the early twentieth century, the concerns and mission of the church were distant from the concerns of the city. Dr. Conn noted, "Churches appear to be in the city but not really of it. City and not church occupies the periphery."[5]

Why must the church be engaged in mission? First, there is a theological reason: the church is the community of the kingdom of God.

> The Church can never possess the King so as to monopolize the Kingdom. The Church is communities resulting from the preaching of the Kingdom. They serve the Kingdom as symbols which show imperfectly what the Kingdom is like. The Church is to bring to visibility for the world fellowship with Christ as King and obedience to Him. The Church is to be "God's colony in man's world, God's experimental garden on earth." She is a sign of the world to come and at the same time a guarantee of its coming.[6]

The church is the people of God in society. It is also the agent of the kingdom. God will use the church as king, prophet, and priest to bring societal transformation. The prophetic role (Joel 2:28–29; Num. 11) will give witness to the truth and declare our faith in public. We will admonish each other toward a resurrected lifestyle. We are priests (Matt. 27:51) and therefore pray and intercede for our community. We have access to our great mediator, Jesus (Heb. 4:14–16). We are admonished and equipped to provide mercy (Heb. 13:16) to a wounded world. We are kingly and will rule (Eph. 2:6); the world will recognize our authority over evil and this world in our role as instruments of justice. We rule as those overcoming the world already, but not yet.

The present rule of Christ is the basic theme of the church and the kingdom. The church brings the people of God together in worship as they acknowledge Christ's reign as King. The church is God's colony. The church is the body of Christ, that community in which Christ dwells, turned in action toward the world (1 Cor. 12:12–27).[7] We also recognize that Jesus Christ is the head of the kingdom, and this will bring great growth to the church in the city as it did in the early stages of the New Testament church (Eph. 1:10, 22–23). The Lord is the evangelist who announces his coming, and he is the herald of the gospel, which is the word of the kingdom. As a result, the church grows and reproduces (Matt. 13:3, 23). The great missionary is Jesus, who is sent by the Father. Jesus is the great shepherd (John 10:11–30), who gathers the people of God from every corner of the earth and promises to deliver them from the Evil One. Jesus ministered the gospel of the kingdom, his rule over all of life, and he was moved with compassion as he saw people who were like sheep without a shepherd (Matt. 9:36). "Shepherding is the mission of the church—crossing frontiers in the form of a servant."[8] Edmund Clowney states:

> Jesus came to gather, and to call gatherers, disciples who would gather with him, seeking the poor and helpless from city streets and country roads. . . . Mission is not an optional activity for Christ's disciples. If they are not gatherers, they are scatterers. Some suppose that a church may feature worship and nurture, leaving gathering as a minor role. . . . Mission is reduced to a few offerings, the visit of several exhausted missionaries on fund-raising junkets, and the labours of an ignored mission committee. Such a church is actively involved in scattering, for the congregation that ignores mission will atrophy and soon find itself shattered by internal dissension.[9]

We follow the example of Christ. He was sent and in obedience came (John 1:1–14), and so we are sent into the world. "Mission expresses the purpose for which Christ came into the world."[10]

The second reason why the church must be engaged in mission is that people from every corner of the world are entering the cities. Urbanization and urbanism are the way of life and the new wave for missions. This process has been going on for the last century, but the church has been slow in responding to it. "A book by James D. Hunter in 1983 notes that 'evangelicals are grossly underrepresented in the large cities.' Only 8.6 percent surveyed by Hunter were in cities of one million or more."[11] Dr. Conn realized that he was in a battle to convince the larger North American evangelical community that God is interested in the cities of his world, and that Paul's theology was profoundly nurtured in urban mission. Paul's missionary labors were centered in the great cities of the Greco-Roman world.

In Acts the Pauline missionaries almost unfailingly go first to the Jewish synagogue and find opportunities to speak and debate at the regular Sabbath services. When they meet resistance there, or even if they do not (16:13–15; 18:2), they sometimes take up residence in the households of individuals: of Lydia in Philippi (16:15), of Jason in Thessalonica (17:5–9), of Priscilla and Aquilla in Corinth (18:2–4).[12]

Conn asks, "How can we recruit personnel for reaching our urban generations when the rural and suburban areas have nurtured their visions of the church?"[13] The church must take on this challenge with vigor and confidence in the power of the reigning Lord. When reading the New Testament, you cannot help but be struck by the fact that most of it was quite purposefully written within a missionary context, and that particular context was mostly urban.

The New Testament made it impossible to distinguish between church and mission. There were no denominational or extra-church structures other than the synagogue that issued strategies for mission. Certainly no parachurch mission organizations were to be found. Dr. Conn noted that "after the first century, [there were] not even separate apostles or evangelists for the unreached."[14]

The apostolic nature of the church has diminished since the apostolic age. This can be seen as we trace a number of shifts in the church's relationship to mission. First, the focus of the apostolate in the Roman Catholic Church changed from sending out missionaries to maintaining the authority of apostolic succession. Then, the Reformation churches shifted their emphasis from mission and evangelism to orthodoxy and the maintaining of truth. Here again, sending out on mission is lost.

Second, the teaching on the Holy Spirit in the Roman Catholic Church was dramatically changed. The Spirit was understood less as the empowerer of the church for prayer and mission and more as the agent of ecclesiastical incorporation. This affected the Reformers as well, as they focused on the Holy Spirit principally as the interpreter of Scripture. The Pentecostal and charismatic churches then moved in another direction, understanding the Spirit as the empowerer of the believer through the charismata. Again, we see a shift that divorces the Holy Spirit from the spirit of mission.

A third shift has to do with the church's role as a sending community. In the nineteenth century, mission was understood primarily as the calling of individuals who were motivated by God to participate in "foreign" missions. Individuals, rather than the church as a whole, awakened to the call of the mission frontier. The individual was called and sent, and that led to a mission focus on saving individual souls. The individual became the agent of the kingdom and of the Spirit, and that limited church-planting strategy. Also, the individual missionary became the agent of mission. "This results in a low view of the church."[15] This did change in the middle of the twentieth century, and the church became much more aware of ecclesiastical responsibilities in church planting.

The establishment of missionary societies by Protestants was due in part, but not entirely, to the failure of missions to emanate from the local church. One reason for the shift in mission responsibility from the local congregation to mission agencies and denominational structures was that the theology of the church became centered narrowly on the church, not necessarily on Christ and his kingdom. The church in Europe, on the whole, was very slow in getting involved in mission work. Another barrier to mission activity was the overwhelming responsibility of maintaining the church. There was a maintenance approach that became stagnant, rather than a focus on mission that would have allowed the church to become more dynamic. Therefore, mission responsibilities were increasingly shifted to mission agencies.

Pragmatically, we might agree with this move. The church was heavily involved with its congregants, and so a survival ideology was formed. The churches could not handle the challenge of mission, which they perceived as being too cumbersome. They found that it was too inefficient for them to carry on the mission mandate; therefore, missions were transferred to a more efficient and pragmatic agency focused on "one thing." The shift from mission to maintenance became a core value in the local church. There was a shift from the New Testament understanding of the church as a body prepared and enabled to serve and become involved in the crossing of urban frontiers to the pragmatic understanding of the church as a body focusing on self-enhancement and solidification.

It is important to realize that this change did not necessarily happen among immigrant and non-English-speaking churches in North America. The Spanish-speaking churches continued to exercise the sending mandate, on a faith basis, and mission from the United States was launched primarily into Latin America and the Caribbean. Other churches from Africa and Latin America continued this mission of planting churches in their own homelands. This mission activity developed spontaneously, and is now taking place in a more organized and intentional manner. We have much to learn about mission from the Spanish-speaking church in North America.

Toward the middle and latter part of the twentieth century, here in the United States, the Holy Spirit was at work in local churches, providing a vision of urban mission. This would break the isolationist or ghetto mentality of the church as a caretaker, rather than a husbandman. It would also shatter the manifestation of the church in mission as one that is out to conquer the world and incorporate others into its own domain. In this movement, the sending of Christians from local congregations (some independent, but many in denominational bodies) revived the apostolic nature of the church. Interestingly enough, some viewed these churches as innovative, creative, and risk takers. Others, however, especially those administering denominational agencies, saw these churches as being disloyal and possibly subversive. Yet these churches were moved by first-century mission history as well as the modern mission movement. They were mostly following the teaching of the New Testament, and the application of biblical principles enabled and empowered the church to pursue this mission challenge. It seemed irregular to see churches reproducing churches, yet they were considered to be refreshing new models of ministry.

In this ever-changing world, the agency of the kingdom and the catalyst for societal transformation is the church. The church must embrace its commitments to the Great Commission in a demonstrative way. The local church must be equipped to handle the numerous missiological challenges that are presented in this increasingly global society. Ray Bakke often speaks about the fifty-two nations living in London. East London is basically becoming Asian; South London is by and large black, housing West Indians, Jamaicans, and Ugandans; and the Arab community is filtering into West London. This phenomenon is occurring in many cities of the world. We are finding the world in our own neighborhoods. This pluralism of religion and culture is now localized in our urban communities, and the mission field has skipped across the ocean into our neighborhoods and local church communities. Look again and note the hand of the missionary God. If we are to carry out our mission responsibility effectively and biblically, the sending nature of the church must be restored.

Mission cannot be allocated to others just because they may have the means or the resources. This is not a pragmatic issue, but one that is centered on the concerns of the Lord of the harvest and the church's faithfulness to the Great Commission. "The Christian answer in face of the urban complexity of life is not a return to the simple lifestyle of rural communities of the 'good old days.' God is at work in the world's urban situation and calls for a lifestyle accountable for his kingdom coming and which he will complete in his time."[16] Churches will have to strategize for a mission movement in their city. It will have to take place in their context and move from that point of reference to other mission frontiers. Churches will become much more the sending platforms for mission activity than ever before. They will use multiple models, not just one. They will go further than the zone of expectation dictates. In other words, they will be faithful to the gospel and sensitive to the context in which they plant churches. Leadership, likewise, will be trained through different vehicles. Multiple models of theological training are essential for the task. Discipleship will take a high priority and will be much more thorough than we have seen in years past. The church consists of the redeemed redeeming the world for Christ.

The Pastor as Shepherd and Church Planter

In order to accomplish the enormous task of mission, churches must review the preparation and selection of pastors and other leaders. The renewal of local churches is essential for this task, and it will take place when kingdom principles are applied, radically restructuring the existing models of leadership into a lifestyle modeled after the servant minister / ministry in the midst of a dynamic and at times impersonal urban context. Churches in North America have become more regional and less local. Location has not been taken as seriously as it should for the mission enterprise. Congregations look for locations with suitable facilities that are accessible by automobile and provide sufficient parking space, but they show little concern for the immediate mission context. Certainly there is a need for churches that might be regional, especially in center-city communities, but this has become all too common. Often this is done because churches focus on the wrong group of people. Most churches are primarily concerned about the people within the church and the people most like "us." They give insufficient attention to their mission context, which could represent a different ethnic, racial, and socioeconomic group. This means that we have followed a church model apart from a mission context. Instead of seriously strategizing to reach the local community, we have transferred people in, in order to get the pews filled, have experienced leadership, and have adequate finances. In this pragmatic move, the mission of the church is short-circuited.

Churches need to strategize with the local community in mind. It may be difficult in the short run, but it will be healthier in the long run. We should not segregate our lives in the interest of ease and comfort while living in a diverse community that needs the gospel. But most churches do not have a clearly defined mission strategy.

Mission work is too often left in the hands of the pastor, who may have a nostalgic vision of the rural or suburban church and lack a missiological dynamic and vision. The pastor and leaders may be in the city, but not part of it.

In this context, the role of the pastor is being challenged. Instead of focusing on meeting the basic needs of the congregation—through preaching, teaching, counseling, administering, and ruling—an increased responsibility will be taken for those in the surrounding community who are more and more culturally distant. This does not mean that pastors will do all the ministry or start new churches, but they will be the strategists, visionaries, and initiators for this calling. We need to equip our pastors with missiological tools, so that the Scriptures will be biblically interpreted and communicated to our new neighbors in the process of contextualization. Charles Kraft refers to his theological training in his book *Anthropology for Christian Witness:*

> [An] important insight that came to me was that my understandings concerning God and His works, including how I understood the Bible, needed to be culturally adapted if they were to speak to the people God had called me to. It came as a bit of a shock that most of what I had learned in Christian college and seminary, in the forms in which I learned it, was inappropriate or irrelevant to the Nigerians I worked with.[17]

William Dyrness, as well, expresses a concern about the relevance of seminary training. "After three years of ministry in North America and this new experience in Asia, I began to suspect that the study of theology in the West was several steps removed from people's lives."[18]

Pastors need skills in interpreting the city and the mission context, so that they and their congregations will be able to form effective philosophies of ministry. Getting acquainted with mission history will alert pastors to mission strategies. They need to reread the Scriptures to see that mission and church-growth principles are really biblical principles properly applied. This ability to be fluid and missiological will give local churches staying power in a transitioning society.

Pastors are placed in the context of mission whether they know it or not. If not, churches will decline and continue to move farther from their context because of the imminent and rapid change of communities. Where will we run, unless we take on the missionary heart of Christ and handle the challenges of transitional communities? These transitions are primarily ethnic, racial, generational, and socioeconomic. Ray Bakke states:

> My urban-pastor colleagues could best find meaning in their otherwise buffeting and discouraging circumstances if they understood the true significance of their roles. They needed to concentrate on their local congregations or neighborhoods, but they also needed to widen their visual lenses in order to see that the *whole world* was coming to their cities. For the first time in nearly 2000 years of Christian history, we could speak realistically of the global mission of local churches.[19]

In her essay, Dr. Baker will lay out more of the specific tools needed by our twenty-first-century pastors and leaders. However, we should emphasize here that the understanding that we are to work out of the Scriptures as the authority for all of life in a mission context is the call for contextualization. In this age, when a continual flow of biblical distortion is entering our churches, it is in the Word of God that we find the transforming power for our communities. Not only is Christ being ignored as the only means and way of salvation (John 16:1–2), but the authority of Scripture is being subverted. Syncretism and liberalism are not necessarily found in the mission enterprise, as often thought. They are found where there is an unbiblical view of Christ and his Word, where evangelism and mission are distorted or omitted.

Donald McGavran once told us that syncretism was not found where evangelism and the saving power of Jesus were proclaimed. There must be a *steady watch and care for our communities*. Pastors, both as gatherers and as watchers, must know their communities. This will entail reading the community formally through census and demographic work and also informally through walking through the community. Visitation is a lost art that must be revived in the city. Technology will not and should not replace the need for face-to-face relationships. It is extremely important that pastors *learn to interpret the community* in a way similar to how they interpret Scripture. In a community where there is a growing population of East Asians, for example, the pastor must know what that transition will mean. Will it mean decline for the church, or will it be a mission challenge that will bring growth and renewal to the church? How we approach people in our context of service will determine the outcome. God desires growth.

How do we apply the Word in light of this sociological phenomenon? How do we communicate the gospel to a people of a different culture and worldview? And how do we as the church of Christ become the agent of the King in this new milieu? The dialogue between the social sciences and theology is rarely reviewed in our educational institutions, but it has to take on greater importance.

Pastors will have a more urgent and profound responsibility in missions. They cannot ignore their function of gathering the flock from within the mission context of the church. "The city, which is the ultimate extension of earthly man and which is therefore capable of evil and good, is both the scene and goal of the Christian pilgrimage. It is therefore the arena of the Christian mission and consequently the context and strategic base of influence for the planting and development of Christian churches throughout the earth."[20] Pastors, along with servant-leaders in the local church, must be trained to model the gospel of the kingdom. Pastors will have to be equipped to understand and apply the holistic vision of the gospel.

The New Relationship Between Sending and Receiving Churches

In this essay, we will be using terms that may cause some difficulty, but our intent is to point out that some nomenclature that is presently used should be abandoned or at least reconsidered. One such set of terms is certainly the "older church" and "younger church" categories. These terms have a history, and at times it has been a negative history. These categories continue to be used today, but seem to have a slightly different edge to them. They are difficult to define, and this will be brought to light in this section. We have also used such terms as "mother church" and "daughter church." The mother church is a church that sends, while the daughter church is the new church being "born." However, these are not biblically defensible categories. Another term we use is "mission church," which is one that is not quite ready to be a "full" and "complete" church. Often denominations do not consider a new start to be a full church until there is more of a self-supporting and self-governing dimension and a number of families are counted; therefore, a mission church is not considered to be a church, and is looked upon as having less in substance and quality than a church.

As the North American sending church becomes more and more dominated by the mission enterprise of the Southern church—the church in Africa, Latin America, and Asia—the language of "younger church" and "older church" is being utilized. Ironically, the younger churches are being started in what are considered to be the new nations. The older churches are mainly Western and Eastern Orthodox churches. How do we define this order? Does geography determine this distinction? Is it based on the historical time line, the chronology of the church? Are the distinctions based on dependency? Which of the churches are more dependent on the others? Dependency is a poor basis for defining churches or drawing conclusions. It may be best for us not to define this global movement in such terms.

Such terminology expresses inherently paternalistic attitudes, held over from an earlier period in the history of modern missions, and thus continue to promote dependency and lead to conflict. In the first phase of modern missions, the sending church in the West was in complete control over the receiving church. The sending church had ultimate power and authority over the mission. There was very little conflict or personal tension, at least visibly, because one was dominant and the other was subservient. This colonial paradigm was oppressive and problematic. The new Christians were considered to be the people being evangelized or the object of the mission group. The leaders, teachers, and experts were those being sent from the dominant mission or sending church. This continued until the early or middle part of the twentieth century, when a second phase began.

In the second historical period, the sending church was still in control, but some consideration was given to indigenous leadership. National leaders were not ignored, but merely tolerated. This was quite frustrating for the national churches. They were part of the mission process, but there was a lingering doubt as to their value in it. Indigenous Christians felt powerless to make a meaningful contribution. This led to a sense that the mission was an employer and the national Christians were employees.

Currently we are in the third phase, in which the "younger" or emerging churches are now clearly in charge and are carrying the major responsibility of the national church. This development of the national churches correlates to some extent with the political climate of the time. As nations became independent, there was a greater opportunity for national churches to become autonomous. Allan Anderson states:

> Africa has witnessed a century of rapid social change with its accompanying industrialization and urbanization, as well as a transition from a pre-colonial period through a traumatic colonial era to an equally traumatic post-colonial order. These factors have affected the formation of new religious movements all over the world, and those in Africa are no exception.[21]

Paternalistic attitudes and practices also lead to organizational tension and conflict between the sending and receiving church. This conflict has at times caused difficulty and sluggishness in the missionary enterprise. When sending churches seek to dominate receiving churches according to the old model, they limit the opportunities for complementary service and partnership. It is still the case, however, that most of the material appearing in mission journals, mission textbooks, and class lectures is authored and published by those from the West.

As we enter the twenty-first century, how shall the process unfold? What should be the response to the new sending churches? Will there be a mutual sharing of resources? Will attitudes of dominance or inferiority or employer-employee relationships be corrected by the church, pastors, and mission societies? It is difficult to determine how we should and will respond to each other, but we must read history and realize that there is much for us to learn from our previous mistakes. David Barrett speaks of the "reaction to mission" principle:

> Barrett thinks that the main cause for the rise of the AIC [African Initiated Churches] movement is socio-political, for he sees AICs as one manifestation of many African protest and resistance movements that arose in the colonial period. He says that the "common root cause" for the whole AIC movement is a reaction to European missions, which exhibited a "failure in love" in their attitudes to African people.[22]

Will the sending church from the South insensitively intrude on the existing North American mission enterprise? Will the priority be control or embracing the opportunity for "our" mission to grow? We will have to rely on a profound spirituality that will embrace the mission of God sacrificially and promote the family of God, unity, and reciprocity as high values. This is a call to humility in Christ. There will, by necessity, be a need for a spirituality that understands the sending God's compassion as we carry out the missionary mandate to reach all nations in partnership with all nations. There must be a reciprocal model of missionary work, based on partnership. The churches must find dependency in each other (1 Cor. 12—"I have need of you"), a *koinōnia* that is significant and presupposes not independence but interdependence (1 Cor. 12:26–27). No longer can one be the donor and the other the recipient.

Another concern will be the status of new missionary works coming from other countries and reaching people of their language and culture in the United States. How will they be treated by their denominations and church fellowships? A recent ethnographic work done by Delia Nüesch-Olver indicated that as Latino missionaries come to reach their particular subgroup, they are stigmatized by their degree of adaptation or assimilation. Many of the denominational leaders who bring these missionaries to the United States do not realize that Latinos have to do cross-cultural work even among their own groups, and that they are unprepared and have few if any support systems. This difficulty is discussed in Nüesch-Olver's article entitled "Immigrant Clergy in the Promised Land."[23] Pastors speak of losing their ministerial status. She notes, "'A Hispanic like me,' said Pastor Hablante, 'will never be elected in this country to the positions of church leadership I had before coming here.'"[24] There is much conflict and loss when immigrant missionaries come to this country.

The Western church cannot provide all the resources, theological training, etc., to the non-Western church. We need each other and must find ways to share our gifts and talents with each other for the advancement of God's kingdom. The gifts and resources are different and should not be compared, one to the other. There must be a change of heart and mind so we can see each other differently and accept one another. We must overcome such categories as mother/daughter, adopted, donor/recipient, and have/have-not.

We must also make structural changes in mission. Mission agencies must have personnel from the minority, national, and international churches involved in their decision-making process. Long-term relationships should be built, leading to mature relationships. In this reciprocal model, we are not necessarily offering similar gifts, but rather the gifts that are necessary and important to each other in the context of evangelizing the world together. There must be more complementary offerings and learning from each other.

Twenty-five years ago, the Lausanne Congress on Evangelism stated that the global Christian mission is a responsibility of the global Christian church and not just a Western missionary responsibility.[25] The call at the conference, as well as for us in the twenty-first century, was for the worldwide Christian church to participate in worldwide mission. We need new partnerships in mission, a global-urban partnership in the spirit of humility. Conn and Ortiz note, "The new wave is distinctive in its location and its accelerated velocity. The wave is breaking on the shores of Africa, Asia and Latin America. And urban metropolises like Mexico City, Seoul and Kinshasa are compressing into a few decades growth that took North American cities over a century to achieve."[26] The future of mission is dependent on humility, mutuality of service and resources, and love for one another as we engage missions globally in the twenty-first century under the lordship of Christ.

Old and New Models for Missionary Enterprise

In my opinion, the new models will not necessarily arise out of this mission era, but rather will come from a reforming of old models—models that are biblical, but need to be contextually sensitive. For one thing, it is important to realize that single models—the one type, one context model—will not accomplish the urban mission task for the twenty-first century. We must consider multiple models as the standard. We must think in multiple forms of church planting, leadership development, community development, leadership selection, stewardship, evangelism approaches, worship, preaching, Sunday school, small groups, and economic development for church plants in the city.

We must keep in mind that the city is dynamic, like culture, and is in constant flux. The urban dynamic needs to help in forming strategies for the city, yet we need to keep our biblical ecclesiology as the authority and principle for all contexts. In the city, there is a diversity of both people and needs. Change and cities go together. The American city is a phenomenon that can only be described in terms of process. The city is a set of interacting systems—political, economic, technological, and sociological—that are constantly changing. This suggests that we need multiple church models for ministry in the city.

The basic foundation and structures are found in the New Testament. First, the church in the New Testament was a *new community*. The members of this new community transcended all earthly barriers—language, culture, socioeconomic status, nationality, vocation, and occupation. It was a community whose members were concerned for others, rather than for themselves. The community was salt, light, body, new creation, etc.

This image of the church challenges the cities that are filled with such diversity. This biblical image of the church should translate into our modern society nicely. That translation might require different forms in different circumstances. It will certainly require a church that is incarnational in its lifestyle. Its members are part of the community in a meaningful way. It is probably multiethnic and multi-socioeconomic and may be multilingual. It takes on the issues of injustice—such as racism, sexism, and oppression—as part of its core values. The new community model is prophetic in that it speaks against evil and social injustice.

The second image of the church is that of *priest*. First Peter 2:9 tells us that the whole church is a priesthood. There may be multiple gifts in the body, with each individual displaying various unique gifts, but the church—both as individuals and corporately—has the office of priest. It will have ministries of mercy and compassion as its major thrust. It will display a lifestyle of prayer, sacrificial giving, incarnational living, and simplicity. The life of the church is one of libation (Rom. 12:1; Phil. 2:17; 4:18; 2 Tim. 4:6). Small groups will be an image of the church in miniature.

The church is also a *pilgrim* (Heb. 13:13). It paves the way, living on the borderline between the "already" and the "not yet." This church is innovative and missiological, giving away its best and seeing the community transformed. It is first local, but it aspires to reach out beyond its boundaries. The regional aspect is missiological in that it wishes to plant new churches in locations where members reside. Small groups are also driven by a mission directive. The church is not to be defined in terms of itself, but in terms of God and the world. It has to cross boundaries into the world.

The church and the city end with a glamorous picture painted by John (Rev. 21:1–6). It is a "Holy City, the new Jerusalem, coming down out of heaven from God, prepared as a bride beautifully dressed for her husband" (v. 2). The city is people; the city is dressed as a bride; the city is being transformed; the city is not going up, but coming down. It is where the nations will be healed because the Lord is making everything new (v. 5). It is already happening, but not yet fully happening. God is transforming the city already and will complete it at the coming of the Lord.

—4—

THE SOCIAL SCIENCES:
TOOLS FOR URBAN MINISTRY

SUSAN S. BAKER

In the U.S., the Immigration Act of 1965 changed the character of immigration guidelines and precipitated a flow of immigrants from Hispanic and Asian countries that has changed the face of many of our cities, especially New York and Los Angeles. As one author noted, "The United States opened itself to becoming a Third World nation."[1]

Is the church ready for this drastic change? Are church leaders prepared and equipped to effectively bring the good news of Christ's transforming power to the many people groups who are ethnically or economically so distant? What do ministry leaders need to learn so they will not be caught spinning their wheels and eventually have to leave their churches (and often the ministry altogether) in frustration and exhaustion? Some organizations, denominations, and seminaries have caught on to the fact that if they are going to send leaders into the city, at least some specialized training is needed. But how effective is it? And what about those ministry leaders who grew up in the city and are pastoring in neighborhoods they once knew well, but are now finding that the neighborhood is changing so rapidly that they are no longer familiar with its people?

Very often when we find ourselves in trouble, we look to the example of others for assistance. We would really like to find a "quick fix" in someone else's life that will make our own problems manageable.

Although we may find those examples inspirational, and they may give us encouragement to continue the race that God has set before us, we soon find that our situation is different in many ways. Those examples are still useful, but we need to start in a different place—with ourselves. We need to reflect on our own history, on what the Lord has been teaching us through our experiences, on what areas are causing us the most problems and why we believe that is so. Therefore, I will begin this essay by letting you walk with me as I reflect on my own life in ministry. The purpose of this is to identify those areas in which I most needed training—areas, I believe, that all people in urban ministry must confront. After identifying these areas, we will approach each one individually. Throughout our discussion, we will raise many questions that will bring us to the Word of God for answers and will also challenge us to use tools not always associated with ministry—those of the social sciences.

Identifying Urban Ministry Issues

Neither my husband nor I had ever been exposed to the city or to other ethnic groups; nor had we ever seriously considered issues such as injustice, poverty, or oppression. We had no urban, missions, or cross-cultural training, yet the Lord brought us into the city over thirty-six years ago to begin a life's work of ministering to the poor and oppressed in inner-city communities.

Throughout our ministry, we have been involved with four different ministry models. We will begin this essay by reviewing these models one at a time and evaluating each one in terms of its strengths and weaknesses in an effort to extract important lessons for all urban ministry workers.

African-American Youth on Chicago's South Side

As students in college, we became involved in a ministry among black youth in the projects of Chicago's South Side. The pastor of this ministry was white, and it was our first exposure to cross-cultural ministry. Basically this ministry was a youth center with numerous programs for the children and a complete Sunday worship time for both the children and their parents. The pastor had a black music director who led all the children in a choir that toured the country numerous times. The Sunday services were contextualized in the areas of music, order of service, and preaching.

Through our exposure to this pastor, we learned the importance of incarnational living, of being a part of the community in which you serve. The early 1960s were not an easy time for African-American communities, especially in major cities of the U.S. Civil rights protests, riots, and gang violence left an aura of tension and danger. Yet this pastor stayed there for over twenty years.

We also began to learn about the existence and nature of oppression and how much the Lord hates oppression. Never having experienced this ourselves, we would get frustrated with people who never seemed to be able to get out of their predicaments. But the pastor started pointing out to us systemic or structural issues that affected his community.

This model of ministry also had its weaknesses. It was independent, tended to be authoritarian, and lacked a commitment to training emerging leaders. The end result was a serious decline in the pastor's personal life as he tried to be everything to everyone, but had no one to hold him accountable for caring for his own life.

Puerto Rican Youth on Chicago's Near Northwest Side

The second model was based on our previous experiences on the South Side, but it was different in a number of ways. This model also focused on children, but it was located in the Puerto Rican barrio on Chicago's Near Northwest Side. Primarily led by my husband, it had a full program of sports, tutoring, summer camping, Sunday services, and personal one-on-one interactions with the children. The major strength of that ministry was a strong commitment to incarnational living. A bonding took place between us and our neighbors that included a reciprocity in meeting needs.

Unfortunately, we fell into the trap of "transplanting" a model. Our ministry was patterned after the one on the South Side, but the differences in context led to a lack of true contextualization. Leadership style was also emulated, and we ended up much like our pastor friend. After seven years, we were totally burned out, just plugging along on sheer grit and a determination not to give up. We had to take some time to evaluate our spiritual lives and find personal renewal in order to continue in ministry.

Church Planting in Chicago Through the Development of Indigenous Leaders

The third model was a church-planting endeavor led by a team of two Puerto Ricans and two Anglos. This model initiated and implemented a strategy to plant a number of churches using trained indigenous leadership. It was during this period that the Lord confronted me with my own sinful attitudes and actions, which were nothing short of what Paulo Freire termed "cultural invasion."[2] This was an extremely difficult time in my life, in which the Lord revealed to me both my sin and his grace as he taught me to be effective cross-culturally.

The strengths of this model were incarnational living, an explicit emphasis on contextualization, team leadership, indigenous leadership development through both formal and informal means, and a missiological emphasis that permeated all decisions. After ten years, there were five churches, an elementary school, a college prep program, a leadership training school, a family counseling center, and an economic development endeavor, all being led by trained indigenous leaders.

The main weakness of this model was that, at least initially, it underestimated the amount of theological training necessary to prepare leaders to serve on a solid foundation.

Multiethnic Church Planting in Philadelphia

The final model, and the one with which we are currently associated, is a multiethnic church plant in Philadelphia. Initially, the plan was to mentor seminary students as part of a church-planting team, with the idea that they would lead the church after graduation. However, for a variety of reasons, we discovered that the students were helpful in the initial phases of starting a new church, but that they were not committed for the long term. This meant that the major leadership reverted back to those with long-term urban ministry experience.

The community in which the church is located is a mix of low-income African-Americans, Hispanics, and some Anglos. This means that our cross-cultural skills are stretched to serve a multiethnic congregation. The Lord has led a number of Asians, as well as Africans, to join the ministry. Besides this ethnic mix, the congregation represents a huge socioeconomic mix, from single moms on welfare to professionals in law and medicine.

The strengths of this model include a conscious effort to meet the holistic needs of a great variety of people; an intentional emphasis on reconciliation along racial, ethnic, and class lines; a solid and growing small group ministry; preaching that is intentionally focused on spiritual maturity; and a strong commitment to training emerging leaders. This ministry has also started other ministries—an elementary school and a community center—and is in the process of developing leaders from within to plant new churches. Also, although congregants come from many areas of the city, the church's focus is solidly on its immediate community.

The major weakness in this model is that because it is so unique, visitors come from all over and many want to join the church. The danger in this is that the people from the community may begin to feel overwhelmed, so that they will participate in the ministries, but not in the church *per se*. The elders and deacons are working diligently to see that this does not happen.

Trouble Spots Identified Through Models

By participating in these models, we were able to identify the areas that are most troublesome to urban ministers—areas that ought to be included in any training curriculum for urban leaders. Four of them immediately come to mind:

1. *The shaping power of culture.* The most important lesson for us actually had to do with ourselves: we needed to understand how deeply our culture had shaped us. Along with that, it became clear just how much the differences attributable to cultural backgrounds influenced the style and content of ministry. An often poorly understood facet of culture is the worldview that underpins it. All urban leaders need to study how their cultural worldview affects both them and others.

2. *The need for incarnational living.* All of the models above promoted incarnational living, yet it is difficult to implement. Its impor-

tance lies in being one with the people you serve, understanding them and the struggles they face, and knowing what issues must be confronted by the Word of God. The bottom line is that ministry must be relevant if it is to be effective. This is usually what we mean by contextualization.

3. *The danger of neglecting your own spirituality.* As we saw in the earlier models, independent ministry can be extremely dangerous as Satan's subtleties can subvert affections that should be for the Lord alone. Also, some form of spiritual accountability ought to be in place for every leader.

4. *The need for evaluation.* This need was not brought out explicitly in the description of models, but many of the mistakes that were made could have been corrected if a process of evaluation had been in place. Leadership, programs, and resources should all be subjected to regular evaluation in order to maintain effectiveness in ministry. With the dynamic transitions that most urban communities are facing, what once worked well may no longer be relevant, and so evaluations must be ongoing.

There are, of course, many other areas that cause concern for urban leaders and which ought to be discussed during a leader's preparation, but these four are responsible for much of the conflict and "failures" we see in urban ministries. Our initial response to all this is often one of despair. It's too much to cope with. How do we do it? We need help. Skills for coping with these tensions will come not only from the Word of God, but through the social sciences as well. We now want to delve deeper into each of these areas and begin to lay out what is needed to avoid the pitfalls that can destroy us.

The Shaping Power of Culture

The most powerful influence of culture is its worldview. One reason for this is that we can't see, hear, or touch it. It is deep-seated, subtle, and taken for granted. The concept of worldview is foreign to many, if not most, of us. So we will begin by defining it.

By *worldview* we mean "the culturally structured assumptions, values, and commitments/allegiances underlying a people's perception of reality and their responses to those perceptions."[3] Another way to define *worldview* is that it is "the basic categories and assumptions people make about the nature of things and the logic that relates these to form a coherent understanding of reality."[4] Conn gives a more expanded definition:

> Worldview . . . becomes the comprehensive belief-framework that colors all of a person's activities. It is a communal direction of the heart, a framework of belief-commitments commonly held by a community of like mind. It includes a person's act of believing, the heart's integrator for all other acts and functions. It includes also the set of beliefs and values flowing from that act of believing.[5]

Worldview is not to be confused with behavior. Our behavior is often conditioned by our worldview, but they are not the same.

It is commonly believed that all Christians operate under a single Christian worldview. What we don't realize is how deeply cultural we are as human beings and how our culture has ingrained us with values and deep-seated assumptions. Some of them are useful and align nicely with the Word of God. Others are sinful, as our culture has been subjected to the evil brought into the world in Genesis 3. And some of our values and assumptions are simply different, and must be recognized as such and not imposed on others.

Characteristics of Worldviews

One of the characteristics of a worldview that Kraft has identified is that "worldview assumptions or premises are *not reasoned out, but assumed to be true without prior proof*."[6] For example, people growing up in white, middle-class society are quite likely to believe, as one of their underlying assumptions, that anyone can succeed in life if he only tries hard enough. They may not consciously say that, but they would probably find themselves looking down on people in poverty and blaming them for being in that situation. This, in turn, affects relationship building and, ultimately, ministry strategy and effectiveness.

Kraft also observes: "In terms of its worldview, *a people organizes its life and experiences into an explanatory whole that it seldom (if ever) questions unless some of its assumptions are challenged* by experiences that the people cannot interpret from within that framework."[7] To better understand this, let's think through the Vietnam War. The U.S. has such a sense of power, that its people cannot fathom that it could lose a war, especially to a small country that most of us had not heard of before. Some Americans even believe that God is on "our side." Because of this assumption, we had to make all kinds of excuses to maintain the façade that we didn't really lose the war. Otherwise, our worldview would have been shaken, and we would have been left in a state of chaos. Paul Hiebert tells us, "There are few fears so great as those which arise when our explanatory systems fail us."[8]

Although Kraft lists a number of other characteristics of a worldview, we will look at only one more: "Of all the problems that occur when people of different societies come into contact with each other, *those arising from differences in worldview are the most difficult to deal with*."[9] If we are used to eating on imported china, with a huge array of flatware laid out on a fine linen tablecloth, we may initially feel awkward or uncomfortable eating from paper plates held on our laps, but we can get used to this type of behavioral difference. However, if our sense of "proper etiquette" tells us that it is wrong to eat in the way that others eat, we will develop a sense of superiority that will cause barriers in relationship building. As you can see, our worldview deals more with *why* we do what we do than with *what* we actually do.

Worldview Universals

There are a number of things that all worldviews address.[10] We won't go into these in much detail here, but we will describe each of them briefly.

First, there is *classification*. Every worldview categorizes reality and establishes criteria by which these categories are defined. One example of this is our concept of family. Most people in the U.S. today tend to think of family as a nuclear family (although that is changing). Other cultures think of family as an extended family, and others go further and think of clans. Almost all people groups recognize the family unit, but the criteria for inclusion in a family may be quite different in different cultures.

A second universal is *the idea of the "self" and the "other."* In a society such as ours, the self is usually an individual, but in many other cultures the self would be considered an entire tribe. To reach such a culture, you would not be effective doing one-on-one evangelism. The tribe as a whole would have to be approached, and that would have to be done through the tribal leadership. We may not run into this in our American cities, but we will run into nonindividualistic views of self, especially with first-generation immigrants.

A third universal is *causality—the forces that produce change.* An example of this can be found in our experiences in Chicago. The community was overrun by gangs, and gang violence was always a concern. Some people believed that gangs were caused by irresponsible parents who let their children do anything, or that there was something innately evil about gang members. To solve the gang problem, their approach was to flood the streets with more and more policemen, make many arrests, and hand out heavy sentences to deter others. However, others saw this approach as putting a Band-Aid on a cancerous growth. They viewed the gang problem in a broader light and realized that members had a deep need for identity and power as they lived in an otherwise invisible and powerless community. In this case, long-range efforts needed to be made to confront the oppressive systems that made gangs such an attractive option.

The fourth universal is *time.* Here we are primarily looking at whether a group organizes its reality with a past, present, or future orientation. The majority American culture is always "saving for the future"—for college, for a house, for retirement, etc. Others have a present orientation and live "paycheck to paycheck." Still others have a past orientation, and put great value on ancestor worship and family traditions. A second consideration has to do with the images that are brought to mind when we think of time. In some cultures, people are always trying to be efficient and "save time." But in other cultures, people don't think about time in terms of hours, minutes, and seconds, but rather talk of sunrises and sunsets. Issues of time are irritating as cultures mix in the city. Urban leaders need to be creative in handling these issues.

The fifth universal has to do with *space*—especially the space around persons and their perception of it. Has anyone ever come up so close to talk with you, that you found yourself backing away? This illustrates an underlying problem of space. We have "personal" areas around us, into which we allow only our most intimate relations (spouses and children, for example); we have areas into which good friends are invited, but not others. When people come from cultures that have different ideas of personal space, relationships between them can be uncomfortable.

The final universal is *the relationship between the "self" and the "other."* The extreme individualism of the U.S. separates the self from the other in almost all areas. Everywhere we hear the slogan, "Look out for number one." The relationship between the self and the other is that the other is useful only if it serves the self, and so the relationship is self-centered. This results in a real inability to build community. Other groups sense responsibility toward the other. Hispanics say "Mi casa es su casa" (my house is your house), and what they mean is that the self is there to serve the other—there is an other-centered relationship.

Layers of Worldview

From this overview, we should be able to better understand why it is so difficult to cross cultures effectively. Most of us do not examine these universals in our lives or even realize that they exist. Now we're asked to understand not only our own cultural worldview, but also the worldview of the cultures to which the Lord has sent us.

This task becomes even more complicated when we realize that our worldviews are not determined solely by our ethnicity, but by other factors as well. Hiebert and Meneses speak of urban worldview themes.[11] A person's worldview—this underlying area of attitudes, presuppositions, and values—is what must be transformed by the blood of Christ. Since we view ourselves as Christians and presume to be guided by a Christian worldview, we are tempted to confuse those pieces of our worldview that are cultural in nature with what is really scriptural. In a Christian worldview, Christ becomes the center of our cultural worldview and permeates every area of it. Conn describes it thus:

The gospel center must always be context-specific. . . . But the center remains center, whether it be Jesus the Messiah (addressed to a Jewish audience) or Jesus as Lord (addressed to a Gentile audience). The gospel "sameness" is not eroded by the gospel's particularization when presented. . . . It is simply being made specifically appropriate.[12]

As Christians, we will not all have the same worldview. What we will have are culturally generated worldviews that are being permeated and transformed by Jesus Christ as the center. Conviction and repentance will be necessary for those areas which are sinful, but many other areas do not need to be uniform for all Christians to celebrate our oneness in him.

The Need for Incarnational Ministry

The second area that often troubles urban leaders is incarnational living. This is especially necessary if we are ministering in communities where the people do not resemble us, or if we are in a transitioning community that seems foreign to us. Men and women training for foreign missions take it for granted that they will have to be at least somewhat incarnational, since their options are limited. But to be incarnational in an inner-city community of the U.S. just doesn't strike us as making sense when we can get there in less than half an hour from a much more comfortable and safe suburban haven.

The primary reason for incarnational living is to better understand the community in which you minister. Incarnational living allows for bonding with neighbors. People are more open when they realize that their community is your community too, that you are dealing with the same issues they are—not from the outside to "help" them, but from the inside because they affect you too.

Besides helping to build relationships, there are two other benefits that come from understanding your community. First, we know that to be holistic in a community, to minister in word and deed, one must know the needs of the community. This is what we call needs assessment, and it cannot be done accurately if we do not understand the community. Second, in order to be relevant in our presentation of the gospel, again in both word and deed, we must contextualize all aspects of our presentation, and this requires an intimate knowledge of the community and its people. Although we are advocating incarnational living, we must remember that being incarnational in itself is not enough; our goal goes far beyond that. Hiebert and Meneses explain:

> The goal of incarnational ministry is not that people understand the gospel. It is that they respond to God's invitation and are transformed by his power. They become new creatures through Christ and members of a new community, the church.[13]

We are going to divide this section into three subsections. First we will present some steps that should help urban leaders in their task of understanding their community. Then we will briefly touch on the reasons for doing needs assessment. And finally we will look at contextualization, along with the dangers that could hinder it.

Understanding the Community

The main purpose of incarnational ministry is to assist us in understanding the community and its needs from the inside. If we don't know the people of the community or what the community is all about, how can we make intelligent decisions regarding ministry strategy? What are the tools that are helpful in bringing about this understanding of the community? In our seminary classes, we have developed a number of steps to gather helpful information. This is a good place to remind ourselves that social science research can only be looked upon as a tool, never as an end in itself. Research must begin with prayer and continue with prayer throughout in order to discern what God is trying to teach us. If we start to put our faith in the research, rather than in God's guidance, the "wisdom" we will gain from the social science analysis may very well be foolishness in God's eye. However, research guided by the Holy Spirit can be of great assistance in discerning God's plan.

Hiebert and Meneses remind us that "we need to use both micro and macro approaches . . . to help us understand this great, complex, and confusing thing we call a city."[14] These two approaches roughly correspond to anthropology and sociology. Sociology looks at the systems of a city and how they interact, while anthropology examines the city more from the street where you meet people and learn who they are. We are going to add two more interrelated, yet distinct disciplines. Demography is the study of populations, their composition, and how they change over time. This is especially important as transitions are being tracked. Also, we need to study both the history of the city and the history of its people groups in order to know why they are the way they are right now.

The first step in understanding a community is one we have already talked about quite a bit, and that is to know your own self. Remember those preconceptions that always seem to be popping up. The second step is to do a walk-through, what Rudy Mitchell has termed "planned awareness walks."[15] This is an exercise that should be done in pairs. It entails a purposeful walk through a portion of your community, during which you make detailed observations. Having a partner helps in identifying questions and interacting on what is seen. More than one walk should be planned, and they should be on different days of the week and at different times of the day, so patterns can be observed. A walk-through is beneficial mostly because of the questions that are raised. Often the questions that come up are based on preconceptions, but that's okay, as long as you resist the temptation to draw conclusions on the basis of those preconceptions.

The next step is to begin to know the individuals who live there. This is where incarnational living is such a help. Shop in the community stores and chat informally with the store owners. Greet people on the street and ask them how they enjoy their community— what they like about it, what they would like to see changed. If there is a park, sit in it for a while and talk with people there. Find out what kind of activities may be planned for that community and participate in them. This is where you are becoming part of the community and why incarnational living is so important. Not only will you be getting to know the people, but they will be getting to know you, too. Try to talk to a variety of people—men and women, young and old—because they will look at the community quite differently.

Another step is to identify the community institutions and interview representatives of them. What schools service the community, and how far away are they? Are there social service agencies or medical facilities nearby? Are there community development corporations, and what is their focus? Ask these professionals what they perceive as the needs in the community and how they are addressing them. Identify other churches in the area, and determine what types of programs they have. Networking is important. The city is not the place to be denominationally protective—we need all of God's people in the city, and there are not enough resources available for us to reproduce programs that are already in place.

The next step is to stand back and take a look at the community as it fits into larger systems—the entire city, the state, the country, and even the world. What are the systems that affect the community, and how do they do it? What happens to a blue-collar community when all the factories relocate to areas where labor is cheaper? What effect does the federal government have on the community when it passes welfare or school lunch legislation? How are teachers selected for schools in the community? What kind of political representation does the community have? What are the major religious forces in the community? These are important questions that directly affect the ethos of the community. After relocating from Chicago to Philadelphia, we were drawn to the North Philadelphia Puerto Rican barrio. It did not take us long to discern that although there were similarities between the barrios of the two cities, there were also major differences—in language, political activism, leadership, religious influence, and even the existence of gangs. These differences were directly attributable to the systemic structures influencing these communities.

Now what about the people groups in the community? An overview of the culture can be obtained through reading materials on that culture. It is also important to know the history of the people's homeland, as well as the interaction between their homeland and the U.S. For example, it is impossible to understand Puerto Rican communities in the U.S. without learning about the colonial relationship that still exists between Puerto Rico and the U.S. Anthropological field work can be done through participant observation and ethnographic interviewing. In this type of research, we learn by sitting at the feet of the culture.

Next we need to review demographic data available for the community. Unfortunately, census data only comes out once every ten years. It is a good place to start, but if you are in a transitioning community toward the end of a decade, you must be wary of these statistics. A good use of the census is to gather data for the last three census periods, compare them, and determine how the community has changed over time. Statistics can also be gleaned from the city's department of vital statistics. Community agencies will often have more up-to-date data because they are needed for grant proposals.

All this information needs to be analyzed by asking two major questions: What information is important to my ministry, and why is it important?

Needs Assessment

One of the benefits of analyzing all this material is that one can gain an understanding of the needs of the community. Door-to-door canvassing of the neighborhood may also be necessary. Without this type of research, valuable resources—both human and material—can be wasted. For example, a church located in a low-income community of Philadelphia decided that affordable health care was needed in its community. Since it had contacts with some Christian doctors and nurses who were willing to give a certain amount of time to a clinic, the church went ahead and set up a clinic, and opened up its services on a sliding-scale basis. However, few people took advantage of their services. It turned out that there was a free clinic less than half a mile away. For poor people, free is better than a sliding scale. The church had made a mistake by not asking people in the community what their needs were. As a result, the clinic lasted only a short time before having to close its doors.

A more subtle issue in doing needs assessment is that of ownership. When community people are consulted and voice their opinions about what needs should be addressed, and then see the church developing programs to help meet those needs, they recognize that they played a valuable and integral role in whatever program ensues.

In turn, they are more apt to support the program and feel more free to offer suggestions along the way.

Contextualization

The concept of contextualization is often misunderstood, and it is fraught with dangers. Let's try to get a grasp on what contextualization is and why it's so important, and then look at some of the dangers to avoid.

Hesselgrave and Rommen describe contextualization as "the attempt to communicate the message of the person, works, Word, and will of God in a way that is faithful to God's revelation, especially as it is put forth in the teachings of Holy Scripture, and that is meaningful to respondents in their respective cultural and existential contexts."[16] Luzbetak describes it somewhat differently when he says, "We understand contextualization as the various processes by which a local church integrates the Gospel message (the 'text') with its local culture (the 'context'). The text and context must be blended into that one, God-intended reality called 'Christian living.'"[17]

Contextualization presupposes that Christian theology has one foot in biblical revelation and the other foot in the historical and cultural context of the people hearing the message. Theology must remain faithful to biblical truth—truth that is understood within a particular biblical, cultural, and historical context—while making that message relevant to the listener. Contextualization is not confined to the message alone. It touches on how we do theology, what Bible translation we use, how we live out the incarnational lifestyle, how we handle church administration, how we plant and grow churches, and what worship style we use.

There are two important points I would like to make here. First, one of the ways our cultural worldview affects us is by influencing how we read and interpret Scripture. For example, two Christians can read what Scripture has to say about stewardship, and yet their conclusions can be quite different because of their cultural conditioning. Some Christians interpret good stewardship as caring for the things that God has provided. Therefore, they are very careful that the church building is not overused, that children are relegated to certain areas of the building, etc. Other Christians may understand stewardship as meaning that we are supposed to use all that God has given to us for his kingdom in every way possible. They do not advocate abuse of the building, but you will find the facilities in use all day, every day.

The other point is that our theology has been built by using the Word of God to answer the questions asked by theologians. Part of contextualization is understanding what questions are being asked and then determining what the Word has to say about them. A theology based on questions that are irrelevant to the listener will soon be discarded as useless.

As important as contextualization is in facilitating relevant communication of the gospel, we must be aware of its dangers. The first danger is that of *cultural relativism or accommodation*. Hesselgrave and Rommen describe this for us:

> False contextualization yields to uncritical accommodation, a form of culture faith. Authentic contextualization is always prophetic, arising always out of a genuine encounter between God's Word and His world, and moves toward the purpose of challenging and changing the situation through rootedness in and commitment to a given historical moment.[18]

Clowney says:

> The Christian answer to relativism is theological: the reality of the Creator God. He is both Creator and Interpreter. Made in his image, we have a relation to his created universe that is not illusory. He is free to reveal himself in time and space, and in the languages of the cultures that develop in human history. Christian theology takes seriously the cultural contexts in which God's revelation is given, and the Christian mission takes seriously the cultural contexts it addresses.[19]

What we're trying to say here is that Satan can easily deceive us as we seek to understand a culture and make Scripture relevant to it. What happens is that we drift closer and closer to a position that says, in effect, that if a culture believes something is right or okay, then who are we to say it isn't? What has happened is that we have forgotten about the authority of Scripture. The biggest task here is determining which pieces of culture are merely different—like using guitars and drums for worship, rather than a pipe organ—and which pieces of culture are sinful and must be brought under the blood of Christ. We must measure everything against the Word of God before we accept it.

A second danger is *reductionism*. In this we find that we have reduced Scripture to only one part of what the Lord has to say to us, and we lose sight of the overall redemptive-historical unfolding of God's complete plan for us. An example of this is found in liberation theology. Many of us have something to learn from liberation theology, as it definitely touches on issues not normally talked about in traditional evangelical and Reformed circles. However, it has reduced the Word of God to only one aspect and has used it to support a political agenda.

Newbigin speaks about this danger:

> Authentic Christian thought and action begin not by attending to the aspirations of the people, not by answering the questions they are asking in their terms, not by offering solutions to the problems as the world sees them. It must begin and continue by attending to what God has done in the story of Israel and supremely in the story of Jesus Christ. It must continue by indwelling that story so that it is our story, the way we understand the real story. And then, and this is the vital point, to attend with open hearts and minds to the real needs of people in the way that Jesus attended to them, knowing that the real need is that which can only be satisfied by everything that comes from the mouth of God (Matt. 4:4).[20]

The third and final danger we will deal with is that of *syncretism*. Conn quotes Douglas and says, "Syncretism was said 'to occur when critical and *basic elements* of the Gospel are lost in the process of contextualization and are replaced by religious elements from the receiving culture; there is a synthesis with this partial Gospel.'"[21] In essence, what we end up with in a syncretistic form of Christianity is a "blend or mixture of Christianity with pre-Christian beliefs and practices relating to supernatural beings and powers."[22] Upon entering a Puerto Rican home, you may see a type of shrine in a corner. On it will be images of Catholic saints and the Virgin Mary, right next to evil-looking spiritist dolls. The families will pray to all of these. In essence, they have just added Christian symbols to their inventory of gods and spirits. This is a visible sign of syncretism.

Although the dangers are real, there is no way to effectively reach our urban communities, with their diverse populations, if we do not contextualize all parts of the ministry. This is difficult, and we can easily be duped by Satan, so we must keep ourselves spiritually alert.

The Danger of Neglecting Your Own Spirituality

The need for spirituality in urban ministry may seem to be a given, and it is not often broached, but all too often the difficulties we face as urban leaders come because of our own spiritual problems. Our cities present an open battleground between God's forces and Satan's forces, and so we must stay focused on our own spiritual well-being in order to ward off Satan's attacks. Robert Linthicum's book, *City of God, City of Satan*,[23] describes that battle, and his last section deals with the spiritual disciplines and the power we receive through them in our ministry. He warns us:

> The most difficult task in urban ministry is to remain optimistic, creative, hopeful, and full of humor. Ministry demands that you give out constantly—and city ministry makes that demand relentlessly. But you cannot give out what you do not have. If you are not replenishing yourself in order to continue the spiritual warfare of the city, then you are exposing yourself to defeat, burnout, and spiritual exhaustion.[24]

The Scriptures admonish us to care for ourselves in Acts 20:28, "Keep watch over yourselves." Just how do we do this when we are so overloaded with responsibilities? Let me make a couple of suggestions.

First, pastors must not be fooled into thinking that they are indispensable, even for short periods. They need to take time away from the ministry to be renewed and refreshed by the Lord. All ministry leaders need to take that one day a month, or one week twice a year, or a portion of one day every week, in which they can concentrate on their own spiritual replenishment.

Second, as we saw in a couple of our models earlier in this essay, pastors need others to hold them accountable. This could be a pastor's elder board, a group of other pastors, or close Christian friends. Linthicum advocates the building of Christian community, the church, as the means to protect ourselves against our own spiritual demise. "If the Gospel is to do anything, it is to change lives. We are to become new creations in Christ. It is our life in community which will most sustain us as we live our new lives. Conversely, lack of community will erode what little faith we have."[25]

We cannot allow ourselves to enter into battle unarmed and unprepared. Urban ministry is intense and frustrating. We have seen throughout this essay how difficult the strains can be, having to deal with constant change and trying to understand people and communities that seem foreign to us. We must recognize where Satan is waiting for us and arm ourselves with the armor of Ephesians 6, or else we will most likely become yet another casualty of the urban war.

The Need for Evaluation

In this, our final section, we will spend some time on evaluation of ministry. Why is evaluation needed? What should be evaluated? How often should we evaluate? How do we make an evaluation? Evaluation is a key component in "staying on top of things." It keeps us from falling into the temptation of following the "that's the way we've always done it" mode of ministry maintenance.

Whenever we are involved in ministry, we ought to be concerned whether we are really doing what we planned to do, and whether what we are doing is an effective use of ministry resources. Notice that I did not say an "efficient" use of resources. Efficiency is not always the best criterion when talking about ministry. Effectiveness implies determining whether what we are doing is significant in building and enhancing God's kingdom.

The first step in evaluation takes place long before the actual evaluation—in fact, it takes place before the ministry even gets started, while it is still in the planning stage. Before any ministry program begins, the expected leaders of that program, in conjunction with the elders of the church, should write out a mission statement and set measurable goals. Exactly what do they expect to accomplish in this program? And exactly how will people be exposed to the gospel through this program? As a part of the planning process, leaders need to be realistic about resources. What will be the necessary staff requirements? Are they to be paid or volunteer positions? What facilities will be required? What finances will be necessary? Will any special equipment be needed? The plan should include a time line that indicates when the first evaluation will be made. Some programs, such as certain training programs, run on a thirteen-week cycle. For such programs, evaluations should be made after each cycle. Other programs run throughout the year (or perhaps throughout the school year). These should ordinarily be evaluated at the end of each year.

One caution should be brought up at this point. Evaluations should be both quantitative and qualitative, and the quantitative should never be emphasized so much that it controls the outcome of the evaluation. Let me give you an example. If your church has a program for new Christians and those who may be seeking, but have not yet accepted the Lord (like an Alpha program), the temptation may be to look at how many people came, or, perhaps more importantly, how many people accepted the Lord during that time. However, qualitative evaluation should also be made. It would look at the spiritual growth in these young Christians. In order to determine how much spiritual growth has taken place, you obviously must know how to recognize it.

Evaluation takes time, and it is often bypassed by churches. This can result in a tremendous waste of resources. For example, if you had four people tied up for three hours a week and a financial commitment of $1,000 a year for a program you were doing in conjunction with three other churches, and after some time had elapsed you realized that all the people utilizing the program were from the other churches, an evaluation would bring up the question of whether the church should continue that program.

Another aspect of evaluation is that no program should be evaluated in isolation from the rest of the church's programs. If one program utilized twelve people from the church for a total of forty man-hours per week, while other programs were struggling to get enough workers, the evaluation might point out that some of those twelve workers could be reassigned to another ministry that needed help.

A temptation in making evaluations, if the church is indeed making them, is to do them a few times until a program starts to run smoothly, and then stop. This will often lead to maintaining programs that may have been relevant and effective at one time, but are no longer relevant or effective, yet are kept around simply because nobody asks whether they still work.

Before finishing this section, let me say a few words about outreach programs. Many churches have day cares, after-school programs, educational and training programs, food pantries, and other outreach ministries. All too often, such ministries slip into meeting the designated need without the participants ever hearing that this is an expression of the love of a God who wants them to be his children and wants to transform their lives.

For example, the community center started by our church had a General Educational Development program. One young man was in the program for two or three years before passing his exams, and just a year or two later was in the hospital on his deathbed. The community center's staff visited him in the hospital and later reflected in shame that they were not sure if he had ever heard the redemption story from them while he was in the GED program. During his last week, the staff members and others from the church made numerous visits to him in the hospital and were very pointed in telling him about God's love. They don't know if he ever fully understood what he was being told or if he accepted the Lord, but this experience certainly made the staff much more aware of their responsibilities to be kingdom builders, not just social service workers. They realized that they might be guilty of having what Conn called world-centered spirituality. "World-centered spirituality considers bodies without souls, and soul-centered spirituality considers souls without bodies."[26] Neither alternative is acceptable if we are to emulate the holistic ministry of Christ himself.

Conclusion

This essay was not meant to be a "how-to" essay. Many social science methods were not even mentioned, let alone discussed in detail. Hopefully, the idea was communicated that the social sciences, when used as a tool in the hands of our sovereign Lord, can be extremely helpful in preparing urban pastors, church planters, and other leaders to be effective in their calling. Urban leaders need training that is specifically designed to equip them as they confront these troublesome areas. We must consider the best way for this to be done. Conn and Ortiz include a whole section (five chapters) in their book *Urban Ministry* on how this can be done.[27] Also, the Greenways have included essays in the present book that detail alternative types of training programs for urban leadership.

Whether their training is formal in a seminary classroom or informal while walking with a mentor side-by-side down the streets, urban leaders must learn how to draw on God's power to combat the many discouragements facing them. They must be prepared to bring the full gospel to the nations coming into our cities.

PART 2

THE CHALLENGES OF
GLOBALIZATION

5

MISSIONS AND THE DOING OF THEOLOGY

PAUL G. HIEBERT AND TITE TIÉNOU

Christian missions challenge the complacency of the church. They call it to look out to a lost and needy world and challenge its tendency to become ingrown and self-satisfied. They call it to admit sinners and challenge its tendency to become a club of the holy. They call it to relate to others and otherness and deal with cultural and religious differences. It should not surprise us that much of the vitality and disturbance in the church today comes from the frontiers of mission.

Unfortunately, as Harvie Conn pointed out, the issues raised by missions are only now appearing in the Christian academy, and there they have led to an academic apartheid.[1] When theology students ask another student what he is doing and he says he is studying missions, there is dead silence or a comment about "showing slides." When mission students ask someone what he is doing and he says he is studying theology, there is an awkward pause or a comment about academic cemeteries. For the sake of the Christian academy, it is important that theologians and missiologists work together, for its existence and that of the church depend on both of them.

Research Traditions

Before we can relate theology to missiology, we need to understand the nature of both. Larry Laudin calls academic disciplines "research traditions"—bodies of knowledge shared by communities of scholars seeking to understand the truth in their fields.[2] Each research tradition is determined by (1) the critical questions it seeks to answer, (2) the assumptions it makes about reality, (3) the body of data it examines, and (4) the methods it accepts as valid means of discovering answers. Different answers or "theories" are offered to key questions, and competing ones are debated until one or the other emerges as accepted doctrine, until it is further questioned. For example, physics, as a research tradition, is the study of the building blocks of the material world, which it assumes is real. It examines material objects using experiments, electron microscopes, ion chambers, and other means to find answers to such questions as What are the basic components of matter? What are the major physical forces? and How do these relate?

Theology is a research tradition. It is a body of knowledge debated by a community of scholars seeking to answer certain critical questions. Because theology is a research tradition, it is an "open inquiry," and it must "treat its sources with *integrity;* it must *integrate* the findings of other disciplines, and it must also require *imagination.*"[3] These factors help us understand the debates among theologians. For instance, in evangelical theology, on the level of theories there is debate between Calvinism and Arminianism, and between premillennial, postmillennial, and amillennial eschatologies. These are genuine debates because the different proponents are asking the same questions and using the same methods. In other words, theology is a research tradition, not because it has arrived at one universally agreed-upon set of answers, but because those in the field are seeking to answer the same questions by using accepted methods of inquiry and examining the same data.

Missiology, too, is a research tradition. It seeks to answer questions related to God's mission in creation and redemption and the church's role in that mission to the world. It ministers to people, and therefore must deal with social and cultural differences. It debates whether churches should be homogeneous or integrated, whether evangelism should include concern for human needs, and whether Christians should dialogue with people of other faiths.

Ways of Doing Theology

How does missiology relate to theology? Before answering this question, we need to clarify what we mean by "theology." We are assuming here that Scripture is divine revelation given to us by God, not our human search for God. Theologies, then, are our attempts to understand divine revelation in our particular historical and cultural contexts. As Millard Erickson points out, it is a second-level activity.[4] It is important, therefore, that we distinguish between revelation and theology, and that we study Scripture carefully, so that our theologies are biblically based. We must keep in mind, however, that our theologies are shaped by the times and contexts in which we live and the questions and methods we use.

There are several ways to do theology, each of which has its strengths and weaknesses. We will examine some of these briefly.

Philosophical Theology

One important research tradition is systematic theology, which uses the assumptions, questions, and methods of modern philosophy.[5] This emerged in the West during the twelfth century, when Greek logic was reintroduced from the universities of the Middle East and Spain.[6] At first, it was seen as "the queen of the sciences," but over time it became one discipline among others in theological education—alongside biblical exegesis, hermeneutics, history, missions, and other disciplines.[7]

The central question that systematic theology seeks to answer is What are the unchanging universals of reality? It assumes that there are basic, unchanging facts, and that if these are known, we can understand the nature of reality. It also assumes that ultimate truth is ahistorical and acultural, and can be fully known. It uses the rules of abstract, algorithmic logic and rhetoric from Greek philosophy, which are propositional in nature, and rejects all internal contradictions and fuzziness in categories and thought.[8] Its goal is to construct a single, systematic understanding of ultimate truth that is comprehensive, logically consistent, and conceptually coherent.[9] In order to arrive at objective truth, it, like the modern sciences, separates cognition from feelings and values, because the latter are thought to introduce subjectivity into the process.

The strength of systematic theology is its examination of the fundamental categories and order in Scripture. In other words, it helps us understand the biblical worldview.[10] It gives us a standard against which to judge our own culturally shaped understandings. In missions, systematic theology is important because it provides the biblical basis for missions and for a sound Christian apologetics that helps us deal with other religions at the philosophical level.

Systematic theology has its limitations. First, because systematic theology seeks to understand reality in universal terms, it faces a difficulty in applying universal truths to particular situations. Universals do not deal with the diversity of human existence. This problem is compounded by the fact that truth must be stated in particular sociocultural contexts. How can the Bible be translated into different languages, each of which views the world differently? How can the church be contextualized in societies that organize groups differently? What is the gospel's answer to problems having to do with the many different beliefs in ancestors, earthly spirits, invisible powers, and divination? In short, how can the one gospel be expressed in different cultures, languages, times, and contexts and remain one gospel?

The search for universals can lead us to overlook the fact that the gospel itself was given to particular people in particular situations. Eugene Peterson writes:

This is the gospel focus: *you* are the man; *you* are the woman. The gospel is never about everybody else; it is always about you, about me. The gospel is never truth in general; it's always a truth in specific. The gospel is never a commentary on ideas or culture or conditions; it's always about actual persons, actual pains, actual troubles, actual sin; you, me; who you are and what you've done; who I am and what I've done.[11]

Christianity does not exist in an abstract form. It has always been incarnated in particular milieus. Age, nationality, gender, church affiliation, and theological bent have a decisive impact on the way in which the gospel is understood and transmitted.

Systematic theology must also deal with the explosion of local theologies that are emerging around the world, as committed Christians formulate their own understandings of Scripture, asking different questions and using different logics.[12] How should we respond to the fact that different theologies are emerging in vital young churches around the world?

The focus on universals has also led theologians to ignore their own particular perspectives in doing theology. All theologies are embedded in worldviews that shape the way theologians see things. This does not mean that we can know no truth. It does mean that we must not equate our theology with Scripture, and must examine the cultural and historical contexts in which we do theology to discern the biases that these introduce into our understanding of Scripture. We must also work in hermeneutical communities in which we help one another check our personal and cultural biases.[13] We must also join in the emerging global hermeneutical community in which theologians from around the world seek to discern God's word for us today. Finally, the stress on universal truth has also led to a divorce between "pure" and "applied" knowledge. This distinction has led to the divorce of theology from missiology and ministry, and a weak sense of mission in systematic theology. As Thomas Finger notes, "Systematic theology arose as a branch of academic study pursued in universities and not primarily as a task of the church involved in the world at large."[14] Missiology is not a division of systematic theology, and systematic theology is not the driving force behind missiology. On the other hand, missions have often appealed to pragmatism to justify their strategies. Both systematic theology and missiology have suffered from this divorce. J. I. Packer writes:

Evangelism and theology, for the most part, go separate ways, and the result is great loss for both. When theology is not held on course by the demands of evangelistic communication it grows abstract and speculative, wayward in method, theoretical in interest and irresponsible in stance. When evangelism is not fertilized, fed and controlled by theology, it becomes a stylized performance seeking its effect through manipulative skills rather than the power of vision and the force of truth. Both theology and evangelism are then, in one important sense, *unreal,* false to their own God-given nature; for all true theology has an evangelistic thrust, and all true evangelism is theology in action.[15]

A second limitation of systematic theology is its difficulty in dealing with history and change. Because it seeks to understand reality in synchronic structural terms, diachronic understandings of change are out of focus. The cosmic drama or plot in Scripture, and the place of events in that drama, are not a part of its agenda. Changes in God's attitudes are often treated as surface phenomena, and not as intrinsic to his essential nature.

Finally, the search for objective truth can lead to a theology that is divorced from the affective and evaluative dimensions of life—from feelings and morality. The result, in education, is a strong emphasis on truth and a weak stress on moral and aesthetic character.[16]

Historical Theology

A second theological tradition to emerge in the West was biblical theology. Reacting to the Scholasticism of post-Reformation theologians, Johann Gabler advocated a new way of doing theology. Spener and the Pietists emphasized theology as a practical science, with a stress on experience and the illumination of the Spirit.[17] In so doing, they advocated a return to the Bible. This gave rise to biblical theology. Their central question was What did the biblical passages mean at the time and to those writing them? In other words, they sought to understand Scripture in its historical context. This led to an emphasis on the unfolding of cosmic history. It assumed that revelation is historical in character—that there is a real world with a real history of change over time that is "going somewhere" and has meaning because it has a plot and culminates in God's eternal reign.[18] This view of theology was fundamental to the Hebrew worldview. To describe ultimate reality, the Jews told and reenacted in rituals the acts of God in their community history.

Biblical theology is "theology that sorts out how the parts of the Bible hang together."[19] It uses the questions, methods, and assumptions of historiography. It draws on the logic of antecedent and consequent causality and accepts teleological explanations. In other words, it views God and humans as acting on the basis of intentions. It is important because it helps us see the big cosmic story in which human history and our biographies are embedded. In doing so, it helps us see God's acts in the confusion of our lives.

Biblical theology has its limits. Because it focuses on diachronic meaning, the fundamental structure of reality remains out of focus—in peripheral vision. Moreover, if we are not careful, it can become a study unto itself, with little application to us today. We focus on the cosmic story, but need to remember that God speaks to us in the concrete settings of human and personal history. Moreover, biblical theology does not always help us discern what in Scripture is historically bound and what are divine principles that need to be applied today.

Tropological Theology

Western Christians, particularly those in academic pursuits, have been deeply influenced by Greek and Hebrew thought. They find it hard to understand Eastern Orthodox theology, which is done in the context of worship and stresses the mystical, sacramental, and iconic nature of truth. The key question that Eastern Orthodoxy addresses is How can we comprehend complex, transcendent truths about God and reality that lie beyond words, logic, and human reason? It assumes that there are mysteries that no theology can unveil. To speak of mysteries that cannot be reduced to words, it uses tropes, such as metaphors, types, myths, parables, and icons, which point to transcendent realities by way of analogy, allegory, type, narrative, and ritual.

One value of tropological theologies is their generative nature. Underlying tropes is the use of analogy between a known reality and one that is being explored. In such analogies, it is clear that (1) there are certain similarities that are the basis for the analogy, (2) there are certain respects in which the analogy clearly does not hold, and to force a fit is to misrepresent the analogy, and (3) there are areas in which it is not clear whether the analogy fits or not. It is this third area that generates a great deal of creative thought and exploration.

A second value of tropological theologies is their integration of ideas, feelings, and response into a living whole. They assume that we must use all our senses—sight, touch, hearing, and smell—to experience truth. They call for emotional and moral involvement with truth that leads to godly character in the theologian. For example, among the Russian Orthodox, the spiritual leader must be "knowledgeable in the Holy Scriptures, just, capable of teaching his pupils, full of truly unhypocritical love for all, meek, humble, patient and free from anger and all other passions—greed, vainglory, gluttony . . ."[20] Theology here is not a cognitive exercise, but a way of living.

Tropological theology is also doxological.[21] It is not an abstract reflection on the nature of truth for the sake of truth itself. It sees theological reflection as an essential element of worship. Christopher Hall writes:

> For the [early church] fathers, the Bible was to be studied, pondered and exegeted within the context of prayer, worship, reverence and holiness. The Fathers considered the Bible a holy book that opened its riches to those who themselves were progressing in holiness through the grace and power of the Spirit. The character of the exegete would determine in many ways what was seen or heard in the text itself. Character and exegesis were intimately related.[22]

Thinking of God must lead to worship and to reflection on life as a daily offering of oneself in service to God.

One of the limits of tropological theologies is their lack of a sense of mission to the world. Another is the difficulty of moving from tropological theologies to the particularities of everyday life and to the contextualization of the gospel in different human settings.

Missiological Theology

Missionaries, by the very nature of their task, must become theologians. Martin Kähler wrote almost a century ago that mission is "the mother of theology."[23] David Bosch notes, "Paul was the first

Christian theologian precisely because he was the first Christian missionary."[24]

Missiological theology is doing theology in everyday life. It reflects on what the Word is saying to our world. Its central question is What is God's Word to humans in their particular situations? Mission theologians assume that mission is the central theme in God's acts on earth, and that all Christians are to be a part of this mission. They also assume that all people live in different historical and sociocultural settings, and that the gospel must be made known to them in the particularity of these contexts. The task of the mission theologian is to translate and communicate the gospel in the language and culture of real people in the particularity of their lives, so that it may transform them and their cultures into what God intends for them to be. Missiological theology deals with matters of God and idols, salvation and damnation, life and death, and disease, hunger, injustice, and oppression. Missiologists begin with questions emerging either out of Scripture or out of human contexts. Reading Scripture raises awareness of sin in lives and societies, and it calls for a response. Encountering human dilemmas raises questions that call for biblical answers.

Missiologists begin by examining the specific human problem at hand in its particular historical and sociocultural context, using empirical analysis and reason to organize their findings. This provides them with an inside or "emic" understanding of the problem, in which they seek to understand the world as the people whom they serve understand it. In the process, they must discover the categories and logic that the people involved use to construct their world.

Emic analyses help us see the world as others see it, but they provide neither a comprehensive understanding of human realities nor a bridge for intercultural communication. Missiological theologians must take a second step and compare different cultures in order to provide a metacultural "etic" grid that enables them to translate between cultures. Here the methods of the human sciences and history, among others, enable missiologists to develop broader generalizations and theories about people and their cultures and histories, based on careful comparisons.

In the second step, missiologists turn to Scripture to throw light on the problems they face in specific human settings. They do so by examining Scripture using the questions, categories, assumptions, and logic that they bring with them. In the process, they must take another critical step, namely, to examine and change their questions, categories, assumptions, and logic in the light of biblical revelation.

The third step is to evaluate the human situation in the light of biblical truth. The logic is that of British and American law, which uses precedent to judge current cases. For the missiologist, the Bible is an accurate record of definitive historical cases of how God worked in particular situations.[25] Much in any culture can be affirmed, for humans are created in the image of God and can create good things. But because all humans are fallen, all cultures and societies are full of sin and stand under the judgment of God.

The final step is missiological. It is to help people move from where they are to where God wants them to be. This process of transformation includes individuals and corporate social and cultural systems. We cannot expect people simply to abandon their old ways and adopt new ones. They can only move from where they are by an ongoing process of discipling and transformation.

One strength of missiological theology is its focus on mission. It takes people seriously, in the particularity of their histories, societies, and cultures. It integrates cognition, affectivity, and evaluation in their response to biblical truth, and defines faith not simply as mental affirmations of truth, nor as positive experiences of God, but as beliefs and feelings that lead to response and obedience to the call of God. It rejects the division between pure and applied knowledge, and sees ministry as a way of doing theology and as a form of worship.

Missiology recognizes that as humans we all live in, and are shaped by, particular cultural and historical contexts, and we can begin only with our existing systems of thought. Recognizing this, missiological theologians consciously reflect on and alter their questions, assumptions, methods, and theories in the light of revelation.

There are limitations to missiological theology. It is easy, in seeking to apply Scripture to human situations, to pick and choose texts with little thought to the underlying theological unity of divine revelation. The result is an easy pragmatism that undermines truth.

Moreover, it is easy to let the methods of human exegesis shape our interpretation of the Bible, and not to examine these categories, logic, and methods in the light of biblical truth. Missiological theology needs both philosophical and historical theology to help it understand the underlying coherence of Scripture.

Complementarity

How do these theologies relate to one another? The Enlightenment sought to build one Grand Unified Theory which integrated all knowledge into one comprehensive system. Today we know that that is not possible. Our human minds are finite and cannot comprehend the full measure of truth even about nature, let alone an infinite God. There is a growing awareness that the "theory of complementarity" offers a way of integrating different, but overlapping understandings of reality into a single, comprehensive understanding of reality.[26] Just as architects make different blueprints for the same building (structural, electrical, plumbing, and so on), and as planners use different maps to map a city (roads, population density, zoning, and so on), so we as humans need to look at reality from different perspectives and through different lenses. Different theologies throw different light on the nature of God, his works, and his revelation.

We need systematic theology to help us understand the questions, assumptions, categories, and logic found in Scripture regarding the structure of reality, knowing that we bring to the task the methods of Greek thought. Gerhard Hasel writes:

> Systematic theology is not made superfluous through biblical [and, we might add, missiological] theology. . . . Systematic theology which takes the Bible as its authoritative source has the function of engaging in a constructive presentation of the meaning of biblical and Christian faith with full usage of information available beyond Scriptural revelation such as history, psychology, sociology, and so forth, as long as such information is subject to the norms of biblical revelation and its truth claims.[27]

We need biblical theology to help us understand the cosmic story unfolding in Scripture, the "mystery" now revealed to us. We need iconic theology in order to transform our theologizing into worship. Here, too, we must put mission at the center of our theologizing.

We need missiology to communicate the transforming gospel into the particular contexts in which humans find themselves, but this needs to build on theological reflections rooted in systematic and biblical theologies, or it will lose its course and its reason to exist.

Finally, we need to make theology—the overall narrative that emerges out of the dialogue between complementary theologies—the center of our Christian life together in the church.[28] Rodger Bassham writes:

> Theology has the task of criticizing and clarifying the church's witness to faith to help it be faithful to the gospel of Jesus Christ and responsive to the context in which the gospel is to be communicated. Finally, a theology of mission must be embodied in the living obedience of faith of individuals and churches as they share in God's plan to unite all things in Christ by the power of the Holy Spirit.[29]

—6—

NEW PATTERNS FOR
INTERDEPENDENCE IN MISSION

SAMUEL ESCOBAR

Harvie Conn's missiology was clearly marked by a dogged commitment to take seriously *the facts* of Christian mission, even when by so doing he would be questioning well-rounded theories that had become the accepted wisdom of evangelical missiology. In the preface to one of his most popular books, he wrote: "This book is an effort at evangelical demythologizing about the city. It looks for grains of truth in the generalizations and tries to shovel away the accumulated snowdrifts."[1] When I moved to Philadelphia, Harvie insisted that I had to see the flourishing ministry of Deliverance Church, an African-American megachurch in the heart of the city, before accepting easy assumptions about the failure of Christianity in urban America. He also put me in touch with Viv Grigg, the New Zealander who went as the typical middle-class missionary to Manila, but immersed himself in the misery of Tatalon and gave us a new way of reading Scripture as a *Companion to the Poor*.[2] Harvie was aware that missiologists had to pay attention to facts even when they were puzzling or paradoxical. He chose a lifestyle that was consistent with his conviction that God has a bias toward the poor, that the present shift of Christianity to the Southern Hemisphere seems to prove the point, and that missiologists had better take notice of this if they are going to remain relevant.

Twenty-five years ago, in that unique moment of missiological awareness that was the Lausanne Congress of Evangelism, evangelicals expressed a dramatic consensus about the urgent need to acknowledge that global Christian mission had become the responsibility of a global church and not only the privilege of the Western missionary enterprise. The Lausanne Covenant expressed it clearly:

> We rejoice that a new missionary era has dawned. The dominant role of western missions is fast disappearing. God is raising up from the younger churches a great new resource for world evangelization, and is thus demonstrating that the responsibility to evangelize belongs to the whole body of Christ.[3]

The Covenant went on to ask all churches to participate in global mission and reevaluate their role continually. For Lausanne, the new forms of partnership had theological and testimonial significance: "Thus a growing partnership of churches will develop and the universal character of Christ's church will be more clearly exhibited."[4] In the face of the urgency of the task, due to the fact that "more than two-thirds of mankind have yet to be evangelized,"[5] the Covenant urged churches and parachurches to pray and to launch new mission efforts.

The Covenant unfolds some of the consequences of taking seriously the new missionary era that has dawned: "Missionaries should flow ever more freely from and to all six continents in a spirit of humble service. The goal should be, by all available means and at the earliest possible time, that every person will have the opportunity to hear, understand, and receive the good news."[6] A note of realism follows in a warning and a call that are especially relevant to the subject we want to explore in this essay: "We cannot hope to attain this goal without sacrifice. All of us are shocked by the poverty of millions and disturbed by the injustices which cause it. Those of us who live in affluent circumstances accept our duty to develop a simple lifestyle in order to contribute more generously to both relief and evangelism."[7]

In the quarter of a century that has elapsed since it was issued, the Covenant's reference to shocking poverty, as well as the call to a simple lifestyle, have become more relevant to our discussion of global partnership for mission. The global situation as we enter a new century is marked by ambivalence. On the one hand, an accelerated globalization process has facilitated communication to the point that we could say that material and technological means are available in order to create and develop transnational and transcontinental partnerships for the recruiting, training, and sending of missionaries. On the other hand, that process is generating a world of economic and social disparities which militate against the possibility of effective and legitimate global partnerships. Given this ambivalent situation, it is time to ask what is implied in the development of new global partnerships.

A Global Church in Mission

Fifteen years after Lausanne, Larry Pate could gather data about the dynamic involvement of Third World churches in global Christian mission. After a brief reference to the gloomy picture that Western missions faced because certain countries were closing their borders to missionaries and other religions were increasingly active, Pate counterbalanced it with a glowing report about "the burgeoning growth of missions by Christians in the Two Thirds world." He stated clearly that "a large part of the future of mission belongs to the missionaries of Latin America, Africa, Asia and Oceania."[8] He also offered a series of statistical studies showing the steady growth of that missionary movement, some valuable case studies, and a directory of Third World agencies that were sending missionaries to other parts of the world.

There has been a steady and significant growth of missionary activity from non-Western countries to other parts of the world. The records we have are approximate and need to be qualified, but in any case they document this growth. Anyone who attends missionary conferences, missionary celebrations, or missiological gatherings knows that representatives of young and flourishing mission organizations from the non-Western world have become more evident also in North America and Europe. We have more nationals sent by non-Western agencies involved in pioneering missionary situations among Muslim, Buddhist, or animistic peoples, and we also have more non-Westerners involved in the new evangelization of Europe and North America and in the promotion and training of traditional Western mission agencies. For example, the figures compiled by Pate show that the number of sending agencies in Latin America went from 61 in 1972 to 92 in 1980 and 150 in 1988. The estimated number of missionaries from Latin America increased from 820 in 1972 to 1,127 in 1980 and 3,026 in 1988.[9] The most recent study available shows that by 1997 there are 284 sending agencies and a total of 3,921 missionaries.[10]

This growth has to be interpreted as more than an imitation of the Western churches or a response to the mobilizing techniques that Western agencies may have developed. Missionary vision and drive have always been connected to movements of spiritual revival, when old churches have been shaken and revitalized. The spiritual vitality of persons, churches, and denominations has nourished the vision and the willingness to obey, and that has made great advance possible in mission. Revival has been the cradle for missionary vocations. Revival has also provided an environment in which new structures for mission have been imagined.[11] A church does not automatically produce missionary vocations in proportion to the number of its members. For example, although half of the Roman Catholics in the world live in Latin America, only 2 percent of the Catholic missionary force come from that region.[12]

The Holy Spirit seems to be especially at work in the periphery of the world, giving Christian people a vision and mobilizing them for local and global mission in spite of poverty, lack of experience, or lack of training. On almost every continent, migrations have brought to cities a legion of mission-minded lay people from Third World churches who make contact with old, established forms of Christendom. These are being rejuvenated by the spiritual warmth and the sacrificial commitment of persons whose parents or grandparents were recent converts from other faiths or from a nominal form of Christianity. If this is the way the Spirit is moving, what needs to be done in order to walk in step with his reviving and transforming activity? What kinds of global partnerships have to be imagined and developed for this new stage of mission history? Obedience to

Christ's commission and the Spirit's missionary drive will keep Christian mission advancing in the twenty-first century, but it will demand a humble and reflective missiological expertise to propose avenues of obedience to biblical imperatives about *the way* and *the style* in which such advance is to take place.

Partnership Within the Framework of Global Disparities

One of the distinctive notes of the Cold War period that followed World War II was the egalitarian socialist dream fostered in part by the utopian Marxist vision of a classless society. Since the fall of the Berlin Wall in 1989, however, it has become evident that the globalization process, driven by the forces of the expanding market economy and Western culture, is left as the most powerful force shaping societies and drawing them into a new world order. A distinctive mark of this new order is the blatant disparity between social sectors or nations with enormous acquisitive power and larger social sectors or nations living in poverty. The prophetic perception of missionaries and missiologists such as Jonathan Bonk and David Barrett, who are among those who have criticized this new order on ethical and moral grounds derived from a Christian worldview, is especially relevant for our missiological reflection. In his effort to confront the serious dilemmas posed by money for Christian mission, Bonk reminds us that two hundred years ago, at the beginning of the Protestant missionary era, the per capita gross national products of the developed and the underdeveloped worlds differed by a factor of less than two; by 1913, the ratio stood at three to one, and it widened to seven to one by 1970. The gap continues to grow at an accelerating rate.[13] Bonk quotes Harvie Conn on this matter:

Missiologist Harvie Conn, addressing delegates to the joint meeting of the American Association of Bible Colleges (AABC) and the Association of Evangelical Professors of Mission (AEPM) held in Chicago in October 1985, argued that the most significant of four pressing issues confronting modern mission endeavours was the growing disparity between shrinking rich populations and the burgeoning poor. He wondered how, as partakers of the wealth and security enjoyed by the relatively few, Western missionaries could sit where the majority of this world's people sit—poor or absolutely poor, with no prospects beyond destitution.[14]

Within this reality, the use of computers and the globalization of information systems available to Christian researchers allow us to have a relatively clear picture of some financial realities to be taken into account as we reflect on partnership. Thanks to these tools, Barrett was calling our attention to some notable contrasts as early as 1983. He pointed out the scandalous disparities within the Christian church at a global level. His figures for that year showed the disparity within the larger global picture:

> Average income at a world level is around $2,400 per person each year. Because Christians are concentrated in the Western world, their average income . . . is far higher at $4,500. Non-Christians average only $1,350. . . . Since lifestyle depends on income, Christians across the world can be seen to live on average at a level over three times higher than non-Christians. . . . There is another factor, however: income distribution is so unequal that, whereas 52 percent of all Christians live in affluence and a further 35 percent are comparatively well off, 13 percent live in absolute poverty.
>
> The degradation and agony of absolute poverty are thus shared by millions of our fellow Christians. Some 109 million Christians live in the world's twenty-six poorest countries. In all developing countries, Christians living in absolute poverty number some 195 million. This is 24 percent of the world's 800 million absolute poor, as well as 13.4 percent of all Christians.[15]

The missiological perspective of Barrett allows him not only to condemn the scandal of disparity, but also to point out the significant fact that the Christian church among the poor is not just a reflection of the abject poverty in which it lives:

How "poor" is the Church of the Poor? . . . Scandalously and outrageously poor. It is surely outrageous that 750 million affluent Christians can continue to allow 195 million brethren in Christ to exist in abject poverty year after year. But from another point of view, . . . this church is largely financially self-supporting, and . . . it has huge potential financial resources. . . . The personal income of the 195 million looks bad enough when expressed as an average of $90 per person per year, but in aggregate it amounts to the huge sum of $19 billion each year. Their churches operate on income of well over $300 million a year, enough to run major relief programs of all kinds.[16]

Side by side with poverty, these churches of the poor show a unique spiritual vitality, which manifests itself in missionary initiative. Barrett adds: "Yet another side of the paradox is that this Church of the Poor is poor only in material goods. They are far from being spiritual paupers. Spiritually it is the Church of the Rich."[17] And he reminds us that some of the more dynamic forms of Christianity today, and the areas where the most rapid church growth is taking place, are to be found precisely in areas of material poverty and destitution. For Barrett,

This Church of the Poor is the only part of global Christianity whose lifestyle is similar to that of Jesus on earth. They are the only Christians who are able with complete accuracy to proclaim, with the Apostle Peter (Acts 3:6): "Silver and gold have I none; but such as I have give I thee: in the name of Jesus Christ of Nazareth, rise up and walk!"[18]

Patterns of a "Stewardship for Survival"

For churches in the world of poverty, and especially for those that are newly formed, life together in Christian community means a continuous effort to prolong the possibility of survival. The self-reliance to which Barrett refers is a fact that catches the attention of unbiased observers. He conducted a massive study of the independent churches of Africa whose vitality and ability to propagate themselves

103

is entirely self-reliant. In fact, it was when they broke away from European or American domination, when they were able to "read the Bible with their own eyes," that theological, financial, and liturgical self-reliance became possible. As missiologists, we must not fall into the trap of idealizing these churches, but neither can we afford to bypass them as we think of global partnerships for mission in the future. Their missionary dynamism expresses a thankful response to their experience of the power of the Holy Spirit and the love of Jesus Christ. The marginal, the lonely, the displaced, and refugees find in these churches "a home for the homeless" and they experience *koinōnia*. The oppressed, who are called *Don Nadie* ("Mister Nobody") because they do not have a name, money, or education, find a community where they may unburden their heart or express their joy in their own way without censorship: the mute speak, and as they speak God's word, they become missionaries. Those who are desperate, because neither psychology nor the fear of police can deliver them from alcohol or drugs, experience the liberating power of the Holy Spirit in the name of Jesus. One can then understand the joyful response by which out of their poverty they become stewards of God's grace and their churches are born with a unique ability to be self-sufficient.

My own experience in Latin America has related to the evangelical and Pentecostal communities that are growing explosively in recent times. The most dynamic among them are either completely free from contacts with Western headquarters or have achieved self-reliance beyond their initial relationship with missionaries. In-depth studies of these churches have helped to clarify the simplistic conspiracy theories provided by both the conservative Roman Catholic hierarchies and the Marxist social science establishment.[19] A well-known Catholic weekly reports: "The Rev. Franz Damen, a Belgian priest who serves as an advisor to the Bolivian Catholic bishop's conference, argues that it is time to lay aside the misinformation and stereotyping of the conspiracy theory. He notes that the Catholic church also receives substantial funding from abroad."[20] In a most enlightening article, Damen proves that in the case of Bolivia, "there is a growing number of sects which have originated in Latin America" and have no connection with the U.S. He also stresses that many churches that were related to North American missions have achieved "an organization, a style, a system of training leadership that are entirely indigenous."[21]

These churches of the poor have what we could call a stewardship for survival. Popular churches planted among the poor cannot depend on a tradition, on the help of the state, on the endowment of rich benefactors, or on a body of professional ministers. They have to be fellowships where members join forces to make the community live, grow, propagate the faith, and survive. The stewardship of the totality of life is experienced as total missionary mobilization. What seems to be more difficult to obtain in the case of developed and established churches is lay mobilization—total participation in the holistic welfare of the Christian community. Among the churches of the poor, such mobilization is the normal lifestyle of the community. No other form of life and ministry is possible. Only after surviving for a certain time does it become possible to speak of patterns of stewardship that involve the community in the great tasks of centrifugal mission. But that experience of voluntary contribution to the survival and growth of the church creates discipline, a new pattern of timing and budgeting, a foundational experience.

What expectations may these churches bring to the table with regard to future partnerships for mission? I must limit myself to pointing out a few. First, these churches would not like to lose the vigor of total mobilization that is characteristic of their missionary patterns. That drive and willingness to be obedient to the prompting of the Spirit is the best contribution they bring to global mission. They may have naïve confidence that "the Lord will provide" or that "he will open a way" even in the most difficult missionary situations. That naïveté may take them to missionary situations that from our Western perspective are disastrous. However, the disposition to obey and the willingness to go are important assets. Their attitude can even affect missionaries from the West who go to live among them!

Second, because involvement in global mission is new, these churches need assistance in training missionaries for participation at that level. However, such training has to be contextual; otherwise, it may stifle spiritual initiative and decontextualize missionaries to the point of making them irrelevant in their own environment and insensitive to the needs of the new places to which they go to work. One serious problem in the development of theological education has been the difficulty of achieving true independence in terms of curriculum design, pedagogical patterns, and content organization. Theological education in the non-Western world has been excessively dependent on Western patterns, not only financially, but also theologically and pedagogically. Missionary education should avoid this pitfall. The tendency in the West has always been to assume that Western training programs and patterns are immediately transferable and translatable. That assumption must be radically revised. I would dare to say that one should start cooperative ventures with the opposite assumption, but work from it in the creative search for adaptation.

Third, participation in global mission requires established and durable institutional structures. Some young churches in the South are fragile and weak, which makes continuous support and care for a missionary effort difficult to maintain. In the enthusiastic or charismatic phase of a movement, institutional structures are secondary, and there is even opposition to them because revival has broken the structures. However, structures are indispensable, though they have to be contextual. This contextuality is very important, considering the framework of disparity that we observed above. Support structures that reflect the needs and demands of an affluent society require drastic revision.

The serious difficulties faced by those who try to reach a workable level of interdependence seem to be related to three factors. First is the lack of a clear ecclesiology, which is an acute problem especially among evangelicals. For instance, interdenominational faith missions without a clear ecclesiology have planted national churches and new denominations. These have no tradition upon which to draw when they face acute pastoral and ecclesiological problems as their numbers grow and their institutions develop. Second, the traditional missionary enterprise has a tendency toward self-perpetuation. And third, we find a lack of acquaintance with, or respect for, the true missionary dynamism of non-Western churches. There is a denomination whose largest churches are ethnic churches in New York that have definite marks of being churches of the poor. However, the leaders of this denomination still base their missionary strategy on the accepted wisdom of Anglo-Saxon missiological think tanks in California.

Before practical advice can be formulated about what is to be done, it is necessary to pose the questions that can help us to understand the problems and to revisit the New Testament model of mission, as well as models of historical missionary obedience. In my observation, the agonizing difficulties of establishing interdependence explain why large mission boards have recently been redefining their missionary strategies and bypassing their national partners. This also explains why missionary structures have been perpetuated, even when the original task to which they were dedicated has been accomplished. Some missiological literature has tried to justify the perpetuation of some missionary structures by affirming the "lack of missionary vision" of the national churches related to those structures.

The basis for a response to the new challenges posed by the need to establish new global partnerships for mission can only be an ecclesiology that serves as the ground for partnership in a way that strengthens the vital communities so that they can carry on a continuous missionary effort. It is understandable that impatience may lead traditional mission agencies to fall into the temptation of creating solid structures in the Western world that would promote the continuity of mission, but also control it. With an adequate ecclesiology, Western and non-Western churches may be able to enter into partnerships characterized by reciprocity and mutuality. After all, that is what characterized the practice and teaching of the apostle Paul.

Mutuality and Reciprocity in New Testament Missionary Practice

Since Roland Allen called our attention to the spontaneous expansion of the church as a New Testament pattern from which we can learn principles that are applicable to the contemporary situation, scholars have better understood the Pauline missionary paradigm. My own study of the Pauline material, coming to it with the questions posed by contemporary missionary situations, has provided me with helpful insights as I explore the practice and teaching of the apostle with regard to finances and mission. Two aspects of it are especially significant and interconnected: his pattern of support for his own missionary work, and his teaching regarding the collection that he organized among the Gentile churches to help the poor Christians in Judea. I have referred elsewhere to the missiological principles of mutuality and reciprocity in the life of the churches, which Paul outlines in 2 Corinthians 8 and 9.[22] In these principles, we come to appreciate the pastoral and missionary creativity of the apostle and its theological roots.

With reference to the collection, Paul's teaching in Romans 15:23–29 comes in the context of his expressed intention to visit Rome on his way to a frontier missionary venture in Spain, which at that time was "the ends of the earth." As an interruption in the flow of this "unreached peoples" kind of discourse, Paul writes, "Now, however, I am on my way to Jerusalem in the service of the saints there" (v. 25). In spite of his plan to evangelize Spain and the sense of urgency he has about it, Paul finds himself on another important missionary trip. The expression "service of the saints" refers to a collection of money that Paul had organized among the Gentile churches in the vast region he had evangelized. He was taking the money to the poor saints in Jerusalem. As Bruce says, "It would be difficult to exaggerate the importance which Paul attached to his work and to the safe conveyance of the money to Jerusalem in the hands of delegates of the contributing churches."[23]

This offering may not seem special to us, but it was something completely new for the Gentile churches. Paul Minear explains:

Financial drives are so routine in our modern churches that we readily overlook the strategic importance of this first drive. It was a startling innovation. Gentile Christians in Macedonia and Achaia had been asked to send money to poor Jewish Christians in Jerusalem. Earlier appeals had been resisted; Paul's authority had been rejected. There were rumours that the whole business was graft.[24]

The resistance of some Jewish Christians to the missionary methods of Paul, who refused to Judaize Gentiles, may have been the source of resentment against Jerusalem. It was probably at Corinth where Paul found the most resistance, and that would explain the long and careful explanations he offers in his second letter to the Corinthians. Minear's conclusion is illuminating:

> Money was thus the root of church conflicts then as now. The heat of conflict, however, had not induced the Apostle to withdraw his request for funds. He had in fact made the gathering of this fund one of the tests of loyalty of the Gentile congregations. He had spent several years at it and had shaped his itinerary to facilitate it. References in five of his letters prove how carefully he planned the solicitation.[25]

In this passage in Romans, as well as in his references to the collection in 2 Corinthians, Paul uses theological language to refer to the financial transaction and theological arguments to explain its meaning. For instance, he refers to the money in question as a *koinōnia* (Rom. 15:26–27), a word with deep spiritual connotations. As Morris says, this is an indication "that the money was not a soulless gift, but the outward expression of the deep love that binds Christian believers in one body, the church (it is used similarly in 2 Cor. 8:4; 9:13)."[26] And in 2 Corinthians 8 we notice Paul's insistence on the voluntary nature of this offering that was to be motivated by love (v. 8). His argument is based on the eager willingness or readiness that the Corinthians had expressed, but which needed completion, for which the apostle was making provision (vv. 10–12). The parallel passage in Romans 15:26–27 twice uses the verbal form "were pleased" to describe the attitude of the believers in Macedonia and Achaia. Paul emphasizes the voluntary nature of this offering: it had to be prepared "as a generous gift, not as one grudgingly given" (2 Cor. 9:5).

What is the theological foundation upon which Paul bases this practice? Setting it in the context of God's saving purpose for humankind, Paul in Romans 15:27 establishes a sense of *mutuality* and *reciprocity* between those who first received the gospel and those who later on were evangelized by them. Paul's own sense of compulsion to evangelize came from the deep source of Christ's love, not from any kind of institutionally governed obligation: "Christ's love compels us" (2 Cor. 5:14). In the same way, spontaneous gratitude to God for the gift of salvation was to be the source of the Gentiles' offering to the poor in Jerusalem. Such is the framework within which we are to understand how the mutual sharing of blessings puts in the same plane the spiritual blessing shared by the Jews and the material blessings shared by the Gentiles. A cultural barrier had been broken along the way, and that was very important for the advance of the mission among the Gentiles, a cause that had in Paul its most outspoken champion. As Leenhardt has shown, "The collection is a manifest sign of the unity of the Church. It shows in concrete fashion that the young shoots were firmly linked to the old trunk."[27] So there are two elements in this holistic view of mission. One is the giving of money, sacrificially in many cases, as an expression of concern for the poor in other lands. The other is the giving of money as a sign of maturity, the completion of the process of evangelization, that the act of offering in itself expresses. In giving, the giver grows and receives a blessing, and the receiver is blessed by the practical help provided for his distress. And the transaction in itself acquires a "eucharistic" dimension (2 Cor. 9:12).

Within this rich framework of mutually belonging to Christ and his body, we are to understand the reference to "equality" in 2 Corinthians 8:13–15. C. K. Barrett says that "the idea is not that the Corinthians and the poor saints in Jerusalem shall change places— poverty in Corinth and luxury in Jerusalem." Rather, Paul "is concerned with fair dealing," that is, "common sense and Christian charity."[28] It is interesting to notice how commentators feel almost defensive about this idea of equality and the reference to the Old Testament as a basis for it. Beware of socialistic temptations! We can safely conclude with Hughes that "the equality proclaimed by Paul is that of the effective display of mutual respect and affection between fellow-creatures and fellow-sinners who by the grace of God have become fellow-believers in Jesus Christ and fellow-citizens of the kingdom of heaven."[29] This is by no means an easy agenda for the days of globalization in which we live.

David Barrett has a fascinating proposal, which is a bit reminiscent of Paul's appeal for equality. I want to conclude this section with it as a challenge to think creatively by revising our assumptions:

> There is plenty of money available worldwide to meet all reasonable Christian global goals and obligations. . . . There is enough to undertake every type of research essential to the prosecution of the churches' life and mission. There is even enough to enable the Church of the Poor to break out of its vicious environment and bring out the rest of humanity with it. It is simply a question of vision, determination, challenge, mobilization, redistribution, management, internal control, and sharing.
> . . . Even the most radical proposal of all—that Christians unilaterally implement a global redistribution of income—is a practical proposition that could have immense global repercussions. A voluntary 10 percent cut in income on the part of all church-member Christians in Europe and North America could produce a 93 percent increase in income on the part of the entire 1.4 billion population of South Asia, or an 82 percent increase throughout Latin America, or an 158 percent increase for every soul in Africa.[30]

The Macedonian Model

The observations about patterns of church life in the non-Western world, especially among the poor, have given me a new appreciation for the piece of missionary education that we find in the "Macedonian model" of stewardship proposed by Paul to the Corinthian church. Within the framework of instructions for his collection that we have been exploring in 2 Corinthians, Paul uses the churches of Macedonia (Philippi, Thessalonica, and Berea) as a model and an incentive to challenge the Corinthians to be obedient stewards. The first nine verses of chapter 8 are an eloquent description of churches that were at the same time poor and generous. Paul's intention is to use those churches of the poor "as a useful measuring rod by which the Corinthians may estimate their achievement in the realm of Christian love."[31]

111

Although it is pastoral and practical, the passage is intensely theological, moving from practice to theology. The generosity of the Macedonians is described with that crucial theological word "grace" (*charis*) (vv. 1, 4, 7). Other key words are also used to describe what, objectively speaking, was a financial transaction: "sharing" (*koinōnia*, as we have already seen) and "service" (*diakonia*) (v. 4). The passage culminates in a Christological statement about the grace of Jesus Christ, who adopted poverty in order to enrich us (v. 9). "The story of Christ is used as in the first instance an example. If the Corinthians are being asked to impoverish themselves for the benefit of others, this is no more than the Lord himself did."[32] Notice how, in four phrases in verse 2, Paul sketches the condition and qualities of the Macedonian churches:

> Out of the most severe trial,
> their overflowing joy
> and their extreme poverty
> welled up in rich generosity.

"The most genuine liberality is frequently displayed by those who have least to give," comments Hughes.[33] Sociologists can only register the fact that the poor are generous and be surprised about it. However, missiology resorts to theology: It is a grace from God, it is the dynamism of the Spirit. Their condition and qualities are sketched in another four phrases in verses 3–4:

> They gave as much as they were able,
> and even beyond their ability.
> Entirely on their own,
> they urgently pleaded with us for the privilege of sharing . . .

The key point comes again as a culmination: "They gave themselves first to the Lord and then to us in keeping with God's will" (v. 5). Here we see the Christological model. The Corinthians are then exhorted to add to their abundance of gifts the one they were missing. Faith, speech, knowledge, earnestness, and love were not enough. There was something they needed to learn from the churches of the poor—the grace of generosity.

In his first letter to the church at Thessalonica, one of the generous churches of Macedonia that Paul mentions above, Paul indicates how to minister to the poor in such a way that they learn to respond to God's grace with generosity. There was definitely no paternalistic attitude in Paul, no assumption that these people were "so poor that they could not give." But there was an incarnational and sacrificial style of ministry. The description of his missionary style emphasizes motivation: "We never used flattery, nor did we put on a mask to cover up greed" (2:5). It also emphasizes sensitivity, which caused him to adopt a flexible tent-making approach to obtaining his support: "Surely you remember, brothers, our toil and hardship; we worked night and day in order not to be a burden to anyone while we preached the gospel of God to you" (2:9). An incarnational and sacrificial style, when imitated by the new believers (1: 6–8), makes them generous in their response to the Lord.

Harvie Conn's urban missiology developed as a reflection on the praxis of all kinds of urban churches in North America and the world, in light of God's Word. What I especially appreciate in his latest books is the attention he pays to what ethnic churches and megachurches in the United States are teaching us about urban mission. In the patient task of gathering data about them and in the tone of many of his comments, I perceive the same sensitivity that Paul the apostle shows as he propounds the "Macedonian model."[34]

Mutuality and Reciprocity in Global Partnerships Today

The Pauline methodology in missionary education, in the practice and teaching of this collection for the poor, is full of suggestions for missionary stewardship in the new global situation. Rather than using the poverty of the Macedonians to make the Corinthians feel guilty, Paul exalts the Macedonian example and shows the possibility of generosity within the framework of reciprocity and mutuality coming from the heart of the poor. Moreover, he crowns his argument with a Christological pointer that actually corresponds to the theological emphasis of the two epistles to the Corinthians. If we could learn from Paul's methodology and return to his theological foundation, we would have guidelines for the many tasks involved in developing patterns of interdependent missionary action in the new global situation. We might be able to correct some of the negative aspects that have developed along the way.

A sacrificial and incarnational missionary style helps the missionary to model in a contextual way how a life of discipline and hard work is a joyous way of responding to God's love and grace. Missionary methodologies and even patterns of support will be chosen in such a way that they do not stifle the Spirit-led response of the poor in their stewardship of survival. The partnership structures are built in such a way that they allow the financially or technologically poor partners to appreciate the value and usefulness of their contribution. To the degree that missionary goals, missionary projects, and missionary education in the new global partnerships are contextual, such an environment of reciprocity is possible. Viv Grigg is a modern missionary whose experience is a real pilgrimage toward a Christlike immersion among the poor in our times. Grigg's vivid account of it is a valuable missiological document, an eloquent case of reflection on praxis.[35]

Missionary pedagogy could benefit from the insights of the Brazilian educator Paulo Freire. When the teacher assumes that the student is an empty vessel that will be filled by the professor from the wealth accumulated in his or her own personal "bank," we have a banking model of education in which students are passive receptors of the treasures imparted by the teacher. In that situation, they may memorize sentences and paragraphs for exams, but will not learn for life. When missionaries see themselves as the bank that has the theological, financial, and missiological resources to be passed on to poor, empty, national vessels, we have a banking model of mission, which, due to inertia or lack of vision, continues in many circles. Missionary partnerships have to avoid the banking approach. Such an approach only stifles the missionary vigor and initiative of non-Western partners. It may turn the partners into passive receptors of the spiritual and missionary plans devised for them at a center in Colorado Springs, Nashville, Wheaton, or Pasadena. But that would not be true partnership in global mission. The time has come for genuine global partnership, following New Testament patterns.

DIVERSITY IN MISSION AND THEOLOGY

WILLIAM A. DYRNESS

Clearly the church is struggling at the turn of the millennium. Christians from all branches of Christendom sit uneasily in the contemporary situation. Our theology seems not to make much difference, even among those calling themselves Christian, and the outreach, at least of the church in the West, is not as effective as it once was. Of all the reasons for this that one might discuss, in this essay I will focus on one aspect of our American cultural situation: what has come to be referred to as our diversity. And by this I refer to all that might be covered under the term *cultural diversity*—our ethnic, religious, and even socioeconomic pluralism. To note just one indicator of our new situation, between 1965, when the immigration laws were changed to do away with quotas based on national origin, and 1994, over sixteen million immigrants entered the U.S. legally, not counting the many illegal arrivals. This figure rivals the earlier waves of immigrants to our country (even if the percentage of foreign-born people was higher in the early 1900s).[1] Or consider a similar indicator: this year, our four-year colleges enrolled more students than ever, but the gap between the richest and poorest students has not narrowed since 1972.

I want to reflect on this reality in relation to missions. Since our situation is much like that of the first century, let me begin with the writings of Paul. Paul, or Saul, as he was originally known, grew up in the midst of a strictly orthodox expression of Judaism—as a Pharisee of the Pharisees, as he put it. But his encounter with Jesus on the road to Damascus radically changed not only his concept of salvation, which was now mediated exclusively through Jesus, but also his views on what we are calling cultural diversity. Christ came to bring salvation, not only to the Jews, but also, by means of a Jewish savior, to all peoples. All people were put on a new footing with respect to God and to each other.

This understanding of things, centering on Christ's death and resurrection, was so radical for Paul that it caused him to revise everything he had previously believed. And it led him at various times to insist on a missionary strategy that appears uncompromising:

> When I came to you, brothers, I did not come with eloquence or superior wisdom as I proclaimed to you the testimony about God. For I resolved to know nothing while I was with you except Jesus Christ and him crucified. (1 Cor. 2:1–2)

That's it, Paul seems to say—take it or leave it. Now we know from other passages that Paul's actual method was much more complicated than this, but Christians have frequently taken their cue from this passage. Missionaries, evangelists, and even theologians have quoted these words for centuries to justify their straightforward presentation of the gospel. But even if this was once an appropriate missionary method, such single-mindedness does not sit well in our increasingly diverse settings. In fact, I want to argue that a closer look at Paul's reflection on diversity suggests a far more complex response to cultural diversity on his part, one that is instructive to us as we begin the new millennium.

Let me begin with a recent discussion of Robert Schreiter on communicating the gospel. Schreiter has thought long and deeply on the implications of diversity for theological reflection. In a recent work, he points out that people's goals in the communication process are in serious conflict: the speaker is primarily concerned with the integrity of the message; the hearers are concerned with their own identity. As he puts it:

The speaker is concerned with getting a message across the cultural boundaries with integrity and lodging it in the world of the hearer in such a way that it will be understood. The hearer, on the other hand, is concerned with finding a place for that message within his or her own world in such a way as to enhance the hearer's identity.[2]

I want to examine this tension between integrity and identity in some detail, because I believe it constitutes the fundamental challenge facing Christians at the beginning of a new century. At the same time, I will argue, making use of Paul's reflection on these things, that responding appropriately to this challenge offers the most promising way forward.

The Integrity of the Message

We begin with the first of these observations: The speaker, the missionary, the evangelist, is concerned with the integrity of the message. And why not? After all, Christians believe unashamedly that the world and its history have been fundamentally altered by God's entrance into human history in Jesus Christ, what G. K. Chesterton called that blow against the backbone of history. Like Paul, Christians whose lives have been transformed by their experience of Christ are anxious that nothing be allowed to obscure the radical, earth-shaking character of that experience. And they want people everywhere to hear about this Savior.

Moreover, throughout history the Christian message has had the greatest impact when it has been offered with integrity, without being compromised by competing ideologies. During the Middle Ages, when the church was in serious need of reform, the proliferating monastic reforms and the new mendicant orders combated the church's accommodation to culture and called Christians back to their primitive calling. The Reformation movements sought above all to free the gospel from the bondage to alien thought forms and cultural captivity, to proclaim the pure word of God.

Later, in the seventeenth and eighteenth centuries, Christians fell back into the habit of accommodating the message to cultural patterns, and, some believe, thereby lost the unique Trinitarian witness to the gospel. In his magisterial study, Michael Buckley notes that Christians used contemporary language and arguments in such a way that God's unique role in creation and providence was lost. One by one, the sciences made their own declaration of independence from first causes, and, says Buckley, "the theologians who had deposited their coin with them found themselves bankrupt."[3]

James Turner notes a similar thing happening in nineteenth-century America. Christians during that century adopted standards of reasoning oriented to a procedural and instrumental view of reality and then sought to employ those in defending Christianity. They sought to assess Christian claims, Turner argues, by using "standards of judgement structured to assess secular truths."[4] Meanwhile, in the revivals of that same century, from Finney to Moody, a simple, heartfelt presentation of the gospel was drawing multitudes into the newly formed Methodist and Baptist churches and enlivening mainline denominations.[5]

Recently this bias toward strict proclamation has received a kind of scholarly support in studies done by sociologists of religion. Beginning with the study of Dean M. Kelley, *Why Conservative Churches Are Growing*,[6] sociologists have realized that the faster growing and more vigorous religious groups in America tend to define their views more precisely, exhibit a wholehearted commitment to their faith, and express an irrepressible missionary zeal. Recent sociologists have developed this line of thinking in two directions. On the one hand, some influential sociologists have propounded a so-called rational-choice theory of religion: religion, like the economy, will thrive most in an atmosphere that promotes a free expression of faith, and where the benefits of adherence are seen to outweigh the objections that might be raised against it.[7]

On the other hand, and more to the point of our argument, other influential sociologists have propounded a so-called new paradigm in the sociology of religion. This has been described in the following terms:

> In a system where religious institutions comprehend not the whole Society but subcultures, modernity, migration, mobility

make it possible for people to found religious associations that are at once self-selected and adapted to present circumstances.[8]

In other words, Christianity will do best when it employs its contextual resources to clearly differentiate itself from other faiths, even as it makes use of current cultural resources to express its identity clearly. This seems to fit well with Paul's insistence on starting from, and holding to, our identity-forming relationship with the crucified and resurrected Christ.

This view has recently been supported by research done by Christian Smith. He found that the vitality of the evangelical segment of the population depends on its ability to form a strong identity over against the dominant culture, while constructively engaging with that culture. His work supports the thesis of the sociologists we have discussed, but he wants to take their thesis further. He agrees that religion survives and thrives in the pluralistic modernized society, but he believes such notions don't go far enough. His research indicates that "in a pluralistic society, those religious groups will be relatively stronger which better possess and employ the cultural tools needed to create both clear distinction from and significant engagement and tension with other relevant outgroups."[9] In a finding that is important to the argument we make below, Smith has found that there is no incompatibility between adherence to a careful expression of one's faith and an engagement with culture. But clearly the strength of a religious community is directly related to the depth of commitment to particular belief structures.

Avery Dulles, a Catholic theologian, has recently cited similar evidence to argue that the Catholic Church, for its part, must also resist the temptation to water down its claims to authority or its insistence on the truth of its teachings. In a noncompromising discussion of these things, Dulles describes in some detail the all-out assault on such claims to authority in our culture: extreme forms of relativism; extreme historicism, which argues that what is true in one era can become false in another; subjectivism, which rejects all objective claims to truth; individualism, which assigns the ability to judge what is right and true to the individual; and an egalitarianism that insists that everyone has the right to his or her own "truth." These all undermine any authoritative teaching, Dulles admits. But the magisterium was never meant to seek popularity. Rather, he notes, the first and indispensable task of the hierarchical leadership is to

> bear witness to the deposit of faith so that the church may always be the "pillar and ground of truth." . . . Its charisma is to adhere constantly to the Gospel of Christ, to discern its implications for the present day and to proclaim it confidently, insistently, in season and out of season, even at the cost of becoming a sign of contradiction.[10]

All of this suggests that Christians are right to insist on the integrity of their message as the starting point of their theological reflection. Not only has this served them well, but the willingness of Christians to hold to their faith even in the midst of severe testing has earned the respect of many who cannot bring themselves to believe that message. Even in the missionary situation, where they deplore cultural imperialism (which we will consider momentarily), national Christians express uniform gratitude for the gospel that the missionaries brought. In Africa, for example, the lack of a center in culture and the diffused spiritual powers often lead to a paralyzing fear. For these people, the news that God has entered history decisively in Jesus Christ and called all powers to account can become relevant in a way that recalls Paul's reference to the Athenians' unknown God. John V. Taylor, who has taught us so much about African Christianity, has this to say about the profound impact of the gospel in Africa: "This discovery that the vague distant creator is the center and focus of every moment of all being is so catastrophic that it may overshadow for a time everything else in the Gospel."[11]

There seems to be good reason, then, not to despise Paul's insistence that we know "nothing but Jesus Christ and him crucified." This is the pearl of great price, for which one should sell everything, and we do not want to compromise this singular call to discipleship. But is this call to follow only Christ—decisive as it is on those ancient and modern roads to Damascus—enough for a full-bodied theology of mission today? More importantly, was it enough in New Testament times?

The Importance of the Hearers' Identity

Remember, our hearers have a different concern. While we are wrapped up with the truth of the message, they care deeply, and sometimes painfully, about their own identity. I have referred to African gratitude for the simple truth of Christ's lordship over the powers. But I must remind us of the damage that Christianity has also done to a sense of identity for the African peoples. Kwabena Damuah, for example, a leading promoter of an African Christianity, argues that the "conflict over the meaning of being African runs through all of African life today—religion, the arts, popular culture and education—so that it is in these areas that many of the struggles over Africa's future in the world are being decided."[12] Testimonies abound of Christians who, having adopted the attitudes and practices of the missionaries, feel bereft of their cultural identity. What do we make of a faith, however successful, that undermines a people's sense of identity, especially of those who have embraced that faith? Does the Christian identity simply eclipse all other identities?

I have a Korean colleague, a Christian leader, who has been concerned for some time about his brother—wanting him to come to faith in Christ. His brother, who lives in Korea, has often heard the message of Christianity. Recently this brother became very ill and finally in the hospital began to pray, telling God that if he recovered he would become an active Christian. But when he was released from the hospital, since he was the eldest brother in the family and therefore under obligation to perform the ceremonies of traditional religion, he came under extreme pressure to perform the rituals that, they believed, expressed their family identity. In the light of the reality and urgency of this identity (who else would perform these rites that held the family together?), the appeal of Christ, made through his brother, lost out. He fulfilled his duty as the eldest son; he did not keep his vow to God.

The question that Christians face, then, is this: How do we connect the urgencies of the quest for identity with the claims of the Christian message? Is there not a relationship between these claims? Must the struggle be settled only in terms of integrity? Or of identity? These questions are, if anything, more urgent now than at any time in recent memory. For one important by-product of our diversity and the globalization of culture and technology is that identities are being challenged on every hand. Immigration threatens host cultures; among immigrants, especially in the second and third generations, questions of heritage and the search for "roots" become central drives. The so-called mestizo identities that emerge lead sometimes to a quixotic quest for racial purity—in its extreme form, to the awful movement we call ethnic cleansing—and sometimes to an embrace of marginality. These are all concerned in some way with truth, but in even more pressing ways they are concerned about the future of their families, sometimes even about their very lives.

In America, these issues are, if anything, more salient than they have ever been. Since the 1960s, as they have been increasingly thrown together, peoples insist more strongly on asserting their ethnic identities. This insistence on recognition, to use Charles Taylor's term,[13] has called forth a reaction on the part of those who fear our national unity is being undermined. We are a people who claim to have forged a unity out of our diversity. But this claim, many believe, is under severe pressure. California, the state in which I live, is poised to become the first state in which the white population will be one minority group among others, but other states will not be far behind. In the Los Angeles School District, well over fifty languages are spoken in the homes of its students. But at the same time, the American ideal is that out of these many, we will form one people—*e pluribus unum*, say our dollar bills.[14] But how are we to be united? And how shall we account for and value the diversity? Clearly this is a central challenge not only for our school districts, but even more particularly for our churches.

The problem in the end is that underlying these discussions of culture and identity lies a paradox: as we earnestly place our initiatives on the ballot to protect our culture, we harbor a nagging suspicion that we do not know who we are. Our claims for recognition are sometimes made to stand for the reality they mean to insist on. Anthony Appiah, in an arresting analysis of these discussions, gives two possible reasons for this uncertainty. First, he points out that we are all creatures of diverse social identities, a diversity that we struggle to understand. And second, as a result, there is clearly a thinning out of our former identities, leading him to wonder if there "isn't a connection between the thinning of the cultural content of identities and the rising stridency of their claims."[15] Clearly, the search for culture-based identities is important, even if we cannot tell how or why.

But if the search for identity is important, so is the quest for finding ways to live together in peace and justice. Accompanying the claims for cultural recognition, which echo literally around the world, are calls for a new kind of assimilation—something that would have been unheard of a decade ago.[16] While we develop the vocabulary of identity and the semantics of diversity, can we learn to speak the language of reconciliation and unity?

In such an atmosphere, Paul's insistence to "know nothing but Jesus Christ" seems positively archaic, or at least irrelevant. But placing this in the larger context of Paul's thought may help us see the relevance. For, in the end, what we find distasteful in the present situation of diversity is not a lack of cultural recognition, but, as Appiah points out, a lack of personal respect. And, for this to be solved, we need to change more than the curriculum or the media, says Appiah, because "culture is not the problem, and it is not the solution."[17] For underlying the calls for recognition are not so much a claim of identity, but the search for one. For Christians, finding our way forward is a challenge, not only for our evangelism and apologetics, but, I will argue, as an opening for our theology as well.

Transformation of Identity

As a means of moving our conversation along, I want to return to the apostle Paul for guidance. I have noted that his encounter on the Damascus road opened new perspectives to him on what we call ethnic identities. But I believe that one can discern two steps in his thinking on these issues, which are instructive for our own situation.

The first moment of truth for Paul, which directly resulted from his encounter with Christ, was elaborated in the book of Galatians. Remember, he had been "a Pharisee of the Pharisees"; one doesn't get any more exclusive than that! Such exclusivism died hard. During the time when this was written, issues of ethnic differences, so important both to Jews and to Greeks, were threatening to derail the fledgling Christian movement. In a famous episode in Antioch, Paul had to rebuke Peter publicly for withdrawing from table fellowship with Gentiles, "for fear of the circumcision faction" (Gal. 2:11–14 NRSV). Apparently, Peter knew he was free from the law as a Christian, but when the conservative Christians from Jerusalem appeared on the scene, he acted differently.

But such behavior, Paul insisted, violated the very center of the gospel. Our identity as Christians now rests on a new basis: "I have been crucified with Christ; and it is no longer I who live, but it is Christ who lives in me" (Gal. 2:19–20 NRSV). Moreover, both Jews and Greeks share in this new status. This puts ethnic differences in a new light. As he explains later, "There is neither Jew nor Greek, slave nor free, male nor female, for you are all one in Christ Jesus" (Gal. 3:28). Ever since this declaration of unity, Christians have consistently claimed that "identification by race, class or sex no longer has any significance because of identification with Christ."[18]

No significance? Clearly Paul, fresh from his encounter with the Jerusalem hierarchy (see 2:1–10), is anxious to celebrate the fact that these divisions present no obstacle to our being accepted in Christ. His point is that all of us, whatever our backgrounds and status, have *equal access to Jesus Christ*. This insight corresponds to our starting point above. Paul is so captivated—indeed, he has been so thoroughly transformed—by his encounter with Christ, that he cannot help himself: we are one in Jesus Christ. This realization, as Taylor notes with regard to African Christianity, for the moment puts everything else in the shade.

I believe that this first insight of Paul lies behind one of the most important modern developments in mission theology: what we call contextualization. In this development, we have elaborated Paul's point that cultural identities and situations present no obstacle to people's ability to hear and respond to the gospel. Missionaries have always known this, of course. But it is only in the last generation that mission theology has explicitly described the relationship between gospel and culture in terms of "contextualization." In the 1970s, missionaries came to realize that Christianity could be understood in terms of any culture, without changing its essential character and without compromising Paul's insistence to know nothing but Jesus Christ and him crucified.[19]

But this discussion, important as it is, does not help us know, positively, what we are to make of the differences between cultures. Clearly, cultures provide no barrier to the communication of the gospel, but do they have a positive role to play in our understanding of the gospel and in the development of our theology? Clearly, our differences do not disappear when we come to faith; indeed, there is strong scriptural support for their presence being in some way intended by God. But in order to know what to make of all this, we need the second step, Paul's second moment of truth. This step I believe we find reflected in the important argument of the book of Ephesians (which I take to be consistent with Paul's thinking, even if one does not grant Pauline authorship). Subsequent to the insights that he had developed in Galatians, Paul continued to come under fire from the Jerusalem Christians, specifically for his support of Timothy and even for taking a non-Christian into the temple. Paul was not hesitant to act on his convictions here—indeed, one might argue that Paul was something of an activist in these matters.

So in Ephesians he returns to the argument of Galatians, but takes it a crucial step further. His subsequent experience and reflection lead him to make the central point in Ephesians 2 in this way: All who were far off, in whatever state they were in, have been brought near because of Jesus Christ (vv. 13–16). He has made them one—this was the argument of Galatians. But then Paul takes a further step that is crucial to our understanding of Christ's work: "And [Christ] has destroyed the barrier, the dividing wall of hostility" (v. 14). Here is the second step for Paul. The new identity that we have in Jesus Christ, in which we have access to God through Christ by the power of the Holy Spirit, takes our differences seriously. Rather than effacing them, this reality removes the barriers that previously existed between them (that is, Paul says, the hostility or enmity between peoples), those awful prejudices and hatreds that lie behind the legal and physical barriers and behind the suspicion and violence. Note carefully what Paul is saying: Because of Christ, we all have equal access to God. But now, further, because of the work of Christ and as an expression of our new identity in Christ, *we all have equal access to each other.*

Paul elaborates on this in chapter 4. After describing the rationale for his Gentile mission in chapter three, he urges the Ephesians to live up to the implications of this new situation. Each of us, he points out, is a recipient of the "grace gifts" of Christ, which he has generously given to his people (4:7). These are given so that God's people might grow into maturity, "to the whole measure of the fullness of Christ" (4:13). However, this maturity does not come to us individually or to us within our ethnic enclaves, but to all of us together, "until we all reach unity in the faith and in the knowledge of the Son of God" (4:13). This happens when the whole body is "joined and held together . . . and builds itself up in love, as each part does its work" (4:16).

Within the unity that is ours because we all share equally in Christ's work (and in his gifts), there is then a necessary diversity that contributes to the building up of the body of Christ worldwide—what Paul calls the joints and ligaments. This means that contextualization of the gospel—that is, lodging it within each of the cultures of the world—while important, is not enough. Something must follow which corresponds to Paul's second great insight in the letter to the Ephesians, a joint and mutually enriched embodiment of the gospel. Because of Christ's work, peace is now possible between the groups, which previously guarded their territory jealously (see 2:15). This allows traffic, mutual exchange, between these parties, whereby each is enabled to enrich the other, and all together can grow toward maturity in Christ. The theological implications of this, it seems to me, are, if anything, more striking than those connected with contextualization. Contextualization emphasizes and values the differences, but it does not allow us to mobilize them appropriately in the service of the gospel. The challenge of the next generation is to move beyond contextualizing the gospel to allowing cultural differences to adorn the gospel.

A colleague at Fuller who is white recently reflected on what it is like to be married to an African-American man. Not long after their marriage some years ago, they visited a photographic exhibition featuring the black experience in America. Included in this exhibit in a local library were scenes of the lynching of a black man. As she stood in front of this picture, she was suddenly struck by the face of this man—she realized with a shock how closely he resembled her new father-in-law. She stood transfixed as Paul's second moment of truth dawned on her—because of her unity with John, and their unity in Christ, these experiences were no longer happening to someone else, but were happening to her! She realized that Christianity is not only a matter of the integrity of the message, but is also equally about the transformation of my identity. In my access to Christ, I also have an irrevocable access to the experience of others. Their gifts enrich me; their sufferings diminish me.

A Theology of Access

What does this mean for our doing of theology? The best guide here, I think, is the theologian Dietrich Bonhoeffer, who was forced to confront his access to others in his struggle against Hitler. His famous account of the small seminary at Finkenwalde, *Life Together*, opens with a reference to a psalm, and references to the Psalms run all through the book.[20] As he notes, he learned to make the Psalms his prayer book; all others, as Luther once said, appeared weak and cold. As he says:

> Whoever has begun to pray the Psalter earnestly and regularly will "soon take leave" of those other light and personal "little devotional prayers" and say: Ah, there is not the juice, the strength, the passion, the fire which I find in the Psalter.[21]

The use of the Psalms as his prayer book had critical implications for Bonhoeffer, for the Psalms embody theologically the point we have just been making. The diversity of the experiences of God's people in these songs of praise and lamentation is important, not only to those who have these experiences, but also to God and therefore to all of God's people. Moreover, they cannot be understood, the psalmist notes, until we enter "the sanctuary of God" (Ps. 73:17).

But this access to the sanctuary of God is not merely a matter of my understanding alone; it decisively affects my worship as well.

For Bonhoeffer, the access we have to each other is the primary means by which we have access to Christ himself. So it turns out that the access we gain to each other through Christ becomes a means by which we come to know more of Christ.[22] As we pray the Psalms, we share in Christ's great high priestly prayer for his people. As David Ford recently commented, "The self that is formed through this discipline is one in community with others who have prayed and continue to pray the Psalms, and so learns the language of this large community."[23] And in this way we can enlarge the community in which our theological reflection is located.

This insight is meant to transform both our life of prayer and our conception of theology. For most of my life, many of the psalms have seemed foreign to me. The experiences related in them have seemed alien to me. So I have focused on those that best reflect my own experience with God. But in hearing Bonhoeffer's elaboration of Paul's theology of access, I have come to realize, with a start, that these other experiences—of grief, loneliness, persecution, thirst, hunger—are not foreign to many of my brothers and sisters in Christ around the world. Believers in the Sudan, Colombia, Kosovo, and Timor are praying these other psalms, and as I read them, I pray their prayers, even as they pray mine.

As an illustration, consider a recent newspaper report of the struggle for survival of women in Burundi today. After years of ethnic strife, many of these women feel caught in the crossfire between ethnic groups, even between government agencies. "We consider ourselves sheep," confessed Innocent Ntiruvakure, a local basket weaver. "We have to follow all the decisions of the politicians."[24] That same day, I was reading Psalm 44, and I came to verse 20:

> If we had forgotten the name of our God or spread out our hands to a foreign god, would not God have discovered it, since he knows the secrets of the heart? Yet for your sake we face death all day long; we are considered as sheep to be slaughtered. Awake, O Lord! Why do you sleep? Rouse yourself! Do not reject us forever. (Psalm 44:20–23)

Those emotions are foreign to me, but they are not foreign to these sisters in Burundi (over 80 percent of which are Christians). And because of Christ, I have access to their suffering and can join with the psalmist in uttering their cries to God. Moreover, this communal reading of Scripture forces me to enlarge the range of my theological reflection. My texts become not only the historical writing and experiences of God's people, but the contemporary stories of believers as well, because these are the record of what God is doing in the world as well. Bonhoeffer's words on this are appropriate:

> A psalm we cannot utter as a prayer, that makes us falter and horrifies us, is a hint to us that here Someone else is praying, not we; that the One who is protesting his innocence, who is invoking God's judgment, who has come to such infinite depths of suffering, is none other than Jesus Christ himself. He it is who is praying here, and not only here but in the whole Psalter.[25]

Bonhoeffer is the theologian of identity because both his experience and, more importantly, his Christology forced him to realize that his involvement with others was essential to who he was as a Christian—it had become a part of his identity. His identification with the Jewish people became for him an archetypal identification with the sufferings of others. His identification with Christ, and therefore with others, and of Christ through these others, continued to change him. It transformed his identity. He saw that Christianity involves not only the integrity of the message, but also, because of that message, mutually transforming identities. As David Ford put it nicely, we "gather ourselves in diverse relationships."[26] Moreover, these relationships are crucial theologically. Because of the work of Christ, they are enabled to reflect and express the inner Trinitarian relationship of the Godhead. As Bonhoeffer put it in his 1933 lectures on Christology:

> Just as Christ is present as the Word and in the Word, as the sacrament and in the sacrament, so too he is also present as community and in the community. His presence in word and sacra-

ment is related to his presence in the community as reality is to figure. Christ in the community is by virtue of his being *pro me*.[27]

So, my experience of Christ, of his being *pro me*, is a function of my experience of his presence in and through the community. This theological insistence has immense significance for our multicultural world.

Notice that what I am arguing relates not simply to the mode of our presentation of the gospel—that we should replace a one-way presentation of the gospel with a kind of dialogue. Dialogue can impose its own tyrannies.[28] Rather, we insist that the center of our message, our access to God through Jesus Christ, implies necessarily our access to others for whom Christ died. This impacts both our method of evangelism and our way of doing theology. It implies a kind of fiduciary structure[29] that, based on the work of Christ, holds on to our connection with other people, whether they are Christian or not. It assumes that what separates us from other people, our enmity and hatred, is far less important than what unites us—that we are both creatures made in God's image and people for whom Christ died.

The challenge to the next generation of mission theologians is to determine whether our theology can truly reflect this transformation. In reviewing the state of theology since World War II, one cannot be sanguine about the answer to this question. Since Bonhoeffer's death and the recovery of his work in the 1960s, there has been a growing gap between peoples of the world, especially between poor nations and rich nations and between the ethnic groups in our own country. Many of the poorest nations reached their current per capita income ten or twenty years ago; meanwhile, ours continues to grow each year. Our per capita consumption has increased steadily (about 2.3 percent annually) over the past twenty-five years. Meanwhile, the growth of consumption in many countries has been slow or stagnant. According to the Human Development Report for 1998, "The average African household today consumes 20% less than it did 25 years ago."[30] In California, the poorest working family today brings home 22 percent less in real dollars than they did in 1969, while the top 1 percent increased their income by 57 percent (to $845,000) from 1993 to 1997 alone![31]

Unfortunately, we have been able to enjoy our growing consumption without a backward glance at those who are left behind, whether they live in Nairobi or South Central Los Angeles. Given that the center of Christianity has now shifted to these poorer countries (and those poorer areas of our own developed West!), people observing Christianity might be forgiven for wondering whether these Christians have been very concerned about the integrity of their message. It clearly has made little difference in their lives; it has not changed their identity. Ironically, those who boast the highest standard of living and display also the greatest spiritual poverty are also the ones who write our theology texts; meanwhile, those with the least often have much to teach us about prayer and dependence on God.

Here then is my thesis: Until we recognize that our ties to Christ give us access to brothers and sisters who are unlike us, to their suffering and their hope, our message will continue to lose its integrity. Worse, unless our theology reflects this larger and more diverse identity, our theology will continue to be the weak and bloodless thing that it has recently become. This is the agenda for theology in the next generation—but could anything be more exciting?

—8—

GENERATIONAL APPROPRIATENESS IN CONTEXTUALIZATION

CHARLES H. KRAFT

When we discuss contextualization, we usually ignore the time factor. I have seen only one brief mention of the differences between first- and second-generation approaches to contextualization in the various studies I have surveyed.[1] We act as if any group that needs to consider whether or not its Christian expressions are appropriate will need to deal with the same things as any other group might. However, situations differ. One of the major ways in which contextualization situations differ has to do with the generation in which they find themselves with respect to the introduction of Christianity. It is important for us to know where a given people group is in their Christian experience before we can speak knowledgeably about the kinds of things that would be appropriate for them.

We often assume that we are working with the first generation of Christians in any given society. But most people are no longer in that generation. So, if we are to be relevant to those who are helping people in the contextualization process, we need to address ourselves to the challenges that face Christians at any point along the way.

In the first generation of a people's Christian commitment, when everything is new and they are just coming out of their pre-Christian experience, the major issues to them may not be concerns about relevance and adaptation to their culture. First-generation Christians

132

are more likely to be concerned about issues of *separation* and *contrast*. Their attention will probably be focused on insuring that they are safe from the revenge of the spiritual powers they have renounced (if they have renounced them). Furthermore, they want to discover which customs they are supposed to reject in order to demonstrate their new faith in contrast to the life of those around them who have not converted.

True, it is important that the newly entered faith be experienced as relevant to at least parts of the lives of the converts. But it is probably too much to expect new converts to develop the energy and insight needed to work out the multitude of details involved in changing their way of life and especially their worldview to fit their new faith. And the converts should not be criticized if they adopt what may eventually look like too much foreignness in the first generation. There will be much adaptation, to be sure, but we shouldn't be surprised if it is quite incomplete at this point, since imitating the outsiders who brought the good news may in their mind be the only way to express their faith.

As we see in Acts 15, even those Jewish Christians who had known Christ for some time had difficulty imagining that Christian faith could be appropriately expressed in Gentile cultural forms. How much more likely is it that those who come to Christ where the gospel is new have the same difficulty of imagining their own cultural forms as vehicles of the new faith. Therefore, they are usually inclined simply to imitate the cultural forms of the outside witnesses on the assumption (often shared by the outsiders) that those forms are God-ordained.

A major problem, however, is the fact that practices that get started in the first generation tend to get "set in cement" and may not be modified or replaced in succeeding generations with more culturally appropriate practices. It seems to be a well-nigh universal tendency for people to regard as absolute, and even sacred, most or all of the cultural forms that the missionaries brought to them. They see to it, therefore, that church members carefully imitate and scrupulously pass on these traditions to newcomers and new generations.

The first-generation problem, on the other hand, is quite different for those who have entered Christianity through a people movement.

When large groups come in with their pre-Christian cultural ways largely intact, they may change their behavior and worldview less than they should. They may simply continue practices that honor their previous gods or that are inconsistent with Christian moral standards, without even knowing that they should change them. It is more likely to be those who convert as individuals or who choose in small groups to go against their previous allegiance who accommodate to the outsiders and change their behavior more than they should.

Either way, there is much contextualizing to be done in succeeding generations. Because of the likelihood of incomplete, inappropriate, or otherwise inadequate contextualization, perhaps we should be looking more to the second, third, or following generations for most of what we seek in the development of appropriate cultural expressions of biblical faith.

Perceiving Relevance

The essence of contextualization (enculturation, localization, or dynamic equivalence), from an evangelical point of view, is the implementation of biblical Christianity in culturally appropriate ways. This is ideally to be done by the insiders of any given society, who perceive the gospel to be relevant and work out ways to express their new faith in appropriate cultural forms. This process is facilitated by the relevant communication of biblical messages to those insiders. But perceptions of relevance differ from generation to generation. What may be considered very relevant in one generation may be looked at in quite a different way by a later generation. Likewise, structures and other forms of expression of the faith that have been worked out as quite appropriate in one generation may be seen as quite inappropriate at a later time.

Given, say, three generations of Christian witness and experience with Christianity, we can assume that there are reasons why the early converts turned to Christ. We can also assume that there are reasons why those of the second and third generations have continued to follow Christ, and why conversions from the non-Christian populace have continued to happen. But the reasons for each succeeding generation will be different.

We can assume that what is appropriate thinking and structuring in the first generation will at best be only partially appropriate for the second, and at worst be totally inappropriate. In addition, whether or not the first Christians did a good job at contextualizing for their time and cultural circumstances, succeeding generations will always have more work to do to complete the task. This is true for at least two reasons: (1) the first generation would not have been able to complete the job even for their generation's needs, and (2) cultural change will have raised some new issues with which to deal.

I advocate, therefore, that the concept of *continuous contextualization* be built into the principles on which any group of Christians operates. This would involve continuous, generation-by-generation reevaluation of church customs and experimenting in one generation with approaches that might well be abandoned in another. This is necessary because the issues are different for each generation, especially in view of the rapid pace of culture change. Even if the contextualization was done right in the first generation, and usually it is not, there will be different issues to deal with in the following generations. Therefore, we need to ask how what might be labeled a "spirit of openness to continual adjustment and change" can be instilled in converts, lest they simply pass on from generation to generation patterns that are culturally and personally dysfunctional.

Dealing with Forms, Meanings, and Empowerment

As anthropologists, we have learned to use the label *cultural forms* to designate all of the parts of culture, including customs, material objects, and cultural patterns such as words, grammatical patterns, rituals, and all of the other elements of culture in terms of which people conduct their daily lives. All of culture, whether surface-level and visible or deep-level (worldview) and invisible, is made up of what we call *forms.*

People, then, as they use and think about these cultural forms, assign meanings to them, usually according to what they have been taught by their parents, peers, and teachers. Although the forms are parts of culture, the meanings belong to the people. They are not inherent in the forms themselves. They are attached to the forms on the basis of group agreements. That is, the people of a society, largely because they have been taught by their elders, agree that certain forms will have certain meanings and, therefore, will be used for certain purposes. When outsiders enter a society, they have great difficulty understanding what is going on because they do not know the agreements of the insiders.

But cultural forms can also be empowered with spiritual power. Such things as material objects, buildings, and rituals can be dedicated and thus convey the power of God (if dedicated to him) or of Satan (if dedicated to him). In dedications, or blessing and cursing, words are used to convey that power. These words are empowered as they are used in obedience to either God or Satan. When cultural forms are thus empowered, they *convey* (not *contain*) spiritual power.

In the Scriptures, we see God empowering such things as the ark of the covenant (Josh. 3:14–17), Paul's handkerchiefs and aprons (Acts 19:12), Jesus' cloak (Luke 8:42–48), and anointing oil (James 5:15–16). But Satan can empower cultural forms also. One passage among many in which it is clear that God recognizes the dangers of satanic empowerment of objects and places is Joshua 7:11–12. There he commands Joshua to cancel that power by destroying captured objects, tearing down altars to pagan gods, and consecrating the land.

Missionary Christianity has been delinquent in dealing with empowerment issues, probably because missionaries haven't known what to do about spiritual power. The fact is, however, that satanic power is usually easy to deal with if it is recognized and handled with understanding and the power of Christ. Material objects that have been dedicated to pagan gods can usually be "cleansed" simply by asserting the authority of Christ to break the power in them. If, however, the object has no other purpose than a religious or occult one, it should be destroyed. Evil power can also usually be removed relatively easily from land and buildings. All that is necessary is for those in authority over them to assert that authority in the name of Christ to break the power that has been bestowed upon them.

There are objects and places that need to be cleansed from evil before Christian activity can take place unhindered. One of several

biblical examples of this principle occurred when King Josiah puri-
fied the temple (2 Kings 23:4–24) from all the abominations of the
worshipers of Baal. Clearly, Josiah removed all evil power from the
temple and from the objects in it. Then, by reconsecrating the objects
and the place to the Lord, he restored God's empowerment to them.

On several occasions, I have heard of, or been consulted about,
mission homes, stations, or churches that have been built on land
that turned out to be infested with evil spirits. One such story comes
from Sierra Leone, where about a century ago the village leaders
deliberately gave some missionaries rights to a plot called Spirit Hill
because they knew it was inhabited by spirits. Missionaries who lived
in the homes built on that land were forced to leave the field by such
things as illness, marriage problems, accidents, and the like until
fairly recently, when someone who understood how to handle satanic
empowerment helped them to break that power. Breaking the power
was relatively easy because of the much greater power of Jesus. It
was discovering the problem that was the hard part, due to the missionaries' ignorance concerning spiritual power. Because of this ignorance, family after family of dedicated missionaries experienced
satanic attacks that could have been prevented.

Evil power also needs to be removed from any objects that have
been dedicated to gods and spirits. Not infrequently, missionaries
and national church leaders are given or buy art objects or work
implements that have been dedicated by their makers or cursed. In
many societies, such dedication is routinely done when the object is
made. And sometimes a curse is deliberately put on the object by
those who wish to thwart God's work. As long as such objects are in
homes or churches, there will be enemy interference. Again, such
empowerment is usually not difficult to break for those who know
what they are doing.

The problem of meaning, however, is much more difficult to deal
with. As pointed out above, meanings exist in people and are
attached by people to cultural forms according to group agreements.[2]
The introduction of Christianity into a society will, of course, involve
both the introduction of new cultural forms and the use of certain
traditional forms in new ways. With regard to the latter, there will
need to be changes in the meanings attached to them. Converts in

the first generation will have to decide what changes to require in the meanings they attach to the traditional forms they retain, as well as the approved meanings of the new forms.

Advocates of the new faith (such as missionaries), since they are outsiders, will not be able to guide all of the choices made by the converts, making it probable that the latter will misunderstand at least some of the meanings intended by the advocates. These misunderstood meanings, then, will likely be passed on to the next generation of Christians, creating a problem (whether or not it is recognized) for the second generation.

Since first-generation converts usually have a primary concern to be differentiated from their unconverted neighbors, they often borrow too many of the cultural forms of the missionaries, on the assumption that those forms are sacred and a necessary part of Christian faith. Such borrowed forms are almost certain to have mistaken meanings attached to them, especially by non-Christians, who have little or no contact with the missionaries or other advocates of the new faith.

Since people in groups change slowly, even highly motivated Christians may not, at least in the first generation, change the meanings of traditional forms sufficiently to assure that the biblical message is being properly communicated. Attempts to "cleanse" words, rituals, and other cultural forms of their pagan meanings often take a long time, even under great pressure. And often there is not enough pressure put on such forms to bring about the necessary changes. For example, Japanese Christians have for several generations used the word *Kami* for God. However, this word is still far from adequate, since it is simply the general word for *spirit* to most people, even to many Christians. Although, for many Christians, the pressure to change its meaning has been reasonably effective, there has not been nearly enough pressure to measurably affect its meaning in the minds of non-Christians and even many Christians, especially new converts.

Recognizing that it is a slow process to change the meaning of traditional forms, many outside advocates have simply introduced foreign words and rituals. In Latin America, for example, after nearly five hundred years of exposure to Christianity, many (perhaps most) of the words and rituals introduced by Roman Catholic missionaries still have pagan meanings. A case in point is the Spanish word *Dios,* which often does not have the same meaning for ordinary people that it had for the Europeans who introduced it. Even after this length of time, *Dios* is usually understood, even by those who call themselves Christians, to be the sun god. Similarly, the name of the Virgin Mary is used to label the moon, and the names of Catholic saints are attached to lesser traditional gods and ancestors. There has not been nearly enough pressure for change coming from inside or outside of the community of those who call themselves Catholics.

What is usually not built into the first-generation concept of Christianity is the need for their understanding of Christian things to be continually developing. This process needs to be calibrated to the growth of the Christian community in its understanding of Scripture and its experience of the presence and power of Jesus Christ. Whenever the expectation of such growth and change is not engendered in the first generation, there will be serious hindrances to increasing the enculturation of the gospel in the second and succeeding generations.

Ideally, new converts need to learn that whatever cultural forms are adopted, adapted, and created in the first generation should be seen as experimental, subject to revision in succeeding generations. Those in the second and succeeding generations, then, should understand that it is incumbent on them to evaluate the first-generation choices in the light of their scriptural understandings and experiences, and to make whatever changes and adjustments seem appropriate.

Since this ideal is seldom realized, Christians of the second and subsequent generations need to be helped to understand the need for them to evaluate and, if necessary, to adjust the cultural forms initiated by the first generation. Even in the occasional cases where the first-generation Christians contextualized well, succeeding generations need to adjust their Christian forms and meanings to *their* reality, a reality that will always differ to some extent from that of their predecessors.

Contextualization and Communication

The process of appropriate contextualization is enhanced by the communication of biblical messages that receptors perceive as relevant to the realities of their life. Receptors have felt needs. Christianity, rightly perceived, relates very well to many of the felt needs of a people.

Receptors, however, attach their own meanings to the messages communicated and, therefore, choose how to use Christian messages in relation to their felt needs. So, we who witness cross-culturally do not have as much control as we would like to have over what our receptors understand and how they use what we present.

Some people are well adjusted in their cultural system; others are not. The former are unlikely to want to change their allegiance when the missionary comes to them with the message of the gospel. Unless there is good reason, such as economic gain or political prestige, the well-adjusted members of a society are not likely to embrace the new faith.

Those who are not making it in a society, however, often jump at the chance to adopt an alternative approach to life, or some part of it. Thus, when foreign ideas are introduced, these convert, hoping to achieve the prestige and status in the new system that eluded them in the traditional system. They have learned to move "up" in the world by moving out of their traditions.

There are other, more legitimate felt needs, though often people are not as aware of these as they might be of the desire to escape from their traditional structures. The need for love, the need for meaningfulness, and the need for forgiveness fall into this category. The need for more spiritual power is also usually there and at a more conscious level.

Historically, Christian witnesses have often given or allowed the impression that satisfaction of these deeper needs comes only at the cost of leaving one's ancestral traditions. That is, people have perceived that only if they become like the foreigners in many ways will they be eligible for such benefits.

Now, moving away from at least some of a people's traditions may well be required at some point for true Christian commitment. And a primary concern of the first generation is differentiation (see below).

What is unfortunate, though, is that people have usually felt that they have to differentiate themselves more by adopting new surface-level cultural forms, usually from Western sources, than by learning to express their deep-level commitments within their traditional way of life.

When this happens, it is because something of the essence of Christianity has not been communicated. Converts miss, usually at least partially because the advocates have not emphasized it, that Christianity is a *process*, requiring continual reevaluation and adjustment as we grow in Christ. Unfortunately, converts often understand their conversion as inducting them into a fairly well defined and permanent state, in which all the rules are set and simply adopted without question, even if the result involves a good bit of poorly understood foreign thinking and behaving.

So, while the messages transmitted may have been relevant, they did not deal adequately with the biblical process of growth. The converts came away with the impression that the cultural forms associated with the first generation were to be forever. These forms are often regarded as sacred, unchangeable, delivered once and for all from heaven to the missionaries and through them to the receiving people. Furthermore, they often feel that these "Christian" forms (including rituals) are magical, containing supernatural power that is available to those who practice them exactly.

There is an important communication principle involved here: When cultural (including language) forms that deal with the supernatural are not understood, they will often be perceived as sacred. People will, therefore, often hold firmly (even fanatically) to these forms, as if the *forms* themselves, as opposed to the *meanings* they convey, were God-given. They will assume that these forms are *magical*, containing power in and of themselves. And people are loathe to abandon or change them, lest they lose the blessing or power that they supposedly contain.

Missionaries down through the centuries have seldom been sufficiently aware of the dangers inherent in such an adoption of their foreign ways to take steps to prevent it. Indeed, many missionaries have assumed, as have their converts, that the foreign ways of worship, organization, education, and theological thinking are God-ordained and thus worthy of adoption by the converts. Only recently have the small percentage of missionaries who receive training for cross-cultural ministry begun to recognize either the need to help people to resist such, often unconscious cultural imperialism or the unbiblicalness of the implicit requirement that cultural conversion accompany spiritual conversion.

The adoption of such "sacred" foreign cultural forms is dangerous because it misleads converts into the unbiblical posture of seeing the essence of Christianity in the *forms*, including the rituals, rather than in the *meanings*. And since the foreign forms/rituals are regarded as magical, invested with power, they are felt to be efficacious only if they are carried out exactly.

Resistance to changing such adopted customs is, therefore, based on spiritual misinterpretation as well as on such things as ignorance of the meaning of Christianity and respect for the advocates and their ways. As Darrell Whiteman points out, this spiritually motivated attachment to Western church customs is probably a greater problem for the first generation than even the common understanding that Christianity requires such customs.[3]

Often, neither the converts nor the missionaries have grasped one of the essential concepts underlying Christianity, that the Christian *meanings* are sacred, not the cultural *forms* used to convey them. Our primary concern, therefore, whether in initial witness or in the continuing practice of the faith, should be that the forms employed be interpreted as conveying the proper meanings. With this in mind, Eugene Nida perceptively contrasts the Islamic concern that Muslims everywhere adopt a large number of "Islamic forms" with the Christian advocacy of what he terms "dynamic obedience" within each cultural context. Nida says:

> While the Koran attempts to fix for all times the behavior of Muslims, the Bible clearly establishes the principle of relative relativism, which permits growth, adaptation and freedom under the Lordship of Jesus Christ. . . . The Christian position is not one of static conformance to dead rules, but of dynamic obedience to a living God.[4]

Different Concerns

To illustrate the different concerns of first- and second-generation Christians, let us take the issue of baptism. Although the first generation of believers in New Testament times baptized converts as adults, what were they to do in the second and succeeding generations, when children were brought up in Christian homes?

Children brought up by Christian parents are in quite a different situation than people who are being converted "out of the world." Adult converts typically have to turn from their non-Christian ways and adopt a new way of life. But children of Christian parents, if they accept their parents' faith, simply affirm the way of life that they were taught as children and continue in it. So, as children of Christian parents, they could be seen as children of the covenant that their parents have made with God.

Soon after the beginnings of Christianity, then, it occurred to the believers that it would be appropriate to develop an initiation ceremony that would function like Jewish circumcision to label each newborn child as participating in the commitment that his or her parents made with God. Hence, rightly or wrongly, the church began to practice infant baptism as a contextualization of Christian initiation for those born into Christian families.

In contemporary contexts, we note the concern of the first-generation converts to demonstrate their differences from the society around them. But at least by the third generation, we frequently find the Christian community sharing a concern with non-Christians to "discover their traditional roots." Such sentiments provide fertile ground for discussions of cultural appropriateness, though resistance to change on the part of entrenched leaders often keeps the discussions from accomplishing much in real life.

First-Generation Concerns: Separation

In the first generation of Christianity, when the gospel is new, converts are usually greatly concerned to make a break with their old ways in order to establish their new identity. Their tendency, then, is to imitate the advocates' ways. Thus, leadership and worship patterns, organizational structuring, biblical and theological training and understandings, and the like tend to be patterned after foreign models, whether or not missionaries have recommended them. The result, then, is *differentiation from*, rather than *contextualization in*, the surrounding culture.

Thus, converts in many places have adopted the kind of clothing used by Westerners and a myriad of other surface-level customs, ranging from housing and eating to courtship and marriage patterns, in their attempts to show supposed differences between themselves as Christians and their non-Christian neighbors.

First-Generation Concerns: Breaking the Power

Many first-generation Christians rightly see the need to break from and reject practices that have traditionally served as vehicles of satanic power. Missionaries, especially those from the West, recognizing that there is a problem, but not knowing what to do about it, usually push people to reject such customs completely. The concern is right, but the way it is usually handled tends to result in what Tippett has called a "cultural void"[5]—a situation in which the local customs are condemned, but nothing is suggested to replace them.

This void leaves most churches planted by foreign (usually Western or westernized) missionaries with an enormous problem. Since no substitute for pre-Christian spiritual power has been provided, large numbers of Christians continue to make use of their traditional power sources. Their commitment to Christ may be quite sincere. But when they need such things as healing, blessing, guidance, and fertility, things their local shamans, priests, and diviners traditionally provide, they feel free to continue their pre-Christian practice of appealing to these traditional practitioners and to the spirits that provide their power.

Several of the problems related to this practice may be illustrated by an experience that our Christian community had while I was in Nigeria. The wife of the village shaman had died quite suddenly. The funeral would, according to custom, last three days, with a great deal of crying, followed by dancing and singing. On the second day of the funeral, the headmaster of our Christian school put the school drum under his arm and led about ninety students to participate in the funeral. This gesture of concern and love by the Christians so impressed the shaman that he started to come to church. He found, however, that the church was filled with his clients—people who, in spite of their commitment to Christ, came to him when they needed a blessing or healing. Since he found no power in Christianity, he soon stopped coming to church.

First-Generation Concerns: Imitating the Powerful

Few things would be more natural than for a receiving group to imitate those who come with greater power, especially if power is their primary concern. In most missionary situations, the outsiders have come with an impressive array of technologically superior machines and implements. Observing such technology, and interpreting it as the result of spiritual power, the receiving groups have naturally assumed the superiority of much of the rest of the missionaries' culture. So, those who converted to Christianity gladly accepted the customs, the cultural forms, recommended by the advocates.

Korean and Japanese Christianity are good examples of this pattern, as are most of the mission-planted churches of Africa, India, the Philippines, and most of the rest of the world. Koreans have developed the art of imitation to such a degree that someone worshiping in any of the churches of Seoul could easily imagine himself in America, except for the language.

Another example comes from the early days of missionary work in Kenya. We are told that the Kenyans, greatly impressed by the technology of the Europeans, sought to discover the secret behind it and focused on reading. They reasoned, perhaps not too inaccurately, that if they could learn to read, they would have access to the Europeans' power. The only flaw in the Kenyans' reasoning was their assumption that they would obtain spiritual power. Although that part of their analysis was wrong, their quest for spiritual power became the motivating factor behind their ready acceptance of Western schools.

The Perseverance of First-Generation Choices

Such first-generation choices would not be a big problem if people understood the importance of making different choices in the second generation. There is, however, in most parts of the world, a pattern of the cultural forms adopted in the first generation persevering into the following generations, whether or not those forms are culturally appropriate. The choices made in the first generation tend to determine the forms in which Christianity will be expressed thereafter. Thus, if the early converts adopt a Western form of Christianity, that form tends to get "set in cement," with the foreign practices seeming to be sacred, even magical, especially because they are foreign.

A major problem arises for second- and third-generation Christians who learn that God wants to interact with them in terms of their own cultural forms. When they attempt to make changes in the direction of appropriate contextualization, they find themselves at odds with the older leaders who insist on preserving the foreign forms adopted by the early converts. They often feel that these forms are right, since the early missionaries were the ones who introduced them, and even that they are sacred and magical. The first generation of Christians tends to assume that the missionaries knew what they were doing when they introduced the forms. I met this kind of attitude in my own ministry in Nigeria. It was felt by Nigerian church leaders and many of the missionaries that I, a young, inexperienced missionary, had no right to question the validity of the recommendations made by the pioneer missionaries who had sacrificed so much to bring the gospel to them.

The assumption of these early missionaries (as articulated to me by one of my contemporaries) was, "We have had two thousand years of experience with Christianity. Therefore, we have a right to tell these people how they should understand the gospel and respond to God." This assumption easily became so basic to the first-generation believers that it never occurred to them to think things through on their own. They never expected to be able to interpret the Scriptures from their own points of view, or to use their own music and musical instruments in worship, or to develop their own requirements for church membership, or to train their leaders in their own ways, or to finance their Christian activities in their own ways, or to do anything else that would signal that Christ and his ways were rooted in their soil, rather than imported wholesale from abroad. They thought that Christianity was supposed to look foreign.

The leaders I worked with had more or less willingly given themselves to what they perceived to be a foreign system. But when some of them learned that they could question and adapt the foreign system and, furthermore, that they could adopt customs and perspectives that came from their own cultural roots, I was accused by my missionary colleagues of undermining what the mission was advocating. And a major piece of evidence against me was the fact that our churches were growing so rapidly! When we left, then, the mission leaders assigned a missionary loyal to the organization (the same missionary who had made the comment about our "two thousand years of experience") to come in and bring our leaders back into line with the westernized system of the mission. He failed in his mission, however, because these leaders had tasted the freedom that comes with experiencing Christianity in their own way.

Baptism can again be used as an illustration. Since the Greek word *baptizō* was transliterated rather than translated into English, its meaning can be argued over forever and the significance of the form exaggerated. The same thing is true of such expressions as "the blood of Christ" and even "in Jesus' name" or "born again." Such expressions and the form of baptism used, since they are so poorly understood, seem sacred and magical and are so used by many Western Christians, especially the more conservative ones.

The Bible is also for many Westerners a magical thing, invested with power of its own, especially if the language is antique and/or academic and sounds theologically sophisticated. Hence, many are attached to versions that they cannot fully understand, but which give the impression that God uses a more sacred form of the language than that spoken by people every day. From such attachment comes the extreme resistance of many to Bible translations in contemporary language. This attitude on the part of missionaries often corresponds to that of non-Western converts who are acquainted with the sacred books of their traditional religion that are preserved in antique, "sacred" language (e.g., the Koran, the Gitas, the Vedas) to settle for minimal intelligibility. They miss the point that most of the Bible was written in highly communicative, even slangy vernacular, and therefore is best represented in translation by that type of language.

So "anticontextual" decisions may be made by first-generation Christians that often are carried on into the second and following generations, even though they are misleading in the practice and communication of Christianity.

Concerns of Second and Following Generations

Although situations differ from society to society, there are a number of common concerns in the second and following generations—some valid, some to be questioned. Legitimate concerns of these generations relate to any lack of appropriateness either to culture or to Scripture that has been passed down to them from the first generation.

Ideally, second and following generations will reevaluate the cultural forms employed by the first-generation converts and make whatever changes are necessary to bring about a better understanding of what God wants to do among them and their people. This habit of reevaluation and the accompanying process of experimenting with new approaches could result in the capturing of more and more of a people's way of life for Christ. Sadly, however, few of the inheritors of first-generation Christianity understand the need for, and the biblical validity of, such adjustments. They prefer to perpetuate whatever the first generation of converts developed in their approach to Christianity in their culture.

Leadership

Perhaps the most important of the questionable concerns are those that relate to the transfer of leadership positions to the younger leaders. The motivations of those who are not yet in power are often somewhat less than biblical. Often those who have prepared to be the next wave of leaders have spent more time in school than did the older leaders and have developed criticisms of how the first-generation leaders have been performing. In addition, they are often impatient to gain for themselves the power that the older leaders have been wielding.

Although second-generation leaders may be critical of the excessive use of foreign cultural forms by the older leaders, the training received by the younger leaders is often designed more to enable them to work within the foreign system than to critique it. When such is the case, a golden opportunity is missed to move the cultural expression of Christianity in the direction of greater appropriateness.

However, when there is discussion of the biblically exemplified relationships of Christianity to culture in the training institutions, there is more hope for change. By studying the ways in which the lists of leaders' qualities in the books of Timothy and Titus relate to their cultural setting, for example, younger leaders can gain insight into the ways in which their cultural leadership ideals can be both incorporated and challenged. Tragically, in many societies the use of schools to train young leaders has led to the appointment of youth to pastoral positions at culturally inappropriate ages, and this has communicated that God is not interested in older men or in working in culturally appropriate ways. Such mistakes can be rectified if training programs seek ways for older and younger leaders to work together, so that the younger ones are sponsored by older leaders when they pastor, either alone or in tandem. In many cultural contexts, it would be appropriate for every pastorate to involve both an older man without academic qualifications, but with prestige in the community, and a younger one who may actually do most of the work.

Second- and later-generation leaders, then, if they develop better cultural and biblical understandings, have a golden opportunity to move things in the right direction.

Relational Aspects of Christianity

Often the need for an initial commitment to Christ is communicated quite well, but the need for growth and developing maturity in the relationship with Christ is neglected. We have usually exported the Western custom of leading a person to Christ and from then on assuming that growth in knowledge will automatically be accompanied by growth in intimacy with Christ and closeness to other Christians. Thus, in a family-oriented society such as Japan, Christianity has come to be known primarily as a classroom, knowledge-oriented faith.

Christians of the second and following generations would do well to study both the relational aspects of Christianity that are presented in Scripture (e.g., John 15) and the relational models that are available in their societies. After this study, practices should be developed that produce growth in these areas. What, for example, are appropriate expressions of love in any given society? And what are the culturally appropriate models of family, friendship, fellowship, recreation, intimacy, and the like that can be adopted and adapted for use in the churches? And what aspects of social life in any given society need to be critiqued and abandoned for scriptural reasons? These issues are often neglected in the first generation, but they can be worked on by succeeding generations.

Music

Worship music passed down from the first generation is often inappropriate. Frequently, the tunes were imported and put with translated words by missionaries and / or first-generation Christians who, in order to distance themselves from their pre-Christian cultural forms, simply adopted foreign musical forms. Perhaps no one taught the first-generation Christians that God could use their music and that there is nothing sacred about Western musical forms. Second-generation Christians ought to be concerned about such inappropriateness (although they often are not), given the importance of music in most societies.

In most societies of the world, people speak tonal languages, and, in many more, music employs a five-note scale, rather than a Western seven-note scale. In such situations, the use of Western music does great injustice to the cause of Christ. Both unconsciously and consciously, the message of foreignness is driven home through music with great force, perhaps more than through any other vehicle.

Second-generation Christians would do well to recognize this and to develop a new and appropriate hymnody. As Roberta King has discovered in teaching African music in Kenya, young Africans, though usually resistant at first to the use of traditional forms of music in worship, can be freed to appreciate and produce truly

African worship music. Year after year, her students have entered her course on African music asking, "Why do we bother with traditional music?" But, by the end of the course, their attitude has usually changed dramatically. They discover both the desire of God to reach their people in terms of their own cultural forms and the relevance and usefulness of traditional music in fulfilling this desire.

Dependence on Literacy

Similarly damaging are the ways in which missionary Christianity has usually been taught to the first generation of converts in societies lacking a tradition of literacy. It was natural for Westerners to introduce such culturally specific forms of education as schools and other educational techniques that are highly dependent on literacy. And there are obvious benefits for those who learn how to read. However, the fact that Christian advocates have largely ignored the rich variety of oral communication forms available in most of the world has again given the wrong impression that God's ways are limited to Western ways. The second and following generations have the opportunity to correct this misimpression by developing the use of oral channels of communication, while not ignoring the use and development of literacy.

The United Bible Societies, Wycliffe Bible Translators, and other organizations that have seen the need to get beyond literacy have recently started to develop creative approaches to the oral communication of Scripture. One of the discoveries coming out of such experimentation is that oral, non-literacy-based communication is often more appropriate in so-called literate societies as well as in those without a long literary tradition. Second- and following-generation Christians can bring great profit to the cause of Christ by working their way out of the captivity to literacy that has characterized much of first-generation Christianity.

Spiritual Power

Although the first generation may have dealt with some power issues, many are usually left for subsequent generations to deal with. This is especially true in the many places where missionary Christianity has largely ignored spiritual power issues and/or simply tried to wean Christians from traditional practices by condemning them. For example, I have heard numerous stories of mission compounds and churches that have been built on land that was infested with satanic power. Those who have lived or worked in these places have experienced various kinds of maladies, from disease to accident to a high level of interpersonal dissension, often without a clue as to where the problems have come from. Taking the land spiritually is, therefore, an important second-generation concern in many parts of the world.

This concern often needs to be brought to the attention of church leaders since, under the influence of Western advocates of Christianity, they have usually become desensitized in this area, at least on the surface. These leaders, like the first generation, would normally be concerned about issues of spiritual power, as would their non-Christian contemporaries. But the fact that their Western mentors do not deal with such issues and, in fact, deal in secular ways with health and emotional problems, has led them either to ignore spiritual power or to deal with it underground. I vividly recall a discussion with a pastor serving under a strongly mission-controlled church who, when he found out that I was knowledgeable about demonization, confessed that he had a secret ministry of deliverance. Most of his colleagues either would have avoided such ministry or, as he did, would have kept their practices secret from church leaders and outsiders, in order to perpetuate the fiction that demonic problems don't exist in their societies anymore.

A major issue is the problem of dealing effectively with demonization among church members. Following the Western custom, the entrance requirements of churches in most parts of the world have simply been a testimony of conversion and some biblical and denominational teaching. The fact that most, if not all, of the people coming out of paganism into Christianity are carrying demons has not been appreciated. Thus, our churches (both overseas and in America) are full of demonized people, and the demons have great opportunity to work from within the churches. Of special concern should be the "cleaning up" of those who come out of non-Christian religions and secret societies. Often, in our ignorance of how demonization works, we assume that conversion gets rid of the demons.

I wish that were the case, but it isn't. Christians of the second and following generations need to give major attention to this problem.

Fortunately, some understanding of these issues is coming into training programs, in both the sending and the receiving countries. Unfortunately, receiving peoples in many places have developed their own ways to deal with these issues. I am appalled to hear stories, both from Korea and from Africa, of Christians attempting to free people from demons by beating them. Some demonized people have even died during such attempts at deliverance. Such practices, and many others that do harm while attempting to free people, need to be taught against, and those who practice them need to be shown better ways of dealing with demonization.

Other Concerns

Such issues as the cultural appropriateness of church government, how the faith is propagated, how the work of Christ is financed, and even, in many places, what language should be used in worship, ought to be reexamined in the second generation, especially if they have not been handled appropriately in the first. In many situations, there has been some contextualization of these concerns in the first generation, but more needs to be done.

Often, the way Christianity was presented and structured in the first generation remains fairly appropriate to one segment of any given population—the westernizing and, often, the more urban segment. More traditional and, usually, more rural segments of the society, however, often find very little that is culturally appropriate in how Christianity is practiced. A challenge that needs to be faced by the second and subsequent generations, then, is to plant churches that are contextualized within traditional and/or rural culture and that, therefore, differ significantly from the more Western and/or urban varieties.

I wonder how many more Koreans, Japanese, Thai, Nigerians, or Indian Americans might come to Christ if they could participate in churches that are more culturally appropriate to their traditional ways than the ones that represent Christ in these places today? I am not saying that churches that are more or less appropriate to the culture of the westernizing segment should to be abandoned. However, there need to be in every society other churches, differing in their cultural orientation, aimed at attracting traditional and rural people.

It is likely that biblical standards that require changes in the culture will need to be addressed more fully in the second generation than they were in the first. The application of biblical standards can mean either the stiffening of standards that were not strongly applied in the first generation or the relaxing of standards that were too strongly applied or that were applied in a too Western manner. In many contexts, for example, much attention needs to be given to discovering and applying moral standards that are both culturally and biblically appropriate. Often the cultural disruption brought about by westernization (largely outside the control of the advocates of Christianity) has resulted in major moral problems. On the other hand, culturally insensitive rules against such things as polygamy, nonchurch weddings, dancing, social drinking of alcoholic beverages, and the like need to be reexamined and, often, modified in the second generation, if Christianity is to be appropriately scriptural. Without such reexamination and change, a major negative reaction against Christianity lies in store for the third and following generations.

Third and Subsequent Generations

The issues mentioned above usually continue to be issues in the third and following generations. As the years go by, however, things that are not dealt with become more and more entrenched and usually become more difficult to deal with. This is especially true in the many situations where biblical understanding of the relationship of Christianity to culture is minimal. For example, where Christianity is treated merely as a religion, even by its adherents, rather than as a relationship, as it is portrayed in Scripture, a deadening nominalism easily takes over in the third generation, if not sooner.

The disease of nominalism speaks of the need for renewal. Renewal is often stimulated by new information and new approaches to old problems. Thus, the cultural sensitivity advocated here, when properly linked to Scripture, can become a source of renewal. So can

154

greater experience of God's power. The latter is transforming Christian experience in Argentina.[6] Third-generation Christians could well be advised to seek new emphases, while praying that these will lead to renewal.

By the third generation, many peoples are expressing nationalistic concerns, especially if they feel that they have been held down by colonial political and religious structures. Often, in reaction to Western domination in government, church, economics, and most other dimensions of life, the intellectuals begin to influence their followers by glamorizing traditional ways of life that they have never really known. Contextualizing in these generations, then, needs to take nationalism into account and to beware of the tendency for people to use Christianity to address concerns that are more cultural than biblical. Down through the ages, for example, national groups that have emigrated out of their home areas, such as Armenians, Eastern Orthodox, Koreans, and Irish Catholics who have come to America, and Japanese or Korean Christians who live in Brazil, have used their Christianity to enhance their ethnic identity. Certain brands of "America first" Christianity fall into this category also.

Nominalism and nationalism, then, are crucial problems that third-generation Christians need to deal with. There are usually also many of the earlier problems that have not been resolved. It is important at this stage for believers not to give up on the need to work toward greater biblical and cultural appropriateness.

Conclusion

We should be concerned about what *meanings* are getting across to those who hear the gospel. The question is how to enculturate Christianity in such a way that people attribute scriptural meanings to the cultural forms employed. First-generation Christians usually do some things right in this regard, but frequently leave much to be done and create much that ought to be redone by later generations.

I have tried to focus on some important issues and to point to the responsibility of the second and following generations to deal with the omissions and commissions of the first generation. Although it is easy to criticize many of the decisions of the first-generation converts and of the outsiders who often misled them, we should sympathize with their position. They didn't know how to do what needed to be done. We can, therefore, give them the benefit of the doubt and ask those of the second, third, and succeeding generations to rectify things.

The sad thing is that these later generations often attain little more understanding of the relationship of Christianity to culture than their predecessors had. They often simply perpetuate the mistakes of the past and even add their own mistakes to them. This enables those around them to continue to misunderstand what Christianity is all about.

I wonder, for example, what might happen in Korea or Japan if a truly appropriate Christianity were developed. Many Koreans, of course, have turned to Christ, but largely to a Euro-American Christianity. But approximately 70 percent of Koreans have not yet come to Christ. Would the 70 percent respond positively to a truly Koreanized Christianity? And what about Japan? Although it will probably be necessary to break through the satanic power to which Japan is committed before anything major can happen there, what kind of Christianity will attract Japanese if the power is broken?

On the other hand, look at what has happened in China. After several generations of missionary contact, followed by a generation or two without outside help, and under very trying circumstances, millions of Chinese have discovered great meaningfulness in Christianity. And, though there are still traces of Western influence, they seem, at least to some extent, to have made the gospel their own, culturally as well as spiritually.

I have sought in this essay to alert us to some of the dimensions of the continuing quest toward more appropriateness that needs to be a part of the way Christianity is presented and experienced. All decisions made in one generation concerning the practice of Christianity within any given culture need to be regarded as tentative and experimental, open to reevaluation and possible change by the next generation. A greater challenge than theorizing this necessity is to get the leaders of younger (or older) churches to act on the theory.

PART 3

SOCIAL ISSUES AND HOW TO ADDRESS THEM

9

THE CHURCH AND JUSTICE IN CRISIS

CLINTON E. STOCKWELL

Justice as Part of the Gospel

Justice is part of the gospel. For many evangelicals and other religious traditions, there have been attempts to separate the mandates of the gospel proclamation from the practice of "doing justice" in the world. Yet, the biblical witness interconnects the proclamation of the gospel with the practice of justice and peacemaking. For Micah, doing justice is by definition doing the will of God: "He has told you, O mortal, what is good; and what does the LORD require of you but to do justice, and to love kindness, and to walk humbly with your God?" (Mic. 6:8).

Implicit in the gospel message is the proclamation of the coming of a kingdom of God "on earth as it is in heaven" (Matt. 6:10). The overwhelming majority of images in the New Testament reflect the notion that individuals who embrace the faith become part of a corporate body, the church. Individuals become part of a redeemed and redeeming community. They become a new people, a holy nation— the "body of Christ" in the world. This kingdom, or rule of God, is indeed the reign of God over the hearts of men. However, God's reign also embraces the whole cosmos.

There are a number of scriptural passages that push us beyond charity to social justice. In the gospel of Luke, Jesus announces his

159

coming by appealing to the prophet Isaiah. Jesus' proclamation functions in many ways as an inaugural address. He proclaims what his vocation is all about, a vocation that embraces responsibility to, in, and for the public realm:

> The Spirit of the Lord is upon me,
>> because he has anointed me
>>> to bring good news to the poor.
> He has sent me to proclaim release to the captives
>> and recovery of sight to the blind,
>>> to let the oppressed go free,
> to proclaim the year of the Lord's favor. (Luke 4:18–19)

While scholars debate the relationship of this passage to the "poor in spirit" passage in the gospel of Matthew (5:3), it is clear that in Luke, Jesus refers to those who are literally poor. Actually, it is possible that the "poor in spirit" in Matthew are not the humble, but the humiliated; not the ones who are of a meek character, but the ones who are broken in spirit, crushed and denied their humanity.

For Luke, these were not merely the spiritual poor, but the economically poor. Specifically, they were the widows, the orphans, women and children, those looked down upon for reasons of race, ethnicity, or nationality. They were the diseased, the political outcasts, tax collectors, and other "sinners"—those assumed to be hopelessly outside the circle of religious and social privilege. In short, the gospel was for these poor, those who were blind, sick, lame, and, on occasion, even dead but brought back to life. These were also people who, for whatever reason, found themselves on the outside of official religious, social, and political institutions.

For Walter Brueggemann, Jesus, like the prophets of the Old Testament, presented what he called an "alternative consciousness." It was his solidarity with the poor that distinguished Jesus from other itinerants of his time:

Jesus is remembered and presented by the early church as the faithful embodiment of an alternative consciousness. In his compassion he embodies the anguish of those rejected by the dom-

160

inant culture, and as embodied anguish he has the authority to show the deathly end of the dominant culture. Quite clearly, the one thing the dominant culture cannot tolerate or co-opt is compassion, the ability to stand in solidarity with the victims of the present order. It can manage charity and good intentions, but it has no way to resist solidarity with pain or grief. So the structures of competence and competition stand helpless before the one who groaned the groans of hurting ones. . . . If the groans become audible, if they can be heard in the streets and markets and courts, then the consciousness of domination is already jeopardized.[1]

The passage from Luke 4 is a declaration of Jesus' position with respect to the dominant culture. It raises other questions as well. What does it mean to be the anointed of God? What does it mean today for individuals and communities who strive to be faithful to the gospel mandate? What is the gospel, and how can the good news be explicitly directed to the poor? Who are the poor, then and now? What does it mean to proclaim release to captives,[2] or, as other passages have it, forgiveness to debtors? What does it mean to let the oppressed go free? Who is it today that is oppressed? How can their freedom be achieved, and how is that freedom connected to the proclamation of the gospel? Finally, what do we mean here by the year of the Lord's favor?[3]

If we are able to answer these questions, and to answer them in the context of the whole of Scripture, perhaps we can find once again a mandate for the faithful everywhere, and reason to be involved in the work of social justice as a manifestation of the gospel.

The gospel is, of course, good news. More academic sources will connect the word (Greek, *euangelion*) not merely to proclamation, verbally declaring that something new is on the horizon, but also to action (*praxis*), and even to the creation of a new world. In fact, one can compare this proclamation with the proclamation in Genesis 1:3–4: "'Let there be light'; and there was light. And God saw that the light was good" (literally "good beyond comparison" in 1:31, *tob m^e'od*). Jonathan Z. Smith describes the uniqueness of the biblical proclamation when compared with other Near Eastern creation stories. Here, Smith observes, the world is created by speech or by proclamation. "The power of the word is respected in most speech. According to many stories, creation is a speech act."[4] Proclamation is thus intimately connected with creative action. The word of proclamation does more than announce good news; it is part and parcel of creating and ushering in the new reality. Gerhard Friedrich makes one of the most powerful theological statements I am aware of regarding the relationship between gospel and new creation:

> He proclaims the victory of Yahweh over the whole world. Yahweh is now returning to Sion to rule. The messenger publishes it, and the new age begins. He does not declare that the rule of God will soon commence; he proclaims it, he publishes it, and it comes into effect. Salvation comes with the word of proclamation. By the fact that he declares the restoration of Israel, the new creation of the world, the inauguration of the eschatological age, he brings them to pass. For the word is not just breath and sound; it is effective power. Yahweh puts His words on lips of His messengers. He it is who speaks through them. With His Word He creates the world, He shapes history, He rules the world. . . . The prophet is sent to proclaim the good news to the poor, and the effect of the proclamation is their liberation.[5]

So, when the apostle John announces that the Word has become flesh and dwelt among us, he is describing the radical invasion of the transcendent into the world of ordinary human history, time and space, freedom and contingency, hope amid hopelessness. John 1:14, of course, is the great verse that describes the Incarnation, that God became flesh in a human person and dwelt among us, sharing our plight and suffering as human beings. The radical nature of the gospel affirms, in word as well as in creative act, that the whole world has changed, that reality has been altered, that something new has begun, and that this something new affects all of us, particularly those who now believe, including those who were once "far off," those often shut out of existing political and economic regimes.

Yet this proclamation was not offered in the abstract. It was proclaimed to people in particular contexts. With regard to Jesus' public ministry, interpreters are now paying more attention to the urban and urbanizing character of ancient Galilee and Judea. Although many of Jesus' parables were agricultural, there was a close connection between the growth of produce and the work that produced them. In Roman Palestine, agricultural and urban worlds were interconnected. More and more, people lived in the cities and towns of Jesus' world. Jesus' travels took him to the many cities and towns in Galilee and Judea. He visited Jerusalem as many as five times. He visited many of the other cities and towns along the way, including Nazareth, Bethany, Capernaum, and the cities of the Decapolis (ten Greek cities). Further, in the gospel of Luke he specifically states his intention to proclaim the gospel to the cities: "I must proclaim the good news of the kingdom of God *to the other cities* [beyond Nazareth] also; for I was sent for this purpose" (4:43). Jesus was clear about his calling and his vocation as one anointed to proclaim the gospel to the poor in the cities. Hope for the cities and a vision for a new societal arrangement are implicit in the gospel proclamation. This new order, the kingdom of God, became an end in itself. It became the ultimate hope, even for cities and cultures that found themselves alienated from the Creator—and from the reigning first-century Greco-Roman global economy.

In this context, Jubilee 2000, the release of the Third World from its indebtedness to the First World, makes perfect sense. From this passage, a clear application of the proclamation of a coming favorable year of the Lord is seen in the movement to forgive impoverished and dependent nations of their debts. At the same time, the gospel is a challenge to mammon in all its forms. It is a challenge that the rich cannot remain satisfied in their prosperity if there are poor among them. If the rich young ruler was challenged to sell his possessions and give to the poor, it is also a challenge to create social arrangements so that, even if there are poor people, there cannot be poverty. The passage that states that the "poor" will "always" be with us requires that our social structures provide for them in every generation. In Deuteronomy 15, the passage Jesus was referring to, the ancient Israelite commonwealth was required to care for the poor. It was never an option; there was never any justification for inaction.

Models of Social Change

Churches Build Community

Churches have often been in the forefront of movements for social change. They are frequently involved in alleviating problems connected with hunger, poverty, and social, economic, and political injustice. There are at least five ways that churches are engaged in the pursuit of social justice in the city. They (1) build community or what some call "social capital," (2) provide social services, (3) participate in activities of advocacy on behalf of poor and marginalized peoples, (4) develop community organization at the local level, including political activism in connection with all levels of government (local, regional, and national), and (5) do community economic development.

Dr. Lowell Livezey, director of the Religion and Urban America Program at the University of Illinois at Chicago, argues that churches, most fundamentally, provide the place and constitute the social linkages that enhance "social capital" and build community in low-income neighborhoods.[6] Social capital theory is in a sense a reaction to other theories of community formation, particularly those of "human capital" and "rational choice."[7]

There are various kinds of capital that exist in even the most devastated urban communities. First of all, there is physical capital. This is the land, the buildings, tools, and the physical infrastructure. While it is true that there is much abandonment of land and buildings in inner-city communities in cities like Detroit, Chicago, and New York, such land is awaiting a new day when market conditions revive or visionaries realize its value. The East Brooklyn churches are "taking back the land" in Brooklyn, New York. Private developers are converting once-abandoned factories and warehouses to loft apartments in downtown Chicago. Land and buildings once abandoned are now being redeveloped, mostly as a social good, but sometimes as a problem for existing residents, causing their displacement.

Human capital is the knowledge and skills of the people in the community. Once individuals have been educated, it is assumed that they will act on the options available to them in a rational way. These are perhaps the "thousand points of light" that exist in every community. Rational choice theory says that such individuals will choose to better their own condition and their neighborhoods as well, and that the barriers that restrain them can be overcome. Strategically, this means that public policy should pay attention to the educational and training needs of individuals, but not to the structures or policies that limit individual choice. If these individuals were prepared, benefits would trickle down, resulting in an uplifting of the community as a whole. As one person said, "A rising tide lifts all boats"— but does it?

Financial capital is the economic resources held by communities or potentially available to them from banks, churches, foundations, or other institutions, such as the National Equity Fund or local community trusts. The problem facing many inner-city communities is that the dollars made by workers in those communities end up being spent outside the community. The result is that economic and financial resources are not maintained in the neighborhood. Residents don't own or control the mechanisms of economic growth, and, for whatever reason, market incentives and government policy have not promoted investment in many low-income communities. So, an important question for many low-income communities is how to get access to financial capital.

A fourth form of capital is political capital. This is the ability or the capacity to exert influence over the political process. Often, people in low-income communities do not control their own destiny because the political officials who represent them are not elected by them. Or, for reasons of social distance, they are not able to impact city hall or the state or national governments to obtain resources. Such communities often have either inattentive or ineffective leadership. Communities sometimes realize that they need to organize and become greater participants in the political process. Otherwise, their voice is not heard, and the capacity to shape the destiny of their own community is restricted.

Social capital is the social glue that can be found in almost all communities. The extent that social capital is operative determines the ability of local communities and their associations to attract other forms of capital to their neighborhoods. Social capital includes the "shared norms, shared understandings, trust, and other factors that make relationships feasible and productive."[8] Social capital is "the stock of knowledge and other resources that enable members of a neighborhood or social network to help one another, especially in relationship to education, economic opportunity, and social mobility."[9]

What churches do best is to build community. Already existing in churches are social networks and connections with organizations and other constituencies in the neighborhood. Churches provide a place for residents to meet, and provide the symbolic language necessary so that the meeting has meaning. Churches provide a place and a mechanism for building relationships, while common problems and common dreams emerge. Social capital theory argues that problems are best solved, not by individuals, but by groups that act together in their own interest. From the standpoint of building community, the church is then able to consider what it must do to address the needs of the community. Human capital allows individuals to escape the community. Social capital builds the community by addressing systemic and structural issues as well as personal ones. Putnam summarizes the importance of social capital for enhancing the capacities for community problem solving:

> In the first place, networks for civic engagement foster sturdy norms of generalized reciprocity and encourage the emergence of social trust. Such networks facilitate coordination and communication, amplify reputations, and thus allow dilemmas of collective action to be resolved. When economic and political negotiation are embedded in dense networks of social interaction, incentives for opportunism are reduced. At the same time, networks of civic engagement embody past success at collaboration, which can serve as a cultural template for future collaboration. Finally, dense networks of interaction probably broaden the participants' sense of self, developing the "I" into the "we," or (in the language of rational choice theorists) enhancing the participants' taste for collective benefits.[10]

Churches Meet Temporary Social Service Needs

Charity or almsgiving has a long tradition in the history of religious communities, particularly in Christian churches. However, social service delivery today has its trappings. On the positive side, the delivery of social services such as food, temporary shelter, medicine, and clothing are very important. Social services are needed and provide temporary relief to the needy. However, there are limits to social service delivery as it is practiced. First, social services do not begin to address the long-term causes of hunger or homelessness. Second, the way services are delivered maintains a "we versus them" relationship, as the server gives something to the recipient, but the recipient is not invited to become part of a community. In the service model, the client is not treated as an equal, or even as a human being with a wide range of needs.

Analyses of social service delivery methods abound. Dieter Hessel argues that social services not only do not address systemic issues, but often legitimate the established order.[11] This system renders its clients dependent on social services, and keeps recipients powerless in the process. Further, if all the church does is give out social services, and it must do at least that, it really misses the deeper calling to build an inclusive community, on the one hand, or to pursue social justice and the equitable distribution of goods and services, on the other hand, including the opportunity to develop skills. We have all heard the wise saying, "If you give me fish to eat today, I will be hungry tomorrow; teach me to fish, and I will eat for a lifetime." The biblical model not only gives what is needed, but invites the stranger into the community. It seeks to redress systemic issues at the level of causation. That in a nutshell is the difference between charity and social justice. Sociologist C. Wright Mills said that we need "sociological imagination." We need to look beyond the obvious, and beyond the symptoms, to see how a problem is created and why the symptoms exist in the first place. "Perhaps the most fruitful distinction with which the sociological imagination works is between 'the personal troubles of the milieu' and 'the public issues of social structure.' This distinction is an essential tool of the sociological imagination and a feature of all classic work in social science."[12]

John McKnight also critiques the social service delivery model. Not only does it create dependency, he argues, but it maintains a culture of professionalism that destroys community. McKnight goes on to argue that we need to shift from a "deficiency" model of delivering social services to an "assets model" that looks at the capacity, potential, and talent of people in communities, despite their challenges.[13] For McKnight, challenges are best solved by the individuals who are most effected. He believes that goals need to be redefined as "recommunalization." By this he means that "the possible future will reach beyond allopathy, therapy, and even deinstitutionalization to what might be called recommunalization—a recognition that it is in person, place and peers that possibilities of regenerative community occur."[14]

As Dutch theologian and political philosopher Abraham Kuyper puts it, if all we do is allow our crumbs to fall from our tables to feed the poor, then "all such charity is more like an insult that beats in the bosom of the poor man (and woman)."[15] For Kuyper, problems facing hungry people will not be solved with charity, but by an "architectonic critique of the social order." Charity which only attends to the symptoms of a problem is "not yet Christian love."[16] In the world, charity at its best raises ultimate questions about how society is structured, how social systems and policies contribute to the problems facing low-income, minority, and disenfranchised groups.[17]

The biblical model of charity differs from the modern social service model in a number of ways. First, charity is not given for its own sake, but contributes to the building of an inclusive community. Second, the early Christian practice of charity exemplified a new social model, where those with abundance not only supplied what was lacking for those who were in need, but welcomed the latter as equals to the table of fellowship. Third, the giving of what was needed to the poor was not just an act of charity, but an expected activity that would and should flow naturally out of a social structure that existed to further justice and insure that justice was the norm. Justice and the pursuit of justice thus constituted the grounding for the giving of public goods.

Churches respond most naturally by delivering social services to the needy. I recall several years ago what James Harper, founder of the Center for Street People, said about his work. Basically, the Center was giving temporary assistance to the homeless in the forms of food, bed in a shelter, and perhaps clothing, but the effect was only (1) to improve their quality of life for that day and (2) to extend their lifetime ever so slightly.

Of course, the biblical message with regard to compassion for the needy is very strong. The gospel of Matthew gives clear tests for discipleship. The great passage in Matthew 25 is actually in the context of the judgment on the nations for failed policies with respect to the vulnerable. In short, the practice of charity was not expected as benevolence, but is portrayed in this passage as a requirement for the nations, based on a higher norm of justice. We know the passage very well:

> For I was hungry and you gave me food, I was thirsty and you gave me something to drink, I was a stranger and you welcomed me, I was naked and you gave me clothing, I was sick and you took care of me, I was in prison and you visited me. (Matt. 25:35–36)

This passage is a challenge to the policies of nations and states, as well as to the practices of churches and even individual believers. Nations and the people in them are judged, not on the basis of some abstract confession of faith, but on the basis of how they lived out the gospel and its calling to be just and compassionate for "the least of these my brethren." In the epistle of James, there are the familiar passages that combine faith and works, and also a description of "pure" religion. For James, religion that is pure and undefiled is "to care for orphans and widows in their distress, and to keep oneself unstained by the world" (James 1:27).

The early church was, of course, dominated by a call to "remember the poor." As one reads the book of Acts, it is clear that St. Paul's purpose was to set up churches in each city of the Mediterranean world. Scholars like Roland Allen have noted the strategic purpose of capturing the cities, even beginning with a house church next to a synagogue, as in Corinth.[18]

What is less known or discussed are the reasons that Paul undertook his missionary journeys. True, his primary purpose was to proclaim the gospel to the Gentiles (nations). But the whole purpose of the gospel was to evangelize individuals and to baptize them into believing communities, which "turned the world upside down." In that context, Paul challenged authorities, bridged nation-states, linked and unified ethnic groups, mollified the class structure by welcoming slaves and free, men and women, and Jews and Gentiles into a new community. As John Perkins has said, "All our works of evangelism, social action, economic development, and justice were on fire, turning and burning around the pivotal priority of preaching the gospel to the poor."[19] Early sociologists of religion, such as Shirley Jackson Case, noticed that early Christianity "triumphed" because it (1) reached the cities, (2) included a diversity of people, and (3) met the spiritual and material needs of the poor and marginal of Greco-Roman society.[20]

However, in addition to spreading the gospel, Paul was also involved in unifying the church, and bringing the congregations throughout the world together by challenging them to respond to needy people with tangible acts of compassion. The churches that Paul founded were important centers in the Roman world.[21] The early church established a beachhead at Antioch, one of the largest cities of the world at that time, with an estimated population of 600,000 people. Antioch was known for its rigid segregation of people by race and religion, as there was a Jewish quarter, a Roman quarter, a Syrian quarter, and so forth. Still, the church appealed to a diverse group of people, as leaders included Lucius of Cyrene (an African), Manaen from the court of Herod, and Simeon Niger (also an African) (Acts 13:1).

At about that time—there were apparently many such economic swings in ancient times—there was the report of a famine in Judea:

> At that time prophets came down from Jerusalem to Antioch. One of them named Agabus stood up and predicted by the Spirit that there would be a severe famine over all the world; and this took place during the reign of Claudius. The disciples determined that according to their ability, each would send relief to the believers living in Judea; this they did, sending it to the elders by Barnabas and Saul [Paul]. (Acts 11:27–30)

Josephus, the ancient Jewish historian, reports that there was a famine in Judea in the late forties of the Common Era, and that food shortages were common, because of "boom and bust" economic cycles.

What is remarkable about this collection is how often it is mentioned in the Pauline letters. In the letter to the Galatians, an early epistle, Paul states that after meeting with the leading apostles in Jerusalem, he was asked, among other things, to "remember the poor, which was actually what I was eager to do" (Gal. 2:10).

Further, at the end of his letter to the Romans, Paul reflected on the mutual obligations that Gentile Christians had with their Jewish brothers and sisters. Following his missionary journeys, Paul mentions gathering the collection as a prime reason for his travels:

> At present, however, I am going to Jerusalem in a ministry to the saints; for Macedonia and Achaia have been pleased to share their resources with the poor among the saints at Jerusalem. They were pleased to do this, and indeed they owe it to them; for if the Gentiles have come to share in their spiritual blessings, they ought also to be of service to them in material things. (Rom. 15:25–27)

Clearly, Paul thought that an exchange between the two races was imperative. He clearly was trying to develop a unified church worldwide, even as tangible needs were being addressed in the sharing of the collection.[22]

In 2 Corinthians, Paul challenges the Corinthians to be like the churches of Macedonia. Paul's "be like us" is tied to a specific model. He notes that despite their "severe ordeal of affliction" and "extreme poverty" (8:2), the Macedonians gave with much generosity. "They voluntarily gave according to their means, and even beyond their means, begging us earnestly for the privilege of sharing in this ministry to the saints" (vv. 3–4). Paul goes on to make one of the great declarations of the significance of the Incarnation, which takes on new meaning when we apply it to economic and social realities: "For you know the generous act of our Lord Jesus Christ, that though he was rich, yet for your sakes he became poor, so that by his poverty you might become rich" (v. 9).

The Incarnation was not just a theological event, but one that challenges our economic and social relationships. Paul was clearly looking to a global church that would share its resources, spiritual and material. In the same chapter, Paul's economic philosophy and doctrine of community follow from his understanding of the person and work of Christ:

> I do not mean that there should be relief for others and pressure on you, but it is a question of a fair balance between your present abundance and their need, so that their abundance may be for your need, in order that there may be a fair balance. As it is written, "The one who had much did not have too much, and the one who had little did not have too little." (vv. 13–15)

This is not too far off the command of political radicals, "to each according to one's needs, from each according to one's means." It is almost as if those on the political left have this biblical passage in mind.

Clearly, there is a theological and human dimension to Paul's economic radicalism. It would be hard to argue from these letters that Paul is supporting a materialist philosophy. On the contrary, the goals for Paul were the evangelization of the nations, a unified network of churches by city, and a just distribution of economic resources, especially food and supplies for people suffering from a severe famine.

The early church had already practiced a form of communitarianism, as related in the book of Acts (chapters 2 and 4). The church in Jerusalem "had all things in common; they would sell their possessions and goods and distribute the proceeds to all, as any had need." As a result, they "ate their food with glad and generous hearts" (Acts 2:44–46). While some were poor, "there was not a needy person among them" (Acts 4:34).

What happened to a church that once cared about the welfare of one's neighbor? Have we forgotten that the gospel is inseparably connected with the practice of compassion and the pursuit of social justice? Have we forgotten what it means to care about our neighbor? A solution can be found again as we revisit the meaning and significance of the Incarnation. For the early Christians, the giving of charity was rooted in social justice. The practice of giving charity contributed to the building of an inclusive community whereby all, rich and poor, were invited to the Lord's Table, and, more broadly, to the sharing of common goods. The original purpose of the diaconate in Acts 6 was to provide the common goods of the community (Greek, *koinōnia*, "holding goods in common").

Churches Advocate for the Poor

For Dieter Hessel, advocacy happens when people with expertise and a high commitment to justice seek to change social structures, laws, policies, and practices so that the poor experience less in the way of destitution or oppression. Many church-based organizations have led the fight for a more just social order by advocating for the less fortunate. Organizations are legion. One need only mention some Chicago-based organizations that can be found in other cities as well. These include the Interfaith Council for the Homeless, Protestants for the Common Good, the Chicago Religious Task Force on Central America, the Justice Coalition of Greater Chicago, the Jewish Council for Urban Affairs, the Community Renewal Society, the Metropolitan Alliance of Congregations, and the United Power for Action and Justice—just to name a few. These organizations are all church-based and advocate changes in government policy. They are headed by informed staff people who work full-time on issues such as housing for homeless people, campaign finance reform, a moratorium on the death penalty, welfare reform, school reform, jobs, funding for affordable housing, and the like.

Advocacy has a rich biblical tradition as well. Most of the sins of ancient Israel were social sins. The rulers and authorities did not speak up to defend the needy. They failed, according to the prophets, because they did not advocate on behalf of the poor or protect them from exploitation or oppression:

Like a cage full of birds, their houses are full of treachery; therefore they have become great and rich, they have grown fat and sleek. They know no limits in deeds of wickedness; *they do not judge with justice the cause of the orphan,* to make it prosper, and *they do not defend the rights of the needy.* Shall I not punish them for these things? (Jer. 5:27–29)

Isaiah's indictment of Jerusalem is very similar. Advocates for the poor were no longer to be found in the city:

> How the faithful city has become a whore! She that was full of justice, righteousness lodged in her—but now murderers! Your silver has become dross, your wine is mixed with water. Your princes are rebels and companions of thieves. Everyone loves a bribe and runs after gifts. They do not defend the orphan, and the widow's cause does not come before them. (Isa. 1:21–23)

With all the talk of "family values" among the pious then and now, it is interesting that the sins that faced the prophets were sins that impacted the way the society was structured. The solution to the problem was more than just the welfare of individuals; it was interconnected with the establishment and maintenance of just social structures. The poor, many of them being "widows and orphans," were to be protected by rulers and authorities. If not, prophets such as Jeremiah and Isaiah advocated for them. In Psalm 82, subtitled "Justice as the Order of the Universe" by the editors of the *Harper-Collins Study Bible,* the call here is to the nations, and to the official representatives or to those who advocate for the vulnerable ones—to ensure that justice is provided for the needy and the weak. "How long will you judge unjustly and show partiality to the wicked? Give justice to the weak and the orphan; maintain the right of the lowly and the destitute. Rescue the weak and the needy; deliver them from the hand of the wicked" (Ps. 82: 2–4).

With over four hundred verses in the Bible dedicated to the welfare of the poor, the just treatment of the poor and the importance of advocates for the poor cannot be understated. Charles Dickens, in one of his investigative pieces in the middle of the nineteenth century, noted that the authorities in London celebrated when they could reduce the rolls and lessen the financial burden of giving relief to the needy. The attitude of the public relief officials in London at the time was that "if the poor creatures were made too comfortable, more would come." For Dickens, the public relief system contributed more to the misery of the poor than to their relief.[23] A corollary strategy of the governing authorities was (1) to make it as difficult as possible for the poor to get relief, and (2) to foster a culture that blames the poor for their poverty, and lays at their doorstep the reasons for their oppression. Too often, churches have also bought into the practice of blaming the victim, even when those on the margin work pretty hard as a rule to "bootstrap" beyond their condition with meager resources.

Shel Trapp, a community organizer in Chicago, minces no words when he argues that "the first excuse out of the enemy's mouth" is, "It's your own fault." He goes further: "It seems that whenever there is an organizing drive on any issue it turns out to be the fault of those oppressed. It never seems to be the fault of those doing the oppressing."[24] In 1996, the president of the United States consented to a bill that would "end welfare as we know it." Many states began a "race to the bottom" to curtail welfare rolls.[25] While many laud the goal of moving people on welfare to work, the bill is fraught with several problems. First, adequate training and time for people to move off welfare is missing. Second, the jobs being created for low-income people are temporary jobs with low wages and no benefits, so they do not really allow such people to move beyond welfare dependency. Biblically, we know that "the workman deserves his wages," and so the question of adequate jobs with livable wages remains. Would not a more biblical goal for welfare reform efforts be to "eliminate poverty as we know it"? If so, then there would be less need for welfare reform. Even so, facts show that most individuals who are poor in this country are children, and many who are homeless today are homeless families, not the usual stereotypes perpetrated by members of the media and policymakers.

Still, there are limits to advocacy. For the most part, advocacy is done by professional activists. These professionals, with good intentions, try to act for others, so as to improve the lot of those on the margins. However, there is a problem in that the poor are sometimes not involved in the process. Professional activists act for the poor or act on their behalf, but the poor are left on the sidelines. A better approach would be to acknowledge the capacities of poor people and to include them in the struggle. The poor can say in the end, "We have done it ourselves." The results would be "good news" on a number of levels.

Churches Organize People Politically

Community organization has deep biblical roots. Ancient Israel organized itself into tribes with distinct boundaries, headquarters, and methodologies to care for the less fortunate. Cities of refuge were established for individuals who were trying to escape vigilante justice. Storehouse cities were established as central places to store grain and other needs of the community. Temples themselves were places where the ancient Israelites were able to give their tithes and offerings, which were in turn given to those who needed help, or kept as a safeguard against famine. Other practices, such as the Year of Jubilee, in which debts were forgiven and lands were returned to their original owners every fifty years, and gleaning, in which the poor were allowed to pick grain or produce on the edge of the field, were encouraged.

One of the great community organization stories is found in the books of Ezra and Nehemiah. There, exiles from the Babylonian captivity were returning home, and the problem of rebuilding the community structures arose. Nehemiah heard that the nobles and officials had set up a stiff tax so that the people were saying,

> We are having to pledge our fields, our vineyards, and our houses in order to get grain during the famine. . . . We are having to borrow money on our fields and vineyards to pay the king's tax. Now . . . we are forcing our sons and daughters to be slaves, and some of our daughters have been ravished; we are powerless, and our fields and vineyards now belong to others. (Neh. 5: 3–5)

Nehemiah's response to this outcry was to take the complaints of the people to the nobles, and to seek a repeal of their taxes, and a forgiveness of the debts of the people due to the heaviness of the taxes and the high interest extracted on loans of money to the people. He then proceeded to organize the community so that the walls of the city were rebuilt, the temple was restored, and the community was organized to protect itself and to operate efficiently. This was followed by some religious reforms, such as the reinstitution of the Sabbath and the separation of returning exiles from intermarriage with people of other nations who worshiped other gods. The restored city and its people then moved to another economy, not based on taxes and usury that benefited the rich and oppressed the poor, but a political economy whereby the needs of the people would be provided for from a common treasury. This was an economic and political transformation.

> For the people of Israel and the sons of Levi shall bring the contribution of grain, wine, and oil to the storerooms where the vessels of the sanctuary are, and where the priests that minister, and the gatekeepers and the singers are. We will not neglect the house of our God. (Neh. 10:39)

Inasmuch as Nehemiah organized a restored Jerusalem to meet its economic and religious goals, so too the apostle Paul set out to organize communities. Gerd Theissen has argued that Paul's primary role was that of a "community organizer." He was not quite a community organizer in the modern sense, but he was one in the sense of organizing institutions throughout the cities of the ancient Roman world. For Theissen, the difference between the wandering charismatics of Jesus' day and the "community organizers" of Paul's day was the urban context.[26] For Theissen, and indeed in the historic experience of the early church, Paul established churches as institutions, and within those institutions appointed and trained leadership, including bishops, elders, deacons, and pastors. For political and historical reasons, these churches avoided conflict with the authorities around it. They were new and small, and lacked the power and resources to successfully "speak truth to power." However, their preference for accommodation (Rom. 13) quickly gave way to animosity because of the church's practice of hospitality to the poor and the refusal to accept Roman authority (Rev. 13). The state became the beast.

Community organizers today build more than institutions; they build community. Community organization in theory and practice began in Chicago. At their best, community organizations represent local constituencies and provide a vehicle for "people's organizations" to act on their own behalf. Many community organizations today are church-based, and have sought to bring people of faith together to address local community issues. Churches are natural constituencies for community organizations for several reasons. First, they generally have values and concerns for the surrounding community. Second, they generally represent that community, especially if the church draws its membership from the community. Third, they generally have resources that can be tapped in any community organization effort. These resources include people, and also space, technology, finances, and connections with other organizations and networks.[27]

Yet the language of community organizations is not the usual language of churches. Organizers frequently talk about issues of power and self-interest, while churches sometimes talk about meekness and the importance of charity. However, organizers know that charity cannot be divorced from justice, and that churches sometimes need to take tough and controversial stands to confront the powers when they act unbecomingly.

For Walter Wink, the powers in the New Testament were rulers, authorities, thrones, dominions, and the like.[28] They were supernatural elements, but, as embodied in institutions, were systems and social structures that human beings faced every day. For Wink, the powers are at once good and fallen, yet redeemable. For William Stringfellow, the powers are those that we contend with on a daily basis. The problem is that the powers can easily oppress and dominate. For Stringfellow, the powers are not just quaint, but real obstacles to a just and whole society:

And if some of these seem quaint, transposed into contemporary language they lose quaintness and the principalities become recognizable and all too familiar: they include all institutions, all ideologies, all images, all traditions, all methods and routines, all conglomerates, all races, all nations, all idols. Thus, the Pentagon or the Ford Motor Company or Harvard University or the Hudson Institute, or Consolidated Edison, or the Diners Club or the Olympics or the Methodist Church or the Teamsters Union are all principalities. So are capitalism, Maoism, humanism, Mormonism, astrology, the Puritan work ethic, science and scientism, white supremacy, patriotism, plus many,

178

many more—sports, sex, any profession or discipline, technology, money, the family—beyond any respect of full enumeration. The principalities and powers are legion.[29]

In the letter to the Ephesians, it seems clear that the power of God in our lives, the power of a God who can resurrect the dead, is ample enough power to transcend other forms of power. Paul prays that the Ephesian church might come to understand

> the immeasurable greatness of his *power* for us who believe, according to the working of his great *power*. God put this *power* to work in Christ when he raised him from the dead and seated him at his right hand in the heavenly places, far above all rule and authority and *power* and dominion, and above every name that is named, not only in this age but also in the age to come. (Eph. 1:19–21)

The issue for us is not that the Bible doesn't speak of power, but how the church deals with power in tangible ways. Power is really a neutral construct. It is merely the ability to do something, or the ability to marshal resources to carry out a task or an objective. I like the way Saul Alinsky sums up the use of power:

> Pascal . . . observed that . . . "justice without power is impotent; power without justice is tyranny." St. Ignatius . . . [said]: "to do a thing well a man needs power and competence." We could call the roll of all who have played out their parts in history and find the word power, not a substitute word, used in their speech and writings. It is impossible to conceive of a world devoid of power; the only choice of concepts is between organized and unorganized power. Mankind has progressed only through learning how to develop and organize instruments of power in order to achieve order, security, morality, and civilized life itself, instead of a sheer struggle for physical survival. Every organization known to man, from government down, has had only one reason for being—that is, organization for power in order to put into practice or promote its common purpose.[30]

Perhaps the biggest problem facing churches is not that they don't understand power, but that they feel they don't have enough of it to make a difference, so it becomes easier to shrink from the fight. Michael Lerner calls this "surplus powerlessness." Surplus powerlessness is "our tendency to see ourselves as more powerless than we really are."[31] And powerlessness corrupts, argues Lerner. It justifies inaction, cynicism, fatalism, and resignation to events thought unchangeable. Surplus powerlessness renders the individual helpless, and sanctions an otherworldly spirituality that divorces itself from the created order:

> It is this surplus powerlessness that kicks in whenever we imagine challenging the ethos of selfishness, materialism, and cynicism in our contemporary world. This ethos seems so big, so built into the ontological structure of necessity, so much a part of the way the world "really is," on the one hand—and we seem to ourselves inadequate and ill-prepared to take on such a world-transformative task, on the other hand—that we fall back into cynicism and despair whenever someone tells us that things could be really different.[32]

For Mary Gonzalez, a community organizer and trainer for the Gamaliel Foundation and the Metropolitan Alliance for Congregations in Chicago, organizing is about "agitation"—not "irritation," but agitation—challenging people to tap into their assets, capacities, and responsibilities as Christians and as citizens.[33] For Gonzalez, churches are places to mobilize power and to act on issues of concern in the real world outside their walls and networks. Christians may pray for the "world as it should be," but we must act in the "world as it is," as faithful and courageous followers of Christ, who challenges the powers and welcomes the stranger in our own time.

Churches that are involved in community organizing do so for a number of reasons. Some act out of a call for justice or the responsibility of being caring and active agents in the community. Some act because their constituency is directly affected by issues that exist locally or beyond. Others act because their interests are at stake, threatened by the actions of the "powers that be." Whatever the motivation, churches have been in the forefront of civil rights issues and many other human rights issues. They have fought for stop signs to prevent accidents; they have taken stands with regard to the death penalty—many now arguing for a moratorium on it, given the plethora of coerced confessions and DNA evidence that has exonerated scores of people once consigned to death row. Churches have organized to challenge toxic waste dumping on Chicago's Southeast Side. They have worked with gangs in Los Angeles and homeless people in Washington, D.C. They have protested U.S. funding of Central American dictatorships. They have often been on the side of justice and have been emissaries for peace.

Organizing is at its best when it involves those most affected by issues that impact a neighborhood in direct action. It is an effective way to train leaders. It is also an effective strategy for a church's social ministry, as well as a successful "church growth" strategy. Mostly, organizing is important because it is a proven way for an organized constituency to address issues of common concern and obtain results that are tangible. Church-based organizations are not only "schools of democracy," but also tangible ways to build the kingdom of God on earth.

Churches Rebuild the City Through Community Economic Development

Another model of social change that churches have been involved with in cities and elsewhere is "community economic development." Bethel New Life, the community development agency of the Bethel Lutheran Church in Chicago, uses as its mission statement this version of Isaiah 58:9–12:

If you put an end to oppression, to every gesture of contempt, and to every evil word; if you give food to the hungry and satisfy those who are in need, then the darkness around you will turn to the brightness of noon. And I will always guide you and satisfy you with good things. I will keep you strong and well. You will be like a garden that has plenty of water, like a spring of water that never goes dry. Your people will rebuild what has long been in ruins, building again on the old foundations. You will be known as the people who rebuilt the walls, who restored the ruined houses.

Many community development agencies today are "faith-based" institutions. Like Bethel, these church-based organizations are recognizing that they, too, have a responsibility for the economic well-being of the poor in their midst. These are the neighbors with whom they are building community. A few years ago, Raul Raymundo, director of The Resurrection Project (TRP) in the Pilsen community of Chicago, said to one of my classes, "We are not just building houses in Pilsen, we are building community." Community development organizations such as Bethel or TRP recognize that their responsibility to people is not narrowly "spiritual," but embraces all of life.

Mary Nelson of Bethel New Life understands the organization's mission as weaving "a healthy, sustainable community on Chicago's West Side." Given the recent trend in cities toward regentrification and the accompanying problem of displacement, many churches have chosen to take a stand for the total well-being of their community and the residents who live and worship there. Like many other church-based agencies, Bethel has taken a stand to reclaim and protect the land and housing for low-income residents. It recognizes that it is not enough to address the temporary problems facing poor people by delivering social services. Rather, longer-term issues, such as affordable housing and training for jobs, must be addressed, so that those who are poor will be able to act independently and self-sufficiently. To date, Bethel has built over eight hundred units of low-income housing and has provided employment opportunity for hundreds.

Models of the church's public presence that emphasize organizing and economic development have as their goals independence and freedom for people (empowerment), not a relationship of dependency and clientage. Unlike national political policies that have either rendered low-income communities dependent or neglected them, community-based organizations, many of which are church based, make a difference by empowering local constituencies to act on their own faith, in their own capacities, realizing their own community goals.

Summary

Isaiah 58:9–12 is a good passage for those who seek to build a foundation for social justice in the city and elsewhere. Isaiah challenges those who think that the solution to problems is found in private acts of charity and fasting. Rather, churches are called to step out and welcome the homeless into their midst as fellow communicants. The call is to end oppression in every form, challenging social structures that render people poor and powerless with new structures that model justice with compassion. The goal is to rebuild the streets and foundations of the city, so that cities and communities everywhere can become more livable.

In Jeremiah 29:7, the exiles of Babylon are encouraged to "seek the welfare [*shalom*] of the city . . . for in its welfare you will find your welfare." This is hard for us, if we see ourselves as exiles or "resident aliens."[34] To seek the welfare (*shalom*) of the city means that we see ourselves as residents within the culture. The word *shalom* in Hebrew generally means "peace," but it can also be translated as "welfare," "prosperity," "harmony," "justice," "salvation," or "deliverance." The Israelites may have been strangers in Babylon, but they were to take Babylon as their home. They were to build houses and live in them, plant gardens, and give their children in marriage.[35]

There are numerous models of church practice in many communities. Churches by definition build social capital and establish networks and relationships, so that communities are able to act on their own dreams in their own capacities. Historically, churches have delivered essential social services, so that the basic needs for shelter, food, and clothing are met. Today, churches are also involved in community organizing, community economic development, and even electoral politics, in order to reshape the social order in a way that looks more like what God wants for human society, a society characterized by a new prophetic spirituality that pursues justice with compassion.[36]

For the Dutch Reformed theologian and politician Abraham Kuyper, Christians cannot run from culture or from the world's problems. Rather, we must reclaim our role in the world as stewards of the earth, as shepherds of the created order. If the world belongs to God as God's creation, then there is nothing that escapes our sight and responsibility. We are "salt and light" in the world, as the gospel says. To be salt means that we function as a preserving agent. To be light means that we know enough from Scripture to be able to show the way to a more peaceable city. For Kuyper, it means that we must operate from some form of "common grace" in the world. Christian faith stems from a profound particularity anchored in the Incarnation, but it also reaches with a universal appeal to the whole created order, due to common grace. Because of common grace, there is nothing that escapes the church's reach or responsibility:

> And for our relation to the world: the recognition that in the whole world the curse is restrained by grace, that the life of the world is to be honored in its independence, and that we must, in every domain, discover the treasures and develop the potencies hidden by God in nature and in human life.[37]

10

DOING THE WORD: BIBLICAL HOLISM AND URBAN MINISTRY

MARK R. GORNIK

A recent debate in *Evangelical Missions Quarterly* between David J. Hesselgrave and Bryant L. Myers highlights the continuing dispute among evangelicals on the relationship between holistic ministry and evangelism.[1] Hesselgrave argues that holistic mission takes away from what he believes is the central Christian responsibility of evangelism, and therefore is not biblical. Myers replies that the whole story of the Bible is about loving God and loving our neighbors, creating holistically oriented Christians. One says proclaiming the word has priority; the other believes that proclamation and deed go together.

So which is it: an integrated approach or a sharp division? Are word and deed to be managed separately, with evangelism or social justice having the ultimate priority? In this essay, I want to consider the relationship between word and deed, and, in particular, community development and witness in urban ministry. I will argue that urban ministry must involve both the proclamation of grace and the work of justice. In making this case, I will first look at some of the historical reasons why American evangelicalism still finds itself debating this issue. Then I will show that Luke's gospel, which joins together the story of Jesus, the coming of the kingdom, and the presence of the Spirit, is by its very character an invitation to holistic Christian witness and discipleship. Indeed, I believe it will become evident that the gospel of the kingdom takes us beyond trying to balance word and deed and leads us to holism. After that, I will offer a series of perspectives or suggestions that are intended to help explain what holistic ministry is. I will conclude with two brief case studies from Baltimore and New York.

This is a most appropriate subject for a collection of essays in honor of, and now also in memory of, Harvie M. Conn. His book *Evangelism: Doing Justice and Preaching Grace*[2] is a classic study, not only showing clearly the biblical basis for holism, but also presenting an approach to ministry that links biblical theology (in the tradition of Geerhardus Vos and Richard B. Gaffin) with a missiological agenda of reflection and action (though perhaps too focused at times on answering evangelical objections). In a redemptive-historical view of revelation, word is necessary to interpret deed, and deed is a privileged redemptive act. Redemptive word and redemptive deed are equally true. And rather than being a series of disconnected events that need to be strung together, they form a single story. In so many ways, the title to Conn's book on evangelism summarizes his mission theology, pastoral practice, and heart as a follower of Christ. This became evident to me very recently when, during some long nighttime drives, my wife and I listened to some of his sermons on tape, many of them more than twenty years old. We laughed a lot, of course. But over and over again, we heard a pastor crying for the church to be the gospel in word and deed, to hear the voices of those who are left out and forgotten.

Other essays and studies reinforce Conn's interest in this subject, which is always driven by his passion as an evangelist and his concern for the outsider.[3] And his final writing project, *Urban Ministry: The Kingdom, the City and the People of God*,[4] coauthored with Manuel Ortiz, strongly continues these interests. This essay, like so much else in my urban ministry development, stands on the shoulders of Conn's profound and distinguished legacy.

How Did We Get Here?

Evangelical movement toward a consensus on holistic mission, chronicled in the important collection of essays and documents by Vinay Samuel and Chris Sugden, *Mission as Transformation: A Theology of the Whole Gospel*,[5] has been very significant. Roger Greenway has added his seasoned and balanced affirmation of the unity of word and deed in *Together Again: Kinship of Word and Deed*.[6] Yet it is clear from the exchange of Hesselgrave and Myers that while some of the intensity of the debate may have diminished, the issue remains. My own experience with many pastors and church leaders formed in the American evangelical tradition is that truly holistic ministry remains problematic, with deed secondary to "evangelism." Apart from the debate, the church asks, how are we to be faithful to the pressing demands of the city? There are many historical reasons for the debate, and while I can hardly cover the entire ground, it is important to note some of these factors.

One clue may be found in the lingering division between body and self that can be traced back to Platonism. Does this explain the continuing evangelical emphasis on the centrality of the "soul"? If so, how is this mediated to contemporary evangelicals?[7] Does it make sense to see some of our problems as an extension of this framework? Is this the reason why an emphasis on saving souls and a concern for the inner person still carry the weight of concern for evangelicals? The whole area of philosophical anthropology and its influence on the church's mission framework remains to be further developed.

A significant reason for the disjunction between word and deed is the historical background of the "Great Reversal," a period of evangelical retrenchment from social issues in reaction to the Social Gospel movement. Running from 1900 to about 1930, it was a period in which, according to George Marsden, "all progressive social concern, whether political or private, became suspect among revivalist evangelicals and was relegated to a very minor role."[8] How much does this legacy continue to shape the evangelical perspective? While any answer must take account of evangelicalism's pluralism,[9] it is possible that evangelical reservations about significant social involvement, let alone the embrace of a progressive social agenda, will be suspect for reasons that go back a full century. Missiologist Wilbert

Shenk also traces the current conflict over evangelical social responsibility to the period of modernist-fundamentalist debate.[10] In reaction to liberal social optimism, evangelicals maintained a focus on individual conversion.

As Andrew Walls observes with regard to nineteenth-century British evangelicalism, "The evangelical paradigm of conversion begins with the personal knowledge of sin, moves to personal trust in Christ's finished work, and issues in a godly personal life."[11] Here are the roots of a missionary faith, but one decidedly individualistic in character. Certainly this history is not without its ongoing legacy in the American church. Reinforcing this history is the American ideal of individualism and a rejection of the social analysis of poverty. Noted Harvard sociologist William Julius Wilson, in his proposals on understanding and addressing inner-city poverty, finds the American emphasis on individual responsibility to be a significant barrier to countering poverty. Individual "character" and "responsibility" constitute the prism through which America predominantly interprets urban dislocation and joblessness, not, for example, the postindustrial destruction of the inner-city job market and family.[12] For evangelicals, with their emphasis on individual change, everything fits right together. In this worldview, it makes sense culturally to emphasize a "personal influence strategy"[13] for social change, rather than lift up a vision of social rights and justice.

It is important to know to whom are we referring when we talk about evangelicals.[14] I have in mind white North American evangelicals. But the larger story is that in the urban church globally defined, there is a much better understanding of the demand for a holistic gospel. Presuppositions shape all of us, as Conn, the student of the apologist Cornelius Van Til, reminded us. We should think, not just in terms of philosophical or theological presuppositions, but also in terms of social beliefs. Is it not likely that we can find in the history of North American evangelicalism a case study of the influence of social location on the reading of Scripture? Where one gets up in the morning makes a difference in the questions we put to Scripture. The suburbanization of so much of the evangelical church leaves it as no surprise that matters of Christian witness are both domesticated and truncated. Without critical assessment and counter witness, context demands it. We now turn to how the biblical text calls forth a more integral or holistic understanding and practice of word and deed, especially in relationship to the poor and oppressed.

Jesus, the Spirit, and the Jubilee

Many biblical avenues of approach are open to us as we seek to build (or better, affirm) a holistic Christian faith. Because God created the world, because Jesus came in human form, and because the world to come is a new creation, our practice of faith cannot be partial or dichotomized. Because the Bible is consumed with a commitment to the poor, the church's life should also be. As but one approach to sustaining a biblical theology of holistic practice, I turn to Luke's gospel and specifically to Jesus' miracles of healing. I do so in great measure because of the central place that Luke held in Conn's writing and thought.

In Luke, Jesus has come to bring redemption to the world, and, quite specifically, to the poor and the city.[15] The paradigmatic text is Luke 4:16–21, where Jesus, in his inaugural sermon, announces the in-breaking reign of God as a time of messianic liberation. Citing passages of Scripture from Isaiah 58 and 61, Jesus proclaims:

> The Spirit of the Lord is on me,
> > because he has anointed me
> > to preach good news to the poor.
> He has sent me to proclaim freedom for the prisoners
> > and recovery of sight for the blind,
> to release the oppressed,
> > to proclaim the year of the Lord's favor. (Luke 4:18–19)

With these words, Jesus announces his ministry of making all things new and restoring right relationships. Jesus is drawing attention to the Jubilee, employing it as an image of God's reign.[16] In the Jubilee, the world is made right for the poor, the outcast, the sick, the struggling, and the unwanted. In the Jubilee work of Christ on the cross, the powers are defeated. Through Jesus, salvation comes to the city.

Quite intentionally, Jesus understands his anointing with the Spirit as equipping him to heal and redeem the fallen urban order, to bring good news to the poor.[17] That the city is the focus of this work is evident in the interpretation that Jesus gives of his calling a few verses later, where he proclaims, "I must preach the good news of the kingdom of God to the other towns [*poleis*] also, because that is why I was sent" (Luke 4:43). The "good news" is the Jubilee message of 4:18–19, a citation of Isaiah 61:1–2. In this text, Isaiah links God's new day for the poor with the promise of urban recovery. "They will rebuild the ancient ruins and restore the places long devastated; they will renew the ruined cities that have been devastated for generations" (Isa. 61:4). Against this background, Jesus understands his life, ministry, and redemptive work as ushering in good news for the city and the forsaken (Luke 9:51). Through his messianic suffering on the cross, Jesus identified with the poor and socially outcast, and called them to live anew in the community of his reign.

Jesus, we read in Luke, was "powerful in word and deed before God and all the people" (Luke 24:19; cf. Acts 10:48). How did the evangelist understand this to be descriptive of Jesus? A significant way was found in the miracles of healing. As Herman Ridderbos, an important interlocutor for Conn, held, "The kingdom of God revealed in miracles signifies the redemption from all evil and the restoration of the whole of life."[18] Jürgen Moltmann also defines a wider creational meaning to Jesus' miracles:

> When Jesus expels demons and heals the sick, he is driving out of creation the powers of destruction, and is healing and restoring created beings who are hurt and sick. The lordship of God to which the healings witness, restores sick creation to health. Jesus' healings are not supernatural miracles in a natural world. They are the only truly "natural" thing in a world that is unnatural, demonized and wounded.[19]

Miracles are signs of the new creation, symbols of the reconciliation of all things in Christ. They are, in Luke's telling, down payments of a new jubilee and outworkings of the Spirit.

The story of the healing of a woman on the Sabbath, found in Luke 13:10–17, offers one window on the holistic shape of the miracles of Jesus. In what follows, I draw particularly on the exegesis of Joel Green in his excellent commentary on Luke.[20] As the story begins, Jesus comes into contact with a woman "who had been crippled by a spirit for eighteen years. She was bent over and could not straighten up at all" (v. 11). Her illness is described in the biblical categories of oppression. This interest is enlarged, for her physical challenge, Jesus diagnoses, has spiritual causes (vv. 12, 16). It is Satan, Jesus says, who has kept her "bound." Thus, in addition to the social oppression she experienced as a woman, her condition is spiritually oppressive.

With this as background, Green observes that "the otherwise unremarkable words, 'there appeared a woman . . . Jesus saw her' (vv. 11–12), become significant indeed, for they portend the materialization of a person otherwise socially invisible."[21] To her as a person, Jesus announces, "You are set free from your infirmity" (v. 12). He brings her holistic liberation and a new beginning. Upon release, her response is to praise God (v. 13). Indeed, as Green notes, she is restored to community.[22]

Many elements of the Jubilee are present in this text. First, there is the interest of Jesus in proclaiming good news in a manner that brings release from oppression (Luke 4:18–19). Second, the Sabbath "today" of 4:21 is linked to the Sabbath context of 7:10–17.[23] Third, elsewhere Jesus characterizes his healing ministry in the same terms as the Jubilee (Luke 7:22). Commenting on verses 15–16, Green gives us an important summary: "The fundamental issue at work in this scene is the divine legitimation of the character of Jesus' mission—liberation and restoration for such poor persons as this woman of lowly status, through which activity he renders present the dominion of God in the present."[24] This, as the biblical writers spoke of often, is *shalom*, one's flourishing with neighbors, world, and God. In fact, peace is an important theme in Luke's gospel, and we are justified in seeing it here. The end result, we should note, is that "the people were delighted with all the wonderful things he was doing" (v. 17).

Here then is a picture of the holistic ministry of Jesus. Christ is in covenant solidarity with the recipients of the gospel. His message and life address the concrete needs of the oppressed, expose and challenge the powers, bring about release, restore to community, and present a witness that causes others to praise God. Put another way, it is the Jubilee made real in the lives of the excluded. In the second part of Luke's narrative, the book of Acts, the followers of Jesus carry on this ministry under the power of the Spirit. What we see in this miracle is a sample of the creation restored, a driving out of oppression under the lordship of Christ. Mission in Luke and Acts joins together word and deed in a seamless manner.[25]

In summary, the story of salvation proclaimed by Jesus in Luke is presented as good news for the city and the world. It is one of approach, of crossing borders, of love and embrace. In response to the multidimensional character of sin, salvation is a message of grace, reconciliation, justice, and healing. It knows no boundaries between social and religious, or physical and spiritual. Nor is it confined to an Enlightenment definition of the world. Deeds and words are parts of a whole. This reality points, as Shenk so well states, to the central problematic of the word-and-deed paradigm:

> The flaw in the "word" and "deed" paradigm is that it has encouraged us to focus attention on the parts rather than on the *whole,* which is God's new order. Once we see and accept this partial way of looking at Christian witness, we never succeed in arriving at the whole. We live in constant frustration trying to achieve balance and defend priorities. But the whole—i.e., God's new order—is always greater than the way we add up the parts. Such arithmetic does not correspond with God's.[26]

The ministry of Jesus enables us to see this.

Beyond Word and Deed

As we have suggested from our study of Luke 13:10–17, the categories of word and deed are at best ineffective and at worst distracting and confusing. For the church as the body of Christ, deeds of justice and mercy are inseparable from its worshiping identity.[27] Communities are more complex, and the kingdom is much broader, seamless, and holistic. Holistic ministry, by the power of the Spirit, is about creating samples and signs of God's new day in everyday settings. Therefore, it is about the restoration of life in its fullness. This is both evangelism and justice. Because the church is to socially embody its belief in Jesus, as Paul's epistle to the Ephesians is an extended meditation, it is through the church that this is to be given expression.

In terms of Christian witness, how can we witness to the kingdom in a way that points to and celebrates the broad urban focus of God? I would suggest some preliminary observations drawn from our brief study of Luke:

1. *Context*. Effective ministry requires understanding and addressing the context. This is a religious, social, political, and economic task.

2. *Spirit*. Because the Spirit's work involves turning persons to Christ and renewing the entire creation, holistic ministry takes place in the Spirit. We should not need the growth of the Pentecostal movement to come to grips with this from a biblical standpoint.

3. *Name and Way*. Holistic ministry, in the name of Jesus, is always the cup of cold water and the renovated house. As done in the name of Jesus, it announces the invitation of his grace and the good news that he is in our midst. It is also always in the way of Jesus, the self-donation of the cross.

4. *Readable Signs*. Holistic ministry establishes signs of the kingdom in the city. An important model of the kingdom is the Jubilee. One of our great urban challenges is to establish signs of the new economic and community order that Christ's mission of Jubilee inaugurated.

Proclaiming grace and doing justice do not come naturally. They are habits that need to be learned and developed. In the global urban context, doing justice requires an increasingly complex set of skills within the fields of community development and community organizing. In the vernacular, this is about more livable local communities where children can grow up. We also need to learn to proclaim grace. As Mark Strom shows in *Reframing Paul: Conversations in Grace and Community*,[28] evangelicals bring a great deal of cultural baggage. More wrestling with the biblical text in concrete communities is required.

193

Embodying Faith

I will conclude this essay with two brief case studies of New Song Community Church in Baltimore and in Harlem. New Song in the Sandtown neighborhood of Baltimore was born in 1986.[29] Sandtown, a community of great joy and hope, is also a place of severe inner-city distress. The broad failure of the modern project has made all words and truth-claims suspect.

Without a holistic faith, there is no gospel in Sandtown. Living out the gospel in this context has meant building a collaborative network of church- and community-based institutions that focus on housing, job development, education, and health care. In 2001, the full-time staff numbered over eighty, of whom more than 75 percent were neighborhood residents. For New Song, seeking the *shalom* of Sandtown means a concentrated effort to eliminate vacant and substandard housing, a K-8 school that has high standards and an excellent record of achievement, a job placement center that links over one hundred residents a year to employment, and a family health center that serves all residents regardless of ability to pay. At the center of all this is a worshiping community.

In ways that form concentric circles outward from the small neighborhood to the city and beyond, the common life of New Song is serving as an attractive and centrifugal witness. In the community, young men have become part of the church and ministry only because of the life of the church. They would never have stepped into a church building unless it dealt with their world. Simply "preaching the gospel" would have failed. At neighborhood-wide house dedications, we find new homeowners and their neighbors praising God on the streets. In the church, we find persons who have had serious substance abuse problems testifying to their new life, a result of Christ and the life of the church representing Christ. And as volunteers have poured into the community from all social strata of the city, New Song has found people with no church relationship whatever drawn into the life of faith and its claims.

That such a life of peaceable discipleship (as fallible and frail as it is) would lead the nations to the presence of God should not surprise us. Israel, Micah and Isaiah emphasized, was to be a model for the nations and thus attract the nations (Isa. 2:2–5; Mic. 4:1–5). Here the observations of Gerhard Lohfink on the exegesis of Justin, Tertullian, and Irenaeus are of significant interest.[30] According to Lohfink, they believed that Isaiah 2, the coming of the nations to the city of God in peace, had been fulfilled in the common life of the church. Yes, the gospel had gone forth to the Gentiles, and the church had been changed (Acts 15:4).[31] But, at the same time, "the eschatological state of nonviolence and peace, prophesied by Isaiah, had already become a reality in the church."[32] In other words, as the social witness of the church to Jesus was very attractive among the nations, it was understood to be the fulfilling of Scripture. It was a hermeneutical and apologetic move.

In 1998, New Song in Harlem was started. Its key pastoral leaders were two former students of Harvie Conn at Westminster, Johnny Acevedo and Jeff White. At that time, in the context of wider developments in New York City, central Harlem was beginning to undergo fast-paced changes. As a world-class city undergoing both a population surge and an economic boom (bubble?), the pressures of gentrification have been felt in all of Manhattan and even in adjacent neighborhoods in Brooklyn, Queens, and the Bronx.[33] As church life unfolds, it is clear that a commitment to the neighborhood demands concrete forms of resistance. Currently, the church is working on community development initiatives and organizing relationships. Only in this way, the church believes, will the gospel of the kingdom be credible.

These commitments have not been barriers to growth, either in numbers or in other ways. People are discovering Christ and becoming disciples in both contexts. In fact, it is impossible to conceive of a parish church in the changing city growing otherwise. Are there tensions between the ministry of the word and the obligations to do justice? In my experience, such tensions rarely exist for the community, but often do for believers who come from outside. The fact that faith must be real amidst everyday life is common sense in the neighborhood. Both churches have taken stands that the church is to exist for the kingdom, the community, and its neighbors, not for itself. This mixes things up, but in the right way.

Without a fully holistic approach to urban ministry, churches are rendered irrelevant and the gospel is denatured. If there is a contradiction or tension between word and deed, it is cultural and self-imposed, not biblical. If there is any hope that ministry will make a difference among the urban poor and in the cities, it will have to be a holistic and embodied Jubilee faith. Holistic ministry in the city is part of the hermeneutic and apologetic of the gospel. It is truth fleshed out. Urban evangelism, as Conn held, must be about heralding grace and doing justice. They belong together as a single story. That is good news for the city, for families, for individuals, and for communities. James characterized the church's responsibility this way: "Do not merely listen to the word, and so deceive yourselves. Do what it says" (James 1:22).[34]

11

JESUS' WORDS TO THE CANAANITE WOMAN: ANOTHER PERSPECTIVE

JOHN S. LEONARD

In this century, the church has the opportunity to become a community that is not based on race, nationality, or social status. The ever-increasing number of immigrants flooding over last century's political borders and the further marginalizing of the church by mainstream society have opened up these doors. Unfortunately, much of the church fails to see the world of opportunity before it. Instead, it is asking, "What is our target group?" This is the modern-day equivalent of the Pharisee's question in Luke 10:29, "Who is my neighbor?"

"Target grouping" has become an unquestioned principle in much of the church-growth literature because it works and it seems natural. But when we call an individual to a radical personal conversion (a Western and especially American way of understanding conversion), that call must also include a radical community conversion. We must call people to repent of their racism, classism, and sexism, because this is the church that our Lord is building. Unfortunately, their sins have been institutionalized, and we define our communal sin with theological and logical arguments.

Christ has been accused of racism and sexism in his dealings with the Canaanite woman in Matthew 15:21–28. It appears that Jesus first ignores the woman's cries for help and calls her a dog. He seems to be targeting a group, while excluding others. This is not the church that Jesus wishes to build. His church is to be as diverse as humanity and should locally reflect its heterogeneous nature. How are we to understand this encounter?

In this essay, I wish to present an alternative interpretation of Jesus' words to the Canaanite woman. In fact, Jesus' words are to be understood and rightly interpreted in exactly the opposite way from their literal meaning. Such communication is commonly used to reinforce one's point. For example, last year a friend remarked to me as we looked out a window at yet another snowfall, "Just what we need, more snow!" It was clear from the context that he was not delighted to see more snow. The correct way to understand his words would be, "I'm tired of snow, and I've had enough of it!"

We should understand the words that Jesus spoke to the Canaanite woman in the same way. The intent of Matthew's gospel and the context in which this passage is found force us to read irony and sarcasm into the words of Jesus. In this essay, we will present three reasons for this interpretation. First, Jesus' words are completely out of character with everything that Jesus teaches in Matthew's gospel. Second, the immediate context around Matthew 15:21–28 requires us to interpret the passage differently. Third, the encounter itself has a teaching purpose for Christ's disciples and the church. What we will discover is that Jesus is ridiculing the conventional theology and wisdom of his disciples when it comes to the inclusion of Gentiles into the people of God. If we listen, we will hear that he is speaking to the church today. He is telling us to leave behind our ethnocentric understanding of the people of God and become his church.

The Universal Themes of Matthew's Gospel

To understand the story of the Canaanite woman, one needs to see how this pericope fits into the larger themes of Matthew's gospel. By looking at the broader strokes of Matthew's work, we will be able to make better sense of the details. The themes that are pertinent to our subject and with which we will deal in this section are: (1) the role of Gentiles in Matthew's gospel, (2) Jesus' teaching on the kingdom of heaven, and (3) Jesus' new category of humanity.

The role and place of Gentiles is an important motif in Matthew's gospel. It is not only the presence of Gentiles in the gospel that is significant, but the fact that they are mentioned in an exemplary way— both as an integral part of Israel's past and as those who responded positively to Jesus' ministry. Matthew wastes no time in introducing Gentiles to his readers. In his first chapter, he includes four Gentile women in Jesus' genealogy. Because the genealogy is located in the first chapter, Amy-Jill Levine argues that the inclusion of these four Gentile women is "thematic" and "programmatic" to the purpose of Matthew.[1] The women mentioned in the genealogy are Tamar, who is the first Canaanite woman we meet in the gospel of Matthew; Rahab, another Canaanite; Ruth; and Uriah's wife. By including these four women in the opening messianic genealogy, Matthew prepares his Jewish readers for the teachings of Jesus—that it takes more than blood relationship to be part of the kingdom of God.

Not only do we find Gentile women in the royal bloodline, but we see Gentiles throughout the gospel responding to Jesus in positive ways. Their responses are even more remarkable when contrasted with the negative response of the Jewish religious and political leaders. In the second chapter of Matthew, we meet the first group of Gentiles who come to Jesus—the Magi. They have responded to an astrological phenomenon and have come to worship the newborn king of the Jews. In contrast, Herod and Jerusalem are disturbed at the news brought by the Magi (Matt. 2:3). The Magi have come to worship the new king and offer gifts to him. By contrast, Herod tries to kill the new king.

The Roman centurion (Matt. 8) and the Canaanite woman (Matt. 15) are unique individuals. Not only are they Gentiles, but they are the only two people in the Gospels who are commended by Jesus for their great faith. They are also members of the nations that are the most despised by the Jewish people. The Romans were hated because they were the present enemy and occupiers of Israel's homeland, and the Canaanites were hated because they were the historic enemy and occupiers of Israel in Old Testament times. The faith of these two members of the despised enemies of Israel stands out in Matthew when it is compared to the unbelief of the people of Israel and the little faith of the disciples.

In Matthew, we find not only that the enemies of Israel are not the enemies of God and can be people of exemplary faith, but also that foreign lands are places of refuge for the Messiah, while the Promised Land is a place of danger. Egypt is not the land of bondage, but the place where Joseph goes to seek protection for his child. The Old Testament narrative is reversed! The destroyer of all male children is not Pharaoh, but Herod, king of the Jews. God delivers his people from the Promised Land to Egypt.

When Joseph and his family returned from Egypt, they could not settle in Judah because Archelaus reigned there. They again had to seek safety by settling in Nazareth in "the district of Galilee" (Matt. 2:22). Later, when Jesus began his ministry, he did so in Galilee because John had been arrested. Quoting from Isaiah 9:1, Matthew reminds us that Galilee is associated with the Gentiles. Isaiah refers to it as "Galilee of the Gentiles" (Matt. 4:15). Later, Jesus would withdraw to the region of Tyre and Sidon for protection from the Jewish leaders. By contrast, he said of Jerusalem, "O Jerusalem, Jerusalem, you who kill the prophets and stone those sent to you!" (Matt. 23:37).

If these new understandings of Gentiles and their lands were not enough to shatter the typical Jewish understanding of the world, then a second theme, Jesus' teaching on the kingdom of heaven, certainly would have been.

Jesus' teaching was kingdom centered. Everything he taught related to the reign of God. Matthew tells us that Jesus began to preach, "Repent, for the kingdom of heaven is near" (Matt. 4:17). The phrase "kingdom of heaven" is used thirty-one times in Matthew's gospel, and it is almost exclusively Jesus who uses the phrase. The kingdom of heaven in the teaching of Jesus is never associated with the political entity or territory of Israel. Could it be that Jesus described this kingdom as a heavenly one to avoid any confusion between the earthly borders of Israel and the reign of God? Jesus' self-designation was "Son of Man," also used thirty-one times in Matthew, which avoided a confusion between Israel's expectations of the Messiah and the task that Jesus had been given. Both of these terms freed Jesus' ministry from the Jewish expectation that the Messiah would come and deliver Israel from its earthly enemies and establish a Jewish territorial kingdom.

Matthew's gospel prepares the way for Jesus' teaching that the kingdom of heaven will not be ethnically based by reporting the angelic visitation to Joseph, where Joseph is told to name the child Jesus. That name is chosen because it describes Jesus' mission: "He will save his people from their sins" (Matt. 1:21). Who "his people" are will be defined by the new categories that Jesus will lay out in his teaching.

The teaching of John the Baptist also opens the way for a new understanding of the kingdom. John does so in two ways. First, he requires that even the Jews be baptized. Second, he tells the Pharisees that they should not trust their heredity, because God can raise up children of Abraham from stones (Matt. 3:9).

In Matthew 13:53–16:20, Jesus separates his kingdom from ethnic Israel by contrasting his "hometown" and "household" with the "assembly" or "church." In Matthew 13:57, he says, "Only in his hometown [or "fatherland"] and in his own house is a prophet without honor." To be a member of a household or a homeland means that there is an association of those who share the same blood or ethnicity. By contrast, Jesus says that he is building his "church," meaning "assembly" or "congregation." No ethnic bonds are required to be a member of an assembly. For Christ's assembly, there are only spiritual requirements.

Jesus' teaching on the kingdom explodes the Jewish ethnic understanding of that kingdom because Jesus does not divide the world into Jews and Gentiles, but into good and evil. Jesus compares men to trees who bear either good or bad fruit (Matt. 7:17–20). Mankind is composed of those who do the will of the Father and those who do not (7:21–23), those who receive the word and put it into practice and those who do not (7:24–27), and those who lose their lives for Jesus' sake and those who choose to save their lives (10:39). There are the sons of the kingdom and the sons of the Evil One (13:38). Mankind is divided into the wicked and the righteous (13:49).

Jesus' standard for being a child of the kingdom has no ethnic characteristics. The Beatitudes all refer to spiritual qualities (Matt. 5:3–10). No one is qualified because of his ethnic origin, and, more importantly, no one is disqualified because of it.

Jesus drives home the nonethnic dimension of the kingdom by redefining the family. In Matthew 12:46–50, when Jesus is told that

his mother and brothers are waiting to speak to him, we would expect
that they would have privileged access to Jesus. But Jesus declares
that blood carries no such privilege. No longer are his mother and
siblings members of his family by right of birth. Rather, his family is
composed only of those who do the will of the Father. Jesus says,
"For whoever does the will of my Father in heaven is my brother and
sister and mother" (12:50). If Jesus' immediate family—his own flesh
and blood—is excluded, then it is clear that no Jew can depend on
his genetic makeup for privileged access to the kingdom of heaven.

The most radical aspect of Jesus' teaching is the one that most
people today take for granted. The radical message that Jesus taught
his disciples was to call God "Father" (Matt. 6:9). In Matthew 23:8,
Jesus says that we all have one Father, and we are all brothers. No
longer is it Abraham who is to be called father, because the members
of Christ's kingdom are not sons of Abraham by the flesh. We, like
Abraham, become part of God's family the same way he did—
through faith.

The universal aspect of the kingdom is seen in the calling of the
disciples. When Jesus calls disciples, he commissions them to be fish-
ers of men (Matt. 4:19). In the Sermon on the Mount, Jesus says that
his disciples are "the salt of the earth" and "the light of the world,"
and they are to let that light shine before men (5:13–16). When Jesus
sends out his disciples on their first mission, he commands them,
"Do not go among the Gentiles. . . . Go rather to the lost sheep of
Israel" (10:5–6). The Jews had a covenantal priority to the gospel,
rather than an exclusive ethnic right to it (see Rom. 1:16). Even Jesus'
instructions in Matthew 10 reveal that the Gentiles will hear the
gospel as well (v. 18).

In Jesus' parables of the kingdom, the universal aspects of his
teaching about the kingdom are brought out. In the parable of the
weeds (Matt. 13:24–30, 36–43), the field represents the world (v. 37).
The kingdom is compared to a net that catches all kinds of fish (13:47),
and the leaven works its way through the whole lump (13:33).

Jesus has even harsher words for Israel in the teaching of his parables. Because they have failed to live out the spiritual qualities of the
kingdom, the kingdom will be taken away from them and given to
others. In the parable of the tenants (Matt. 21:33–44), he says, "There-

fore I tell you that the kingdom of God will be taken away from you and given to a people who will produce its fruit" (v. 43). In the parable of the wedding banquet (Matt. 22:1–14), Israel is the one who refuses to come to the banquet. Therefore, in verses 8 and 9 we read, "The wedding banquet is ready, but those I invited did not deserve to come. Go to the street corners and invite to the banquet anyone you find." Jesus reiterates this universal understanding of the kingdom in response to the faith of the centurion: "Many will come from the east and the west, and will take their places at the feast with Abraham, Isaac and Jacob in the kingdom of heaven. But the subjects of the kingdom will be thrown outside" (8:11–12).

Jesus' teaching on the final judgment is that Israel will hold no favored place, but will be summoned with all the other nations before the Son of Man: "All the nations will be gathered before him" (Matt. 25:32). When the judgment is pronounced, the people will be divided—the sheep will be separated from the goats according to their deeds and not according to their national origins.

Jesus has redrawn the boundaries of the kingdom. No longer can the Jews claim a birthright that exempts them from the demands of the kingdom. All mankind in Jesus' teaching has equal access to the kingdom, and they must all come to the kingdom in the same way. Could it be that Paul's statement in Galatians 3:28—that there is neither Jew nor Gentile, slave nor free, male nor female—is taken from Jesus' teachings on the kingdom of God?

Finally, Matthew ends his gospel with the Great Commission (28:19–20). Jesus commands his disciples to preach the gospel to every nation. In light of all the above, a literal interpretation of his words would probably be mistaken. It is more likely that Jesus is reinforcing his teaching that the new family of God is made up of "whoever does the will of my Father in heaven" (12:50).

The Structure and Placement of the Narrative Text in Matthew 13:54–16:20

Is there structure to Matthew's gospel, and does that structure help us discern his meaning and purpose? Gospel studies have swung widely on this question since the middle of the nineteenth century.

Early scholarship, believing that there was no structure to the teachings of Jesus, described the gospels as collections of pearls on a string. More recent scholarship has discerned a high degree of arrangement of the material found in the Gospels, and many have concluded that the intricate structure reveals purpose. David Bosch writes, "Today scholars agree that the entire gospel points to these final verses (Matt. 28:19–20). All the threads woven into the fabric of Matthew, from chapter 1 onward, draw together here."[2] A key turning point in understanding Jesus' message and ministry is revealed in the section of Matthew's gospel where the encounter with the Canaanite woman is found. Matthew 13:54–16:20 prepares the reader for Matthew 28:19–20.

Matthew 13:54–16:20 can be called the hinges of the gospel of Matthew. This section should be read and interpreted as a unit, because of (1) the literary devices that mark the boundaries of this section, (2) the internal structure of the passage itself, and (3) the passage's strategic place in the gospel of Matthew.

Literary Markers of Matthew 13:54–16:20

The passage should be considered as a unit because it opens and closes with clear markers that tell us a major transition has taken place. Matthew 13:53 ends the previous section with the statement, "When Jesus had finished these parables, he moved on from there." So important is this phrase to one school of Matthean scholars that they see Matthew structuring his entire gospel around its use.

The phrase "from that time," cited by the narrative school as the key literary device for structuring Matthew,[3] marks the end of our section (Matt. 16:21). Both schools have discovered important structural features in the text of Matthew, but neither group has proved that its approach represents the overarching structure of the gospel. The very fact that neither school has won a consensus of scholarly opinion indicates that neither solution fully explains Matthew's structure. One would agree with Gundry when he writes, "We should avoid imposing an outline on Matthew. It is doubtful that the first evangelist thought in terms of one."[4] But although we cannot discern an overall structure, passages like the Sermon on the Mount are highly structured. Matthew 13:54–16:20 is another intricately designed section of Scripture and must be interpreted as a unit to be properly understood. Each story in this section is affected by the episodes around it.[5]

Commentators who believe that Matthew had access to Mark's gospel have noted that beginning in Matthew 13:54, Matthew returns to Mark's order of material. Bruner writes, "Matthew no longer creatively alters the order of Mark's Gospel."[6] Could it be that Matthew himself was aware that this section of Scripture comprised a unit?

Internal Themes and Structure of Matthew 13:54–16:20

Besides the presence of these markers setting the boundaries of our section, there are also strong internal themes running through Matthew 13:54–16:20 that require us to handle this passage as a unit (see fig. 11.1).

The most obvious theme in this passage is "bread." Lucien Cerfaux describes this section and its parallel in Mark 6:31–8:26 as "La section des pains."[7] Doyle entitles this section of Scripture "Bread"[8] because of the frequent use of the term "bread." In all its forms, "bread" occurs twenty times in the gospel of Matthew, with fourteen of those occurrences being in Matthew 14:17–16:12.[9]

As part of the bread theme, the eucharistic formula "took bread" is used three times (Matt. 14:19; 15:26, 36). The phrase "ate and were satisfied" is again a reference to bread. It is found only twice in Matthew's gospel, both times in our section (14:20; 15:37).

A second theme that runs through this passage is that of compassion. In Matthew 14:14 and 15:32, Jesus has compassion on the crowds. Of the four times in Matthew's gospel that Jesus is described as having compassion, two are found in our section. Not only is the theme of compassion in this section, but also the opposite characteristic—the lack of compassion. We see the lack of compassion in the disciples in their desire to send the crowds away (14:15) and in their sending away of the Canaanite woman (15:23). Could Jesus have been responding to a nonverbal request of the disciples when he says, "I do not want to send them away hungry" (15:32)? It is only in our passage that the disciples ask to send people away. We also have two other clear demonstrations of the lack of compassion in this section. The first is when our Lord describes the Pharisees as

Figure 11.1. The Structure of Matthew 13:54–16:20

The Chiastic Structure	A. At Nazareth confession of Jesus (13:54–58) + John the Baptist an example of a prophet without honor—death (14:1–12)	B. The feeding of the 5,000 (14:13–21) + a disciple = little faith (14:28–33)	C. Jesus heals many (14:34–36).	D. The tradition of the elders (15:1–20)	D. The Canaanite woman (15:21–28)	C. Jesus heals many (15:29–31).	B. The feeding of the 4,000 (15:32–39) + the disciples = little faith (16:5–12)	A. Peter = confession of Christ (16:13–20) + the prediction of what it means to be the Christ—death (16:21)
THEMES								
Bread, Loaves, Crumbs	(14:17) loaves (14:19) loaves			(15:2) bread implied by "eat"	(15:26) bread (15:27) crumbs		(15:33) bread (15:34) loaves (15:36) loaves (16:5) bread (16:7) bread (16:8) bread (16:9) loaves (16:10) loaves (16:11) bread (16:12) bread	

Eat to Their Full		(14:20)			(15:37)	
Only Asking for Crumbs				(15:27) crumbs		
Compassion		(14:14) Jesus			(15:32) Jesus	
Lack of Compassion		(14:15) the disciples	(15:5) the Pharisees	(15:23) the disciples (15:23–26) Jesus = words		
No Faith	(13:58) people of Nazareth					
Little Faith		(14:31) Peter			(16:8) the disciples	
Great Faith				(15:28) the Canaanite woman		
Taking Offense	(13:57) people of Nazareth		(15:12) the Pharisees			
Jesus' Withdrawals		(14:13)		(15:21)		
Revelation That Jesus Is the Son of God		(14:33) the disciples				(16:16) Peter

people who say to their parents, "I cannot help you because I have pledged all I have to God" (15:5, my paraphrase), and the second is our Lord's treatment of the Canaanite woman.

A third theme that runs through this narrative is the contrast between little faith and great faith. In Matthew 14:31, Jesus rebukes Peter, addressing him as "you of little faith." In 16:8, Jesus again rebukes the disciples by describing them as "you of little faith." By contrast, the Canaanite woman is praised by Jesus as having "great faith." The people in Jesus' hometown are cited for their unbelief (13:58).

Another important contrast is found in the two pericopes on either end of Matthew 13:54–16:20. The first takes place in Jesus' hometown; the second takes place at the northern limit of Jesus' ministry, Caesarea Philippi. In the first story, the people from Jesus' hometown ask, "Isn't this the carpenter's son?" (13:55). In the second, Peter confesses that Jesus is "the Christ, the Son of the living God" (16:16).

When this section of Scripture is looked at as a whole, a chiastic structure can be seen (see fig. 11.2). Along with the chiastic structure, there are linear relations in this section as well. The pericope of Jesus' rejection in Nazareth (13:54–58) and the pericope following it, John the Baptist's beheading (14:1–12), are joined together by the connecting phrase "at that time," and John's beheading is an example of a prophet who is without honor in his own house (13:57).

Figure 11.2. A Chiastic Structure [10]

A. Jesus' confession at Nazareth (Matt. 13:54–58)

   + an example of what it means to be a prophet without honor (14:1–12)

   B. The feeding of the 5,000 (14:13–21)

      + a disciple's little faith (14:28–33)

      C. Jesus heals many (14:34–36)

         D. The tradition of the elders (15:1–20)

         D. The Canaanite woman (15:21–28)

      C. Jesus heals many (15:29–31)

   B. The feeding of the 4,000 (15:32–39)

      + the disciples' little faith (16:5–12)

A. Peter's confession of Christ (16:13–20)

The pericopes of the clean and the unclean (Matt. 15:1–20) and the Canaanite woman (15:21–28) are also linked. There is the use of the conjunction "and,"[11] and the theme of clean and unclean continues in connection with the Canaanite woman. There is a connection between clean and unclean foods in Peter's vision (Acts 10:9–17) and the taking of the gospel to the Gentiles. Peter interprets his vision to Cornelius this way: "But God has shown me that I should not call any man impure or unclean" (Acts 10:28). Hill writes, "Note the connection between the question of clean and unclean and the mission to the Gentiles in the Pauline churches. Thus the link between the two stories seems to be generally accepted by scholars."[12]

The Strategic Placement of Matthew 13:54–16:20

A third reason why we should consider this passage as a unit is the placement of this narrative passage in Matthew's gospel. In this section, several themes reach their climax. Perkinson writes of the encounter with the Canaanite woman, "The pericope falls at the beginning point of the transition. It is strategically placed near the epicenter."[13] The most important theme reaching its climax in this section is the identification of Jesus as "Son of God." We find this confession used twice in our passage. The disciples in the boat after Jesus calms the storm confess, "Truly you are the Son of God" (14:33), and Peter, in answer to Jesus' question, responds, "You are the Christ, the Son of the living God" (16:16).[14]

A second theme that reaches a climax in this section is Israel's rejection of the Messiah and the Messiah's rejection of Israel. The rejection of Christ is literally brought home in the pericope of Jesus returning to his hometown. It is at Nazareth that, for the first time in Matthew's gospel, the people "took offense at him" (13:57). In 14:2, Herod hears of Jesus' fame and believes that he is John the Baptist raised from the dead. The political powers take offense at Jesus. In 15:12, the disciples tell Jesus, "The Pharisees were offended when they heard this [the words of Jesus]." In 15:1, we are told for the first time in Matthew that "some Pharisees and teachers of the law came to Jesus from Jerusalem." These represent the religious establishment. This is the only place in Matthew's gospel where this term is used to describe the response of people to Jesus' teaching. The response of Jesus to the people's taking offense is to withdraw. We are told that Jesus "withdrew" in 14:13. The withdrawal of Jesus is a response both to the people of Nazareth taking offense at him and to the beheading of John. In 15:21, Jesus withdraws again in response to the Pharisees' taking offense at him (15:12).[15] This will be the last time that Matthew uses the term "withdraw" to describe Jesus' movements.

Israel's rejection is also expressed in the geographical movement of Jesus throughout Matthew's gospel. In this narrative, we come to the limits of Jesus' travels and the shift where Jesus turns back toward Jerusalem. The first Jewish threat to Jesus is at Jerusalem. King Herod and all Jerusalem are disturbed (Matt. 2:3). Jesus' family withdraws to Egypt. The second implied threat is Archelaus, and the family withdraws to Galilee (2:22). The third threat comes also from Judea. John was baptizing "in the Desert of Judea" (3:1) and was arrested by Herod (4:12). Jesus withdraws to Galilee to begin his ministry. When a fourth threat comes from Galilee, Jesus' hometown (12:15), and he hears of John's death (14:13), Jesus withdraws "to a desolate place." The only other time in Matthew that the phrase "to a desolate place" is used is when the Spirit leads him "into the desert" after his baptism (4:1). The next threat is the coming of the Pharisees and the teachers of the law from Jerusalem. This is the first time in Matthew that the leaders of the Jews have come from Jerusalem to see Jesus. As a result, Jesus withdraws to the Gentile territory of Tyre and Sidon (15:21). It is at Caesarea Philippi, probably the most northern point of Jesus' travels, that Jesus will begin to move toward Jerusalem.

Finally, there is the shift from "hometown" and "house" (Matt. 13:57) to "church" (Matt. 16:18). As explained earlier, the mission to restore Israel ends in this section. Jesus now turns his attention to building his congregation.

Based upon the above findings, we should consider Matthew 13:54–16:20 to be a vitally important unit in Matthew's gospel. Therefore, the interpretation of any part of this section must depend on how it fits into the entire section. When we consider Matthew 15:21–28 from this perspective, it opens up possibilities for seeing

Jesus' words in a completely different way, a way that would cause us to see our shortcomings instead of trying to see them in Jesus.

The Words of Jesus in Matthew 15:21–28

The first three responses of Jesus in Matthew 15:21–28, when taken at face value, are problematic. Is this the Jesus of whom Matthew, just a few chapters earlier, said, "A bruised reed he will not break, and a smoldering wick he will not snuff out" (12:20)? My translation of the four responses of Jesus are:

1. But he did not answer her a word.
2. But he answering said, "I was sent only to the lost sheep of the house of Israel."
3. But he answering said, "You cannot take the children's bread and feed it to the dogs."
4. Then answering, Jesus said to her, "O woman, great is your faith. Let it be as you desire."

Most commentators take one of two approaches to this text. Jesus is either learning something about his ministry or testing the faith of the woman. But neither approach fits into our understanding of Jesus or his teaching. Beare writes, "The attitude attributed to Jesus in the atrocious saying of verse 26 is completely out of keeping with everything else that is reported of him."[16] Since this is the case, we must see the passage differently.

The master teacher who amazed the crowds with his teaching (Matt. 7:28, 13:54) is being the master teacher in this pericope. Doyle is right when he states that discipleship is the central theme around which Matthew's gospel is shaped.[17] Accordingly, we must see these verses from another viewpoint if we wish to understand them.

Jesus is preparing his disciples for the mission to which they will soon be commissioned. They have been with him for some time, and now he wants to see what they have learned. Jesus places three tests before his disciples in Matthew 13:54–16:20. The first is found in 14:16, where Jesus tells his disciples to give the crowd something to eat. Another test is found in the question that Jesus asks his disciples in

16:15, "But what about you? . . . Who do you say I am?" The other test in this section is found in 15:23, in the silence before this desperate woman who cries out for help from Jesus.[18] When teachers are silent, it is not because they are not sure how to respond. They are waiting to see how their students will respond.

What lesson does Jesus want to teach his disciples? The recurring lesson that Jesus teaches his disciples by way of negative example is that they are not to be like the Pharisees.[19] Jesus particularly stressed that the Pharisees were people who lacked mercy and compassion. In Matthew 9:13, Jesus tells the Pharisees, "But go and learn what this means: 'I desire mercy, not sacrifice.'" Again, in 12:1–7, in response to Jesus' healing of a man on the Sabbath, the Pharisees plot to break the sixth commandment in order to protect the fourth. To them again Jesus says, "I desire mercy, not sacrifice" (v. 7).

This lack of mercy in the Pharisees was not just toward tax gatherers, sinners, and the sick whom Jesus healed on the Sabbath; their lack of mercy extended even to their own parents. When their parents came to them for help, there was no help to give.

In Matthew 23, Jesus pronounces seven woes on the Pharisees. He prefaces those woes with a general remark concerning their character (23:1–11). Their lack of mercy for others can be seen in their unwillingness to lift a finger to help those upon whom they have laid a heavy burden (v. 4). In the fourth woe, Jesus commends the Pharisees for tithing the smallest spices of the garden, but condemns them for neglecting the more important matters of the law, namely, "justice, mercy and faithfulness" (v. 23). In the narrative that we are considering, Jesus warns his disciples, "Be on your guard against the yeast [teaching] of the Pharisees and Sadducees" (16:6). Their teaching leads to using the first table of the law, to love God, as the grounds for breaking the second table of the law, to love your neighbor.

In contrast to the Pharisees, Jesus is moved with compassion. Twice in our section, he is said to be moved with compassion: in 14:14, he heals the sick; in 15:32, he says, "I have compassion for these people," and so he feeds them. Jesus has compassion on the crowds in 9:36 when he sees that they are like sheep without a shepherd. We may conclude that all that Jesus did was, in one sense, motivated by his compassion for people. He never drove a wedge between compassion for people and devotion to God, as the Pharisees did.

Thus, Jesus expected his disciples to be people of mercy and compassion. In Matthew 5:7, Jesus teaches that the merciful are blessed. In the parable of the unmerciful servant (18: 21–35), it is unthinkable that one who had been shown mercy would not show mercy to others.

With the silence in 15:23a, Jesus, the master teacher, is placing another test before his disciples. He waits for a response from them to the desperate Canaanite woman.[20] What have they learned? "Send her away, for she keeps crying out after us" (v. 23b). Notice the continuing action of the disciples, with the use of the imperfect verb "they keep asking" and the present participle "saying" (in v. 23). This structure parallels the action of the woman. "She keeps crying" is an imperfect verb also, followed by the present participle "saying" (in v. 22). One may well ask, which of the two parties was more adamant?

The disciples heard the noise and asked Jesus for relief, but they did not hear her desperate cries for help, even when her cries were reminiscent of one of the disciple's very own pleas. The cry of the woman in verse 22, "Lord, Son of David, have mercy on me!" and again in verse 25, "Lord, help me!" is similar to Peter's cry in the preceding chapter, "Lord, save me!" (14:30). Did Peter hear the echo of his own cries for help in the screams of the woman?

To make sure that we hear the woman's cry as an echo of Peter's cry, Matthew places the woman and Peter in the same position before Jesus. In Matthew 14:30, we read that Peter was "beginning to sink." A better translation would be "beginning to drown." The same word is used to describe what is to happen to the man who has a millstone placed around his neck and is thrown into the ocean. Literally, he will be "drowned" in the depths of the sea (Matt. 18:6). Harrington suggests that Psalm 69 (especially verse 1) is the Old Testament background for Peter's cry.[21] Peter's position in the water is the same as the psalmist's: "Save me, O God, for the waters have come up to my neck" (Ps. 69:1). Peter's head is approximately in the same position before the Lord as the woman's head when she "knelt" before him (Matt. 15:25). Once again, the translators have sanitized the translation. The woman is not coming like the Magi, "bowing down." She is desperate![22] She falls at Jesus' feet, just as the servant in the parable of the unmerciful servant "fell on his knees" and begged, "Be patient with me" (18:26). Based on Matthew 18:33, "mercy" is a good dynamic equivalent for "patience." Our Lord's point in this parable is, "Shouldn't you have had mercy on your fellow servant just as I had on you?" (18:33). Peter and the other disciples in this story prove themselves to be just like the unmerciful servant.

This was not the first time that the disciples had asked the Lord to send people away. They had previously asked Jesus to send the crowds away so they could buy something to eat (Matt. 14:15). In 15:32, Jesus states that he does not want to send the crowds away hungry. Perhaps he was responding to the disciples' unspoken desire that the crowds be sent away. Later, the disciples would rebuke those who had brought their children to Jesus (19:13). The disciples may have been responsible for sending more people away from Jesus than they brought to him.

Could the church likewise today be the obstacle that keeps men and women away from the Lord? Are we any better than the disciples? Do we hear in the cries of people of different races our same cry to the Lord for help? Or do we just want them to go away? I believe that the reason that many of our churches are so homogeneous is that we have sent the other kinds of people away. We still have not learned to see how much alike all people are.

Today many of our churches are filled with channelers who speak for God. But do we need another word? Jesus is silent because he has already told us what we should do and is waiting for our obedience to his commands.

Jesus' silence is easy enough to explain, but how can we explain his words that appear to violate everything that he is trying to teach about mercy? One thing is clear: both phrases, "I was sent only to the lost sheep of Israel" and "It is not right to take the children's bread and toss it to their dogs," make absolutely no sense in the present context unless we see these words as a teaching device. While the disciples have voiced what they want Jesus to do with the woman— "Send her away!"—Jesus gives voice to their motivation. He expresses the disciples' motives.[23]

Supporting this interpretation is the fact that we are not told to whom Jesus is speaking. Is he answering the woman or the disciples, or is he musing to himself? In any case, Jesus' words should not be interpreted as a rejection of the woman's request.

To correctly interpret the next two statements of Jesus, we need to understand the teaching device that Jesus uses. Jesus' teaching has been shown to resemble that of a sage.[24] Most of Jesus' discourses in the Gospels consist of proverbs, aphorisms, and parables. One of the remarkable qualities of Jesus' teaching is that he often quotes conventional or traditional wisdom and then turns that wisdom on its head. For example, "You have heard that it was said, 'Love your neighbor and hate your enemy.' But I tell you: Love your enemies and pray for those who persecute you" (Matt. 5:43–44). James G. Williams comments that Jesus employed the technique of paradox to disorient his audience and to negate tradition.[25] This type of aphoristic wisdom is known as "counter-order," which Williams defines as "employing paradoxical speech to call into question a given tradition and to express the worth of another dimension or reality that is seen to stand against the traditional order."[26] Witherington writes that counter-order aphorisms "were often meant to challenge prevailing assumptions that Jewish Wisdom had traditionally inculcated."[27] Melchert writes, "He offers parables and aphorisms that question the status quo and evoke a counter-order view."[28] We should see the two statements in Matthew 15:24, 26 as counter-order aphorisms, because everything in the context cries out to the reader to "listen and understand."[29]

When Jesus says, "I was sent only to the lost sheep of Israel," we have to hear irony in his words and see them in the light of what Matthew has been saying about Jesus' reception among the Jews. Herod tries to kill him; the Jews plot his death. The cities don't believe, despite his miracles. He is rejected in his hometown. John the Baptist is killed by Herod. Jesus can rightly say to the Jews that they are the renters of the vineyard who have mistreated the servants of the landlord and want to kill the son, so the vineyard will be theirs (Matt. 21:33–39). In the context of the passage, we need to read, "I was sent to Israel, but look at the difference in the reception. It is just as I told you. Gentiles are more willing to repent than the Jews" (see Matt. 11:20–24).

Theologically, the statement "I was sent only to the lost sheep of Israel" is true. Jesus was sent only to Israel. But heresies always contain some truth. This heresy is that the restoration of Israel was to be an end in itself. What this statement leaves out is that the sending of the Messiah to Israel would result in the coming of the nations to the Lord. The Old Testament prophets foretold that the nations would come to Jerusalem as a result of the Messiah's reign (see Isa. 2:2–4; 11:10; 19:19–25; 25:6–8; 60:3–14; 66:19–21; Mic. 4:1–4; Zeph. 3:9–10; Zech. 8.20–23). The Canaanite woman, along with the other Gentiles in Matthew's gospel, the Magi and the Roman centurion, are the first-fruits of the Messiah's reign. They have already begun to come.[30]

The mystery is that even Israel's rejection of her Messiah would not keep God from fulfilling his promise to Abraham—that all nations would be blessed in him (see Paul's discussion of the rejection of Israel in Romans 9–11 and what that means to the Gentiles).

Jesus' words also tell us about Israel's covenantal position. God is true to his promises. For this reason, when Jesus sent his disciples out on their first preaching tour, he told them that they were not to go among the Gentiles or enter any town of the Samaritans: "Go rather to the lost sheep of Israel" (Matt. 10:5–6). The covenantal priority of Israel was also respected by Paul, for his practice was to go first to the Jews and then to the Gentiles (Rom. 1:16).

Therefore, "I was sent only to the lost sheep of Israel" should not be read as exclusive words, for the sending of the Messiah meant the coming of the world to him. The problem was that they became exclusive words to the Jews, and they hid their prejudices behind theological half-truths. Theological truths spoken in the wrong circumstances are false. Too often the church has used one theological truth to wash its hands of its calling before God. Those who hold to the Reformed faith can be guilty of a similar misuse of the truth. We misuse truth when we stress the sovereignty of God to the exclusion of the Lord's mandate to evangelize or to pray.

Jesus' second statement, "It is not right to take the children's bread and toss it to their dogs" (Matt. 15:26), is not gospel truth, but traditional wisdom. It is a proverb from Jewish folk wisdom. We cannot hide behind the use of the word "puppies." To such attempts Scott and Martin respond, "Given the tortured nature of so many of the 'apologetic' interpretations and the fact that it is impossible to find plausible affirmative references to people as either little dogs, puppies, or house pets, attempts to explain away Jesus' rudeness on the basis of positive historical precedent seem doomed to failure."[31] The words sting.

The meaning of the proverb needs no explanation. Most societies have similar proverbs. The French say, "Manger le pain des Français" ("Eat the bread of the French"). It expresses well the proverb of our text. The French use it to explain why immigrants have come to their country. It expresses the loathing that some of the French have toward immigrants, for if they eat the bread of the French, there will be no bread for the French.

In the same way, you cannot take the children's bread and feed it to the dogs, because the children must be fed. To feed it to the dogs is to take it away from the children. In a world of limited resources, there is only enough bread to feed one group; all other groups must go without. So the proverbial wisdom of the Jews under normal circumstances seems to make very good sense in normal times. But with the coming of the Promised One, times would never again be normal.

In this new economy of the kingdom, the traditional wisdom becomes the foolishness of men, for the message of Matthew 13:54–16:20 is that there is bread enough for all. More than enough! One no longer needs to make a choice between one group and another. The two miraculous feedings that envelop this pericope, when examined closely and taken together, teach clearly and unmistakably that there is enough bread for all people—both Jews and Gentiles.

In the first feeding story, five thousand men (plus women and children) were fed (Matt. 14:21). After all had eaten "and were satisfied" (v. 20), there were still twelve baskets of food left over. Although we should avoid numerology, the number twelve is significant because it represents the twelve tribes of Israel. The feeding of the five thousand is the feeding of a Jewish crowd. It teaches us that there is more than enough bread for the children of Israel.

In Matthew 15:29–39, four thousand men (plus women and children) were fed (v. 38). They also ate "and were satisfied" (v. 37). And when they had finished, seven baskets of food were gathered up.

Who were these people? We have an indication of what kind of people they may have been in verse 31. We are told that in response to the healings of Jesus, they "praised the God of Israel." This indicates that this was a Gentile crowd. Jesus was teaching his disciples and the church today that there is not only enough bread for the Jews, with much left over, but also enough bread for the Gentiles, also with an abundance left over. The seven basketfuls left over might symbolize the seventy nations of Genesis 10, or they may signify completeness or wholeness. In any case, for both Jews and Gentiles there was an abundance.

The words of the Canaanite woman, that even the dogs eat the crumbs that fall from their masters' table (Matt. 15:27), are identified by Perkinson as "messianic words."[32] But these are not the promises of the Messiah. Her words are a woefully inadequate view of life in the kingdom. In Christ's kingdom, all are invited to join the Master at the table—not simply to get by on crumbs or rations, but to eat to one's fill (see Matt. 8:11).

Jesus, by the graphic illustrations of the abundance of the two feedings, taught his disciples that the wisdom of this age is not the wisdom that children of the kingdom are to use. This teaching is doubly reinforced by the stark contrast between the abundance that is available to the children of the kingdom and the "not enough" economy of the Pharisees.

The story that precedes the encounter with the Canaanite woman is introduced with a reference to bread. The Pharisees ask him why his disciples "don't wash their hands before they eat" (Matt. 15:2). Jesus' response is that the Pharisees use their tradition to break the commandment of God. He illustrates this by showing how, under their system, they do not have enough to help their own parents (v. 5). Under the teaching of the Pharisees, there is nothing extra, for there is never enough. One need not concern oneself with father, mother, brother, sister, or neighbor, and certainly not Gentiles, because it is only to God that one is really responsible. Thus, the Pharisees used their theology to justify their lack of mercy.

Jesus draws on traditional wisdom with his statement, "It is not right to take the children's bread and toss it to their dogs," and it is clearly ridiculous in light of the events that surround this passage.

There is obviously enough for this woman; there is no need to send her away. Her request can be granted because there is enough for all.

Another way to look at this saying is to ask, When is it right to take the children's bread and feed it to the dogs? We feed the children's bread to the dogs when the children have had enough to eat, when they do not want any more food.

This is exactly what Matthew has been saying! The children of Israel have had enough, and have made that clear by rejecting Jesus at Nazareth (Matt. 13:57), by beheading John (14:10), and by taking offense at Jesus' teaching (15:12). The children are fed up with the bread and want no more of it. Israel has pushed Christ away, just as children push their plates away when they are no longer hungry. So it is time for others to eat. The same teaching is presented in the parable of the wedding banquet (22:1–14).

We know that children have had their fill of food when they start playing with it. We see an example of the children playing with the bread in Matthew 14:22–32, where Peter asks Jesus if he can join him on the water. How necessary was a walk on the water for Peter? Maybe he was asking Jesus for a sign, but even that was not necessary. Jesus condemned the Pharisees as "a wicked and adulterous generation" because they were looking for a sign (16:4). Peter was playing with the power of God when he asked to walk on the water. The children had had their fill.

There is a clear reference to the Lord's Supper in the two feedings. In the gospel of John, John turns the feeding into a eucharistic meditation (John 6). At the Lord's Table, all who come in faith are invited to come and eat. The only ones who are excluded are those who take offense at the Lord and do not see their desperate need of him. We are not only supposed to welcome all who come, but are also to go out and invite all to come.

This teaching speaks volumes to the church. How often has the church used the very same logic in deciding its priorities? In the budget of every church, you will find the teaching of the Pharisees at work. We too often make sure that there will be enough for us. The children will get their bread, whether they need it or not.

Could we be filled with the same ethnocentric sins as the Pharisees and the disciples? Do the ethnic terms in the names of our churches make it clear what kind of people will be seen as children and what kind of people will be seen as dogs?

The woman's response to Jesus shows great faith. She is not offended by the Lord's words, for she most likely expected this treatment from Jews. Instead, she responds, "Yes, Lord, but even the dogs eat the crumbs that fall from their masters' table" (Matt. 15:27). She realizes that it is a small thing for which she is asking. What the Lord can do for her represents only the crumbs.

In verse 28, Jesus finally addresses the woman directly: "Woman, you have great faith! Your request is granted." Jesus addresses her with great compassion and admiration. Her great faith is to be seen in contrast to the little faith of the disciples. Immediately before and after this pericope, the disciples are described as people of little faith—Peter in 14:31, and the disciples as a group in 16:8. The disciples are described as "dull" or "lacking understanding." This lack of understanding and little faith are combined in 16:5–12. The disciples think that Jesus is talking to them about bread because he is concerned that they do not have any. Jesus rebukes them and reminds them of the two feedings. He asks them why they are concerned about bread when they have the bread factory with them.

One should not overlook Jesus' declaration that it is not what goes into a man that makes him unclean, but what comes out of his heart (Matt. 15:17). It is this explanation of what is clean and unclean that introduces the story of the Canaanite woman. Has not Jesus, with this pronouncement, broken down the differences between Jews and Gentiles? Mankind is no longer divided along kosher lines, the clean and the unclean. It should not be overlooked as well that when Peter was being prepared to take the gospel to Cornelius, the Roman centurion (Acts 10), he had a vision involving clean and unclean food. The inclusion of the Gentiles is preceded by the declaration that kosher eating is not what makes us clean.

How then should we interpret Matthew 15:21–28? What are the lessons for the church today? Jesus is preparing his disciples to go out and make disciples. He has led them to this Gentile region to teach them that they must have compassion on all peoples. It is not Jesus who is being tested, but his disciples. When Jesus paused to let them speak, they should have implored him to hear this woman's cry. When Jesus stated that he had been sent only to the lost sheep of Israel, the disciples should have protested that that mission did not preclude receiving those who come to him, but rather that this, too, is a sign that he is the Messiah. To Jesus' use of Jewish folk wisdom, the disciples should have responded, "This is not what you have taught us; this is not what we know! You are the bread of life, and there is enough blessing for all. Remember the twelve baskets full of bread! Lord, have mercy on her!"

What does this passage say to the reader and the church today? Maybe it is hard to hear the words of Jesus spoken to the Canaanite woman. We do not like to have our prejudices exposed. But here we have them! We hide our sin behind theological half-truths and conventional wisdom. Through this narrative, Jesus calls us to a new way of looking at the world. We are not to suppose that the resources of God, spiritual or physical, are limited and must be rationed to those closest to us. The spiritual resources of God are never lacking.

We are to be people of compassion. We are not to be like the Pharisees and use our religion to separate us from reaching out to others. The first and greatest commandment can never be used to break the second great commandment. We are called to make disciples the same way that Jesus made disciples, and these disciples are to come from all the nations of the earth, forming one body, his church.

PART 4

LEADERSHIP DEVELOPMENT TO MEET NEW CHALLENGES

—12—

GETTING DAVID OUT
OF SAUL'S ARMOR

ROGER S. GREENWAY

In 1 Samuel 17, there is the fascinating story of the young man David preparing to engage the giant Goliath in mortal combat. King Saul tries to put his equipment on David: a coat of armor to protect the body, a bronze helmet to cover the head, and a heavy sword strapped on the hip. Such equipment suited Saul's way of fighting, and he believed that it was the best. But Saul's armor did not fit David, and it would have been useless against a giant like Goliath.

David was wise enough to realize this. "I cannot go in these," he said to Saul. David recognized that heavy armor did not fit the way he had learned to fight. David had to be free to engage the enemy in ways that were best suited to him. Alone in the wilderness, David had learned how to defend his sheep and kill attackers with simple weapons. He had proved his ability by single-handedly killing a lion and a bear. In order to defeat the giant, David had to use weapons with which he was proficient. If he had been forced to use Saul's armor, the story might have ended with a dead David and a defeated army. But freed to fight in an appropriate way, David slew the giant.

The Message

There is a message here for everyone concerned about leadership development for churches and kingdom institutions in the city: Trust God, and insist on training that is appropriate to your religious and social context. Education should fit the needs and expectations of the people for whom it is designed. Urban "giants" are many, and, like Saul's soldiers, many of God's good evangelical people wring their hands, wondering how to overcome them. Promising "Davids" appear now and then, but when they are forced to wear "Saul's armor," they become frustrated and disappear. People wonder why. Inappropriate educational programs are a large part of the answer.

The issue we face is this: traditional seminaries—and I have particularly in mind schools that are conservative and evangelical in theology—are not able or willing to make the necessary changes to prepare an adequate number of people to serve effectively in urban contexts and minister in churches representing a wide spectrum of races, languages, cultures, and religious backgrounds. Writing on the basis of their experience and research, two professors at Fuller Theological Seminary in Pasadena offer this critique: "We share the conviction that traditional theological education is not well suited for the equipping of urban Christian leaders. . . . Traditional forms produce nonfunctional or dysfunctional graduates."[1] If that assessment is accurate, and there is evidence that it is, God's urban people must look hard and fast for alternative ways to develop leaders. They should not expect seminaries to provide them.

A Faculty's Dilemma

A few years ago, I was invited to give an address before the faculty of a seminary that was much larger than the school at which I teach. That seminary was the principal training school for ministers of a denomination with more than a million members. The denomination seemed incapable of producing enough leaders for ethnic congregations. Fingers were pointed at the seminary for failing to recruit and retain minority students. Pressure was building up to ordain minority leaders without the benefit of seminary training because churches needed them and the academic process failed to produce them. Since I had done some writing about theological education for urban ministry, and most of the ethnic congregations were urban, the seminary invited me to come down and address the problem in front of the faculty.

I knew beforehand that I would be walking through a virtual mine field. Heated discussions about the issue had gone on for several years. When I looked at the fifty academics gathered in the paneled faculty room, I could see by their faces that defenses were high. This was a theologically conservative school, and for many of them academic traditions and theological orthodoxy were closely related. They had heard enough liberal ideas coming from "urban types," and any hint that theology or tradition might be downgraded in the curriculum could start a fire.

The first thing I did was to sketch my personal journey in training urban workers. I talked about my years as a missionary pastor in Colombo, Sri Lanka, where Christians were a small minority and opportunities for evangelism abounded. There was no Protestant seminary of any kind there, and all ministerial students had to go abroad for training. Most went for long periods to schools in England or the United States. When they came back, they discovered that they had become "decontextualized." They felt like foreigners in their own land. They had learned a good deal, but what they had learned was designed to prepare leaders for churches and institutions in the West. Little of what they had been trained in addressed the religions, cultures, and needs of Sri Lanka. They needed to reintegrate themselves into the Sri Lankan context. Some of them became so frustrated that they left the country and never returned. Sensing the need for indigenous training, I fought to get a seminary started in Sri Lanka. But it was not until years later that such a school was begun.

I went on to describe my seven years in Mexico City, where my main assignment was to teach in a Presbyterian seminary. Nearly a million people were moving every year to Mexico City, but where do you think the main focus of the seminary was? It was on rural churches in distant villages, where empty houses testified to the exodus of families to the city. New neighborhoods, containing tens of thousands of people, were springing up overnight all around Mexico City. But there were virtually no workers trained to gather in the urban harvest. I saw that the seminary where I taught was entrenched in a rural orientation, and my response was to begin a new institution dedicated to training urban workers. Its graduates were not considered qualified for ordination in the Presbyterian denomination, but they knew how to evangelize, start churches, and minister the gospel among urban people.

Then I told the faculty about the Center for Urban Theological Studies (CUTS) in Philadelphia, an inner-city training school that offers an accredited bachelor's degree through Geneva College and master's degrees through Westminster Theological Seminary. For some twenty-five years, CUTS has been a source of spiritual enhancement for the evangelical community of Philadelphia. The school is located in the heart of the city. Classes are held in the evening, and the style of teaching is geared to the needs and expectations of urban people. In order to enroll, students must already be in church leadership, because the aim of CUTS is to strengthen the people whom God has chosen and raised up for leadership.

I was honest with the faculty about the problems facing my own denomination, the Christian Reformed Church in North America (CRCNA), and the denominational seminary where I taught. We too struggled with the challenge of making theological education helpful and accessible to a wider variety of students. Our record was not great. Almost the same number of pastors and evangelists were being ordained who had not passed through seminary as the number of those who had gone the traditional route. On Sundays, the CRCNA worshiped in twenty-two different languages, yet only a fraction of those languages were represented in the student body. Where would leaders for all those different groups come from? Where would they be trained?

Common Ground

At that point, I detected a rising level of interest in what I was saying. I proceeded to lay out three points that I called "our common ground." First, it is our avowed intention to be loyal to the Scriptures as the revealed and authoritative Word of God, and every proposal we make should be scrutinized on the basis of Scripture. Second, we value our theological traditions, those we share with all Christian churches and those of our particular denominations. We acknowledge that many denominational traditions are largely cultural, such as styles of music and liturgy, pastoral roles and congregational expectations, forms of ecclesiastical organization, and educational standards for ordination. Third, we desire to be obedient to the Lord by proclaiming the gospel to everyone, building up churches and training effective leaders among people of different races, national origins, languages, economic conditions, educational levels, and cultural traditions.

As faculty members, we grimace when we hear charges that seminaries are insensitive to minority concerns. We want to say to the churches that what drives the curriculum is ministry, and not mere loyalty to the "academy." But we have accreditation standards to meet, traditions to respect, and constituencies that tend to oversimplify the issues.

Then I raised the burning question: Can seminaries like ours reasonably be expected to deliver the kind of training that leadership among the urban masses requires, training that is biblically based, theologically valid, *and contextualized to urban realities that are marked by ethnic diversity, cultural pluralism, wide educational differences, enormous social and economic problems, and rapid change?* Like it or not, the evidence does not point to a positive answer.

Probing the Matter Further

To probe the matter further, additional questions need to be considered:

1. Is it realistic to expect a seminary serving a denomination that has a European background and has traditionally required a high level of academic education, to adapt its curriculum so as to develop for leadership persons representing ethnic communities whose "ladders" to leadership are not academic credentials, but years of demonstrated godliness, powerful preaching, and pastoral effectiveness?

2. Are most seminary professors equipped by training and experience to provide the kind of education that gives leaders among urban and minority people the kind of preparation they need, namely, a sufficient knowledge of Scripture and theology to make them competent ministers of the Word, while not deculturalizing them to the extent that they lose their identity and acceptance among their people?

3. Are seminaries willing to infuse urban concerns and perspectives throughout the curriculum to the extent that urban issues are addressed from the standpoint of many disciplines—biblical, historical, theological, and pastoral, as well as missiological—and by all faculty members?

4. Are faculty members willing to change and adapt their teaching styles to meet the needs of people from other cultures, people who learn differently, and people who have difficulty with North American English and cannot write adequate notes during a traditional lecture?

5. Can urban ministry experience and education become part of all students' training for ministry, not merely in a token way, but with enough depth to equip leaders to analyze, evaluate, and address urban realities with both theological integrity and cultural sensitivity?

6. Given the fact that seminaries are expected to train missionaries for overseas assignments as well as for ministries in North America, can the focus in the missiology departments be shifted from rural/suburban-oriented education to a more urban emphasis, with greater attention given to ethnic diversity and cultural differences, in order to equip a higher percentage of missionaries for service in major urban centers?

7. Are seminaries disposed to require as seriously that faculty members be personally ministering regularly in churches and missions in order to better relate their teaching and writing to people and their current needs as they are to require scholarly research and writing?

A Vision with Three Options

What I have in mind for leadership development in the city requires the kind of structure that is freed from the encumbrances of traditions of marginal relevance to urban people, and that is driven by the single vision of delivering contextually appropriate training that is biblically and theologically sound and enhances the ministry ability of men and women who show spiritual maturity and are respected workers in their churches. I consider this to be one of the great educational "frontiers" of the twenty-first century, and we are just beginning to see it.

The options before us, as I see them, are these: First, we can maintain the "single cookbook" approach, try to force it on everyone, and let those who refuse to conform leave if they please. Second, we can try to change and adapt the traditional academic institutions by tinkering with curriculums and browbeating professors into showing more urban and ethnic sensitivity. Third, we can adopt the principle of "new wine in new wineskins" and strike out in creative new directions. We can respect traditional academic institutions as valid vehicles of education for the majority culture in North America and as options for persons of all cultures who choose them.

But alongside the traditional institutions, we can develop new forms of leadership training that are more church- and ministry-based, that build in a simple and straightforward manner on the authoritative Word of God and how it applies to people's lives, that preserve the essentials of traditional ministerial education, but place an equal emphasis on personal godliness, prayer, preaching, evangelism, servant leadership, and sensitive pastoral ministry in particular cultural contexts.

We have tried the first two options; let's consider the third.

An Unhappy Marriage

Some years ago, John M. Frame, then professor of theology and apologetics at Westminster Theological Seminary in Escondido, California, proposed a "New North American Model" for ministerial training.[2] Frame began by reflecting on the early history of Protestant ministerial training in North America, beginning with the period when young men who felt called by God to the ministry would be trained by an individual pastor. Often they would live in the pastor's home, he would teach them what pastors needed to know, and they would accompany their teacher-mentor as he went about his pastoral duties. After a time, this model was replaced by a formal type of training. Under the influence of the German university system, theological training was institutionalized and at the same time *academicized.*[3] Ministerial education was married to the academy.

In 1848, a book appeared, entitled *The Power of the Pulpit,* authored by the Rev. Gardiner Spring, who had served for thirty-four years on the board of Princeton Theological Seminary. Spring compared the generation of seminary-trained ministers with the earlier generation that had been pastorally trained. Although Spring acknowledged that it was too late to turn back the clock, "he reluctantly concluded that the older generation was notably superior to the younger in pastoral effectiveness and spiritual maturity."[4] As a way to improve seminary training, Spring urged that (1) professors maintain close supervision not only over seminarians' academic progress, but also over their spiritual and social development; (2) that the seminary faculty itself be composed of people with extensive pastoral experience; and (3) that no students be ordained without first having an apprenticeship with an experienced minister.[5]

Spring's proposals fizzled, and seminaries actually became less involved with the social and spiritual development of students. The academic demands on professors made it impossible for them to be more involved in pastoral ministry, and rising academic standards pushed nonacademic concerns into second place, "lest an institution's scholastic respectability be compromised."[6] Some argued that since, in principle, spiritual development was the work of the church and not of an academic institution, it was inappropriate to expect a seminary to include spiritual nurture in the curriculum.[7]

Frame went on to point out that, in the course of time, some of what Spring pled for has been adopted by North American seminaries. Before being hired, most professors are expected to have pastoral experience. Most seminaries require some kind of "internship" year before granting a Master of Divinity degree. But, at the same time, two of the most frequent complaints among seminarians themselves are: (1) the academic side of the curriculum receives the most attention and is the most rigorously tested, and (2) the spiritual development of seminarians is neglected to the point that many regard their time in seminary as "desert" years, almost barren of spiritual vitality. On the basis of his own observation, Frame said:

> It seems to me that most seminary graduates are not *spiritually* ready for the challenges of the ministry. Seminaries not only frequently "refuse to do the work of the church," they also tend to undo it. Students who arrive expecting to find a "spiritual hothouse" often find seminary to be a singular test of faith. The crushing academic work-load, the uninspiring and unhelpful courses, the financial agonies, the too-busy professors, the equally-hardpressed fellow students all contribute to the spiritual debilitation. I have known a number of students who have stopped going to church while in seminary, and others who wander from church to church in a fruitless search for genuine Christian fellowship, yet unwilling (some of them would say "unable") to give enough of themselves to others to make such fellowship possible.[8]

Is this what the urban and ethnic churches want for themselves? I doubt that they do, although some of them unfortunately are fixated on getting "accredited" degrees for themselves and their leaders. If they want them, let them pursue them. But I propose that urban churches set the academy aside, with everything it entails—degrees, accreditation, Ph.D.'s, credit hours, and traditional curriculum—and focus unrelentingly on the needs of the churches, the skills required for ministry, and the biblical standards for leaders of God's people.

Beyond what needs to be said regarding its weaknesses, I see no point in attacking the academy. Leave the academy to those servants of God whom he has gifted and disposed to serve him in that sphere. And let the denominations whose culture and tradition require a particular kind of "learned ministry" continue to support their schools and benefit from what they produce. Without question, gifted scholars are an asset. Churches ought to draw upon them frequently for teaching and insight, and sometimes for correction. But the marriage of the academy to ministerial preparation has produced too many unhappy children, who have been foisted on churches everywhere as though there were no other way to train leaders. As urban and ethnic churches multiply in North American cities, and as more leaders are needed to serve them, the opportunity arises to develop new models of leadership training that maintain certain elements of the old, while adding many that are new. I hope that urban churches will rise to the occasion, and that time-honored institutions of the cultural majority will not stand in their way.[9]

Putting Together a Training Community

My proposal for most urban churches is that they encourage their younger leaders to obtain college degrees, but that for further education they drop the academic model altogether and develop their own leadership development program. John Frame proposed that "we dump the academic model once and for all" for everyone.[10] I do not go that far. Traditions in white, middle-class churches are too deeply embedded to make this a viable option. Furthermore, there are values to be preserved in traditional theological education, and the defense of biblical orthodoxy will always require scholars of high caliber. But in the light of all the facts, I believe that the wisest course of action for most urban, ethnic churches is to develop alternative programs of leadership training, contextualized to their needs.

Cannot the two approaches be blended and offered under the same roof? I do not believe so. Almost every urban educational institution I know that tries to meet the requirements involved in academic degrees and at the same time provide the kind of training that urban churches need is *frustrated and in danger of failing on both scores*. Instead of chasing after the standards set by the academy, which has its own priorities and expectations, urban churches should focus on the basic training that God's Word requires of spiritual leaders and the needs of their people. Faithfulness to Scripture and to sound theology are not the issue, but rather the appropriateness of the process by which urban churches train ministers.

Character, Skills, and Knowledge

First, churches should focus on *character development* and the qualifications for church leaders given in Scripture, notably in 1 Timothy 3:1–13, 1 Peter 5:1–3, and Titus 1 and 2.[11]

Second, they should focus on developing the necessary *skills* for ministry, because, according to Scripture, church leaders must be able to shepherd the flock, feed the sheep, defend against "savage wolves," "preach the Word . . . correct, rebuke and encourage," "do the work of an evangelist," and give spiritual oversight in a humble, servant-hearted manner (Acts 20:28–29; 1 Tim. 3:2; 4:16; 5:17; 2 Tim. 4:2–5; 1 Peter 5:2).

Third, they must impart *a knowledge of God and his Word,* as indicated in 2 Timothy 3:14–17, Titus 1:9, and 1 John 5:18–21. This knowledge of God and his Word must be closely linked to Christian character, because, as John Frame points out:

Knowledge of God, "knowing the Lord," "knowing the truth," in Scripture are never mere academic attainments. To "know God" in the Bible is to be God's covenant servant and therefore to be obedient to God (Jeremiah 22:16). Thus, the "knowledge of God" is of a piece with the traits of Christian character. . . . This covenantal knowledge, of course, involves "knowledge" in the more conventional modern sense of the term—i.e., knowledge of facts. The covenant servant must know who God is and what God has said and done. But even such factual knowledge is the gift of the Spirit (1 Corinthians 2:11, 12:8), when pursued and discovered in its proper covenantal context. And factual knowledge pursued and discovered outside of that context is of no spiritual value: the devils also believe and tremble (James 2:19ff.).[12]

The trouble with the traditional way of training for the ministry is that it is so heavily weighted toward academic accomplishments that the "weightier things," such as diligence in prayer; evidence of a loving and gracious spirit; obedience to the moral standards of Christian living; spiritual power in teaching, preaching, and evangelism; and the ability to exercise authority without pride, receive scant attention. Yet these are the most important things to be measured in persons preparing for Christian leadership. They are the things that spiritually perceptive members in most ethnic and urban churches look for in their leaders. The expectation of spiritual, servant leadership is ingrained in most urban congregations, and this expectation must be preserved and encouraged. It should be central in any ministerial training program for the city.

What form should an alternative program take? One thing to avoid is a "cookie cutter" approach that offers one answer for every church and community. Urban church leaders need to come together to discuss what they need in their situation, with their resources, and in terms of their goals. They need to form associations, or partnerships, of like-minded people who share the goal of a contextualized urban training program for their churches and are determined to achieve the goal without becoming dependent stepchildren of educational institutions wedded to the academy.

Teachers

Teachers do not necessarily need high academic degrees, but they do need to be fully conversant with the Scriptures, sound in doctrine, and rich in ministerial experience. They need to be people of high and noble character, good role models, and "able to teach." Not everyone, with or without a Ph.D., is skilled in teaching teachers, and the teaching of teachers is what leadership development is all about (2 Tim. 2:2). The subjects they are asked to teach should be related to their field of experience and sought after by the churches to meet their needs.

Learners

Learners in such training programs are already exercising their spiritual gifts, and they are drawn to the programs by the desire to enhance their abilities to minister. The fruits of the Spirit are evident in their lives. Their fellow church members respect them for the service they already render and for their sense of calling to greater ministry. During the course of their training, they engage in serious discussions with their mentors, peers, and instructors regarding their personal needs. They deal with their sins and weaknesses, and they seek to grow stronger in every area of spiritual life. Spouses and older children are involved in the training as well, because they too are part of the ministry. Many a person has floundered in ministry because of family problems.

Curriculum

The curriculum in the urban program is developed in the opposite way from the academic model. Notice the difference in figure 12.1.

Figure 12.1. Contrasting Educational Models

Academic Model

KNOWLEDGE ➡ Skills ➡ Character

New Model

CHARACTER ➡ Skills ➡ Knowledge

In the new model, Christian character receives primary attention. Practical assignments in ministry come at the beginning of the educational process instead of at the end. The nature and length of each part of the development process are tailored to the needs, background, and progress of each participant.

First there is evangelism, including individual witnessing and group endeavors, under the guidance of skilled evangelists. Until they have actually led people to Christ, students proceed no further. Training then moves from "Evangelism 101" to visiting prisoners in jail, teaching Bible classes at various levels, visiting sick persons in the hospital, ministering to bereaved persons, carrying responsibilities for the oversight of church and mission programs, and eventually preaching in the pulpit.

Books and Other Learning Tools

At each stage, appropriate books and other materials are assigned. Courses offered by "distance education" may be included. Whatever the students study is discussed by the group. The more advanced the stage, the more the students become aware of their need for additional instruction in Scripture and theology, and incrementally more instruction in these areas is given. At the advanced stages, the help of seminary instructors, by private arrangement or through partnerships with seminaries, is beneficial. The instructors must be prepared to adapt their style of teaching to the experience levels of the urban students and the variety of ways in which the students learn.

Graduation

When is graduation? The number of "earned credit hours" has nothing to do with graduation from the program. Readiness for ministry is the determining factor. In the model that he suggests, John Frame says that "no person will 'graduate' unless the teachers are convinced that he has the character, skills and knowledge which the Scriptures require of church officers."[13] When the mentors and instructors are convinced that a person is ready to leave the program, a diploma or some other certificate of achievement is granted. In the urban institute that I started years ago in Mexico City, we gave students grades, but we told them repeatedly that no matter how high their grades might be, they would not graduate unless they had been personally involved in planting a church in the city.[14]

Basic Seminary Communities

From China to Latin America and elsewhere, a great deal of the growth of the church in recent years has come about through various forms of "basic communities." Meeting in small groups, often in private homes and without the benefit of highly trained teachers or clergy, God's people have grown in faith, spirituality, and witness. I suggest networks of "basic seminary communities" as the way to develop contextualized programs of leadership development for urban churches. These basic seminary communities can be the answer to the needs of churches in the city that are economically poor or culturally isolated, cut off from mainstream theological education and looking for an approach that fits their needs.

In order for basic seminary communities to make a collaborative training program work effectively, there is a major hurdle that must be crossed. It is the hurdle of *trust and reconciliation* between racial and ethnic communities in the city. Mistrust and alienation make it difficult to propose concrete leadership development programs that can stand on their own and make a broad impact in the city.

In an enlightening discussion of this issue, Sidney H. Rooy writes, "Theological education for urban mission is of little value and can expect little blessing unless it is based on the solid rock of God's reconciliation with man and His demand that man be reconciled with his brother."[15] That is well said, because many a promising urban initiative has run aground because of feuding between Christian leaders. If urban churches are to pursue a new vision for leadership development that fits their needs and is not "borrowed armor," they will need to reach out and be reconciled to one another to a much greater degree.

What Would Harvie Say?

As I finished writing this essay, I asked myself, What would Harvie Conn say about these proposals? Harvie spent most of his life serving the academy. Yet he was always looking for better ways to spread the gospel and grow the church among the masses. His heart was with God's "little people" and their needs, as his role in the founding and development of CUTS illustrates.

I think that if Harvie read this, he would smile, his eyes would twinkle through his thick glasses, and with his contagious laugh he would say, "Go for it!"

13

SEMINARIES: TIME FOR A CHANGE?

EDNA C. GREENWAY

Many of the ideas for this essay are taken from the text of a study committee report for the Synod of the Christian Reformed Church.[1] The committee was assigned the task of examining alternative routes used to enter the ordained ministry in the church. As a member of the committee, I participated in the development of the final piece. Due to the fact that this report will likely be buried in the archives of the church, it will never have the wider audience that it deserves. However, most of the issues raised deserve a wider audience and hopefully will provoke the kind of discussion that will contribute to the enhancement of seminary education.

Traditionally, seminaries have been scholarly institutions. Although many schools claim to train pastors and ministry practitioners, much of the thrust of seminary teaching and learning is scholarly. Seminary professors themselves are scholarly folk. They have studied hard and long in their areas, and their teaching reflects a scholarly disposition. Urban leaders can be helped by a scholarly approach to biblical studies, but they need to expand their understanding of the city through practical means as well. In the past, many seminary professors came from rural, small town, or suburban areas. Today, even though fewer and fewer church leaders have rural backgrounds, this "rural" tendency still exists to some extent. In general, the rural mind-set is reflected in their lectures.

The seminary world has begun to recognize the importance of preparing men and women for gospel ministry in the metropolitan areas of the world. In the past decade, many seminaries have introduced an urban component into the curriculum. It usually consists of a course or two focused on urban ministries and some sort of practical urban experience. From Mexico City to Manila, Seoul to Singapore, Aix-en-Provence to Amsterdam, Lagos to Lima, no one has to argue for the importance of preparing for urban ministry. Even some seminaries in nonurban areas offer courses in urban ministry.

What Must the Seminary of the Future Look Like?

First of all, the seminary of the future will be an institution where teaching and learning take place among a diverse population. Throughout the world, seminaries are attracting students from within their countries and students from other countries as well. This student diversity presents the seminary with a number of cross-cultural challenges.

Some questions arise. In which language should the courses be taught? How much language support should be offered to students? If professors are available who know the second language, should an international student be allowed to write course papers in his or her own language? What kinds of cross-cultural orientation should be made available? Additional considerations include financial support, housing, and relocating students and their families to the new country and then returning them to the home country after their studies are completed.

Faculties and administrators in North American seminaries often consider such questions to be mainly North American issues. However, we are seeing more and more students throughout the world who long for advanced programs in seminary education. They travel to other countries to obtain the training they desire. Students from Africa are studying in Seoul, Korea. Students from Bangladesh and Pakistan are studying in Manila, and students from many countries in Latin America are traveling to Costa Rica and Mexico City for urban training. The questions above are faced by schools through-out the world.

Seminary faculties and staffs need to be cross-culturally oriented in order to understand minority and international students. Professors must be constantly alert to the cultures of the students in the classroom. Cross-cultural misunderstandings occur frequently enough even with professors and administrators who try to be aware of the concerns of minority and international students. An international office or an advisor for international students is a sign to newly arrived students that their needs are taken seriously.

Different Models for a New Seminary Culture

The Technological Model

The electronic age is rapidly influencing the seminary. Virtual libraries, online courses, and chat rooms with professors available are all new technological possibilities.

Second-career students, students from other lands, and other categories of nontraditional students are interested in this new mode of seminary course delivery. One of the leaders in the area of online courses is Asbury Seminary in Wilmore, Kentucky. Their Web site details the information needed to enroll at Asbury and how to begin their program. Students can earn credits for up to one-third of their Master of Divinity degree while remaining at home. Asbury's Master of Arts degree can be completed entirely through online courses. These courses can be accessed in North America and anywhere in the world where necessary computer and Internet equipment are available. Asbury Seminary gives students access to chat rooms and also provides students with online consulting time with the professors.

Bethel Seminary in St. Paul, Minnesota, has courses online to fulfill the requirements for a Master of Arts in Children's and Family Ministry. The program combines on-campus weeks with online courses.

Fuller Seminary in Pasadena, California, has an online campus that offers six courses from the School of World Mission. Fuller Seminary offers special information for international students who are interested in online courses.

More and more seminaries are offering such courses and programs for their nontraditional students. Will such programs be the wave of the future for an urban and diverse world? They certainly will be used in urban centers around the world where technology is available to support such endeavors. As the virtual library that is available to students is expanded to include hyperlinks to a growing number of important resources, these resources will be available in many new places. At this time, there are still places in the world where such technology is not available. This will change, however, and in the course of this century, even remote rural areas and small towns will have the technological capabilities that are now considered the norm in urban centers.

In order to succeed, distance learning and online courses require a certain dynamic interaction between professors and students far away. Most professors find that they have to present their material in new and exciting ways to maintain the interest of students who are miles away.

The greatest advantage of this model is that it makes advanced education available globally. Students who cannot leave home, relocate their families, and leave their local ministries will be the ones who benefit most from online courses.

Traditional students who prefer the classroom model may not want to take online courses. Such students need the on-site support of a professor and fellow students in the classroom. In my opinion, the convenience of learning in one's own home with the use of library resources on the computer will in time impel even reluctant learners to try the new model. Many nontraditional learners find themselves taking night courses or concentrated summer school courses. How much easier it will be to take courses using the online model!

The U.S. Seminary Link with Overseas Site Model

A second model of the future is one that has been used successfully for fifteen years. Dr. James Grier of Grand Rapids Baptist Seminary, now part of Cornerstone University, is the director of the Christian Worldview Institute and the World Missions Center. Fifteen years ago, under Dr. Grier's direction, Baptist Seminary planned a seminary program with sites in six Asian countries: Myanmar, the Philippines, Thailand, India, Hong Kong, and Singapore. Twice a year, professors from Grand Rapids Baptist Seminary go to each of these sites for two weeks. The visiting professor teaches one course during the two-week period, and a professor from an Asian country teaches another course. This enables students to take two courses at a time. The professors live on-site with the students during the two weeks in which the courses are taught. The adjunct Asian professors are expected to know the language of the dominant group of the country where the instruction is given.

Students receive a Master of Arts degree in religious studies from Grand Rapids Baptist when they have completed the program. The Hong Kong school offers courses that allow a student to begin the Master of Divinity program. All sites have the approval of the accrediting organizations.

Will programs such as this be the wave of the future? A program like the one just described is a credible alternative to having students move to a different culture to take seminary courses. Students are able to live at home during most of the year and at the same time have the opportunity to study for two-week periods during the course of the year. Students are able to continue in their ministries or vocational work and not move their families. This plan is far less costly to the North American institutions than to pay for the student and his family to move to a new culture.

North American Models Which Serve an Urban and Diverse Community

The Center for Urban Theological Studies

This model, located in Philadelphia, Pennsylvania, began in the 1970s when Harvie M. Conn offered Saturday classes to urban church leaders at Westminster Theological Seminary. The initiative led to the formation of the Center for Urban Theological Studies (CUTS), located in the Hunting Park area of North Philadelphia. Urban students have the opportunity to take college and seminary courses in the city. Seminary professors, as well as urban practitioners, teach in the CUTS program. CUTS has played a vital role in the training of African-American urban church leaders in Philadelphia.

Degrees from both Geneva College in Beaver Falls, Pennsylvania, and from Westminster Theological Seminary are granted yearly to urban students of all ages. Many of the graduates form the core of workers in the urban churches of the metropolitan area. Other graduates are ministering in urban centers throughout the world.

Seminarians from Westminster Theological Seminary's suburban campus who are interested in urban ministry are encouraged to take courses at the CUTS city campus. This gives them the opportunity to learn along with students from the city. Together the students address urban issues.

Even though CUTS has had its share of struggles, it has remained a dynamic model of urban ministry for almost thirty years. Harvie Conn's dream is a reality and a source of blessing for the urban church worldwide.

As this is being written, CUTS is going through a period of self-assessment. CUTS would like to receive accreditation in its own right and not depend on Westminster Theological Seminary and Geneva College for accreditation. CUTS also wants a professorial staff that will mirror the student population. CUTS expects that experienced professors skilled in urban ministry will be found to teach the classes.

Another cause for concern is finances. New sources of revenue must be sought, so that this urban model can continue to flourish in Philadelphia. Without adequate funding, the expansion of programs and courses is impeded. Churches help to provide financial support, but far larger funding grants are needed. Grant proposals must be written and submitted periodically to ensure the continuation of such ministries.

Another difficulty is finding professors who are urban-oriented and will give their time on weekday evenings and on Saturdays to teach at an urban training center. It is a sacrifice that only a few are willing to make.

A Church-Based, Seminary-Facilitated, City School

Emmanuel Gospel Center, located in South Boston, Massachusetts, is a model whose mission is to understand and help nurture the vitality of the church in the context of the urban community, especially Boston's low-income and immigrant communities, where the work of the church is so critical. Emmanuel Gospel Center provides resources to help churches operate effectively at the grassroots level. For many years, Emmanuel Gospel Center offered opportunities for seminary students from Gordon-Conwell Seminary to participate in urban internships.

A new program being launched by the center is the Boston Education Collaborative. The church-based collaborative provides a way for urban Christians to pursue postsecondary education. Partnerships are being developed with colleges, Bible institutes, technical schools, and seminaries. These institutions help to provide faculty for the new initiative.

This type of effort may be part of the answer to providing urban seminary education for nontraditional students who are not likely to attend seminary on a full-time basis. One of the degrees offered by the collaborative is a Master of Divinity through Gordon-Conwell's Center for Urban Ministerial Education.[2]

The Center for Urban Ministerial Education

The founding director of the Center for Urban Ministerial Education (CUME) at Gordon-Conwell Theological Seminary in South Hamilton, Massachusetts, is Dr. Eldin Villafañe. It was established in Boston, Massachusetts, to serve a multilingual and multicultural constituency. Courses are offered to pastors and churches in five languages: English, Spanish, Portuguese, French (Haitian), and American Sign Language. This school offers diploma and degree programs (M.A. and M.Div.) in urban ministries.

CUME now coordinates a new program called the Contextualized Urban Theological Education Enablement Program (CUTEEP) in Boston. Dr. Villafañe is the executive director and Dr. Bruce Jackson is the program director. This program was established by a grant from the Pew Charitable Trust. Their brochure states:

The calling of CUTEEP is to strengthen urban theological education institutions and programs that are attempting to be contextual. Such institutions and programs work with local leadership to develop curricula that present the scope of historic Christianity within the context and stresses and joys of urban life. The resources of the community are considered an asset and are used, tapping into the expertise and wisdom of God's people. The theology, curriculum, teaching methods and academic policies of these programs are informed by the context of ministry.[3]

In order to maximize the training of urban church leaders, CUTEEP encourages various theological institutions and programs (Bible institutes, colleges, and seminaries) to form collaborative partnerships, where there is dialogue, shared resources and faculty, and mutual affirmation of each institution's unique place and calling.

Through the Pew foundation, CUTEEP has given grants to several urban projects in North America. The organization also provides technical assistance and consultants to the grant recipients. Conferences are held for the grantees and others who are involved in the planning. Workshops are held in various regions, and research and publications are facilitated.[4]

Seminary Consortium for Urban Pastoral Education (S.C.U.P.E.)

S.C.U.P.E. is a Chicago-based program used by several Midwestern seminaries for students who want an inner-city internship. It provides an enriched cross-cultural educational opportunity for seminary students who are not able to participate in an urban ministry internship in the area of their regular seminary.

The Apprenticeship School for Urban Ministry (TASUM)

TASUM is a program that no longer functions, but it played a major role in preparing urban ethnic leadership. It was a special arrangement between Calvin Theological Seminary in Grand Rapids, Michigan, and Spirit and Truth Fellowship in Chicago (Humboldt Park), Illinois. During the early 1980s, Manuel Ortiz, now director of the Urban Program at Westminster Theological Seminary in Philadelphia, initiated this program. Seminary professors from Grand Rapids traveled to Chicago on weekends during the regular school term and offered courses for urban workers. Both African-American and Hispanic church leaders participated in the program. The program terminated in the early 1990s. To this day, the fruits of the TASUM program are shown through the leadership development of the Spirit and Truth Fellowship Hispanic churches in the Humboldt Park area of Chicago.

Accreditation

The standards required for accreditation by the Association of Theological Schools (ATS) and regional agencies, such as the North Central Association or the Middle States Association, must be faced when a seminary plans an urban program. Some schools fear that proposing an innovative urban/ethnic track will cause the accrediting agency to look unfavorably upon the school's entire accreditation.

Until schools feel free to plan courses and programs that are innovative and also responsive to the needs of urban and ethnic ministries, we will be restricting the ministry of the seminary and shortchanging the urban church. The mission of the seminary should be to prepare church and kingdom leaders for the twenty-first century, many of whom will minister in urban centers and among diverse people groups throughout the whole world.

In actuality, accrediting organizations may allow for more creativity than the institutions realize. It has been my observation that some seminaries have been overly cautious about initiating urban programs. Or is it that they are not motivated strongly enough to meet the needs of the urban church and take risks to meet those needs?

The Traditional Seminary and Practical Options

What can we do for the seminary that does not have the money or the resources to have special programs for urban or cross-cultural and ethnic ministry? There are several options that can be added to existing courses.

To allow students to receive training that will expand their horizons to the cultural diversity and the urban world around them, it is important that the seminary give students the opportunity to see new cultural realities firsthand.

Students must leave the classroom and go out on the streets. They need to experience the sights and smells, the delights and the fears, the pains and the joys of cross-cultural and urban life.

Here is a list of suggested experiences and assignments:

1. Students will arrange for religious conversations or dialogues with persons from other faiths. Preferably, this can take place face-to-face, but it may be over the Internet. The Internet is more impersonal, but it is a "safer" way for strangers to interact.
2. Students will visit Moslem mosques, Buddhist temples, Hindu ashrams, and other places where people from other religions worship.
3. Students will visit rescue missions, shelters for the homeless, and inner-city clinics, and if possible they will become involved in these ministry programs.
4. Students will become involved in weekly youth programs in urban churches.
5. Students will teach ESL classes to newly arrived immigrants or tutor urban students from minority communities.
6. Students will gain exposure to city systems, social agencies, court systems, and political offices and institutions.

To maximize the value of such assignments, the experiences should be shared ones. Everyone learns more when feedback sessions involve everyone.

Other Programs and Sites of Urban/Cross-Cultural Seminary Training

In preparing a list of models and resources, there is always the risk of overlooking some important ones. Except for the Grand Rapids Baptist Seminary at Cornerstone University, the other models mentioned in this essay are not really seminaries. They are institutions that are quasi-seminaries and are often accredited through an existing seminary.

There are many seminaries in the United States and throughout the world that have excellent urban programs. Among them are

Fuller Theological Seminary in Pasadena, California; Alliance Seminary in Nyack, New York; and Providence Seminary in Winnipeg, Manitoba, in Canada. In Philadelphia, Westminster Theological Seminary gives M.A., M.A.R., M.Div., and D.Min. degrees in urban mission. Gordon-Conwell Theological Seminary in the Boston area provides urban training through the Center for Urban Ministerial Education. Eastern Baptist in Philadelphia and Northern Baptist in Chicago are well known for their urban programs. There are two overseas sites in Manila—Asia Theological Seminary and Alliance Biblical Seminary. These schools offer masters degrees in urban ministry. Trinity Evangelical Divinity School in Deerfield, Illinois, has an urban presence in the inner city of Chicago. Trinity has also launched a D.Min. in urban studies in Taipei, Taiwan.

Can the Seminary of Today Train Leaders Who Meet the Needs of an Urban and Diverse World?

It is my opinion that seminaries will meet the needs of an urban and diverse world only if successful models are explored and expanded to contextualize to the specific sites. To train leaders overseas, the Grand Rapids Baptist model is working well in different countries. To train national leaders in North America, models like CUTS (Philadelphia) and CUME (Boston) are good. Variations of these models can be contextualized for each particular urban center. When all is said and done, it takes a group of devoted people who are future-minded and dare to take risks, to seek God's will in preparing men and women to bring the gospel to the cities of the world.

A song we often sing in our inner-city church is one that points to the need for urban workers. Urban seminaries and training programs could well take this as their theme song:

> The city is alive, O God,
>   with sound of hustling feet,
> With rapid change and flashing lights
>   that pulse through every street;
> But oft there's inhumanity
>   behind the bright façade,

And throngs with empty hungering hearts
   cry out for help, O God.

Is it your will, O loving God,
   that races live in strife?
That loneliness and greed and hate
   should mark a city's life?
Do you desire one person's wealth
   to keep another poor?
Must crime and slums and lost abound?
   O Lord, is there no cure?

O God, inspire your church today
   to take Christ's servant role,
To love the world, to hear its claims,
   to sense its yearning soul,
To live within the marketplace,
   to serve both weak and strong,
To lose itself, to share its dream,
   to give the world its song.[5]

—14—

AN INQUIRY INTO URBAN THEOLOGICAL EDUCATION

GLENN B. SMITH

Introduction

This inquiry and the story presented in this essay are rooted in three assumptions. First, the French-speaking world of fifty-one political entities is in dramatic motion. Political, economic, technological, and educational partnerships pepper the globe as we begin the third millennium.[1] La Francophonie is but one more example. Second, urbanization in this network of countries is exploding. We can identify some forty cities in the network with 500,000 or more people.[2] The consequences, as we will see, are enormous. These realities are only beginning to preoccupy the church in these countries. Third, preparing practitioner-leaders for the authentic contextual mission of the church in these cities must be rooted in a new reflection, with fresh actions that bring together the national church, mission societies, and theological institutions into a concerted partnership.

The purpose of this essay is to examine how the broader missiological challenges of this unique context gave birth to an emerging partnership dedicated to the theological education of practitioner-leaders in large French cities. Urbanus, an initiative of partners of an evangelical faith in the Protestant tradition, is working in these cities to develop thoughtful, practical, and contextualized curriculum with the intent of raising up the next generation of men and women who will lead the church in holistic kingdom mission. This essay will also examine the results of the qualitative and quantitative study of the training of people presently working in francophone cities.

The essay is divided into three sections. The first section will familiarize the reader with the francophone world. In the second section, we will examine four missiological challenges facing urban mission in this commonwealth of nations. Alongside each challenge, the implications for Protestant theological education in the urban francophone setting will be explored. Finally, we will suggest how the research and the model of partnership could serve the cause of the kingdom of Jesus Christ elsewhere in the urban world.

La Francophonie

The francophone world represents a commonwealth of fifty-one French-speaking political entities with a population of 500 million people (see fig. 14.1). This network is centered primarily in Africa (twenty-nine countries), yet spreads across the globe into the Americas (six entities), Europe (eleven countries), Asia (four countries), the Middle East (one country), and Oceania (three countries). Although French is considered a super language (i.e., a tongue of which there are at least 100 million speakers), only 180 million people (2.5 percent of the world's population) use it on a daily basis. Apart from France, every one of these countries has at least one official language in addition to French. But each major city or capital area in the French world is a multilingual metropolis that benefits from the *penser-français,* a cluster of ideas based on the historical richness of the French language as a cultural way of life, a way of examining problems and finding solutions. French has traditionally been the language of philosophical questions, diplomacy, and freedom.

The original concept of La Francophonie, this worldwide network of French nations, was first proposed in 1880 by the geographer Onesime Reclus, the son of an evangelical pastor. However, it was not until 1985, at the initiative of Leopold Sedar Senghor of Senegal, in close cooperation with François Mitterand of France and Brian Mulroney of Canada, that a new initiative was launched. Now La Fran-

Figure 14.1. The Francophone (French-Speaking) World

Legend

#	Country	Capital	#	Country	Capital	#	Country	Capital
1	Albania	Tiranë	18	Equatorial Guinea	Malabo	37	New Brunswick	Fredericton
2	Belgium	Brussels	19	France	Paris	38	Poland	Warsaw
3	Benin	Porto-Novo	20	Gabon	Libreville	39	Quebec	Quebec
4	Bulgaria	Sofia	21	Guinea	Conakry	40	Republic of Congo	Brazzaville
5	Burkina Faso	Ouagadougou	22	Guinea-Bissau	Bissau	41	Romania	Bucharest
6	Burundi	Bujumbura	23	Haiti	Port-au-Prince	42	Rwanda	Kigali
7	Cambodia	Phnom Penh	24	Ivory Coast	Yamoussoukro	43	Saint Lucia	Castries
8	Cameroon	Yaoundé	25	Laos	Vientiane	44	São Tomé and Príncipe	São Tomé
9	Canada	Ottawa	26	Lebanon	Beirut	45	Senegal	Dakar
10	Cape Verde	Praia	27	Luxembourg	Luxembourg	46	Seychelles	Victoria
11	Central African Republic	Bangui	28	Macedonia	Skopje	47	Switzerland	Berne
12	Chad	N'Djamena	29	Madagascar	Antananarivo	48	Togo	Lomé
13	Comoros	Moroni	30	Mali	Bamako	49	Tunisia	Tunis
14	Democratic Republic of Congo	Kinshasa	31	Morocco	Rabat	50	Vanuatu	Port-Vila
15	Djibouti	Djibouti	32	Mauritius	Port Louis	51	Vietnam	Hanoi
16	Dominica	Roseau	33	Mauritania	Nouakchott			
17	Egypt	Cairo	34	Moldova	Chisinau			
			35	Monaco	Monaco			
			36	Niger	Niamey			

September 1999

cophonie is increasingly viewed as a linguistic, geographical, and spiritual community of emerging world-class cities rooted in the French language and French culture. In most cases, the capital city is a leading city. In most places outside of the North Atlantic corridor, French is only spoken in the capital.

In the mid 1990s, a study was undertaken for denominations and mission societies working in cities of La Francophonie. The purpose of this survey was to measure the quality and quantity of the training that missionaries receive and how this influences strategies and work in French urban areas.[3] The survey underscored an issue that is increasingly a matter of concern in the church: the small number of urban ministry practitioners in large cities. Interestingly, only 70 of the 179 North American denominations and mission societies that answered the survey work in the urban centers of La Francophonie. They represent only 751 urban missionaries out of a total of 10,415 Protestant missionaries in the fifty-one French countries. In other words, even the mission societies that would be interested in an urban-based research project have only a small percentage of their practitioners working in cities of 500,000 or more people.

The research illustrates what denominations and agencies perceive that their practitioners do in urban ministry, in comparison with what the missionaries themselves perceive they are doing. It examines the typical training of an urban worker and the specific training that one might receive. In both cases, the practitioners themselves confirmed what their organizations required before sending them into ministry in a large French-speaking city.

Missiological Challenges and Implications

This network of French-speaking cities and countries presents four major challenges for a holistic understanding of Christian mission and the educational preparation of urban ministry practitioners. It should be underscored that at the present time there are more missionaries in Kenya than in the entire French-speaking world.

Challenge One: Secularization and Postmodernism

The world-class cities of the North Atlantic French world are highly modernized. Secularization, the process by which religion is marginalized in society, is an ever-present reality. Furthermore, postmodernism has its intellectual and architectural roots in Montréal and Paris. Figure 14.2 describes the urban populations and the number of Protestant churches in these cities.

Figure 14.2.

Population and Number of Churches in Selected Francophone Cities, 2000

City	Population	Churches	Ethnic Population	No. of Ethnic Churches
FRANCE				
Paris				
Paris	2,152,330	95		
Ile-de-France	8,507,736	244	1,300,000	100
Lyon				
Lyon	412,000	10		
Region	902,000	28	148,000	4
Marseille				
Marseille	872,000	31		
Region	500,000	39	96,000	6
BELGIUM				
Brussels	970,000	38	254,000	18
QUEBEC				
Montréal				
Island	1,900,000	56		
[English pop.]	500,000	180	400,000	89
Region	1,000,000	58		

Sources: The Census Bureau for Canada, France, and Belgium; Annuaire de la France protestante, 1999; Annuaire 1999 des Assemblées de Dieu en France; Eglises au Québec, 1999 (Christian Direction, Inc.)

The roots of modernism and postmodernism, with the ensuing secularization, are found in the eighteenth century, when European philosophy placed its confidence in the power of reason to provide a foundation for knowledge. This confidence is often referred to as rationalism. The idea that divine revelation is essential was gradually discarded. For over two centuries, the debate has raged about how to use reason alone to find truth and morality. This move toward rationalism created an implicit trust in science as the answer to all of humanity's problems.

There are four essential features of this culture of rationalism, with corresponding challenges to urban mission. First, rationalism interprets all reality scientifically. This brings the double consequence of separating work from the home and the growth of cities as a result of the mechanization of this work. Individualism saw its birth at this juncture. Lesslie Newbigin adds, "But we shall not be wrong, I think, if we take the abandonment of teleology as the key to understanding the whole of these vast changes in the human situation."[4]

Second, a sharp distinction is made between personal values and objective knowledge. A dichotomy between the private and the public worlds becomes fundamental to modern Western culture.

Third, in medieval Europe, a stable order was based on revelation. But with the Enlightenment era came a rational, scientific, and never-ending bureaucratic approach to reality. The consequences of modernity included unprecedented economic activities, the exponential growth of technical skill and knowledge, education, exploding urbanization, rootlessness, communication and information technologies (CITs), and the separation of work from home, including the mechanization of work. Tradition began to be viewed with suspicion.

Fourth, all (scientific) knowledge was therefore viewed as acultural and ahistorical. It provides answers for everybody, everywhere.

The cultural consequences of such an approach to reality in the francophone urban milieu is most dramatically seen in the recent decline in the presence, influence, and power of the Roman Catholic Church in the city. For example, the number of priests in Québec rose from 4,000 in 1930 to 5,000 in 1945, and then to 8,400 in 1960. But today, there are fewer than 3,000 priests, and their average age is 63. Although Quebeckers still maintain the highest level of religious commitment in North America (79 percent still consider themselves Christian, and 50 percent identify themselves as profoundly committed to their faith), religious practice is the lowest on the continent. Only 15 percent go to a religious service once a week, and only 5 percent in the urban centers.[5] Spirituality has been completely privatized in Québec society, and institutionalized religion is scorned. Montréal is filled with empty cathedrals.

Joseph Moody has shown that from 1861 to 1905, the population of Paris grew by 100 percent, but the number of parishes grew only by 33 percent and the number of priests by 30 percent.[6] Os Guinness describes the result:

> The churches were neither ready nor able to cope with the explosion. . . . There is no more striking sight in the environs of Paris and other cities than the little church, intended for a village but now feebly serving a sprawling urban area. Inadequate in itself, it is marooned from the main currents of modern life and left to its own irrelevance.[7]

French-speaking cities represent the clearest examples of this process of marginalization.[8] Such authors as Os Guinness, Peter Gilbert, Langdon Gilkey, and Peter Quek emphasize the evolving nature of this trend in Western societies. Far from being a philosophy or conscious ideology (i.e., secularism), this process is understood as "(1) the decline of religion; (2) conformity with this world; (3) the disengagement of society from religion; (4) the transposition of beliefs and patterns from the 'religious' to the 'secular' sphere; and (5) the desacralization of the world."[9] At a time when there is an increasing need to think theologically and missiologically, it is crucially important to understand the intricacies of this approach to reality, particularly in world-class metropolitan areas, where religious beliefs and values for a large number of people and subcultures are no longer a means for integrating and legitimating all dimensions of life. The social significance of faith has been pushed to the sidelines as a way of bringing integration to life.[10]

Numerous authors have devised theories to explain the process of secularization—this intersection within modernity of an increasingly industrialized and scientific society, religious faith, and the decline of religious practices. Some link this process entirely to industrialization and urbanization. Others tie it more directly to the conflict between science and religion.

The past prestige of faith has lost out to technology and the modern economy. Certainly there are exceptions to this process and the extent of its influence. But it is real. Church structures have been increasingly marginalized.[11]

In the last century, cracks began to appear in the trust that people were willing to put in rationalism and the modern project. A new movement appeared called Romanticism, which tried to capture the God-consciousness in each of us. One philosopher wrote in reaction to the scientific rationalism of his age, "Man is weak if he looks outside himself for help. It is only when he throws himself unhesitatingly on the god within that he learns his own power." Even the painters and the poets of the movement called Symbolism depicted the despair of a world gone wrong in thinking and science. There was no hope within or without for them.

The discussion of postmodernism started in the French world through the works of philosopher Jean-François Lyotard, after the universities in Québec had ordered its study.[12] Philosophers like Lyotard said that nothing can be known with certainty, history is devoid of purpose, universal stories or quests for truth had to be abandoned, and everything is relative. Truth is elusive, inward, subjective, and even polymorphous. The metanarrative of modernity had come apart. Lyotard wrote:

What I am arguing is that the modern project (the carrying out of universality) was not abandoned, forgotten, but destroyed, liquidated. There are many modes of destruction, many names which figure as its symbols. Auschwitz can be considered as a paradigmatic name for the tragic incompletion of modernity.[13]

It is very important to recognize postmodernism, not just as a cultural phenomenon to be seen in movies, music, and magazines, but as a social, economic, and political transformation. Each group, even each person, claims to have a unique take on reality, which is equally valid. The social forces that foster the postmodern condition are above all new communications media and the consumer marketplace. Modern commitments to science, to democracy, and to progress, once strong, now corrode in the new context.

The new communications media help to globalize the world. This means that we actually do things more and more from a distance, not that we become more of a global village. Superficially, we are more in touch with each other. But what these links do is to expose us to other ways of doing things, upsetting our treasured traditions and leaving us to believe that they are only particular options and local orientations. When Lyotard wrote *The Postmodern Condition*, he stressed the role of communication and information technologies (CITs) in transforming "knowledge." They do nothing to discourage the view that anything goes.

The consequences are more than evident. Multiple worldviews and manners of expression, tensions between order and disorder, symbols, the flux of life: all these define the new order. All have been deconstructed. Ernest Gellner clearly states the reason: "Post-modernity would seem to be rather clearly in favour of relativism, in as far as it is capable of clarity, and hostile to the idea of unique, exclusive, objective, external or transcendent truth. Truth is elusive, polymorphous, inward, subjective."[14]

As urban cultures began to evolve, neither Protestant nor Roman Catholic churches were able to help their parishioners face the changes that were occurring. Contributions to culture were minimal. Yet what are the implications of this contextual reflection for our actions in urban francophone mission? In a very real sense, it means that we need to rethink three fundamental horizons involved in theological education and learning:

1. Our own cultural perspectives as we approach reality.
2. The biblical texts.
3. The world-and-life views of urban dwellers.

A fundamental renewal of practical education for practitioner-leaders should incorporate a critical-realist approach to these horizons.[15]

Our own cultural perspectives. The first horizon deals with how we perceive reality. Bernard Lonergan reminds us in *Method in Theology* that the interpretation of issues (hermeneutics) and the study of history are foundational to life. By this he means that the way we create meaning enters into the very fabric of human living, but varies from place to place and from one age to another. The issue deals with how we interpret reality.[16]

One school of thought affirms that there is a real world that exists quite apart from the consciousness of persons. This is often referred to as *realism*. On the other side, *nonrealism* denies this and maintains that what exists is the result of what one person or a group of people think. There are obviously nuances of opinion within each school of thought. For example, one perspective within realism is materialism, which affirms that all that exists is what we see. Christians reject this kind of realism, yet they affirm that a real world exists that God created—totally distinct from the Creator—and that real events take place in time and space. Therefore, before we can examine how we read, interpret, and apply Scripture in our missiology, we need to look closely at the ways in which people approach meaning itself and pursue understanding of any subject, including a city. This takes us to the heart of the first horizon.

As many authors have shown, there are at least three schools of thought as we consider reality. There is the rather optimistic approach to knowledge, including interpretation and action. Proponents of this view believe that issues can be studied "objectively" and tested "empirically." The material world exists, and our minds can perceive and understand this reality. This model is sometimes referred to as *ontological, naïve,* or even *uncritical realism.*

Like an increasing number of writers, I believe that the approach known as *critical realism* is an appropriate method to lead us out of our present muddle. This is a way of describing the process of knowing that acknowledges the reality of the thing known, as something other than the knower (hence "realism"), while also fully acknowledging that the only access we have to this reality lies along the spiraling path of appropriate dialogue or conversation between the knower and the thing known (hence "critical").[17]

Elmer Thiessen summarizes this quest: "Our knowledge is always partial and particular, but it is not just that. There is a non-relative goal to our search for truth, and there are criteria by which to assess the adequacy of our human constructions in relation to this goal, although this is admittedly a complex process."[18] These criteria include the ability to interpret all empirical data with consistency, breadth, simplicity, fruitfulness, and pragmatic considerations.[19]

We illustrate this approach to urban mission in figure 14.3. The arrows illustrate that acquiring knowledge is not a simple process of interpreting objective reality, as the positivists assume in their naïve realism—the first arrow. Nor is it determining reality through one's own sense-data, as do the postmodernists through their relativism—the second arrow. Rather, the third level of reflection illustrates that the observer sees reality evolving within the stories and worldviews. The hallmark of critical realism, then, is its insistence on integrating together the empirical (data), the intelligent (the questioning and answering), and the rational (the grasp of evidence as sufficient or insufficient, and the personal act of commitment) as a whole to enter into true judgment.[20] Practitioner-leaders need a thorough introduction into such readings of reality in their contexts.

Figure 14.3. Interpreting Reality

A group of Christians ➡ studies their neighborhood often by listening to the stories of the community.

⬅

They reflect on what they hear, realizing that their claims about the world are not the only ones that exist.

➡

Through new stories, they can challenge these worldviews.

The biblical text. The second horizon deals with the biblical text. In the fundamental renewal of practical urban theological education, instruction in the second horizon means that we will need to learn how to take critical-realist inquiry into consideration as we read a biblical text. Educating practitioner-leaders must be rethought at this juncture. We do not just read a text, nor are we obligated to totally deconstruct it to find its meaning. I suggest that all texts represent worldviews in the narrative genre. Better still, the telling of stories brings worldviews to light. I think that it can be clearly shown that conversations in particular and human actions in general are "enacted narratives." In this sense, life itself is a story, a video of all that transpires. The overall narrative is the basic category, while a particular incident or an encounter with a person can be understood only within that category.

What do we mean when we say that life is a narrative? What does it mean that societal character is best understood as formed, unfolded, and revealed in a story line? Susanne Johnson gives a succinct glimpse of the question when she states that a narrative is an account of characters and events in a plot moving over time and space through conflict toward resolution.[21]

The world-and-life views of urban dwellers. The third horizon means that we need to learn how to listen to the worldviews of the city. This reading informs practitioners, as they pursue shalom among the populations of the city where the church pursues the cause of the rule of God. The hard work of teaching practitioner-leaders, this third horizon, is often neglected in urban ministry. It is critical if we are to have an authentic encounter with the peoples and the cultures of the city.

Urban ministry practitioners need to be able to identify worldviews in order to reflect and act in their particular context. Worldviews are primarily lenses with which we look at the world. Generally speaking, they are the series of presuppositions that groups of people hold, consciously or unconsciously, about the basic makeup of their society. Tom Wright illustrates worldviews when he compares them to the foundations of a house: vital but invisible.[22] He states, "Worldviews may be studied in terms of four features: characteristic stories; fundamental symbols; habitual praxis; and a set of questions and answers. These presuppositions interact with each other in a variety of complex and interesting ways."[23] By studying the intersection of these big themes, the urban ministry practitioner can unearth the worldview of the context under study.[24]

A critical-realist approach to mission in an urban context, then, acknowledges the essentially "storied" nature of human knowing, thinking, and living within the larger model of worldviews and their component parts. The practitioner acknowledges that all knowledge of realities external to oneself takes place within the framework of a worldview, of which stories, symbols, characteristic human behavior, and answers to the fundamental questions of life form an essential part. This approach to mission in the city attempts to tell new stories about the God of Jesus Christ in the world and tests them in the urban setting by seeing what sort of fit they have with the stories already in place. Mission in the city today is best conceived of as the telling of stories that bring worldviews into articulation.[25]

Challenge Two: Structural Poverty

On the other hand, the cities of the French-speaking portion of the Two-thirds World find themselves in deep structural poverty. Seven of the ten countries in the world on the lowest human development index are French speaking. Ten of the forty largest cities of the world with a significant population living in slums or squatter settlements use French as the language of urban life. The continuing devaluation of the currency used in French Africa will only accentuate this reality.

For the American reader, there is no closer example of the complexity of this deep structural poverty in La Francophonie than the country of Haiti. To understand the complexity of the situation, four sociodemographic realities need to be grasped.

First, for the past three decades, the average annual rate of growth in the agricultural sector (which employs 74 percent of the workforce) has been stagnant. From 1965 to 1973, there was a 0.3 percent decline; from 1973 to 1983, there was a 0.7 percent rise; and in the turbulent decade since the overthrow of the Duvalier regime on February 6, 1986, chaos has reigned, as evidenced by the inability of the World Bank to report verifiable figures in the World Development Report.[26]

Second, every social indicator now ranks this nation as unquestionably the poorest in the Western Hemisphere. Haiti is referred to in Canada as part of the Fourth World! The World Bank (one's least favorite source to quote, along with the IMF) states that less than 1 percent of the population controls 46 percent of the national revenue, only 2,700 families receive 72 percent of all revenue in the country, and 80 percent of Haitians live in absolute poverty, earning less than $150 a year.[27] The parameters shown in figure 14.4, reproduced for comparative purposes with another poor country from French-speaking Africa, give us insight into the state of the institutions and values that are an integral part of the Haitian world-and-life view.

Figure 14.4. Statistical Comparison of Haiti, Rwanda, and North America

	Haiti		Rwanda	Canada	USA
Indicators	1989	1999	1999	1999	1999
Population (in millions)	5,360	7,395	8,155	29,942	271,648
Area in square kilometers	27,750		26,338	9,976,186	9,159,123
Density (inhabitants per square kilometer)	193.2	266.5	223.3	3	29
Birth rate (per woman, age 15–40)	no data	4.6	5.8	1.6	2.0
Infant mortality (per 1000 births)	119	82	125	6	7
Life expectancy	53.0	54.4	42.1	78.9	76.7
Number of doctors per 1000 people	0.11	0.09	0.04	2.1	2.6
Illiteracy rate (m)%	62.4	52.0	30.9	9.6	8.9
Illiteracy rate (f)%	no data	58.0	48.0	9.6	8.7
Education % 12–17	48.3	43.9	36.4	no data	no data

Sources: *L'état du monde, 1999* (Montreal: Boréal, 1999); 1987–1988 report published in 1989

Third, one must never underestimate the gravity of the under-nourishment of the Haitian people. The daily caloric intake in 1989 was at 84 percent of levels recommended by the United Nations. This means that there is a deficit of 300 calories and 42 grams of protein on a daily basis.[28] More than one author attributes the high birth rate to the medical consequences of these facts. They claim that the simple lack of protein alters the functions of the liver, and especially folliculine, therefore stimulating reproductive capacities.[29]

Finally, migration within the country and emigration make all census figures highly suspect. It is reported that Port-au-Prince has grown from 750,000 to 3.1 million since 1979, and that Cap Haitian has grown from 40,000 to 750,000 in the same period. Infant mortality rates are still the highest in the hemisphere at 82 per 1000 births, but the rate has declined from 119 in the past decade. Some one million Haitians live in major urban areas in Canada and the United States. But the Haitian government still claims that there are only 7.18 million people in the country.[30] Simple demographic projections based on the government's own figures would put the population of the country at 10–12 million.[31] The question is, Who will count and how? It raises the question, Why have a low number? I believe that civil authorities want to give outside donor nations the impression that birth control is working. But, as the chart shows, the birth rate is 4.6 children for every woman 15–40 years of age.

To understand the Hatian worldview, it is critical to grasp how the volatile mix of superstition, fatalism, paternalism, population explosion, illiteracy, malnutrition, and AIDS are affecting this people. Furthermore, Laënnec Hubron[32] illustrates how voodoo runs throughout the nation's economic and social framework.[33] A dialectic goes on between the poor, taxed by superstition and voodoo, and the dominant classes, who use this belief system to oppress the poor. Everything from "spells" on the tap-tap (taxi) to protect it, to participation in the national lottery (three per day), provides a lens on living in Haiti.[34]

All of these factors surface in the Haitian urban context. More than 55 percent of urban dwellers live in absolute poverty. The causes are extensive unemployment and underemployment: 90 percent of the urban population earn less that $150 per annum, and only 20 percent receive the official daily wage of $3. Other causes are inadequate and unaffordable housing and inadequate municipal infrastructure—only 21 percent of city dwellers have access to sewers and drinking water. Automobile emissions, open waste, and the persistent use of charcoal continue to make ecological concerns a large preoccupation of nongovernmental agencies involved in transformative community development.

There are very simple, yet profound missiological implications to this challenge across the French-speaking portion of the Two-thirds World. For example, two centuries of independence in Haiti did not amount to much when the rest of the "civilized" world placed sanctions on the country for pursuing freedom.[35] Couple that with a world-and-life view (voodoo) that enforces an ironclad fatalism throughout the culture and historical rivalry among racial/color groups in the country,[36] and you find yourself in a society that totally exteriorizes evil and scorns personal responsibility. The result is the debilitating poverty that we witness.

Poverty affects one's identity and one's vocation. Each time I teach at the Faculty of Theology at the Université Chrétienne du Nord d'Haiti, I thoroughly enjoy interacting with my students on a theology of creation. It establishes a level playing field. Genesis 1–3 is the greatest democratizing creed in history. My students always clap after that lecture! One's identity is restored because we are all made in the image of God, children of the Creator. Our vocation is also restored because we all are called to use the gifts that God gave and to be partners in the stewardship of the creation mandates (Gen. 1:26–2:15).

When I first taught urban theology and missiology, I was struck by how difficult it was to communicate the essence of God's project and the role of cities in the biblical narrative. I had seen resistance and hesitancy before (the age-old rural bias of much of the Christian church), but never of this magnitude. For those who live in urban squalor, seeing the possibilities of God's project are often dimmed.

Slowly, I began to understand the Haitian view of space. A dear friend helped me to understand that "territory" for a Haitian is the island. Hatians do not think in terms of personal/private space. Henry Hogarth states:

> The most telling expression used by traditional, rural Haitians that describes the inherent separateness between themselves and the urban dwellers is: *M'ap tounen andeyò*—I'm returning outside. No less significant is: *m'pral nan payi'm*—literally, I'm going to my country, meaning, of course, I'm going home. Both expressions indicate the sense that the Haitian countryman or woman has in regards to what is considered home, "country": the hills, the plains, the valleys of the rural area. Home is definitely not the city.[37]

But he goes even further, and this is what I began to see: "One might even infer that the average Haitian countryman does not relate much to the notion of Haiti as nation-state or *res publica*."[38] This raised very interesting questions for me as I tried to teach both urban theology and missiology. But it became even more critical when we began to wrestle with holistic urban community development. As we tackled biblical texts dealing with *place*, their enthusiasm for cities and neighborhoods grew. We began to explore the reality of a biblical theology of creation as the basis and orientation for all mission in the city.

I wonder if the horrific state of so much urban space across the French world and the globe is not in large part due to a perspective of distance that exists toward place. It is certainly worth more reflection, in my opinion. Also, Haitian Christians want to see change for the whole. To bring local changes for local success is hard to grasp. This seems to fit in with the fatalistic framework as well.

Unquestionably, the biggest missiological implication has to do with the nature of evil and the role of the conscience. The way that evil is exteriorized in Haitian culture is a massive form of disempowerment. (*Pas faute mwen*: "It's not my fault, but what can I do?") As we wrestled with the contextualization of the good news in the Haitian urban context, I was struck by how my students initially did not want to touch the subject, but then suddenly warmed to the ideas and offered amazing insights into the world-and-life view of people at this point.

Now I certainly do not want to flee into the arms of the introspective conscience of the West.[39] Yet the general inability (1) to see oneself as a sinner, or (2) as one sinned against, or (3) as responsible for one's destiny aggravates the misery of two centuries of poverty. Dr. William Hodges initially described this phenomenon.[40] Jules Casseus[41] and Raymond Fung[42] have brought a good theological balance to the issue by stressing that a biblical perspective will hold the interiorization and the exteriorization of evil together. "We are sinners and we are sinned against." This thinking is absent both in the culture and in the discourse of much of the church in Haiti. A recent article by Henry Hogarth gives interesting psychological insights into these issues.[43]

No authentic mission encounter with cultures of poverty will transform cities unless these biblical realities are translated into fresh actions.

Challenge Three: Cultural, Religious, and Ideological Diversity

Cultural, religious, and ideological diversity is an ever-present challenge for the church in these countries, especially in the city. Eleven French countries have significant Muslim populations; seven have large populations holding to tribal belief systems. The French-speaking countries of Asia (Cambodia, Laos, and Vietnam) are significantly Buddhist. As we have already emphasized, the French countries of the North Atlantic are secularizing to a significant rate, and the church, particularly in the city, is being increasingly marginalized in public life.

To begin to understand this challenge and the ensuing missiological implications, we need a clear definition of the issues. Keeping the words *plurality* and *pluralism* distinct helps us to get to the heart of the issue.

Cultural diversity refers to the presence of peoples from other countries or ethnic backgrounds. Although Canada, for example, has tended to define itself historically as two founding nations, the image of a true mosaic reigns supreme today. Among the approximately 200,000 students in the five school boards of the Montréal Island School Council, there are 168 countries represented. A formerly European immigration has shifted to a truly global movement. This is true right across the North Atlantic French-speaking world. Figure 14.5 illustrates this for the world-class cities of the North Atlantic corridor.

Figure 14.5. Francophone Immigration Patterns

City	1960 Population	1960 Immigrant %	2000 Population	2000 Immigrant %
Montréal	2,200,000	20.0	3,400,000	27.0
Paris	8,486,000	6.8	10,660,000	13.3
Bruxelles	620,000		970,000	21.5
Lyon	886,400	8.8	1,314,000	8.6
Marseille	797,900	8.7	1,372,000	12.2

Source: The Census Bureau for Canada, France, and Belgium

Furthermore, some 37 percent of the residents of Abidjan Côte d'Ivoire are immigrants from non-Ivorian ethnic groups.

Religious diversity is also the order of the day. For example, the old paradigm of English Canada being Protestant and French Canada being Roman Catholic has fundamentally changed. Although 82 percent of Canadians still identify themselves as Christians, the diversity in religious affiliation in Canada, according to the 1996 census, is quite striking.

The fact that 16 percent of Canadians opt for "none" or "other" in the religion category is a dramatic change. From 1961 to 1981, this figure rose from 1 percent to 7.3 percent. Today in British Columbia alone, 20.5 percent of the population has no religious affiliation. In fact, Vancouver displays the most marked religious disaffiliation of any Canadian city.

Plurality also has a third dimension—often referred to as ideological pluralism. At the level of one's basic assumptions about the way the world operates, a former consensus of basic beliefs has given way to what we often refer to as relativism. Today, life in our cities encourages us to be "tolerant"—to realize that there are several ways to believe and to live, and that all are equally valid.

Throughout much of history, most human beings have found themselves in a uniform cultural context throughout their lives. Today, we constantly encounter people of different cultures, religious beliefs, and lifestyles through technology, such as television and the Internet. Rapid transportation takes us to other places in a matter of hours, and instant communication systems unify the globe. The suggestion now is that a plurality of beliefs is justified in intellectual, cultural, and religious life. Any assertion that one group has an exclusive claim to truth is viewed at best as a unique perspective and at worst as arrogant and imperialistic.

It is important for urban Christians to grasp the historical, philosophical move to this advocacy of diversity that we now call pluralism. It is absolutely essential that urban theological education incorporate explicit contextual instruction on the issues of plurality and pluralism.

It is not hard to see that pluralism, in this sense, is an ideology or philosophy of life. In this sense, it does not just describe a state of affairs (plurality), but prescribes a bias for a state of affairs in which relativism reigns. In the modern city, pluralism reigns.

Yet to understand how pluralism is advocated, we need to see how issues get discussed. Increasingly, people make a distinction between the public world of facts and the private world of values. In the former, we discuss "truth" and issues that are viewed as objective and verifiable. This is what we know. In the latter world, we find beliefs and issues that are subjective. This is what we believe. Religion, as a value system, therefore, is excluded from the public world of facts in the primary institutions of community building.

The Christian who wants to engage pluralism in the diversity of urban society has a huge task, but a noble ambition. The process of engagement must begin with a commitment to contribute to the development of a common public culture. This means that we will want to articulate that nucleus of values, those "rules of the game," and those crucial institutions that must be for all a source of profound inspiration for life in society and the glue for unity and social coherence in our culture. This common public culture obviously includes a commitment to the United Nations Universal Declaration of Human Rights. There are some fundamental values we will want to uphold, such as democracy, freedom, equality, and solidarity. The "rules of the game" include civility and a respect for minorities. All Christians will be committed to the public good because the Creator poured out his common grace on all the cosmos as part of his care for it.

But our task will include entering into dialogue with other partners in the diversity of today's cities. We are not suggesting a mere exchange of ideas with those of various points of view, nor are we promoting a polemical engagement that would result in accusations of proselytism. Dialogue in today's pluralistic environment is a serious no-holds-barred interaction between competing truth-claims.

Such a dialogue is rooted in the development of full, mutual, intellectual understanding and a respect for differences of nuance and subtlety, particularly in the area of those diversifying "lived values" within a culture of many ethnic groups. It includes the development of attitudes and mentalities within the common public culture that will welcome the variety of different cultures and lifestyles within a society and sees this as an enrichment of human life. But this dialogue is a process where respectful exchange of views will take place, not merely where opinions are tolerantly shared. In the years ahead, dialogue will be the operative form of urban mission and, therefore, an essential concern of urban theological education.

Challenge Four: Curriculum Development

Theological education in the French-speaking world has not kept pace with these missiological challenges. Although there are marvelous examples of innovation to deal with these emerging realities, much of the curriculum is not preparing men and women for urban ministry.

Today there are some 5,000 theological establishments in the fifty-one countries of La Francophonie.[44] Some interesting curricular issues are being discussed in the emerging partnerships of the French world. But, as we saw at the beginning of this essay, much of the training continues to be quite traditional.

No school has influenced the francophone world as much as L'Institut Biblique de Nogent, in the inner suburbs of Paris. Established in the early 1930s, the guiding pedagogical principle was that a student would graduate with a three-year degree after studying each of the sixty-six books of the Bible. The school continues to work primarily on that basis and centers all theological education around the traditional axes of Bible, theology, history, and pastoral ministry. Nogent's curriculum continues to circulate primarily in schools in Europe and French West Africa. On the other hand, Institut Biblique Européen has a totally different orientation, centered around the Bible, history, the gospel, and culture. It has one of the most innovative approaches to theological education that I have encountered in any language. The boldest moves in francophone theological education have been made in Montréal through the Faculty of Theology at the Université de Montréal and the Mennonite Brethren school, École de Théologie Evangelique de Montréal. Over the past decade, a university-accredited program has emerged, rooted in evangelical hermeneutics and practice. A student can now graduate with an undergraduate degree in evangelical studies that includes thirty credits in praxeology. The Institut Biblique Européen has been integrated into this degree program. A student studying in Paris gets a Québec diploma. A student studying in Montréal can take courses in Paris. This is bold because of the historic *laïcité* (the strictly secular character) of French education. The six government-recognized schools in Haiti are doing excellent innovative work while staying within the traditional denominational approaches. The events since the fall of Duvalier in 1986 have placed a great cultural strain on the schools to teach in a changing context. We know, for example, that only 55 percent of the schools in French-speaking Africa offer courses in Islam. Furthermore, schools located in Muslim areas are less likely to include such a course in the curriculum.

But how do practitioners view the education they received in light of the urban ministry they are now pursuing? Let us return for a moment to the study we mentioned at the beginning of this essay.

Research and Partnership for the Kingdom

The researchers did not simply take a quantitative approach, although statistics represent an important factor in the research. They also investigated the experience of practitioners in French urban areas—this represents the qualitative section of the study. This allowed the perspectives of denominations and mission societies to be compared with those of practitioners.

Although the relationship between training and strategy is at the heart of this study, this must be placed in the larger context of the specific needs of missionaries working in La Francophonie. To help understand these issues, statistics were gathered on:

1. Missionary presence in French urban areas,
2. Missionary activity in French urban areas,
3. Investment in training by practitioners, and
4. The urban ministry of trained and untrained practitioners.

The *quality* and *quantity* of the practitioners' training, the strategies for urban mission, the capacity to implement them on the field (*effectiveness*), and the links between training and execution (*efficiency*) in French urban areas are, from a theoretical point of view, subjective. For this reason, the research team was not explicitly testing a hypothesis in this research. They were analyzing data related to these areas. However, a scientific value to the quantitative and qualitative approach that produced the data has been given. Recognized concepts were used to build the theoretical model. Throughout the study, the team attempted to be as explicit as possible concerning the methods and the theoretical models employed. But, as they stated, "We have proceeded with caution and tried to remain as faithful as possible to the findings. We are all students whose knowledge is evolving."

The survey results highlighted three critical issues.

First, from the survey one sees that agencies believe that practitioners are involved in typical urban initiatives, although ministries of compassion appear surprisingly low on the list of activities. Only 15 percent pursue such strategies across La Francophonie. In light of the second missiological challenge we highlighted, it is obvious that new innovations in holistic ministry education and the study of social justice are needed.

Second, the survey indicates that a real distinction is made (or required) between formal theological education, in terms of both time and content, and a more contextual, sociological, and hands-on orientation. Yet both agencies and practitioners perceive a difference in the ability of someone to choose a strategy, implement it, evaluate its effectiveness, and work independently based on the extent of one's training, particularly in the more practical issues. In statistical terms, agencies think that 40 percent of their practitioners with such practical training are excellent or very good in choosing pertinent urban strategies, versus 14 percent of those without the background. (Practitioners themselves are much less optimistic: only 15 percent with the background are excellent or very good in choosing a strategy, compared with 11 percent without the training.) Agencies think that 50 percent of their people are excellent or very good at implementing strategies with a practical background, compared with 21 percent without it. (Again, practitioners are less optimistic: only 15 percent of the trained people see themselves as excellent or very good at implementation.) But the greatest discrepancies appeared when the question was asked, "How would you rate a formally trained practitioner in their capacity to be self-initiating and autonomous in their ministry-learning once they are on the field?" Sixty-two percent of the agencies rated their people as excellent or very good. Fifty percent of the practitioners themselves say the same thing. However, this percentage drops to 29 percent for untrained workers, in the eyes of their agencies, and 23 percent for the practitioners themselves. A new approach to integrating traditional curriculum with new subjects to prepare people for urban ministry must be high on the agenda of all concerned across La Francophonie.

Third, analysis of the statistics indicates that there is a correlation between the level of urban training and work in an urban context. (It will be important to explore the nature and limitation of such a correlation.) The research seems to indicate that:

1. The level of training does not positively correlate with its quality.
2. The knowledge of how to choose a strategy does not necessarily mean that one will be able to do it.
3. Two years and $4,000 are the maximum that one would need to spend in preparing a practitioner for the city.

Conclusion

The research reviewed in this essay continues to orient a partnership of thirty-five international partners representing denominations and mission societies; sixty regional partners in French-speaking Europe, West Africa, Central Africa, the Great Lakes region of Africa, the French Caribbean, and Québec; and some thirty schools that have now committed themselves to urban theological education that is practical, contextual, and pertinent. In the areas where the other ten super languages of our globalizing planet are spoken, new reflection and new action are needed to equip practitioner-leaders to participate in the spiritual transformation of all of life in the cities of the world.

PART 5

GOD'S MESSAGE TO THE NATIONS

15

AFRICAN THEOLOGY FROM THE PERSPECTIVE OF HONOR AND SHAME[1]

ANDREW M. MBUVI

African theology has been characterized by two concerns. On the one hand, it has been struggling to find aspects of the African Traditional Religions (ATR) that could inform the Christian faith and make it uniquely African. On the other hand, it has been struggling to make the Christian faith relevant to African Christians. While these are not necessarily mutually exclusive and distinct concerns, and in fact should be complementary, the two processes have, on the whole, been taking place separately—at the local and grassroots level for the latter, and at the scholarly level for the former.

This in no way denies the fact that the two processes have informed and affected each other. Grassroots theologizing has been carried out via oral traditions in the local churches, while the interest in ATR seems to come primarily from universities, seminaries, and Bible schools.[2] Within the latter, the focus has been on using philosophical categories to interpret the African Christian experience. But, just as in the use of ATR, the primary goal is to arrive at a uniquely African theology that is appropriate in addressing the pertinent issues of the African Christian situation, while at the same time seeking to remain faithful to the biblical revelation of God. A third area of interest is in symbolism, which involves theological expression through art, music, drama, rituals, dances, etc.[3]

The concern to address a distinct culture and to remain faithful to the gospel has been an integral part of Christianity since its beginning. We can see it in Acts 15, when the church ventured out of Jerusalem and had to preach the gospel to the Gentiles. It faced the new challenges of whether to impose circumcision on the Gentiles and whether to adopt a Greek concept of the *Logos* to formulate its Christology. The struggle was to make the gospel relevant to such situations by discontinuing a practice that was binding on one community, but a stumbling block to the other community in the transmission of the gospel message, or by adopting something that was loaded with other meanings and give it a new Christian meaning. The letters of Paul are classical examples of the gospel meeting new and different situations and addressing them.

In this essay, we shall use the social science model of honor-and-shame values in an attempt to articulate an approach to African theology that explores the cultural affinities of the African and biblical worlds while remaining both relevant and meaningful to the peoples of Africa and faithful to the Scriptures.[4] Our working definition of culture is articulated by Robert Wuthnow as "the symbolic-expressive aspect of human behaviour," which takes into account "verbal utterances, gestures, ceremonial behaviour, ideologies, etc."[5] And, as Richard Niebuhr notes, it "is not possible to refer to a culture as evil or even necessarily have a Christian culture."[6] We thus agree with the anthropological view that culture is primarily "ideational"; that is, the essence of culture is found in its worldview and thought patterns, which in turn influence observable behavioral patterns.[7]

If it is true that the African man or woman in his or her Christian experience will not have far to go before he or she begins to tread on familiar ground, as Mbiti puts it,[8] then it makes perfect sense to begin with the sociocultural tenets that are similar in the two cultures. Thus, we interpret the gospel from an African perspective. The result hoped for, then, is the development of an interpretation that enhances the unique aspect of the African Christian *experience* and that contributes to the better understanding and sharing of the faith on the African scene.[9]

Most of the studies, though, have concentrated on ATR with the hope that these would provide the foundation for a uniquely African theology. This essay seeks to stimulate discussion in this area by promoting the cultural approach as a more viable alternative to achieving the desired end, and also contribute to the ongoing discussion of African theology.

A study carried out by Ernest McFall among the Nuer of Sudan concluded that it seemed to be very sensible, because of the similarities, to introduce the message of salvation to the Nuer through the Old Testament. Unlike many Western studies of his day on African societies and religions, McFall said that "if it can be shown that certain things in the African cultures are similar to those of the Hebrew culture, then the way may be open for the increased realisation of the extent to which the Holy Spirit can speak to the African in and through his culture without the intermediary of the Western cultures."[10] Aware of the many elements of Nuer culture that are not compatible with the faith, and thus need to be rejected,[11] he concludes his study by stating that "the culture of the Nuer is similar in many ways to that of the Hebrew culture, primarily because the *core* of each culture is similar to that of the other."[12] The contention of this paper is that one of the primary core values that underlie both the African culture and the biblical cultures is that of honor and shame.

Tite Tiénou, focusing on the evangelicals of Africa, believes that if a "theology of culture" developed for Africa, "we could win back precious theological ground we have lost. In so doing we would also help the churches to come out of their cultural ghettos and confront African culture with the Gospel at all levels."[13]

Kwame Bediako captures the essence of the current task of African theology when he states that "African theology in the post-missionary era is as much a response to the missionary underestimation of the value of the African pre-Christian religious tradition, as it is an *African* theological response to the specific and more enduring issue of how the Christian Gospel relates to the African culture."[14] It is with the second aspect that this paper is concerned.

Honor and Shame: Toward a Working Definition

Honor and shame are values found in all societies, but they tend to be more pronounced and evident in some cultures than in others. Generally speaking, honor and shame seem to be less important in areas of social control in Western cultures than they are in Mediterranean and African cultures.

E. R. Dodds postulates that one can discern a shift from a "shame culture" to a "guilt culture" in the first three centuries of Greek culture.[15] A similar phenomenon has been identified in the Germanic languages. The word *guilt* is first known to have been used in the Germanic languages in Old English in 1593; it is associated with the rise of the Puritans and their focus on subjective guilt. This date, according to D. Riesman, marks the transition from a "tradition-directed" society, motivated by shame, to an "inner-directed" society, motivated by guilt.[16] In the years that followed, Christian missionaries would leave from Europe and later America, and bring to Africans a gospel that placed a strong emphasis on guilt. This required an Anglo-Saxon system of education for the African before an appreciation of Christianity, as presented by the Western missionary, could be achieved. This, in turn, required the African to be more Western in his or her thought patterns and lifestyle in order to be able to comprehend the Christian message from the missionary.

Fred Welbourn, following Erikson, defines shame as "the obverse of *autonomy*—the feeling which a child experiences when, at the appropriate stage, he fails to control his bowel-movements, to co-ordinate his muscles sufficiently to stand up and walk." Guilt he describes as what is felt when "a child uses his newly found autonomy to display his *initiative.*"[17] What Welbourn misses in his otherwise eye-opening study is that, in his concentration on the subjective aspect of shame, he does not do justice to how shame functions in the group. This is crucial in distinguishing shame more clearly from guilt, which is essentially a subjective evaluation of an action.

Gerhart Piers, whose work is considered the standard in the field of psychoanalysis, distinguishes shame from guilt by arguing that whereas "guilt is generated whenever a boundary . . . is touched or transgressed, shame occurs when a goal . . . is not being reached. It thus indicates a 'shortcoming.'"[18] Building on this distinction,

M. Lynd refers to Franz Alexander, who believes that guilt "gives rise to the feeling that 'I am no good' in contrast to the feeling of shame 'I am weak' or inadequate. A sense of guilt arises from a feeling of wrongdoing, a sense of shame from a feeling of inferiority. Inferiority feelings in shame are rooted in a deeper conflict in the personality than the sense of wrongdoing in guilt."[19] But shame and guilt do reinforce each other in given situations.

Shame, then, is much broader than guilt and involves more than a subjective, introspective perspective on self. It is heavily influenced by the external forces that define the goal that is to be achieved. But this distinction between the internal nature of guilt and the external nature of shame does not mean that shame is not internalized. On the contrary, as Agnes Heller puts it, this is a moot question, since "shame is a feeling and as such an internal occurrence."[20] Her suggestion is not to question whether shame can be internalized, but rather to question whether the external authority (e.g., rituals, habits, codes, or rosters of behavior represented by the "eye of others") has been internalized.[21] For it is not simply the fear of being put to shame that makes shame a central factor in social control, but its internalized authority. Laurenti Magesa, a Roman Catholic priest from Tanzania, argues that guilt in African religion is "the psychoanalytical/moral stage of development where a person 'owns up to' personal worthlessness or shame. In this case, shame is the primary factor in the recognition and confession of guilt."[22]

For this reason, it is meaningful to study African theology in terms of the sociocultural similarities between the world of the Bible and that of African culture. This approach is similar to that taken by Harry Sawyerr in his first major publication, *Creative Evangelism: Towards a New Christian Encounter with Africa.*[23] Mbiti refers to this approach as "Contact Theology, a Theology built upon areas of apparent similarities and contact between Christianity and traditional African concepts and practices."[24] While we hope this will shed light on some important aspects of understanding Scriptures relevant to the African church, it will more importantly illuminate the central issue of identity, which has been considered crucial for African theology.[25]

The Vocabulary of Honor and Shame in the Bible

Both the Old and the New Testaments are very sensitive to the concerns of honor and shame, even though they are the products of largely distinct cultures—Jewish for the Old Testament, and Hellenistic for the New Testament.

Old Testament Perspectives

At the very beginning of the story of humanity's creation and existence, we encounter Adam and Eve in the Garden of Eden, where they are "naked" (*'arom*) and have no "shame" (*boshah*) (Gen. 2:25). Shame in this incident is not merely a feeling of embarrassment, but a reflection of a deeper reaction to the realization of the breaking of a boundary set by God. Thus Geerhardus Vos, in his discussion of this incident in *Biblical Theology*, comments:

> The shame arising from nakedness is in its sexual form the most primitive mode in which the loss of innocence reveals itself. . . . Shame would then be the instinctive perception of the degradation and decay of human nature. . . . It should be noted, however, that the shame and fear operate with reference to God. The man and woman hide themselves, not from each other, but from the presence of God. The divine interrogation reduces the sense of shame and fear to its ultimate root in sin.[26]

Vos is correct in identifying shame as the "most primitive mode" of reaction to "loss of innocence," but I would go even further than that. It is not only in the "sexual form," but in the totality of human being. The nakedness here described is not simply a reference to the sexual oddity of the broken boundary, but is symbolic of the whole framework of the relationship of humanity with God. Any sin bares our nakedness before God (Isa. 47:3; Rev. 3:18). Whether this "vertical" element of shame in relation to God, as opposed to a "horizontal" one in relation to other people, is present in African cultures is difficult to determine.[27] But this could be the crossroads: here the gospel could be communicated to the African community as a new dimension from God, building on the already existing horizontal aspect.

While guilt may be subsumed under shame, shame is the most basic reaction to the loss of innocence. This essay, then, operates on the premise that shame may be more basic than guilt in describing the human dilemma.[28] Shame describes the condition of the rejected people of God, who, because of their sin, find themselves without God's presence and fellowship. This in turn also hampers relationships with one another, as the Garden narrative illustrates. The ultimate removal of shame, then, becomes the perennial struggle of humanity, a battle that people by themselves cannot overcome. Only God, as the "significant other" to whom glory and honor belong, can remove humanity from this dilemma and struggle. Only through ascribed honor can humanity be restored to perfect fellowship with God. And this happened through sacrifices and covenants, both in the Scriptures and in ATR.[29]

The word for "honor" or "glory" in the Old Testament is *kabod*, whose primary meaning is "weight," but also "glory" as a reputation marker. Thus, when one has *kabod*, one has "a heavy reputation," a very positive public recognition. Its opposite is *qalal*, which means "to diminish, dishonor." And, as earlier mentioned, since the family is the basic unit of community life, the honor of parents is stressed (Ex. 20:12). Honor maintains the unity of the family and underlines the responsibility of every generation in the household—children, parents, grandparents, etc.

Among the prophets, Ezra is "ashamed" (*bosh*) to ask for protection from the king for his journey back to Jerusalem from exile (Ezra 8:22). Job was ashamed by the behavior of his friends, who had come to comfort him, but who ended up being more trouble for him (Job 6:20; 19:3–5). Harvest and abundance, a sign of blessings from the Lord, is a sign of the absence of shame (Ezra 2:26–27). David, by refusing to join his troops in victory over his mutinous son Absalom, and instead mourning his death, shamed the victorious troops and dishonored them (2 Sam. 19:5).[30] Israel's greatest shame would be for her to put her trust in another country, instead of the Lord (Isa. 3:26; 20:3; 30:3–5). The result would be exile, a shaming judgment where exiles were often stripped naked and publicly humiliated by their captors.[31] Jeremiah 2:25–26 describes this common scenario in the life of the nation of Israel: "But you said, 'There is no hope. No! For I have loved aliens, and after them I will go.' As the thief is *ashamed* [*bosh*] when he is found out, so is the house of Israel *ashamed* [*bosh*]; they and their kings and their princes, and their priests and their prophets" (NKJV). The sense of Israel's communal shame is also vividly displayed in the prophet Hosea's marriage to Gomer, with Gomer depicting the unfaithfulness of the people of Israel in their relationship with God.[32]

New Testament Perspectives

In the New Testament, the primary terms for honor are *doxa* and *timē,* and they can mean "honor," "glory," or "esteem." *Timē* means "proper recognition which a man enjoys in the community because of his office, position, wealth, etc., and then the position itself, the office with its dignity and privileges."[33] This recognition, whether it be given to a man, state, or deity, "must be distinguished from that of another," for honor is shown because of the sphere of one's control and influence.[34]

The use of *timē* in the sense of showing honor is rare in the New Testament (Acts 28:10; Rom. 12:10; 1 Tim. 6:1). Honor within the domain of marriage is the husband's responsibility to his wife: "Treat them [women] with respect [*timē*] as the weaker partner" (1 Pet. 3:7). *Doxa* is honor reserved primarily for God, and is used especially in doxologies (1 Tim. 1:17; 6:16; Rev. 4:11). But while the general culture of the New Testament viewed "the exchange of goods, services, and prestige, in proportion to the socially assigned 'worth' of each participant," and as the process that made "ancient society work," Christianity showed a significant discontinuity with this hierarchical thought (Rom. 13:7–8, esp. v. 8, "Let no debt remain outstanding, except the continuing debt to love one another").[35] Christianity subverted the concept of honor and shame held by a society that "enforced the unwritten rules of these continual transactions."[36] This subversion of what is honorable or shameful is extremely critical to the gospel message, as we will see later in the exegesis of the parables of Jesus, and also in interpreting the death of Jesus on the cross.

Aischunē is the New Testament term for shame, and in the Hellenistic world it was used to signify that which is undesirable. Paul in 2 Corinthians 4:2 says, "We have renounced secret and shameful ways." In this passage, he is referring to the whole sinful nature of human beings as shameful, as the rest of the passage goes on to show. Dodds, referring to the Greek culture in general, states that the "application to conduct of the terms *kalon* and *aischunē* seems also to be typical of shame-culture. These words denote, not that the act is beneficial or hurtful to the agent, or that it is right or wrong in the eyes of the deity, but that it looks 'handsome' or 'ugly' in the eyes of public opinion."[37] This then marked out what one could or could not do, depending on one's relationship to the group. Therefore, for "a citizen to be treated as an alien was to be put to shame. For a slave or a freedman to put on airs like a freeborn citizen marked him as shameless. For an emperor to give performances like an actor or musician as Nero is said to have done, was a public shame."[38]

Honor and Shame in African Societies

Briefly, honor and shame are group values underlining strong kinship ties and giving high value to ancestry. The individuals in an honor-and-shame culture tend to be what are called "dyadic" personalities. The dyadic personality "always needs others to learn and to continue to know who he or she is."[39] And since honor is a scarce commodity, it is obtained at a cost and can be either ascribed or achieved. The honor-and-shame culture is characterized by an ongoing "challenge-riposte," usually in the public domain (the male zone), as opposed to the domestic domain (the female zone). The male is the embodiment of honor, while the female is the embodiment of positive shame. In such a culture, honor is also controlled and dispensed by individuals called the "significant other."[40]

We now turn to selected East African societies. How do honor and shame function in them? Our survey is not comprehensive of all the societies of Africa, but the evidence in African literature, both Christian and non-Christian, indicates that these categories are reflective, *mutatis mutandis*, of many African societies.

Among the Abagusii of Kenya, *ensoni* is a feeling of "sexual shame" and is considered "to be at the core of their morality." In this community, the attitude of *ogosika*, "respect or honor," is more important among males, while for the females it is avoidance of sex.[41] In Kinyarwanda, a cognate (*isoni*) is used for "shame." This is supplemented by the much stronger *ikimwaro,* which is weightier in emphasis and has guilt included in it. The former could be used of children when they wet themselves, but the latter would be used if they could not control their bowel movement at the appropriate stage.

This distinction is true also of other societies in Africa. The Baganda of Uganda differentiate between *ensonyi* (a cognate of *esoni* and *ensoni*) and *okuswala,* "to be ashamed" or "out of proportion." Some from New Guinea differentiate between "shame of the skin" for minor transgressions and "deep shame" for weightier matters.[42] Among the Kalenjin of Kenya, *kochong* ("shame") designates both guilt and shame, while to lack *konyit* ("respect" or "honor") is to be shameless.

In these African groups (and probably also other African societies), there is a distinct absence of the expression of guilt. Even when included in the expression for shame, guilt is only described in terms of the relationship to the community. The emphasis is on its function as a social control, thus making it useful in the preservation of social equilibrium.[43]

In Africa, the focus is undeniably on the importance and centrality of the community. The individual functions in direct relation to the codes set up by the community. The family is the basic unit of organization and forms the core of community life. Every member of the family is responsible to uphold the "good name" or honor of the family. But while the nuclear family is important in this culture, even more important is the extended family, which includes uncles, aunts, cousins, grandparents, the living dead, the unborn, etc. And since the family constitutes the very fabric of African societies, one can only imagine the devastation that the evangelical missionaries to Africa caused when they forced polygamists to divorce their wives (with the exception of the first wife) before being accepted into Christian fellowship.[44]

The next larger group is the clan, which is made up of several extended families. And beyond that is the larger society, which goes as far as the tribal boundaries. The clans thus provide the organizational structure for the larger community.[45] Mbiti's slight reversal of Descartes' philosophy of *cogito ergo sum* captures the meaning. It becomes *cognatus ergo sum,* "I am, because we are; and since we are, therefore I am." This is descriptive of an African philosophy of existence and epistemology, which has been uncritically accepted by African Christian scholarship across the board, as well as being representative of African thought patterns.[46] It has been used by such writers as Mulago from the Congo, who relates ethics to community life and what he calls "co-responsibility." He rightly argues that it accords well with the Christian message.[47]

This *sensus communis,* as a vital element of African society, is also reflected in some sayings of African tribes. For example, the Akamba of Kenya use the expression *Mundu ni andu* ("A person is a person only in relationship to other people"). The Xhosa of South Africa say, *Ubuntu: umuntu ngamuntu ngabantu* ("A person is a person only because of people"). The Ewe of Ghana in West Africa put it this way: *Amenove nye awu* ("Your neighbor is your covering / clothing"—thus, without him you are naked, exposed, and vulnerable). The Saboats in western Kenya express it thus: *Samis murya kupo (kap)chi* ("However rotten a person [literally, a rat] is, he belongs to a family / household"). This strong community orientation elevates the role of honor and shame to a significant level. It is an element of social control, affecting gender roles and political organization, and provides a framework for all aspects of life in African societies.

Gender roles are well illustrated and articulated by a Ghanian proverb which says, "A woman is a flower in a garden: her husband, the fence around it."[48] The woman is viewed as the owner of domestic beauty, tender, radiant, and vulnerable, needing the protection of the man (cf. 1 Peter 3:7). The garden represents the woman's domestic domain, while the man's domain is in the public arena, where he defends and protects his "flower." The honorable man protects the woman and keeps intruders away.

In this framework, the public sphere, as the domain of the male, becomes a zone of challenge and conflict. This conflict was symbolized, and even resolved, in wrestling matches, competitive traditional dances, etc. Here were opportunities for the young men to impress the young ladies. It is still not uncommon to witness serious fights for women among African men in their quest for honor and respect. Another arena was the elder's court, where the wisdom of the elders was put to the test and displayed by the difficult cases that were brought to them to judge.

The clear distinction between the male and the female domains is illustrated by a proverb from the Lugbara of Uganda, which says, "The man dies in the wind, the woman in the house."[49] The man dies protecting his wife in the conflict zone, while the woman dies in the homestead, the place of no conflict. Again, in this social order, the man has found his identity outside in the public arena, while the woman has found hers in the domestic arena.

Part of the measure of a man's honor was how well he had provided for his family (through such practices as hunting and gathering). If the woman then made it a habit to leave her domain, she would be said to have no shame, while for the man to be too much in the homestead meant he was too "womanly" and therefore without honor. So a woman who lost her "shame" was an embarrassment to her husband and spoiled the husband's and family's name. On the other side, the man who had no honor, because he failed to provide for his household, brought shame to the family name. It was normally up to the family, elders, clan, or chiefs to deal with such a one who had deserted his or her societal duties.[50]

Stereotypical group labeling is also a common feature in African societies, as it was in the biblical world (see John 1:46 and Titus 1:12). For example, among the Akamba of Kitui in Kenya, the members of the clan called *mbaa matha* are derided as generally stupid and are described as being so uncivil that "they hunt beetles with bows and arrows."

In the political arena, shame and honor are vital factors in social control and therefore in political organizations in African societies. Magesa notes that social control through "shame, the fear of taboos, or the upholding of dignity is also the reason behind the formation and maintenance of the various sodalities. . . . Blood friendships, secret societies, age grades, and joking relationships play a conspicuous political role, each one at its own level, in African societies."[51] This right to disgrace or honor someone publicly for reasons of social control rests with an officeholder who, in turn, is also constrained by the eye of the public.

There is thus no denying that honor and shame are at the core of the value system of African societies, just as in biblical cultures. How then do these core values of honor and shame shape Christianity in the African scenario? We will now consider the points of contact with the biblical culture that can help to inform and challenge some aspects of Christianity that are present on the African continent today.

Expressions of Honor and Shame in African Christianity

The three areas that we will focus on now are evangelism, Christology, and ecclesiology. These have been radically altered from the form in which they were handed over by the Western church to the African church. The dynamism of the concepts of honor and shame in the culture, with their deep-rootedness in the thought forms of Africans, continues to shape the church in Africa. These thought patterns and cultural elements continue to emerge and to shape the concept of the gospel as it is experienced on the African continent. The concluding words of McFall's study are useful in this respect:

> One who has been brought up in a clan or tribal way of life will be able to comprehend more fully the clans and tribal life of the Hebrews. One who has his marriage arranged by his kin will have a better understanding of Abraham sending his servant to obtain a wife for his son, Isaac. . . . One who sacrifices his cattle in order to placate God will better be prepared to understand the significance of the Hebrew sacrifices and the ultimate sacrifice of Christ.[52]

The parables of Jesus recognized and sought to make use of the cultural categories of honor and shame. But his was also an understanding that went beyond these categories and even subverted or inverted them.

This element of subversion or inversion becomes central in Paul's development of Christology. Paul speaks about Jesus in a hymn, using honor-and-shame language: "Who, being in very nature God, did not consider equality with God something to be grasped, but made himself nothing, taking the very nature of a servant, being made in human likeness" (Phil. 2:6–7). Jesus, though God, assumed the form of the lowest person in the social hierarchy. He became like the scum of the earth so that he might save the scum of the earth. As he says in Luke 4:18–19, he came to give good news to the poor, release the captives, and give sight to the blind and liberty to the oppressed. These rejects and liabilities of society with whom he identified are those for whom the Son of Man came. Forsaking his glory and honor, he descended to the most ignoble level of manhood, to be a slave with no honor. Thus, in the words of Neyrey, "Honour and shame, then, are not only integral parts of the language patterns which describe the facts of Jesus and his disciples, but a basic element in the way the Christian story perceives and deals with suffering, rejection, and death."[53]

There is no doubt that Africa is the home of some of the most abject poverty on this planet. Many Africans suffer from the ravages of disease, blindness (both physically and spiritually), and the bondage of injustice, poverty, and oppression. It is for these that Jesus came, not only to give them eternal life, but also to restore them to fullness of life here on earth. For as Jesus healed the sick, gave sight to the blind, cast out demons, forgave the sins of prostitutes, and gave them a new chance in life, so he continues to do the same on the African continent.

But when the Bible came to the African, it came via the Western church, which in many respects is culturally more distant than the African from ancient Mediterranean culture. The points of contact were lost. Only later—especially with the growth of independent churches and later with the rapid growth of Pentecostal and charismatic churches—did these elements resurface. These churches recognized how the Scriptures and African cultures converged, and thus allowed the Scriptures to speak to the people in their cultural reality.

This is probably best reflected in their evangelism. These churches emphasize the reality of the spiritual world; in many respects, evangelism is defined as the plundering of the devil's domain to save sinners for the kingdom of God. Thus, "power evangelism" has become a popular term in these circles.[54] This is nothing more than challenge-riposte, transferred into the spiritual realm (actually not transferred anywhere, since the spiritual and physical worlds are not separate) and manifested in the cosmic confrontation between Christ and the evil powers.

While traditionally in African religions, the ancestors, gods, and spirits were the intermediaries to God, the introduction of Jesus into the scene brings a challenge that must be met. And just like the challenge of Elijah to Baal on Mt. Horeb, Christ is presented as challenging these other intermediaries, who in biblical terminology are the devil and demons. This emphasis on the phenomenological aspect of Christianity in Africa is reminiscent of first-century Christianity, where the spiritual and the physical worlds were not impervious to each other.

These African independent churches and charismatic churches lay a great deal of emphasis on casting out demons and healing the sick through prayer, miracles, etc. And they do this because they find such a close affinity between the biblical worldview and theirs. In fact, some of these activities have found increased acceptance even in mainline and missionary churches, which strongly indicates that this reality fits the basic model not only of the social fabric of life (honor and shame), but also its religious fabric.[55]

By bearing upon the cross the shame he did not deserve, Jesus gave to humanity what they did not deserve: the honor of God. For honor is not ultimately *horizontal*, before people, but *vertical*, before God. But God did not leave Jesus in the tomb. Instead God raised him on the third day and exalted him to the place of highest honor by seating him "at the right hand of the Majesty in heaven. So he became as much superior to the angels as the name he has inherited is superior to theirs" (Heb. 1:3–4). And by calling us his siblings/brothers, he makes us coheirs with him.

No greater honor can humanity receive than that which Christ, by dying on the cross, has obtained for them. In this sense, Jesus has become greater than the spirit beings, greater than the gods, and greater than the ancestral spirits of the Africans. Transcending the second level of the cosmos,[56] he disarmed and paraded the evil forces in his crucifixion and took them captive, baring their shame in public (Col. 2:15). That which was intended to be shame for Christ turned out to be his glory and the shame of his enemies. He has sat down at the right hand of God, and in the presence of God intercedes for Christians who need no other intermediary.

On the whole, the African pastor is the embodiment of poverty. In a society where honor is judged by material wealth and power, he finds himself rather inadequate to confront the powerful politicians or businessmen who boast of more wealth, better education, and a more influential position. Whatever the challenge may be from the pastor, it is viewed as no threat, since he does not operate at the same level of authority. Thus, the church in Africa has been unable to influence, to any significant degree, the social, economic, or political realms of African society, as Bnézét Bujo complains.[57]

Coupled with this pastoral ineptitude is the fact that most of the people in the church are women, while the political, economic, and other public spheres remain the domain of men. And beneath the element of shame that belongs to women in the public sphere, there are the manifold forms of fear that keep them back from public confrontation. Because of their place in the domestic center (positive shame), they generally do not see themselves as able to influence the public sphere of male dominance. So, despite the staggering growth of the church, the influence on life outside the church and outside charitable concerns is almost negligible. This is one area where the gospel needs to inform the African church with its inversion of honor and shame, redefining that which is honorable and showing how the honor of Christ removes all barriers (Gal. 3:28).

One of the reactions that has taken place in this respect among the Pentecostal/charismatic groups has been the prosperity gospel. As described by Ojo, "one of the interesting developments in recent years in the Charismatic movements is the continuing emphasis on prosperity and success. What sustains this economic quest for material resources is partly the present deteriorating economic situations in Africa."[58] The solution to mass poverty from the charismatic perspective starts from the basic premise that "people cannot escape from the poverty until they are conscious of it, and if people can be helped to reflect on their situations, changes will follow."[59]

An area where Africans have faced some of the greatest challenges is in the area of leadership. The concept of a leader in African traditional society was associated closely with divine influence and the closeness of such individuals to the spirits and gods. Not unlike Egypt, where the Pharaoh was a form of, or an incarnation of, a god, the chiefs and kings in Africa south of the Sahara were viewed as possessing sacred power as a result of their position, which made them semidivine.[60]

This situation has been heightened by the fact that the traditional social control of shame, or the fear of violating taboos,[61] has lost its controlling power within the realm of leadership, as the closely knit tribal communities of rural areas are replaced by the intertribal urban centers, from which most of the African leaders emerge. The social control of shame and guilt that was so vital in political organizations in Africa would prove to be useful in this regard if appropriated from a biblical perspective.

By clearly directing people to the correct dimension of honor and shame as the *vertical* relationship with God, rather than the *horizontal* relationship with man, we can affirm that God is the true "significant other" who ascribes honor to us even when we do not deserve it. The true power, honor, and glory reside with God and not humankind. We need to eliminate any sort of sacral overtones that might reside in the minds of Africans concerning leadership and instill "an understanding of power that secures its source beyond the reach of human manipulation, at least conceptually, and so transforms the exercise of power in human community from rule to service."[62]

Conclusion

Whether one agrees or not with what has been presented in this essay, the basic point must remain clear. As the theological field in Africa begins to take shape and find its place in the global theological arena, it must continue to seek out the most effective means and methodology of expression. This essay presents only one perspective suggested for consideration.

—16—

THE POWER OF THE GOSPEL IN KOREA (1882–1912)

SUNG-IL STEVE PARK

Christianity in Korea has received much academic attention in recent decades.[1] One of Christianity's most remarkable features is its amazing rate of growth since the introduction of Protestant missions to Korea in the late nineteenth century. This is so atypical for Northeast Asia, that the phenomenon has taken on an enigmatic quality that remains elusive to investigations inspired merely by the social sciences. Undeniably, when the church grew, a supernatural factor was at work. On the other hand, the supernatural power of the gospel unfolded in Korea in a recognizable and concrete shape. In retrospect, we can discover the key features of Korean Christianity that not only built a vigorous church, but also became an important force in the making of modern Korea.

Because present-day Korea is marred by denominational posturing and theological strife, we often forget the amazing history in which the gospel reformed hearts and society alike. The eschatological vision of "Thy kingdom come" was planted in the hearts of the missionaries and the early Christians in Korea. Unlike the "otherworldly" mind-set of many minority Christians in their largely hostile society, Korean Christians developed a consciousness for national renewal when it was confronted by international hostility. A nation

296

that was literally falling apart, inside and out, latched on to the doctrine of hope and transformation, rather than comfort and escape.

Early History of the Korean Protestant Church

The early history of the Korean church has received diverse evaluations. Often the grid determines the result; therefore, the importance of perspectives cannot be underestimated. Thus far, the historiography of the Korean church has been dominated by two perspectives or evaluative grids. The first perspective is the dogmatic or doctrinal grid that attempts to describe the early church in Korea in terms of its theological posture or doctrinal integrity. This approach is typical of the conservative camp. The second grid, not surprisingly, is a sociological one. It attempts to evaluate the significance of the early Christian movement in terms of its visible impact on the society or influences on the nation's political life. This approach, developed by theological liberals, often undermines or ignores the transcendental dimension of what the church is. Neither perspective can do justice to the complexity of a Christian movement developing and expanding in a new context. Both are reductionistic in their own ways. The first overlooks various contextual concerns; the second loses sight of the supernatural redemptive work of God, without which the church cannot be comprehended. The situation begs for a more balanced approach.

First, we must go beyond a narrowly theological evaluation. Because Korea today stands as a major constituency of Reformed Christianity in the world, some Reformed writers have asked this important question: Is the Korean Presbyterian Church truly Reformed? Sang-Kyu Yi, a conservative scholar, raises the question and then offers this evaluation in his essay "The Reformed Theology in Korea":

To some extent, we have critiqued liberal theology or neo-orthodoxy by setting the boundaries of orthodoxy. However, we have not carefully established clear theological boundaries between fundamentalism, conservatism, evangelicalism, dispensationalism, mysticism, pietism, or Pentecostalism. Under the banner of Reformed Christianity, we have, in fact, embraced what resembles dispensationalism or fundamentalism. The Korean Presbyterian Church claims the Reformed heritage, but in reality one detects widespread vestiges of fundamentalism, dispensationalism, and pietism.[2]

That essay attempts to identify Reformed Christianity mainly as a monolithic theological entity, with its complete development traceable in European history during the past five centuries or so. Theologically, a truly Reformed church is that which correctly adheres to the seventeenth-century Reformed confessions. Yi concludes that the Korean Presbyterian Church from its earliest stage lacked Reformed distinctives.

However, while it is good to be mindful of confessional orthodoxy and theological correctness, one should not overlook another factor that is significant for obtaining a balanced historical evaluation. A distinction must be maintained between the burden of the seventeenth-century Reformed churches in Europe and that of the twentieth-century missionary churches taking root in Asia. The distinction is between the need for theological acuity and elaboration in the context of competing theological movements within a largely Christian world and the need for theological extraction in the context of competing worldviews within a non-Christian world. It is unfortunate, as Sang-Kyu Yi says in his essay, that the Reformed church in Korea has been somewhat slow over the years to demonstrate a high degree of commitment to solidifying its confessional stance. However, one should not be too quick to fault the early Christians in Korea for being more concerned about theological extraction and the dynamics of spiritual conviction, conversion, and commitment.[3]

A narrowly theological evaluation, such as the one presented above, can impoverish the outlook of the Christian community. If we fixate on the relative lack of theological "sophistication," we may sadly fail to observe the numerous evidences of God's marvelous work in Korea. If, instead, we fully appreciate the providential hand of God at work in the historical development of the Korean church, we discover a rich inheritance worth sharing with the Christian church at large. Unfortunately, the conservative theologians in Korea have generally been slow to give credit where it is due. They have been too tentative to address the sociopolitical dimension of the gospel transformation and reluctant to cultivate a theological understanding of church renewal informed by the contextual dynamics as well as the biblical mandate.[4]

We should recognize that the fruit of the gospel proclamation in Korea was in effect the realization of the demands of the Reformed worldview.[5] It is an example of how the gospel transforms the society as well as the heart when God brings a revival on a land. At its core, the Korean church has operated with the conviction that it is the business of God to convert and renew individual hearts, which in turn leads to the building of a civil society and a nation. Essentially, this reflects the eschatological vision of the kingdom of God.

Second, we must dispute the position that the Korean church, in the final analysis, grew mainly as a sociopolitical struggle of liberation from foreign oppression. Daniel J. Adams asks the familiar question, "Why has the church grown in Korea and what are the factors that have contributed to this growth?"[6] He points out that in the early period of Christianity in Korea, there were two pivotal events typifying the growth paradigms. One was the great revival of 1907; the other was the Independence Movement of 1919. The first, he believes, was a movement focused on "quantitative growth through building up of the Church," while the second event "emphasized qualitative maturity through the strengthening of national consciousness."[7] With that distinction in place, Adams attributes the growth of the church in Korea to a timely paradigm shift that occurred sometime between the two key events. Describing this paradigm shift, he says, "[The] shift was away from ecclesiology and concern with the institutional church, to nationalism and concern with the recovery of national identity. It is this paradigm shift which has enabled Christianity to become truly Korean."[8]

Adams is quite perceptive to point out two key issues or features of Christianity in Korea, yet he is misguided to think that a decisive shift in paradigm indeed took place. A better analysis would be to see both the experience of, and the continuous desire for, spiritual awakening and the aspiration for nation building as parallel tracks, which together are signs of a vibrant piety. They have been, from the very beginning of Protestant missions in Korea, the major driving forces of church growth. In fact, these two motifs are often indistinguishable in their manifestation, because they have been blended together in the consciousness of most Christians in Korea. Neither of these features is merely quantitative or qualitative, as Adams suggests. Together, they have played an enormous role in mobilizing a large number of people at a high level of commitment.

A Roman Catholic Contrast

As we begin to investigate the way in which spiritual renewal and the movement toward nation building converged in Korea and to appreciate the timeliness of the Protestant missions, we can find a helpful contrast by looking at the Roman Catholic missions that began about a hundred years prior to the Protestant endeavor. A student of history would be astonished at the difference in the level at which these two new belief systems were received. The former, although experiencing noticeable growth, faced massive persecution that choked its development; the latter, however, enjoyed sustained growth that ultimately converged with the national consciousness.

While the nation under the rule of the Yi Dynasty was steeped in Confucianism, a few progressive Confucian scholars opened their eyes to the "teachings of the West." Catholic ideas trickled in from China, where Roman Catholicism had been firmly established since the last quarter of the eighteenth century. Yi Byok was one of those Confucian scholars who appreciated the merits of the "faith practice of the West." He began to teach attentive listeners regularly, and with the help of Yi Seung-Hoon, who was baptized by a Jesuit priest during his visit to China, established a house church in 1785 at Myong-Dong, where now stands the famous Myong-Dong Cathedral, the mother church of all Catholic churches in Korea. By 1800, there were over 10,000 Catholic adherents in Korea, and in 1863 nearly 20,000 were reported to have embraced the faith.[9] The numerical growth may seem unimpressive, but it is significant in the light of an extreme persecution that developed and lasted over a century, producing over 10,000 martyrs, including several foreigners.

Regarding the new faith, an antagonistic Confucian scholar stated that it "believes in Heaven [*chun*, a transcendental reality or being], but dishonors the king and parents, and it deceives the people with the idea of an afterlife of heaven and hell; therefore, as it stirs up the whole world, its effect is worse than a disastrous flood or an attack of ferocious beasts."[10] This was more than an individual opinion. A sincere hatred of what is foreign dictated the political policy and fueled the terrible Catholic bloodshed that continued until the last and most staunchly isolationist regent, Taewongun, relinquished his power in 1873.

Initially, the difference in receptivity seems to stem from the difference in strategy. For example, Don Baker points out that the bloody fate of the early Catholics in Korea was the result of a slow political contextualization. They established themselves as a conflicting ideology to that which built and maintained the nation under the Yi Dynasty. In other words, it was an ideological force that undermined the nation building.

Catholics, even before Catholicism was explicitly outlawed, met secretly to read Christian books. They created an unauthorized organization and gave unauthorized titles, such as "sinbu" and "kyobu," to its leaders. They refused to perform rituals such as *chesa* in the manner the government told them to perform them. Moreover, they performed their own rituals, such as baptism and the mass, which the government had not given them permission to perform. And, worst of all, they looked to the Pope in Rome and his representatives in Beijing rather than to the King of Korea for advice on their moral and ritual obligations. This was a departure from the traditional relationship between the state and religious communities which the Korean government could not tolerate.[11]

But the Protestant missions were able to avoid clashing with the government. Commenting on the successful contextualization of Protestant missions in Korea, Adams writes that the Protestant movement in Korea "sought to preserve Korean culture and champion the aspirations of the Korean people in the face of [Japanese] oppression."[12]

However, in the final analysis it is difficult to attribute the difference in reception to the difference in strategy. Both the Catholics and the Protestants sought to Christianize people. Yung-Jae Kim correctly points out that the major difference between them was the radical difference between their historical contexts.[13] In other words, the difference was more a matter of context than content. At the end of the eighteenth century, Catholicism represented an ideology that undermined the traditional Korean way of life, firmly supported by the Confucian monarch. However, the Protestant missions at the end of the nineteenth century represented an ideology that could strengthen and rebuild the nation as it suffered under the threat of Japanese imperialist oppression. The fact is that in the late nineteenth and early twentieth centuries, the old Korea was fading away. Such a time brought about a truly extraordinary receptivity to a new faith planted in the soil of an age-old culture. At the eclipse of the old regime and the old way of life, Christian faith offered a new worldview, accompanied by hope for a sweeping transformation. Divine providence had set the stage for the gospel to make a remarkable landing. This was the context for spiritual awakening and nation building.

Steps Toward Spiritual Awakening and Nation Building

First: Translation of the Bible into Hangul, the Korean Phonetic Alphabet, and the Rise of a Literate People

In the last quarter of the nineteenth century, under King Ko-Jong's rule, Korea's international policy decidedly turned away from isolationism. This change was really a succumbing to the advancing world powers that were driven by global expansionism. Woefully ill prepared to navigate through the current of the new international order, Korea stepped out when Japan first coerced the Korean government to enter into an international treaty in 1896. Soon delegates poured into Korea from the United States, the United Kingdom, Germany, Italy, Russia, France, and other countries. Suddenly, the door to the Korean mind was wide open to international influences. At this time of "things falling apart," and the questioning of traditional values and culture, the nation as a whole was beginning to experience a serious identity crisis. At this opportune moment, the Bible landed in Korea in written codes that were truly Korean.

Before a formal Protestant missionary stepped onto Korean soil, Bible translation work began simultaneously in northeastern China and in Japan. The Scottish Bible Society's John Ross and John McIntyre were commissioned to work in the Manchurian region of China, and soon their attention was drawn to the people of Korea. Many Korean merchants traveled through that area, and the missionaries began to expose them to the gospel. Ross's confidence in the power of the written Word drove his effort to translate the Bible into Korean using the Korean alphabetic script (*Hangul*), helped by the merchants who came to Christ. By 1882, the team succeeded in printing the gospel according to Luke. Within a year, Matthew, Mark, and Acts were printed. They completed the translation of the New Testament by 1887 and proceeded to print 3,000 copies.[14] A legendary story of Suh Sang-Ryun begins with his role as an assistant to Ross for Bible translation. He brought copies of the translated gospels into Korea in 1883 and was instrumental in establishing the first Protestant church in his hometown of Sorae. Sorae Church was truly an indigenous church, established by an evangelistic effort of a Korean convert to Christianity. So pervasive was the effect of this indigenous outreach that within a few years fifty households out of the fifty-seven in Sorae joined the church.[15]

Meanwhile, Yi Soo-Jung, an assistant to a Korean delegate to Japan, decided to remain abroad following his official duty, hoping to acquire a greater knowledge of Western thought. He came in contact with an American Presbyterian missionary, George W. Know, and a Methodist missionary, R. S. Maclay. After he was baptized in 1883, he was urged by Henry Loomis of the American Bible Society, stationed in Japan, to translate the Bible into Korean. He successfully translated Luke by 1885.[16] This translation played an important role as Horace G. Underwood of the Northern Presbyterian Church and Henry G. Appenzeller of the Methodist Church, often mentioned as the first official missionaries to Korea, began their work in 1885. When they landed in the port city of Inchon, they carried Yi Soo-Jung's Luke in their hands.

From the standpoint of evangelism, the immediate availability of the Bible in the native language is an incomparable advantage. The Korean church enjoyed this advantage from the time of its conception. Because of this availability, missionaries endeavored to establish the Korean church as a literate church. Utilizing the so-called Nevius Plan of missions, the early stage of Korean missions was successful due to the early settling of the Scripture as the center of Korean Christian experience. The plan, often understood as the three-self policy, was adopted in 1890.

> In 1890 Dr. John L. Nevius, a Presbyterian missionary working in China, received an invitation to Korea from a group of seven young missionaries who were just beginning their work in [Korea]. They asked him to give them two weeks of instructions in missionary methods.... To those two weeks of meetings and to the application of those principles . . . many missionaries in Korea attribute much of the rapid growth of mission work in that country. There were only 100 communicants at the time these principles were adopted, but [by 1958] there [was] a full grown, self-propagating, self-supporting and self-governing church of 800,000 members.[17]

At the heart of the Nevius Plan was an uncompromising emphasis on the authority of God's Word. The ability to propagate, support, and govern themselves would stem from the native people's ability to study the Word and become proficient in it.

The tremendous growth of the Bible-reading population in Korea was an orchestrated development. First of all, in God's providence, there was the invention of the Korean phonetic alphabet under the royal commission of King Se-Jong (1418–1450) during the golden era of the Yi Dynasty. This logically coherent and aesthetically pleasing phonetic system was largely abandoned by the Confucian society which, offended by its easy use by the uneducated, stubbornly held on to an exclusive use of Chinese characters. The missionaries' decision to translate the Bible into *Hangul* (the phonetic language) proved to be a brilliant strategy that impacted not only the church, but even the national destiny. Missionaries made a concentrated effort to teach people how to read *Hangul*. The Presbyterian Assembly in Korea, consisting of the missionaries, agreed upon the principle that all Christian publications would be published in *Hangul*.[18] Soon it was a common sight for people of all ages and genders and social classes to gather together, with each one carrying his or her own text of the Bible to read and study. The first newspaper in Korea was published by an outstanding Christian leader and physician, Suh Jae-Pil, and his paper was an all-*Hangul* publication. The pervasive use of the language helped to awaken the national identity of Korea. The redis-covery of *Hangul* by the Christian missions was an important block for nation-building, as well as the spiritual awakening, for it pro-moted literacy and developed a biblically literate church. As a result, Bible reading became a centerpiece of Korean piety.

Second: The Establishment of Social Institutions and the Rise of Indigenous Leadership

In 1884, Horace N. Allen, an American Presbyterian missionary, arrived in Korea. Since the government did not allow missionary activities, he came as an official physician of the American Consulate in Seoul. However, within a few months of his stay, a fateful event turned him into a celebrity at the royal palace. A riot erupted when the Progressive Party, consisting of social elites, clashed violently with social conservatives, and Min Yung-Ik, a relative of King Ko-Jong, was critically wounded in the struggle. The palace sought help from Dr. Allen, and miraculously Min's life was saved. As a result of this fortunate turn of events, the king granted permission for Allen to establish the first medical hospital in Korea in 1885.

Although Allen did not attempt from the beginning to evangelize openly, he played a pivotal missionary role by successfully earning the trust of the royal court, which in turn opened the door for the future influx of American missionaries. Allen and others were seen as allies in advancing the social system of a nation that desperately needed such advancement. Medical missions became a huge part of the early missions in Korea. Long-term patients were particularly susceptible to the gospel presentation. Along with a demonstration of Christian charity, medical missionaries taught the Bible and provided counseling in the hospital rooms of many medical clinics that opened their doors in Korea.

At the same time, early missionaries focused on leadership development for a nation in decline and played a crucial role in introducing modern education. Many reform-minded people flocked into the church, since the church was virtually synonymous with education. The newly founded *Dokleeb-Shinmoon* (*The Independence News*) commented that every advanced nation successfully utilized three institutions—schools, churches, and newspapers—for educating its people, and it urged diligent use of them.[19] Within fifteen years, the Presbyterian missions alone established 229 Sunday schools (for literacy and basic education as well as Bible teaching) with 9,090 students, and 32 churches operated weekday schools with 665 students.[20] By 1910, Christian schools dominated the popular education of this nation. "Korea had more students in Christian schools than in Government schools."[21] In other words, Western Christian education began to replace the traditional Confucian education system. In this way, the gospel made a tremendous impact in raising an educated population in the old nation as it came into the new world.

On the other hand, Christian schools did not aim to train the existing social elites. The Nevius Plan of missions adopted by the Presbyterian Assembly in 1893 offers a good indication of their approach. It argued that it would be more effective to begin evangelizing the nation by targeting the working class rather than the upper class. In fact, the specific mention of women and children as the primary target groups is telling.[22] Appenzeller took a handful of young students and officially started Bae-jae School with royal consent in 1886. In the same year, Mrs. M. F. Scranton established the first women's educational institution in Korea, Yi-hwa School. Underwood founded Kyung-shin School when he brought a few orphans under his wings to care for them.[23] These early schools offered room and board to students of various ages. Arrangements were made for those who demonstrated exceptional abilities to go abroad for higher education;[24] and they returned to become key leaders in the modern nation of Korea.

A Christian organization that made a significant contribution was the YMCA. It was organized in 1903 under the leadership of P. L.

Gillet. The founding members became illustrious in the early history of modern Korea. Many of them were leaders of the Independence Movement.[25] The organization drew much support from abroad, as well as within Korea. The YMCA building at the heart of Seoul became a center of the modernization of Korea in terms of Christian and vocational education, cultural activities, and sports. Numerous other youth-oriented organizations thrived in various parts of the nation, aiming at similar results.

Third: The Great Revival and the Emergence of the National Christian Network

The world's superpowers' menacing march toward colonialism heavily impacted Korea during the dying years of the Yi Dynasty. The eclipse of the dynasty seemed immanent when Japan won a decisive victory over China in the Sino-Japanese War of 1894–95. In the minds of the rulers of the Yi Dynasty, the real superpower in East Asia was China, and they leaned heavily on China as the center of gravity. "They saw Japan's victory with the westernized military system and weaponry and began to question the Confucian value system that had been the fundamental basis for the consciousness of the Korean people for centuries. At this juncture, the gospel of Christianity was introduced by western missionaries."[26] For the Korean nation as well as the church, the years between 1885 and 1910 were indeed a time of great turmoil. At the same time, a remarkable growth of the church was taking place.

The nation was quickly swept away in the imperialistic expansionist policy of Japan. While Korea was rapidly weakened by internal political factions, foreign powers sought to spread their influence over the nation. After Japan defeated China, a new rivalry arose between Japan and Russia. But it was the Japanese moment. Even before Japan defeated Russia in the war of 1905, it seemed to have the upper hand in Korea with its aggressive interference in Korea's internal affairs. When a pro-Russian party took control of Korean politics with the support of the royal court controlled by Queen Min-Bi, the Japanese sent assassins into the palace and murdered her. After this event in 1895, an open resistance developed in Korea and began clashing violently with the Japanese imperialists. The last reigning king of the Yi Dynasty, Ko-Jong, was in a vulnerable position when he publicly declared Korea's political independence from Japan. In constant fear of losing his life, Ko-Jong relied on loyal missionaries, such as Allen, C. Weber, and Underwood. Missionaries became personal bodyguards of the king.[27] In order to understand the situation from a missions perspective, it is crucial to realize that unlike other colonized nations in the world (or at least in Asia), Korea's adversary was Japan, not a Western nation. While many nations received Western Christian missionaries along with the political and military aggressors from the same countries, Korea's missionaries did not come from an imperialist nation. For Korea, Western missionaries were allies who sympathized with the frail nation as it was threatened by a newly developing military giant in East Asia. Many missionaries sympathized with the Korean independence movement. This support intensified in the later years of Japanese occupation, when persecution against the church became severe and increasingly inhumane.

In 1905, Korea practically lost its national sovereignty when Ito Hirobumi, an emissary from Japan, came and forcefully drew out a "Protectorate Treaty."[28] Japan had already shipped an occupying force into Korea and had completely taken over its foreign and domestic affairs. In 1907, Ko-Jong was forced to relinquish his throne, and he was succeeded by his son, Sun-Jong, who was made a puppet king. At the same time, the national military was dissolved. As the final act of erasing Korean nationhood, Japan completed the annexation of Korea in 1910, and on August 29 of the same year, Sun-Jong was forced to give up his throne and his country.[29] While these things were happening, the church in Korea experienced something remarkable.

The early Christians in Korea suffered along while the whole nation lost its national sovereignty. They expressed their loyalty to the nation and to King Ko-Jong with songs and public prayers. In 1906, on the birthday of the king, Christians gathered together for a prayer service, and a special song written to encourage the king was circulated among the people that day.[30]

It is true that many sought Christian fellowship out of their patriotism and an earnest desire to seek the strengthening of the nation. Syngman Rhee, who was later the first president of the Republic of

Korea, was one such person. He grew up in a Confucian home and was steeped in Confucian values. However, in 1905, just prior to his matriculation at George Washington University, he was baptized. At that time, he expressed his reasons for his commitment to his newly found faith, as well as for his going to America:

> He chose to study in America . . . to "raise the moral standard of the Korean people who were in a beastly low state of morality through Christian education." And he made his pledge that he would devote himself to Christian education of his people. Defining Christianity as "God's way" while Confucianism as "a human way," he characterized Christianity as a religion that befitted the contemporary new era because it had "a principle of reform . . . within the church." He hoped that with its "dynamism for reform" . . . Christianity would help his people to gain "a power to do new things out of their own accord" so that his country might regain independence. His wish was to a make "a perfect Christian country" of Korea.[31]

This strong nationalistic tendency in the early church was regarded by some missionaries as an unhealthy development.[32] However, Christian missions in Korea from the very beginning was a nation-building endeavor. The nation building, however, was not merely a political development; rather, it was a real effort to transform the culture by reshaping the mind and the faith of the people. The missionaries and the early Christians alike, at the sight of a miserably failed nation—along with its dysfunctional sociopolitical culture and a traditional religion that trapped able people within the class and gender structure—looked for real reform, so that while the nation fell, a new people would emerge and a new independent nation would be established under a new order.

Amazingly, a timely supernatural revival accelerated the transformation of the people. Contrary to Adams's argument mentioned earlier, the Great Revival of 1907 did not represent a narrowly spiritual paradigm of church growth later replaced by the paradigm of nationalism; rather, it was a divine fueling of an emerging nationwide Christian movement that was equally committed to spiritual renewal and nation building.

Yong-Kyu Park argues that the great Korean revival should not be pinpointed to 1907, since there were signs of renewal as early as 1903.[33] Many people in various locations throughout the country reported a fresh experience of the Holy Spirit touching their hearts. A pattern began to emerge: the revival was characterized by teaching of the Word through *Sa-Kyung-Hye*—a public gathering for Bible teaching and preaching—and then came convictions of sin, leading to rigorous prayers of repentance, public confessions, and a renewed zeal for evangelism.

Robert Alexander Hardie, a medical missionary commissioned by the Southern Methodist Church, was the primary instrument for stirring up the missionaries in Wonsan in 1903. Many trace the origin of the great awakening of Korea to Hardie's own spiritual transformation.[34] He had experienced a spiritual renewal and began to publicly confess that failures had occurred in his work due to his pride and slowness to seek the filling of the Holy Spirit. He had been commissioned to lead a weeklong Bible study and prayer time for a group of missionaries who desired a spiritual refreshing. During the meeting, Hardie himself was overwhelmed by the powerful movement of the Holy Spirit. Not only the missionaries, but also other Korean Christians who witnessed Hardie's confessions, were shaken by the visible breaking down of a person who suffered, according to his own words, the agony of confessing his own failures and pointing out the reasons for them. He confessed the pride that caused him to look down upon the natives, the callousness of his heart, and his lack of faith.[35] He stated that, though a missionary, he experienced the deep conviction of sin leading to a real experience of repentance for the first time in his life.[36] This phenomenon spread from person to person, as many continued to flock to *Sa-Kyung-Hye* meetings and prayerfully committed themselves to forsaking sins and reforming lives. Soon a renewal movement, characterized by Bible study, prayer of repentance, and evangelism, was spreading all across the nation.

The peak of this phenomenon is what has become known as the Great Revival of 1907. The outbreak of renewal, documented and reported by many as a truly remarkable season of spiritual harvest, originated at the winter *Sa-Kyung-Hye* (Bible training class) for men.[37] About a thousand men gathered in Pyongyang's Jang-Dae-Hyun Church. Pyongyang was the stronghold of Presbyterian missions. The meetings continued for two weeks, characterized by great spiritual intensity. The Bible classes met during the morning hours, concentrating on study and prayer. During the afternoon, they scattered throughout Pyongyang to evangelize, and each evening over 1,500 people gathered to hear the gospel being preached. From the first night, unbearable agonies of the heart came upon many who sought and begged for forgiveness from God and others.[38] But the day referred to as the Korean Pentecost was yet to come. On the night of January 14, over 2,000 men had gathered to hear the gospel preached. The message was followed by a time of spontaneous prayer. It is reported that the simultaneous praying of the 2,000 men did not seem chaotic or out of character. It was as if many hearts were in perfect harmony as utterances merged together into a thundering sound of a mighty waterfall.[39] This spontaneous vocalized prayer of a body of believers has become known as *Tongsung-Kido,* a common practice of the Korean church even today. This mode of prayer became a notable trait of the Great Revival of 1907.[40] That event of January 14 turned into an all-night affair. About 500–600 men remained to pray through the night. After numerous waves of louder and calmer episodes of corporate prayer, people began to confess their sins publicly. This continued for hours. As people were deeply convicted by their sins and filled with unbearable remorse, they poured out confession upon confession. Those who were present uniformly report that it was as if a tornado had swept through that place, leaving none unaffected by the powerful movement of the Holy Spirit.[41] This peak experience continued into the next day and spread beyond that meeting into many Christian schools, where young men and women were affected and renewed. A leader who emerged out of this movement was Kil Sun-Joo, a gifted speaker and a deeply spiritual man.

Under the leadership of figures such as Kil, the churches began to organize a nationwide network in order to continue the promotion of spiritual renewal. In 1909, a sweeping evangelistic movement— "A Million Souls to Christ"—was set in motion. This movement was a momentous event for the Korean church, not in terms of its level of success, but as an orchestrated mobilization across denominations and regions. One can hardly doubt the effect of this movement on the subsequent nonviolent uprising for independence known as "the March One Movement" of 1919. Its scale was enough to cause panic among the Japanese regime, which began from that moment on to systematically persecute the church. Many Christians were imprisoned and martyred until the Allied defeat of Japan in 1945.

One must notice the irony in this piece of Korean history. When their national identity was stripped away from the people, the church became the cradle of national consciousness. The church in Korea was truly a Korean church, not a Western institution. The church experienced remarkable growth during this period. Between 1900 and 1910, the Protestant believers increased by 825 percent. By 1910, there were 140,158 Presbyterians and 70,525 Methodists registered as church members.[42]

Furthermore, another event of tremendous significance took place in 1907. Missionaries relinquished a significant portion of the organizational leadership of the Korean Presbyterian Church and passed it into the hands of the Korean leaders when the first presbytery of Chosun (i.e., Korean) Presbyterian Church was founded. This event was supernaturally orchestrated with the Great Revival that energized the national church leaders. Also, it was the fruit of a diligent leadership development effort exerted by the Presbyterian missionaries who established Pyongyang Theological Seminary in 1902 with Samuel A. Moffett as its first president. The first group of graduates came out in 1907, and in order to ordain them into ministry, it seemed appropriate to establish a presbytery. On September 17, 1907, at the same place (Jang-Dae-Hyun Church) where the Great Revival broke out earlier that year, thirty-three missionaries and thirty-six Korean ruling elders assembled for the first presbytery meeting. They ordained seven graduates of the seminary into ministry, one of whom was Kil Sun-Joo.[43] With regional subgroupings in place to support adequate mobilization, the presbytery was indeed a national organization. When the first General Assembly was organized in 1912, the subgroups naturally became seven regional churches (i.e., presbyteries), which, when taken together, made up a national church (i.e., the synod). Once again, the years between 1907 and 1912 were a time when Korea relinquished its national sovereignty to Japan. Meanwhile, the national church was formed with its leaders in place and was organized into a relatively sophisticated form of government that modeled both unity and plurality. Whether the timing was intentional on the part of the leaders of the church or not, in God's sovereign providence the national church emerged as the only nationwide network of Koreans when the nation of Korea was no more.

Between 1882 and 1912, during the first thirty years of the Christian movement in Korea, the identity of the Korean church was shaped. It was a church molded by a great spiritual awakening, whose piety strongly demonstrated a historically grounded desire to rebuild their people and eventually their nation.

Conclusion

The Korean church, now over a century old, has become a major body of Protestant Christianity in the world. To this day, churches are thriving and deeply committed believers fill their pews. Over a quarter of the whole population of the Republic of Korea is considered churched.

The Christian community is divided into numerous denominations and theological persuasions, but the majority of the Christians in Korea are relatively conservative evangelicals, often Presbyterian, composing a somewhat cohesive entity. Moreover, the Protestant church in Korea is still shaped by two dominant motifs: an urge for spiritual vitality in the tradition of the Great Revival of the early twentieth century and a constant concern for nation building. The latter gradually shifted focus over the past century, particularly in the South, from independence from Japan to resistance to Communism, and then from industrialization and military dictatorship to democratization, and finally from class struggle to the reunification between the North and the South. Nevertheless, the Korean church has always been a patriotic entity. At the most crucial junctures in its history—there were many national tragedies and upheavals during the twentieth century—Christians in Korea, time after time, have mobilized themselves according to the familiar paradigm of the Great Revival to pray for their country.

In the same way, Christian leaders are still in the forefront of promoting social justice and ethical responsibility. One can easily hear them speaking about these issues in the context of national destiny. Also, Christian leaders are the first ones mobilized to assist famine victims in North Korea and to speak out for North Korean refugees moving across its northern border into China. Every Sunday, the pastoral prayers ringing from the vast majority of the Korean pulpits are dominated by the themes of spiritual fervency and national security and prosperity. These are the twin towers of Korean Christianity, the markers left by the wildfire of church growth during the first thirty years of Protestant missions.

A great challenge lies ahead, however. Mere good manners has gradually replaced true spiritual renewal and is becoming a dominant culture in the Christian community. Forgetting the central pieces of the Great Revival, many are falling into sensationalism as church communities try to recreate the emotion without the proper dynamics of spiritual renewal. Rather than hungering for the truth of God's Word, great crowds seem to follow the fascinating images of material success and technological refinement that the numerous megachurches are more than capable of offering. The concern for nation building, which must be grounded in the eschatological vision of kingdom building, informed by the proper biblical worldview, has been, in some sectors of the Christian community, replaced by the feeling of self-satisfaction at the sight of the symbols of religious success or, in other sectors, hopelessly secularized. The secularizing can be seen, on one hand, among theological liberals, who have lost the vision of the transcendence as they bluntly equate the kingdom vision with ethnocentric nationalism or various manifestations of liberation thinking. On the other hand, too many theological conservatives have become used to expending their energy on church and denominational politics rather than on kingdom seeking.

"Thy kingdom come, thy will be done!" is the transformational motivation for the church in all ages and in all nations. It is the power of the gospel that brings sinners to repentance and then produces societal transformation. For so long, Christianity in Korea has reflected that power. It is the power of the gospel that is worth remembering and worth promoting wherever the Word is preached.

NOTES

Introduction

1. Erik Davis, e-mail sent to Westminster Theological Seminary faculty and staff, 27 August 2001.

2. Personal letter from Harvie Conn to Dr. and Mrs. Edmund Clowney, 30 December 1989.

3. Harvie M. Conn, "Normativity, Relevance, and Relativism," in *Inerrancy and Hermeneutic,* ed. Harvie M. Conn (Grand Rapids: Baker Book House, 1988), 185–209.

Chapter 1: Mission, Missions, Theology, and Theological Education

1. Harvie M. Conn, "Contextual Theologies: The Problem of Agendas," *Westminster Theological Journal* 52 (1990): 55–58.

2. David Bosch, *Transforming Mission: Paradigm Shifts in Theology of Mission* (Maryknoll, N.Y.: Orbis Books, 1991), 489.

3. Edward Farley, *Theologia* (Philadelphia: Fortress Press, 1983), 31.

4. Conn, "Contextual Theologies," 58.

5. Werner Jaeger, *Early Christianity and Greek Paideia* (London: Oxford University Press, 1961), 74.

6. Farley, *Theologia,* 39.

7. Ibid., 99–149.

8. Bosch, *Transforming Mission,* 490.

9. Ibid., 492.

10. R. Pierce Beaver, "The American Protestant Theological Seminary and Missions," *Missiology* 4 (January 1976): 85.

11. Norman Thomas, "Globalization and the Teaching of Mission," *Missiology* 18 (January 1990): 14.

12. Ibid.

13. Bosch, *Transforming Mission,* 349–62.

14. Farley, *Theologia.*

15. Max Stackhouse, *Apologia: Contextualization, Globalization, and Mission in Theological Education* (Grand Rapids: Eerdmans, 1988).

16. Ibid.

17. Gerald H. Anderson, "Facing the Realities of the Contemporary World in Mission," in *Educating for Christian Missions,* ed. Arthur L. Walker Jr. (Nashville: Broadman Press, 1981), 50–51.

18. Nancy Gibbs, "Answers at Last," *Time*, 17 December 1990, 45.

19. Peter Steinfels, "Apathy Is Seen Toward Agony of the Homeless," *New York Times*, 20 January 1992, A1.

20. David Barrett, "Annual Statistical Table on Global Mission: 1992," *International Bulletin of Missionary Research* 16 (January 1992): 27.

21. Glenn Smith, "Reaching Canada's Cities for Christ," *Urban Mission* 8, no. 1 (September 1990): 33.

22. Lesslie Newbigin, *Foolishness to the Greeks* (Grand Rapids: Eerdmans, 1986); id., *The Gospel in a Pluralist Society* (Grand Rapids: Eerdmans, 1989).

23. Newbigin, *The Gospel in a Pluralistic Society*, 235.

24. Stackhouse, *Apologia*.

25. Harvie M. Conn, "Contextualization: Where Do We Begin?" in *Evangelicals and Liberation*, ed. Carl Armerding (Phillipsburg, N.J.: Presbyterian and Reformed Publishing Company, 1979), 90–91.

26. See Charles Kraft, *Christianity in Culture* (Maryknoll, N.Y.: Orbis Books, 1979); Louis Luzbetak, *The Church and Cultures* (Maryknoll, N.Y.: Orbis Books, 1988); John R. W. Stott and Robert T. Coote, eds., *Down to Earth: Studies in Christianity and Culture* (Grand Rapids: Eerdmans, 1980).

27. See David Hesselgrave, *Communicating Christ Cross-Culturally* (Grand Rapids: Zondervan, 1978).

28. William J. Larkin Jr., *Culture and Biblical Hermeneutics* (Grand Rapids: Baker Book House, 1988).

29. Harvie M. Conn, *Eternal Word and Changing Worlds: Theology, Anthropology, and Mission in Trialogue* (Grand Rapids: Zondervan Publishing House, 1984), 211–60.

30. Tite Tiénou, "Contextualization of Theology for Theological Education," in *Evangelical Theological Education Today: Agenda for Renewal*, ed. Paul Bowers (Nairobi: Evangel Publishing House, 1982), 42.

31. Ibid., 43.

32. Ibid., 48.

33. Don Browning, "Globalization and the Task of Theological Education in North America," *Theological Education* 23, no. 1 (autumn 1986), 43–44.

34. Jose Miguez-Bonino, "Global Solidarity and the Theological Curriculum," in *Global Solidarity in Theological Education: Report of the U.S./Canadian Consultation held at Trinity College, University of Toronto, Canada, 12–15 July, 1981*, ed. U.S./Canadian Consultation on Global Solidarity in Theological Education (Geneva: Programme on Theological Education, WCC, 1981), 22.

35. Noriel C. Capulong, "Globalization of Theological Education: From Whose Perspective?" *The Auburn News*, spring 1990, 1–4.

36. David Schuller, "Globalization in Theological Education: Summary and Analysis of Survey Data," *Theological Education* 22, no. 2 (spring 1986): 54.

37. S. Mark Heim, "Mapping Globalization for Theological Education," *Theological Education* 26, supp. 1 (spring 1990): 22–23.

38. James Cone, *A Black Theology of Liberation* (Maryknoll, N.Y.: Orbis Books, 1986).

39. Miguez-Bonino, "Global Solidarity," 22.

40. Bosch, *Transforming Mission*, 494–96.

41. Ibid., 496.

Chapter 2: Urbanization and Evangelism: A Global View

1. This and other material was delivered at Luther Seminary in Minneapolis on April 14, 1998, as part of the Aus Lecture Series, and appeared in *Word and World* 19 (summer 1999): 225–35.

2. Fredrick Norwood, *Strangers and Exiles: A History of Religious Refugees* (Nashville: Abingdon Press, 1969).

3. Martin Kähler, *Schriften zur Christologie und Mission* (1908; reprint, Munich: Chr. Kaiser, 1971), cited in David Bosch, *Transforming Mission: Paradigm Shifts in Theology of Mission* (Maryknoll, N.Y.: Orbis Books, 1991), 489.

4. Alice Baum and Donald Burnes, *A Nation in Denial: The Truth about Homelessness* (Boulder: Westview, 1993).

5. Martin Luther, *On the Councils and the Church (1539)*, in *Luther's Works*, vol. 41, ed. Eric W. Gritsch (Philadelphia: Fortress Press, 1966), 9–178.

6. Raymond J. Bakke, "Urban Evangelization: A Lausanne Strategy since 1980," *International Bulletin of Missionary Research* 8 (1984): 149–54.

Chapter 3: The Church and the City

1. Robert C. Linthicum, *City of God, City of Satan: A Biblical Theology of the Urban Church* (Grand Rapids: Zondervan, 1991), 17.

2. Harvey Cox, *The Secular City: Secularization and Urbanization in Theological Perspective* (London: SCM Press, 1966), 273.

3. Harvie M. Conn, "Genesis as Urban Prologue," in *Discipling the City: A Comprehensive Approach to Urban Ministry*, ed. Roger S. Greenway, 2d ed. (Grand Rapids: Baker Book House, 1992), 15.

4. Ann Witkower, "Latinos Bring New Flair to European Missions," *Christian Mission, A Journal of Foreign Missions*, summer 2001, 6.

5. Harvie M. Conn, *The American City and the Evangelical Church: A Historical Overview* (Grand Rapids: Baker Books, 1994), 11.

6. Ralph W. Christensen, "Church Renewal and the Kingdom of God" (unpublished paper, n.d.), 1.

7. Harvie M. Conn and Manuel Ortiz, *Urban Ministry: The Kingdom, the City and the People of God* (Downers Grove, Ill.: InterVarsity Press, 2001), 143.

8. David J. Bosch, *Witness to the World* (London: Marshall, Morgan and Scott, 1980), 248.

9. Edmund P. Clowney, *The Church*, Contours of Christian Theology (Downers Grove, Ill.: InterVarsity Press, 1995), 159–60.

10. Ibid., 161.

11. Harvie M. Conn, *A Clarified Vision for Urban Ministry* (Grand Rapids: Zondervan, 1987), 17.

12. Wayne A. Meeks, *The First Urban Christians: The Social World of the Apostle Paul* (New Haven: Yale University Press, 1983), 26.

13. Conn, *Clarified Vision*, 17.

14. Harvie M. Conn, unpublished notes, 1981, 3.

15. Ibid., 2.

16. Christensen, "Church Renewal," 12.

17. Charles H. Kraft, *Anthropology for Christian Witness* (Maryknoll, N.Y.: Orbis Books, 1996), xiii–xiv.

18. William A. Dyrness, *How Does America Hear the Gospel?* (Grand Rapids: Eerdmans, 1989), 5.

19. Raymond J. Bakke, *The Urban Christian: Effective Ministry in Today's Urban World* (Downers Grove, Ill.: InterVarsity Press, 1987), 9.

20. Francis M. DuBose, *How Churches Grow in an Urban World* (Nashville: Broadman Press, 1978), 110.

21. Allan Anderson, "A 'Failure to Love'? Western Missions and the Emergence of African Initiated Churches in the Twentieth Century," *Missiology* 29 (July 2001): 276.

22. Anderson, "Failure to Love," 276, quoting David Barrett, *Schism and Renewal in Africa: An Analysis of Six Thousand Contemporary Religious Movements* (Nairobi: Oxford University Press, 1968), 97, 154, 184.

23. Delia Nüesch-Olver, "Immigrant Clergy in the Promised Land," *Missiology* 29 (April 2001): 185–200.

24. Ibid., 187–88.

25. John Stott, ed., *Making Christ Known: Historic Mission Documents from the Lausanne Movement, 1974–1989* (Grand Rapids: Eerdmans, 1996), 28.

26. Conn and Ortiz, *Urban Ministry,* 65.

Chapter 4: The Social Sciences: Tools for Urban Ministry

1. Robert Pastor, "The Impact of U.S. Immigration Policy on Caribbean Emigration: Does It Matter?" in *The Caribbean Exodus,* ed. Barry B. Levine (New York: Praeger, 1987), 253.

2. Paulo Freire, *Pedagogy of the Oppressed,* trans. Myra Bergman Ramos (New York: Continuum, 1989).

3. Charles H. Kraft, *Anthropology for Christian Witness* (Maryknoll, N.Y.: Orbis Books, 1996), 52.

4. Paul G. Hiebert and Eloise Hiebert Meneses, *Incarnational Ministry: Planting Churches in Band, Tribal, Peasant, and Urban Societies* (Grand Rapids: Baker Books, 1995), 42.

5. Harvie M. Conn, *Eternal Word and Changing Worlds: Theology, Anthropology, and Mission in Trialogue* (Grand Rapids: Zondervan, 1984), 318–19.

6. Kraft, *Anthropology,* 55 (emphasis in original).

7. Ibid., 56 (emphasis in original).

8. Paul G. Hiebert, *Cultural Anthropology,* 2d ed. (Grand Rapids: Baker Book House, 1983), 356.

9. Kraft, *Anthropology,* 57 (emphasis in original).

10. Ibid., 68–106.

11. Hiebert and Meneses, *Incarnational Ministry,* 313–20.

12. Conn, *Eternal Word,* 196–97.

13. Hiebert and Meneses, *Incarnational Ministry,* 373.

14. Ibid., 261.

15. Rudy Mitchell, *Studying Urban Communities* (Boston: Emmanuel Gospel Center, 1994).

16. David J. Hesselgrave and Edward Rommen, *Contextualization: Meanings, Methods, and Models* (Grand Rapids: Baker Book House, 1989), 200.

17. Louis J. Luzbetak, *The Church and Cultures: New Perspectives in Missiological Anthropology* (Maryknoll, N.Y.: Orbis Books, 1988), 69.

18. Hesselgrave and Rommen, *Contextualization*, 31.

19. Edmund P. Clowney, *The Church*, Contours of Christian Theology (Downers Grove, Ill.: InterVarsity Press, 1995), 177.

20. Lesslie Newbigin, *The Gospel in a Pluralist Society* (Grand Rapids: Eerdmans, 1989), 151.

21. J. D. Douglas, ed., *Let the Earth Hear His Voice* (Minneapolis: World Wide, 1975), 1216–23, as quoted in Conn, *Eternal Word*, 176.

22. Kraft, *Anthropology*, 376.

23. Robert C. Linthicum, *City of God, City of Satan: A Biblical Theology of the Urban Church* (Grand Rapids: Zondervan, 1991).

24. Ibid., 235.

25. Ibid., 265.

26. Harvie M. Conn, *Evangelism: Doing Justice and Preaching Grace* (Grand Rapids: Zondervan, 1982), 57.

27. Harvie M. Conn and Manuel Ortiz, *Urban Ministry: The Kingdom, the City and the People of God* (Downers Grove, Ill.: InterVarsity Press, 2001).

Chapter 5: Missions and the Doing of Theology

1. Harvie M. Conn, *Eternal Word and Changing Worlds: Theology, Anthropology, and Mission in Trialogue* (Grand Rapids: Zondervan, 1984).

2. Larry Laudin, *Progress and Its Problems: Towards a Theory of Scientific Growth* (Berkeley: University of California Press, 1977).

3. J. Andrew Kirk, *What Is Mission?* (Philadelphia: Fortress Press, 2000), 18–19.

4. Millard J. Erickson, *Christian Theology* (Grand Rapids: Baker Book House, 1986).

5. For instance, B. B. Warfield, in *The Right of Systematic Theology* (Edinburgh: T. and T. Clark, 1897), made systematic theology and scientific theology synonymous. For him, there can be but one theology.

6. Thomas N. Finger, *Christian Theology: An Eschatological Approach,* vol. 1 (Scottdale, Pa.: Herald Press, 1985), 18–21. Systematic theology is based on the resurgence of Platonic realism that gave rise to Scholasticism and later the humanistic school of Erasmus, culminating in the Enlightenment. For a historical summary of its emergence, see Daniel P. Fuller, "Biblical Theology and the Analogy of Faith," *International Journal of Frontier Missions* 14 (1997): 65–74. See also G. R. Evans, A. E. McGrath, and A. D. Gallway, *The Science of Theology* (Grand Rapids: Eerdmans, 1986), particularly pp. 62–173.

7. Mark Young, "Theological Approaches to Some Perpetual Problems in Theological Education," *Christian Education Journal*, n.s., 2, no. 1 (spring 1998): 78–79.

8. An algorithm is a formal, logical process which, if carried out correctly, produces the right answer. Algorithmic logic is sometimes called "machine" logic because it is the basis on which calculators and computers work and can be done faster and more accurately by these than by people.

9. Finger, *Christian Theology*, 1:19, tells us that Peter Lombard founded systematic theology when he sought to disengage key theological questions from their original biblical contexts and to arrange them in a logical sequence of their own that would provide a comprehensive, coherent, and synthetically consistent account of all the major issues of Christian faith and demonstrate the rational credibility of Christian faith. Evans, McGrath, and Gallway, *Science of Theology*, 71, 132, indicate

that Lombard's *Sentences,* written in the 1140s, provided the form for much of later Medieval and Reformation theology.

10. Some argue that there is no biblical worldview, but only a series of world-views in biblical history. This is to argue that there is no deep, underlying unity and coherence in Scripture. Surface cultures change rapidly over time, but the deep cognitive, affective, and evaluative assumptions underlying them often persist for centuries. We argue, for example, that our modern worldview has its roots in Greek and Roman thought and in the Bible. Worldviews are these enduring themes that persist with variation over long periods of time. In the Old Testament, God prepared a people through whom he could send his Son. In it, he also prepared a worldview that could adequately comprehend and communicate the gospel. He started with Abram and his pagan worldview, but taught him about the nature of God by revealing himself not just as *el,* but as a unique and distinct *el*—as *El Elyon, El Olam,* and *El Shaddai.* Later he revealed himself to Moses and the people of Israel as *Yahweh* and to the prophets as the coming Messiah. Similarly, he took the ideas of sin, sacrifice, forgiveness, and peace and gave them new meaning in the emerging Hebrew worldview. When the people and their understandings of God were ready, God revealed himself fully in Jesus Christ, who must be understood in the light of that worldview.

11. Eugene Peterson, *Leap over a Wall: Earthly Spirituality for Everyday Christians* (San Francisco: Harper San Francisco, 1997), 185.

12. Western systematic theology was a product of Western intellectual history. Calvin, Luther, and their successors not only appealed to *sola Scriptura,* but also used logic, rhetoric, and other methods to shape their theologies. In so doing, they allowed Scholasticism in through the back door. G. Ebeling, in *Word and Faith* (London: SCM, 1963), 82–83, notes:

> What was the relation of the systematic method here [in the post-Reformation period] to the exegetical method? Ultimately it was the same as in medieval scholasticism. There, too, exegesis of holy scripture went on not only within systematic theology but also separately alongside of it, yet so that the possibility of a tension between exegesis and systematic theology was *a priori* excluded. Exegesis was enclosed within the frontiers fixed by systematic theology.

Western philosophical and scientific methods use abstract logic based on digital (well-formed Euclidian) sets and interval numerics. Christians in other parts of the world use fuzzy logic based on analogical (fuzzy) sets and ratio numerics (cf. Paul G. Hiebert, *Anthrolopological Reflections on Missiological Issues* [Grand Rapids: Baker Book House, 1994], 107–36). Others use concrete functional logic. For example, in Africa one central theological question is What are the ultimate relationships in the cosmos? This question is reflected in African worldviews and philosophies: "Things stand in relation to one another by a *union* and *ofica.*" Meaning in many African philosophies is gained not by understanding a logical progression, but by grasping the relation of the parts to the whole. Each system of logic is internally consistent and rational.

13. In the free church tradition, the doing of theology is the task of the church as a hermeneutical community, not of experts who make the final decisions. The

priesthood of all believers is a radical doctrine, and one can argue that the Reformation is only now seeing the full implementation of its fundamental premises. The involvement of all Christians in Bible study and interpretation does not reject the importance of experts in various fields, who bring deep insights into the understanding of Scripture. It does mean that theologizing is the ongoing task of the church as it seeks to understand what God is saying to it in its particular contexts. Moreover, it is the task of the leaders to facilitate and formulate the community consensus. We see this process at work in Acts 15, where James summarizes the debate over the admission of Gentiles into the church.

Today the theological dialogue is becoming increasingly global. Theologians in one part of the world can help those in other parts of the world see their own cultural and historical biases, and to read Scripture with fresh eyes. This dialogue is not easy, for it involves not only new answers given to old questions, but also the doing of philosophical theology in new ways. Theologians around the world are asking different questions, employing different categories, and using different logics. This raises the need for a metatheology, a theology on how to do theology that is rooted in Scripture, guided by the Holy Spirit, and done by the church seeking to follow its Lord.

14. Finger, *Christian Theology*, 1:20–21.

15. J. I. Packer, "What Is Evangelism?" in *Theological Perspectives on Church Growth*, ed. Harvie Conn (Nutley, N.J.: Presbyterian and Reformed Publishing Company, 1977), 91.

16. This disappearance of moral curriculum is most evident in modern American universities. In 1896, Maine Agricultural College, which became the University of Maine the next year, defined its task as: "It shall be the duty of Trustees, Directors and Teachers of the College to impress upon the minds of the students, the principles of morality and justice, and a sacred regard for truth; love of their country; humanity and universal benevolence; sobriety, frugality, chastity, moderation and temperance, and all other virtues that are ornaments of human society." Today this sounds archaic. Universities are no longer known for teaching "sobriety, frugality, chastity, and temperance."

17. Evans, McGrath, and Gallway, *Science of Theology*, 170–71.

18. We use the term "plot" here in the way that Paul speaks of the "mystery" now revealed to us (Rom. 16:25; Eph. 1:9; 3:3; 6:19; Col. 1:26). That is, there is real history that is moving in a direction, and it is part of a cosmic drama that gives it meaning. That drama is the story of God creating a perfect world, redeeming the lost who turn in faith to him, and restoring creation to perfection in which all will bow before Christ the Lord in his eternal kingdom.

19. D. A. Carson, "'Worship the Lord Your God': The Perennial Challenge," in *Worship: Adoration and Action*, ed. D. A. Carson (Grand Rapids: Baker Book House, 1993), 16.

20. Michael Oleksa, "Introduction," in *Alaskan Missionary Spirituality*, ed. Michael Oleksa (New York: Paulist Press, 1987), 14.

21. Doxology is not absent from Western systematic theology. Geoffrey Wainwright authored a textbook entitled *Doxology: The Praise of God in Worship, Doctrine, and Life: A Systematic Theology* (New York: Oxford University Press, 1980), with the purpose of seeking a "liturgical way of doing theology." However, the doxological dimension of theology is not a major concern in much of systematic theology.

22. Christopher A. Hall, "'Augustine Who?' A Window on the Greek Christian World," review of *The Bible in Greek Christian Antiquity*, ed. by Paul M. Blowers, *Christianity Today*, 18 May 1998, 67.

23. Martin Kähler, *Schriften zur Christologie und Mission* (Munich: Chr. Kaiser Verlag, 1971), 190, cited in David J. Bosch, *Transforming Mission: Paradigm Shifts in Theology of Mission* (Maryknoll, N.Y.: Orbis Books, 1991), 16.

24. Bosch, *Transforming Mission*, 124.

25. Unlike French law based on the Napoleonic Code, which is unable to deal adequately with the changing times, British law is able to apply unchanging principles to ever-changing situations.

26. See A. Grunbaum, "Complementarity in Quantum Physics and Its Philosophical Generalizations," *Journal of Philosophy* 54 (1957): 713–27; D. M. MacKay, "Complementarity in Scientific and Theological Studies," *Zygon* 9 (1974): 225–44.

27. Gerhard Hasel, "The Relationship Between Biblical Theology and Systematic Theology," *Trinity Journal* 5 (August 1984): 127.

28. It is this kind of dialogue that Harvie Conn initiated in his pioneer work, *Eternal Word and Changing Worlds* (1984).

29. Rodger C. Bassham, "Mission Theology: 1948–1975," *Occasional Bulletin of Missionary Research* 4 (April 1980): 58.

Chapter 6: New Patterns for Interdependence in Mission

1. Harvie M. Conn, *A Clarified Vision for Urban Mission* (Grand Rapids: Zondervan, 1987), 9.

2. Viv Grigg, *Companion to the Poor* (Monrovia, Calif.: MARC, 1990).

3. John Stott, ed., *Making Christ Known: Historic Mission Documents from the Lausanne Movement, 1974–1989* (Grand Rapids: Eerdmans, 1996), 33 (par. 8).

4. Ibid.

5. Ibid., 33 (par. 9).

6. Ibid.

7. Ibid., 33–34 (par. 9).

8. Larry Pate, *From Every People* (Monrovia, Calif.: MARC, 1989), 5.

9. Ibid., 19.

10. Ted Limpic, *Catálogo de organizaciones misioneras iberoamericanas* (Miami: Comibam, 1997), 191.

11. Howard A. Snyder, *Signs of the Spirit* (Grand Rapids: Zondervan, 1989).

12. COMLA, *Memorias del COMLA-4* (Lima: Ed. Paulinas, 1991), 267.

13. Jonathan J. Bonk, *Missions and Money* (Maryknoll, N.Y.: Orbis Books, 1991), 4–7.

14. Ibid., 4.

15. David Barrett, "Silver and Gold Have I None: Church of the Poor or Church of the Rich?" *International Bulletin of Missionary Research* 7 (October 1983): 147–48.

16. Ibid., 148.

17. Ibid.

18. Ibid.

19. David Stoll, *Is Latin America Turning Protestant?* (Berkeley: University of California Press, 1990); David Martin, *Tongues of Fire: The Explosion of Protestantism in Latin America* (Cambridge: Basil Blackwell, 1990).

20. *Latinamerica Press*, 29 June 1989, 2.

21. Franz Damen, "Las sectas: ¿Avalancha o desafio?" in *Cuarto intermedio, Cochabamba,* May 1987, 54.

22. Samuel Escobar, "Biblical Basis for Intercultural Ministries: A Latino Perspective," in *Missions Within Reach,* ed. Enoch Wan (Kowloon, Hong Kong: China Alliance Press, 1995).

23. F. F. Bruce, *Paul: Apostle of the Free Spirit* (Exeter: Paternoster Press, 1977), 319.

24. Paul Minear, *The Obedience of Faith: The Purposes of Paul in the Epistle to the Romans* (London: SCM Press, 1971), 3.

25. Ibid.

26. Leon Morris, *The Epistle to the Romans* (Leicester: InterVarsity Press, 1988), 520.

27. Franz J. Leenhardt, *The Epistle to the Romans: A Commentary* (London: Lutterworth, 1961), 370.

28. C. K. Barrett, *A Commentary on the Second Epistle to the Corinthians* (New York: Harper, 1973), 226–27.

29. Philip E. Hughes, *The Second Epistle to the Corinthians,* New International Commentary on the New Testament (Grand Rapids: Eerdmans, 1962), 310.

30. David Barrett, "Silver and Gold," 151.

31. C. K. Barrett, *A Commentary on the Second Epistle,* 222.

32. Ibid., 222–23.

33. Hughes, *The Second Epistle to the Corinthians,* 288.

34. Harvie M. Conn, ed., *Planting and Growing Urban Churches* (Grand Rapids: Baker Book House, 1997).

35. Grigg, *Companion to the Poor.*

Chapter 7: Diversity in Mission and Theology

1. Philip Gleason, "Melting Pot Redux," *Books and Culture,* July–August 1999, 10.

2. Robert J. Schreiter, *The New Catholicity: Theology Between the Global and the Local* (Maryknoll, N.Y.: Orbis Books, 1997), 35. See also his earlier work, *Constructing Local Theologies* (Maryknoll, N.Y.: Orbis Books, 1985).

3. Michael Buckley, *At the Origins of Modern Atheism* (New Haven: Yale University Press, 1987), 358.

4. James Turner, "Secular Justification of Christian Truth Claims: A Historical Sketch," in *American Apostasy: The Triumph of Another Gospel,* ed. R. J. Neuhaus (Grand Rapids: Eerdmans, 1989), 15. See my discussion of these mistakes in William A. Dyrness, *The Earth Is God's: A Theology of American Culture* (Maryknoll, N.Y.: Orbis Books, 1997), 60.

5. See Nathan Hatch, *The Democratization of American Religion* (New Haven: Yale University Press, 1989).

6. Dean M. Kelley, *Why Conservative Churches Are Growing: A Study in Sociology of Religion* (New York: Harper & Row, 1972).

7. This view is associated most closely with Rodney Stark and L. R. Iannaccone. See L. R. Iannaccone, "Why Strict Churches Are Strong," *American Journal of Sociology* 99 (1994): 1180–211. Stark applied this theory to the growth of the early church in *Conversion to Christianity* (New York: Harper, 1994).

8. The new paradigm is best set forth in R. Steven Warner, "Work in Progress Toward a New Paradigm for the Sociological Study of Religion in the United States," *American Journal of Sociology* 98 (1993): 1060. See also Robert D. Woodberry and Christian S. Smith, "Fundamentalism et al.: Conservative Protestants in America," *Annual Review of Sociology* 24 (1998): 49–50.

9. Christian Smith, *American Evangelicalism: Embattled and Thriving* (Chicago: University of Chicago Press, 1998), 118–19.

10. Avery Dulles, "Orthodoxy and Social Change," *America* 178 (20–27 June 1998): 16.

11. John V. Taylor, *The Primal Vision: Christian Presence amid African Religion* (London: SCM, 1963), 122.

12. Kwabena Damuah, Ph.D. diss., Howard University, 1971, quoted in Kwame Bediako, *Christianity in Africa: The Renewal of a Non-Western Religion* (Maryknoll, N.Y.: Orbis Books, 1995), 25.

13. See Charles Taylor, *Multiculturalism and the Politics of Recognition* (Princeton: Princeton University Press, 1992).

14. See Nathan Glazer's poignant description of this dilemma in relation to the New York City school system in his chapter entitled "Just How Much 'One Nation' Are We as Against 'Many Peoples'?" in *We Are All Multiculturalists Now* (Cambridge: Harvard University Press, 1997), 26.

15. Anthony Appiah, "The Multi-Culturalist Misunderstanding," *The New York Review of Books,* 9 October 1997, 31–32.

16. See, for example, Glazer, *We Are All Multiculturalists Now.*

17. Appiah, "Multi-Culturalist Misunderstanding," 36.

18. See G. W. Hansen, "Galatians, Letter To," in *Dictionary of Paul and His Letters,* ed. Gerald Hawthorne, Ralph Martin, and Daniel Reid (Downers Grove, Ill.: InterVarsity Press, 1993), 332.

19. Roman Catholic missiologists discussed these issues during the 1960s in terms of what they called "indigenization." But Protestants began to speak of this as "contextualization" only during the 1970s. See Charles H. Kraft, *Christianity in Culture* (Maryknoll, N.Y.: Orbis Books, 1979), and the collection of papers edited by John R. W. Stott and Robert T. Coote entitled *Down to Earth: Studies in Christianity and Culture* (Grand Rapids: Eerdmans, 1980).

20. The first chapter begins, "Behold, how good and how pleasant it is for brethren to dwell together in unity!" (Ps. 133:1 KJV). Dietrich Bonhoeffer, *Life Together,* trans. John W. Doberstein (London: SCM, 1954), 7.

21. Dietrich Bonhoeffer, "Prayerbook of the Bible," in *Dietrich Bonhoeffer, Works,* vol. 5, *Life Together and Prayerbook of the Bible,* ed. Geffrey B. Kelly (Minneapolis: Fortress Press, 1996), quoted in David Ford, *Self and Salvation: Being Transformed* (Cambridge: Cambridge University Press, 1999), 251.

22. Bonhoeffer spells this out more carefully in *Christ the Center,* trans. John Bowden (New York: Harper and Row, 1966).

23. Ford, *Self and Salvation,* 251.

24. Ann M. Simmons, "Tribal Strife Is Set Aside for Survival in Burundi," *Los Angeles Times,* 24 October 1999, A18.

25. Bonhoeffer, *Life Together,* 31.

26. Ford, *Self and Salvation,* 99.

27. Bonhoeffer, *Christ the Center,* 59.

28. Cf. John Durham Peters, "Dialogue's Supposed Moral Nobility Can Suffocate Those Who Prefer Not to Play Along," in his book *Speaking into the Air: A History of the Idea of Communication* (Chicago: University of Chicago Press, 1999), 159.

29. The phrase is from F. LeRon Shultz, "'Holding On' to the Theology-Psychology Relationship: The Underlying Fiduciary Structures of Interdisciplinary Method," *Journal of Psychology and Theology* 25 (1997): 329–40. Shultz, quoting James Loder, argues that this reflects the dual nature of Christ, rather than, as we are arguing, the work of Christ in breaking down barriers: "The logic of Chalcedon provides us with the relationality needed to relate God's self-revelation to God's creation" (p. 337).

30. United Nations Development Project, *Overview of the Human Development Report for 1998*, 1.

31. Mark Arax, Mary Curtius, and Soraya Sarhaddi Nelson, "California Income Gap Grows amid Prosperity," *Los Angeles Times*, 9 January 2000, A1, A16. The figures are from a study done by the California Policy Institute.

Chapter 8: Generational Appropriateness in Contextualization

1. R. Daniel Shaw, "Contextualizing the Power and the Glory," *International Journal of Frontier Missions* 12 (1995): 159.

2. See Charles M. Kraft, *Communication Theory for Christian Witness*, rev. ed. (Maryknoll, N.Y.: Orbis Books, 1991).

3. Darrell L. Whiteman, "Contextualization, the Theory, the Gap, the Challenge," *Missiology* 25 (1997): 3–4.

4. Eugene A. Nida, *Customs and Cultures* (Pasadena: Wm. Carey Library, 1954), 52.

5. Alan R. Tippett, *Introduction to Missiology* (Pasadena: Wm. Carey Library, 1987), 200.

6. See C. Peter Wagner and Pablo Deiros, *The Rising Revival: What the Spirit Is Saying Through the Argentine Revival* (Ventura, Calif.: Gospel Light, 1998).

Chapter 9: The Church and Justice in Crisis

1. Walter Brueggemann, *The Prophetic Imagination* (Philadelphia: Fortress Press, 1978), 88.

2. These are "bonded slaves," according to Brueggemann, *The Prophetic Imagination*, 83.

3. This is probably a reference to the year of Jubilee, when debts were cancelled and lands were restored every fiftieth year. For more information, see John Howard Yoder, *The Politics of Jesus* (Grand Rapids: Eerdmans, 1972); Robert B. Sloan Jr., *The Favorable Year of the Lord: A Study of Jubilary Theology in the Gospel of Luke* (Austin: Schola Press, 1978).

4. Jonathan Z. Smith, "Word (in traditional religions), power of," in *HarperCollins Dictionary of Religion*, ed. Jonathan Z. Smith (San Francisco: HarperCollins, 1996), 1139.

5. Gerhard Friedrich, "*euangelizomai*," in *Theological Dictionary of the New Testament*, vol. 2, ed. Gerhard Kittel, trans. Geoffrey W. Bromiley (Grand Rapids: Eerdmans, 1964), 708–9.

6. Lowell Livezey, lecture to students and staff of the Chicago Metropolitan Center, 24 March 2000.

7. Important discussions of social capital can be found in James S. Coleman, "Social Capital in the Creation of Human Capital," *American Journal of Sociology* 94, supp. (1988): S95–S119; Robert D. Putnam, "Bowling Alone: America's Declining Social Capital," *Journal of Democracy* 6 (January 1995): 65–76.

8. Ronald F. Ferguson and William T. Dickens, "Introduction," in *Urban Problems and Community Development*, ed. Ronald F. Ferguson and William T. Dickens (Washington: Brookings Institution, 1999), 5.

9. Ibid.

10. Putnam, "Bowling Alone," 67.

11. Dieter Hessel, *Social Ministry* (Louisville: Westminster/John Knox Press, 1992), 145ff.

12. C. Wright Mills, *The Sociological Imagination* (New York: Grove Press, 1959), 8.

13. See John P. Kretzmann and John McKnight, *Building Communities from the Inside Out: A Path Toward Finding and Mobilizing a Community's Assets* (Evanston, Ill.: Center for Urban Affairs and Policy Research, Northwestern University, 1993).

14. John McKnight, *The Careless Society: Community and Its Counterfeits* (New York: Basic Books, 1995), 139. See also John McKnight, "Professionalized Service as Disabling Help," in *Disabling Professions*, ed. John McKnight, Ivan Illich, Jonathan Caplan, and Harley Sharken (London: Marion Boyers, 1978).

15. Abraham Kuyper, *The Problem of Poverty*, ed. James W. Skillen (Grand Rapids: Baker Book House, 1991), 77.

16. Ibid., 51.

17. For other theological treatments of justice, see Reinhold Niehbuhr, *Love and Justice: Selections from the Shorter Writings of Reinhold Niehbuhr* (Louisville: Westminster/John Knox Press, 1978); Emil Brunner, *Justice and the Social Order* (London: Lutterworth Press, 1947); Paul Tillich, *Love, Power, and Justice* (New York: Oxford University Press, 1954).

18. See Roland Allen, *Missionary Methods: St. Paul's or Ours* (Chicago: Moody Press, 1959).

19. John Perkins, *A Quiet Revolution: The Christian Response to Human Need, A Strategy for Today* (Waco: Word, 1976), 221.

20. Shirley Jackson Case, *The Social Origins of Christianity* (Chicago: University of Chicago, 1923); id., *The Social Triumph of the Ancient Church* (New York: Harper and Row, 1933).

21. Wayne A. Meeks, *The First Urban Christians: The Social World of the Apostle Paul* (New Haven: Yale University Press, 1983).

22. This theme is developed well by Keith F. Nickle, *The Collection: A Study in Paul's Strategy*, Studies in Biblical Theology (Naperville, Ill.: Alec R. Allenson, 1966).

23. Charles Dickens, "The Frozen Out Poor Law," *All the Year Round: A Weekly Journal*, n.d., 446–49.

24. Shel Trapp in *Disclosure: The National Newspaper of Neighborhoods* (Chicago: National Training and Information Center), January 2000, 3.

25. Merrill Goozner, "Study Finds Urban Areas Lag in Trimming Welfare Cases: Illinois Among the Worst in States Faltering in Task to Cut Load," *Chicago Tribune*, 19 February 1999, North Sports Final edition, 8.

26. Gerd Theissen, *The Social Setting of Pauline Christianity: Essays on Corinth* (Philadelphia: Fortress Press, 1982), 35ff.

27. Evangelicals are slowly warming up to community organizing. See Marilyn Stranke, *Christians Supporting Community Organizing: A New Voice for Change Among Evangelical, Holiness and Pentecostal Christians* (Los Angeles: Center for Religion and Civic Culture, University of Southern California, 1999).

28. Walter Wink, *Naming the Powers: The Language of Power in the New Testament* (Philadelphia: Fortress Press, 1984), and subsequent volumes on the powers.

29. William Stringfellow, "Traits of the Principalities," in *A Keeper of the Word: Selected Writings of William Stringfellow,* ed. Bill Wylie Kellerman (Grand Rapids: Eerdmans, 1994), 205.

30. Saul David Alinsky, *Rules for Radicals* (New York: Random House, 1971), 52.

31. Michael Lerner, *The Politics of Meaning* (Menlo Park, Calif.: Addison-Wesley, 1996), 52ff.

32. Ibid., 53.

33. Presentation to students and staff of the Chicago Metropolitan Center, 10 March 2000.

34. Stanley Hauerwas and William H. Willimon, *Resident Aliens* (Nashville: Abingdon Press, 1989).

35. This is explicated by Jack L. Stotts, *Shalom: The Search for a Peaceable City* (Nashville: Abingdon Press, 1972); George W. Webber, *Today's Church: A Community of Exiles and Pilgrims* (Nashville: Abingdon Press, 1979); Bruce W. Winter, *Seek the Welfare of the City: Christians as Benefactors and Citizens* (Grand Rapids: Eerdmans, 1994).

36. For contemporary evangelical statements, see Jim Wallis, *The Soul of Politics* (Maryknoll, N.Y.: Orbis Books, 1993), and Ronald J. Sider, *Just Generosity* (Grand Rapids: Baker Book House, 2000).

37. Abraham Kuyper, *Lectures on Calvinism* (Grand Rapids: Eerdmans, 1994), 31.

Chapter 10: Doing the Word: Biblical Holism and Urban Ministry

1. David J. Hesselgrave, "Redefining Holism," *Evangelical Missions Quarterly* 35 (July 1999): 278–84; Bryant L. Myers, "Another Look at 'Holistic Mission,'" *Evangelical Missions Quarterly* 35 (July 1999): 285–87.

2. Harvie M. Conn, *Evangelism: Doing Justice and Preaching Grace* (Grand Rapids: Zondervan, 1982).

3. One of the earliest must be Harvie M. Conn, "Can I Be Spiritual and at the Same Time Human?" *The Other Side* 9, no. 5 (September–October 1973), 16–19, 42–47.

4. Harvie M. Conn and Manuel Ortiz, *Urban Ministry: The Kingdom, the City and the People of God* (Downers Grove, Ill.: InterVarsity Press, 2001).

5. Vinay Samuel and Chris Sugden, eds., *Mission as Transformation: A Theology of the Whole Gospel* (Oxford: Regnum, 1999).

6. Roger S. Greenway, *Together Again: Kinship of Word and Deed* (Monrovia, Calif.: MARC, 1998).

7. See Phillip Cary, *Augustine's Influence on the Inner Self: The Legacy of a Christian Platonist* (Oxford: Oxford University Press, 2000).

8. George M. Marsden, *Fundamentalism and American Culture: The Shaping of Twentieth-Century Evangelicalism: 1870–1925* (New York: Oxford University Press, 1980), 86.

9. For the reasons, see Christian Smith, *American Evangelicalism: Embattled and Thriving* (Chicago: University of Chicago Press, 1998), 86.

10. Wilbert R. Shenk, "The Whole Is Greater Than the Sum of the Parts: Moving Beyond Word and Deed," *Missiology* 20 (January 1993): 67.

11. Andrew F. Walls, *The Missionary Movement in Christian History: Studies in the Transmission of Faith* (Maryknoll, N.Y.: Orbis Books, 1996), 83.

12. William Julius Wilson, *When Work Disappears: The World of the New Urban Poor* (New York: Knopf, 1996), 159–60.

13. Smith, *American Evangelicalism*, 187–203.

14. Manuel Ortiz, "Who Are They Talking About?" *The Banner*, 28 August 2000, 27–28.

15. See Conn and Ortiz, *Urban Ministry*, 116–37.

16. The benchmark study in this regard is John Howard Yoder, *The Politics of Jesus: Vicit Agnus Noster*, 2d ed. (Grand Rapids: Eerdmans, 1994), 28–75.

17. On the place of the Spirit, see Matthias Wenk, *Community-Forming Power: The Socio-Ethical Role of the Spirit in Luke-Acts* (Sheffield: Sheffield Academic Press, 2000).

18. Herman Ridderbos, *The Coming of the Kingdom* (Philadelphia: Presbyterian and Reformed Publishing Company, 1962), 68.

19. Jürgen Moltmann, *The Way of Jesus Christ: Christology in Messianic Dimensions*, trans. Margaret Kohl (Minneapolis: Fortress Press, 1993), 98–99.

20. Joel Green, *The Gospel of Luke*, New International Commentary on the New Testament (Grand Rapids: Eerdmans, 1997), 520–26. For what an African Pentecostal reading of this text might look like, see Ogbu U. Kalu, "The Third Response: Pentecostalism and the Reconstruction of Christian Experience in Africa, 1970–1995," *Journal of African Christian Thought* 1, no. 2 (December 1998): 12.

21. Green, *Gospel of Luke*, 522.

22. Ibid., 523.

23. Ibid., 524.

24. Ibid., 525.

25. See Albert Tizon, "Understanding Deeds as Proclamation in the Missional Task of the Church: A Luke-Acts Guide," *Phronésis* 7, no. 1 (2000): 35–51.

26. Shenk, "The Whole Is Greater," 74.

27. See the provocative essay by Stanley Hauerwas, "Worship, Evangelism, Ethics: On Eliminating the 'And,'" in his book, *A Better Hope: Resources for a Church Confronting Capitalism, Democracy, and Postmodernity* (Grand Rapids: Brazon, 2000), 155–62.

28. Mark Strom, *Reframing Paul: Conversations in Grace and Community* (Downers Grove, Ill.: InterVarsity Press, 2000).

29. For a larger presentation, see Mark R. Gornik, *To Live in Peace: Biblical Faith and the Changing Inner City* (Grand Rapids: Eerdmans, forthcoming).

30. Gerhard Lohfink, *Jesus and Community: The Social Dimension of the Christian Faith* (Philadelphia: Fortress Press, 1984).

31. Ibid., 172–73.

32. Ibid., 173.

33. Nationally, many neighborhoods are facing this problem, which is creating real tension. For one view of this, see Michelle Cottle, "Boomerang," *The New Republic*, 7 May 2001, 26–29.

34. I am grateful to Allan Tibbels for his comments on this essay and to Sue Baker and Manny Ortiz for their patience.

Chapter 11: Jesus' Words to the Canaanite Woman: Another Perspective

1. Amy-Jill Levine, *The Social and Ethnic Dimensions of Matthean Social History* (Lewiston, N.Y.: Edwin Mellen Press, 1988), 59.

2. David Bosch, *Transforming Mission: Paradigm Shifts in Theology of Mission* (Maryknoll, N.Y.: Orbis Books, 1991), 57. This school reads Matthew as a gospel on discipleship and sees the outline of the book built around the five major discourses. They see an attempt on the part of the author to present Jesus as the new Moses with his new Pentateuch. See Francis Wright Beare, *The Gospel According to Matthew* (Oxford: Blackwell, 1981), and John P. Meier, *Matthew*, New Testament Message (Dublin: Veritas, 1980). The internal structure that would justify the division of Matthew into five discourses is the use of the phrase "And when Jesus finished these sayings" and its variations to mark the end of each discourse. Accordingly, Meier divides Matthew as follows (p. xii):

1–2	Introductory Infancy Narrative	
5:1–7:28	The Sermon on the Mount	discourse 1
10:1–11:1	The Missionary Discourse	discourse 2
13:1–53	The Parables	discourse 3
18:1–19:1	The Church Life Discourse	discourse 4
24:1–26:1	The Discourse on the End	discourse 5
26:2–28	The Climax—The Death-Resurrection	

3. This second school of scholars—see Jack Dean Kingsbury, *Matthew: Structure, Christology, Kingdom* (Minneapolis: Fortress Press, 1975); Augustine Stock, *The Method and Message of Matthew* (Collegeville, Minn.: Liturgical Press, 1996)—divides the gospel into three sections. For this school, the phrase "from that time on" marks the "beginning of a new phase in the life of Jesus" (Kingsbury, *Matthew*, 8). Using this criterion, Matthew's gospel is structured in the following manner:

1:1–4:16	Prologue
4:17–16:20	The Proclamation of Jesus the Messiah
16:21–28:20	The Suffering, Death, and Resurrection of Jesus the Messiah

This structure is found in B. Rod Doyle, "Matthew's Intention as Discerned by His Structure," *Revue biblique* 95 (1988): 34–54.

4. Robert Gundry, *Matthew: A Commentary on His Literary and Theological Art* (Grand Rapids: Eerdmans, 1982), 10.

5. Levine, *Social and Ethnic Dimensions*, 155, marks off the passage from 13:53 to 16:13 for similar reasons.

6. Frederick Dale Bruner, *Matthew, A Commentary*, vol. 2 (Dallas: Word Publishers, 1990), 520. Also see Meier, *Matthew*, 158, and Elaine Mary Wainwright, *Towards a Feminist Critical Reading of the Gospel According to Matthew* (New York: Walter de Gruyter, 1991), 217.

7. Lucien Cerfaux, "La section des pains: (Mc vi, 31–viii, 26; Mt xiv, 13–xvi, 12)," *Recueil Lucien Cerfaux I* (Gembloux: Editions J. Duculot, 1954), 471–85. See also Wainwright, *Towards a Feminist Critical Reading*, 100.

8. Doyle, "Matthew's Intention," 44. It should be noted that each of these authors is referring to a narrower passage in Matthew. They begin with 14:13 and end at 16:12.

9. There are nineteen references to bread or loaves. Matthew 15:27 speaks of crumbs. The other references to bread are in the temptation story (4:3–4), Jesus' teaching on prayer (6:11; 7:9), David's taking the bread of the presence (12:4), and the Lord's Supper (26:26).

10. We have taken the chiastic structure from Wainwright, *Towards a Feminist Critical Reading*, 100, and added the two sections in bold print.

11. "Dermience, in her article 'Péricope,' in which she provides an excellent analysis of this pericope from the perspective of redaction criticism, comments on Matthew's use of 'and' at the beginning of the pericope instead of 'but' which is found at the beginning of the Markan pericope. She gives as the reason for the change: 'To tie the story of the Canaanite woman to that which precedes it'"— Wainwright, *Towards a Feminist Critical Reading*, 100 (my translation). See also Gundry, *Matthew*, 310.

12. David Hill, *The Gospel of Matthew* (Grand Rapids: Eerdmans, 1972), 253.

13. Jim Perkinson, "A Canaanitic Word in the Logos of Christ; or the Difference the Syro-Phoenician Woman Makes to Jesus," *Semeia* 75 (1996): 61–85.

14. The phrase "Son of God" is used nine times in Matthew's gospel. It is used twice by Satan during the temptations in the wilderness, but each time it is preceded by "if" (4:3, 6). The demons identify Jesus with the title once (8:29). The high priest uses the title in his interrogation of Jesus (26:63). The crowds mock Jesus on the cross with the same phrase used by Satan (27:40), and they use the same phrase against Jesus that the chief priest used (27:43). Finally, the centurion uses the title as a confession: "Surely he was the Son of God!" (27:54).

15. "Withdraw" is used to describe strategic retreats by Jesus or his family for his protection. We find the term in Matt. 2:14, where Joseph withdraws with his family to Egypt to protect Jesus from Herod. Later, when Joseph returns with his family to Judea, God warns him about Archelaus ruling in Judea, and the family withdraws to Galilee. In 4:12, when Jesus hears about the arrest of John, Jesus withdraws into Galilee to begin his ministry. In 12:15, when the Pharisees respond to Jesus' healing on the Sabbath by taking counsel on how they might destroy him, Jesus withdraws.

16. Beare, *Gospel*, 343.

17. Doyle, "Matthew's Intention," 39.

18. Jesus has prepared his disciples for a visit to Tyre and Sidon with his remarks in Matthew 11:20–24. In that passage, Jesus curses the cities of Galilee and says that if Tyre, Sidon, and Sodom had seen the same miracles, they would have repented long before.

19. In the Sermon on the Mount (Matt. 6:1–18), Jesus says that we are not to give, pray, or fast like the hypocrites (one can read "Pharisees" for "hypocrites"). In Matthew 23:2–3, Jesus says, "The teachers of the law and the Pharisees sit in Moses' seat. So you must obey them and do everything they tell you. But do not do what they do, for they do not practice what they preach."

20. By introducing the woman in 15:21 as a "Canaanite," Beare states, "Matthew's word has overtones of the derogatory use of the term in the Old Testament. . . . They ought to have been exterminated" (*Gospel*, 341).

21. Daniel. J. Harrington, *The Gospel of Matthew* (Collegeville, Minn.: Liturgical Press, 1991), 224.

22. The woman is desperate because her daughter is "suffering terribly from demon-possession" (Matt. 15:22). It seems that this was a particularly horrible case of demon possession. More severe cases of demon possession seemed to be associated with Gentile regions. For example, in Matt. 8:28–34, Jesus casts demons out of two men and into the herd of swine. These men were Gentiles or at least were in a Gentile area.

23. F. F. Bruce, *The Hard Sayings of Jesus* (Downers Grove, Ill.: InterVarsity Press, 1983), 111, suggests that perhaps Jesus had a twinkle in his eye as he spoke to the woman.

24. See Ben Witherington, *Jesus the Sage: The Pilgrimage of Wisdom* (Minneapolis: Fortress Press, 1994); C. F. Melchert, *Wise Teaching: Biblical Wisdom and Educational Ministry* (Harrisburg, Pa.: Trinity Press International, 1998); C. E. Carlston, "Proverbs, Maxims, and the Historical Jesus," *The Journal of Biblical Literature* 99 (1980): 87–105; James G. Williams, *Those Who Ponder Proverbs* (Sheffield: Almond Press, 1981).

25. Williams, *Ponder Proverbs*, 57.

26. Ibid., 47.

27. Witherington, *Jesus the Sage*, 164.

28. Melchert, *Wise Teaching*, 206.

29. The only time in Matthew's gospel when Jesus tells us to "listen and understand" is in 15:10, when he introduces the parable of the clean and the unclean.

30. We are not told how the Canaanite woman heard of Jesus. Most likely, she heard reports that were being spread about him, since "news about him spread all over Syria" (Matt. 4:24). From the woman's words, it appears that she knew a good bit about Jesus—and at the same time knew so little. The text says that the woman was crying out, "Lord, Son of David, have mercy on me!" Regardless of how she heard of Christ, like the Roman centurion she came to Christ for help. It should not go unnoticed that no Pharisee or other Jewish leader ever came to Jesus and asked for healing for either himself or a family member.

31. C. Scott and J. Martin, "Matthew 15:21–28: A Test-Case for Jesus' Manners," *Journal for the Study of the New Testament* 63 (1996): 21–44.

32. Perkinson, "Canaanitic Word," 65.

Chapter 12: Getting David out of Saul's Armor

1. Edgar J. Elliston and J. Timothy Kauffman, *Developing Leaders for Urban Ministries* (New York: Peter Lang Publishing Co., 1993), 1.

2. John M. Frame, "Proposals for a New North American Model," in *Missions and Theological Education in World Perspective*, ed. Harvie M. Conn and Samuel F. Rowen (Farmington, Mich.: Associates of Urbanus, 1984), 369–86.

3. Ibid., 369.

4. Ibid., 370.

5. Ibid.

6. Ibid.

7. Ibid.

8. Ibid., 371–72.

9. The proposals in this chapter should not discourage academically gifted men and women from minority groups from pursuing higher degrees in theology or from joining theological faculties. Nor should seminaries reduce their efforts to recruit more minority faculty members. The intention of these proposals is to assist churches in urban and ethnic communities whose leadership needs, for whatever reason, are not served by traditional institutions.

10. Frame, "Proposals," 377.

11. Frame suggests these three areas of spiritual qualification for the ministry. Ibid., 372–74.

12. Ibid., 373–74.

13. Ibid., 382.

14. See the chapter entitled "Seminaries and Bible Schools," in Roger S. Greenway, *An Urban Strategy for Latin America* (Grand Rapids: Baker Book House, 1973), 182–96.

15. Sidney H. Rooy, "Theological Education for Urban Mission," in *Discipling the City: Theological Reflections on Urban Mission,* ed. Roger S. Greenway (Grand Rapids: Baker Book House, 1979), 185.

Chapter 13: Seminaries: Time for a Change?

1. "Report from the Committee to Examine Alternate Routes Being Used to Enter the Ordained Ministry in the CRC," in *Christian Reformed Church in North America Agenda for Synod, 2000* (Grand Rapids: Christian Reformed Church in North America, 2000), 271–350.

2. *The Ministries and Missionaries of the Emmanuel Gospel Center* (Boston: Emmanuel Gospel Center, 1999).

3. *Contextualized Urban Theological Education Enablement Program* (Boston: Center for Urban Ministerial Education, n.d.).

4. Ibid.

5. *Psalter Hymnal* (Grand Rapids: CRC Publications, 1987), 597–98.

Chapter 14: An Inquiry into Urban Theological Education

1. See map on page 254.

2. Determining the population of large cities is an increasing challenge! This is certainly true in La Francophonie, where the problem is compounded when one is attempting to establish the number of people who use French on a daily basis. For the purposes of this research, main figures representing the population estimate of the city was the point of departure. The percentage of people who use French on a daily basis was based on estimations given by the Haut Conseil de la Francophonie. For further clarification, see "L'univers francophone," *La Presse,* 15 March 1997, B6–7. The reader will notice that two Algerian cities are on this list, in spite of the fact that the country recently withdrew from La Francophonie. Furthermore, certain large cities in countries like Cambodia, Egypt, and Democratic Republic of the Congo are absent from the list because the number of people who use French in those metropolitan areas is too small to compare with others on the list.

3. A full copy of the study, *Survey of Mission Agencies Working in La Francophonie,* including the methodology and the results, is available from Direction Chrétienne Inc. (Write to dcicdi@total.net.)

4. Lesslie Newbigin, *Foolishness to the Greeks* (Grand Rapids: Eerdmans, 1986), 34.

5. Glenn Smith, *How Unique Is Québec's Religious Climate Anyway?* (Montreal: Christian Direction, 1997).

6. J. Moody, *Rechristianization of Religion in Modern European History* (New York: Macmillan, 1964), 89.

7. Os Guinness, *The Gravedigger File* (Downers Grove, Ill.: InterVarsity Press, 1983), 59.

8. Peter Berger, *A Far Glory* (Toronto: Free Press, 1992), 36.

9. Peter Zuck, "The Promise or Peril of Religion in Modern Society: An Examination of the Secularization Theory," *Crux* (June 1987): 26–27.

10. I think that this definition of the process goes a long way to respond to the questions raised by Harvie M. Conn in "Any Faith Dies in the City," *Urban Mission* 3, no. 5 (May 1986): 6–19. Also see F. Dumont, "Du Catholicisme Québécois," chapter 12 in *Une foi partagée* (Montreal: Bellarmin, 1996), for an insider's view of the question of marginalization.

11. Any discussion of secularization, however, must consider religion and its relationship with the "modern project." Too often, religious faith is reduced to "human contact with the divine" or a denominational affiliation. This reductionism is another example of how our culture has divided the secular from the spiritual. The discussion of secularization is greatly enhanced when we link religious belief and worldview issues. Religion includes that which one holds to be of ultimate importance. As Paul Tillich said, "Religion is the substance of culture and culture the form of religion." From a biblical point of view, no one can escape the religious aspect of life, as God is ever present in the affairs of all people and cultures. One can do with the Creator what one wants—worship, love, hate, or run—but God cannot be ignored. The sense of God is still what Calvin referred to as *semen religionis*, the seed of religion. Because of the threefold aspect of the modern project, secularization implies a decline in the ability of traditional beliefs to bring meaning to life for large numbers of individuals and cultures as a whole. This means that secularization is not just a philosophy or a conscious ideology (i.e., secularism). It includes the reshaping of the religious components of a worldview and initiates the transfer of beliefs and values from the religious sphere to the secular sphere. It leads to the desacralization of the world.

12. For an excellent analysis, see David Lyon, "Post-modern Canada," *Ecumenism,* June 1997, 12–14. I am grateful to the author for permission to incorporate his reflections into the following paragraphs.

13. J. F. Lyotard, *Le postmodernisme expliqué aux enfants* (Paris: Les Éditions Galilée, 1988), 32 (my translation).

14. E. Gellner, *Postmodernism, Reason and Religion* (New York: Routledge, 1992), 24.

15. I would encourage the reader to consider the contributions of Ben Meyer, Tom Wright, and Paul Hiebert to this discussion.

16. Bernard Lonergan, *Method in Theology* (Toronto: University of Toronto Press, 1994), 81.

17. N. T. Wright, *The New Testament and the People of God* (Minneapolis: Fortress Press, 1991), 35. Ben Meyer explains this further when he states, "Here the adjective, *critical,* implies a thoroughgoing valorization of the scholastic adage, 'being becomes known through the true.' Reality, that is, comes to light not through acts like looking at a tree or kicking a stone but through the act of judgement, by which reflective intelligence climaxes the discursive and often laborious process of trying

to find out what is true. The noun 'realism' signifies that, as the strict correlative of truth, reality is the goal of the drive to know" (*Critical Realism and the New Testament* [Alison Park, Pa.: Pickwick Publications, 1989], 197–98).

18. Elmer J. Thiessen, "Curriculum after Babel," in *Agenda for Education Change,* ed. John Short and Trevor Cooling (Leicester: Apollos, 1997), 167.

19. Wright, *The New Testament and the People of God,* 178. In an earlier paragraph, he adds to our understanding on this point when he states that a good hypothesis must include data, "it must construct a basically simple and coherent overall picture: and finally it must explain or help to explain other problems" (99–100).

20. Ben Meyer, *Reality and Illusion in New Testament Scholarship: A Primer in Critical Realist Hermeneutics* (Collegeville, Minn.: Liturgical Press, 1994), 142.

21. Susanne Johnson, *Christian Spiritual Formation in the Church and Classroom* (reprint, Nashville: Partheon Press, 1997), 88.

22. Wright, *The New Testament and the People of God,* 125, but also pp. 109–12 and 122–26. See also N. T. Wright, *Jesus and the Victory of God* (Minneapolis: Fortress Press, 1996), 137–44.

23. Wright, *Jesus and the Victory of God,* 138.

24. But, as Wright and Meyer have already illustrated, it is also the same way that we analyze the biblical texts.

25. Wright, *The New Testament and the People of God,* 65. See also Meyer, *Reality and Illusion in the New Testament,* 65. He affirms that "it seeks (that is) to be true to itself, and to the public world, while always open to the possibility of challenge, modification and subversion."

26. Sauveur Pierre Étienne, *Haïti: L'invasion des ONG* (Montreal: Les Éditions du CIDIHCA, 1997), 118–19. In 1999, the World Bank produced a two-volume study entitled *Haiti: Les défis de la lutte contre la pauvreté* (Washington: World Bank, 1998), which was the best effort in three decades to describe the extent of the challenge.

27. *Haiti: Les défis de la lutte contre la pauvreté,* 130.

28. Étienne, *Haïti,* 115–16.

29. Jules Casseus, *Pour une église authentiquement haïtien* (Limbé: Séminaire Théologique Baptiste d'Haïti, 1987), 13.

30. The most recent government statistics can be found on the Web site of the Ambassade d'Haiti in Washington, D.C., at www.monumental.com/embassy/haitil~l.htm.

31. The last official census was in 1981. The population at that time was 5.989 million people. Even this figure is contested. I have been told that many census takers in that year were told to stop counting in certain neighborhoods of Cap Haitian. The Institut Haïtien de Statistiques et d'Informatique (IHSI) established the population at 6.486 million in 1990. They estimate urban annual growth at 4 percent and rural growth at 1.1 percent. Demographics is not rocket science. Just add the numbers. In the 1998 State of the World's Population Report of the United Nations Population Fund, we find identical percentages, but the same insistence on the population of the nation.

32. Laennec Hubron, *Dieu dans le vaudou haïtien* (Paris: Payot, 1972); id., *Les mystères du vaudoo* (Paris: Gallimard, 1993).

33. Charles-Poissant Romain has written a very good article examining the religious dimensions of Voodoo. It is entitled "La religion et le développement paysan en Haiti," *La nouvelle revue du monde noir* 1 (1986): 149–61.

34. There are several good books and articles on this theme, including Lawrence Harrison, "Voodoo Politics," *The Atlantic Monthly*, June 1993, 101–7, and several articles devoted to Haitian culture in the quarterly review entitled *Spring: A Journal of Archetype and Culture* (spring 1997). The book by Laënnec Hubron, *Comprendre Haïti: Essai sur l'état, la nation et la culture* (Paris: Éditions Karthala, 1987), also gives great insight into the issues.

35. Étienne includes an interesting historical perspective on the economic consequences of independence in *Haiti: L'invasion des ONG*, 121–27.

36. "The class and racial/color relations and conflicts gave rise to political relations and structures of domination that in turn conditioned the reproduction of the social and economic structures of Haiti." A. Dupuy, *Haiti in the World Economy* (Boulder, Colo.: Westview Press, 1989), 184.

37. Henry Hogarth, "The Garden and the Gods," *Spring: A Journal of Archetype and Culture* 61 (spring 1997): 62.

38. Ibid.

39. Krister Stendahl, "The Apostle Paul and the Introspective Conscience of the West," *Harvard Theological Review* 56 (1963): 199–215.

40. W. H. Hodges, *A Philosophy of Christian Mission* (privately published), 17–23. Interestingly, Lawrence Harrison picks up on Hodges' perspective in "Voodoo Politics," 106.

41. Casseus, *Pour une église authentiquement haïtienne*, 81–83.

42. Raymond Fung, "Évangeliser les victimes du péché," in *L'évangile et le monde urbanisé*, 4th ed. (Montreal: Direction Chrétienne, 1994), sec. II, 3–8.

43. Hogarth, "The Garden and the Gods," 61–82.

44. This count is based on an informal mailing list that the Overseas Council has compiled.

Chapter 15: African Theology from the Perspective of Honor and Shame

1. I want to thank Dr. Harvie Conn of Westminster Theological Seminary for encouraging me to publish this, and for reading a couple of earlier drafts of it and offering very helpful insights.

2. Tite Tiénou, *The Theological Task of the Church in Africa*, 2d ed. (Achimota, Ghana: African Christian Press, 1990), 49–51.

3. John Mbiti, "The Biblical Basis for Present Trends in African Theology," in *African Theology en Route*, ed. Kofi Appiah-Kubi and Sergio Torres (Maryknoll, N.Y.: Orbis Books, 1979), 84.

4. These are not the only sociocultural categories that social scientists have identified and used in studies of communities. Others include value, patrons and clients, grace, etc. And this is also not to say that honor-and-shame categories are more important than the others. But they are more apparent in African culture, just as they were in the Mediterranean world.

5. Robert Wuthnow, James Hunter, Albert Bergesen, and Edith Kurzweil, *Cultural Analysis in the Work of Peter L. Berger, Mary Douglass, Michel Foucault and Jürgen Habermas* (Boston: Routledge and Kegan Paul, 1984), 3. The definition of culture remains ambiguous even in the social sciences, as this particular study shows.

6. Richard Niebuhr, *Christ and Culture* (New York: Harper & Row, 1951), 32.

7. William J. Larkin Jr., *Culture and Biblical Hermeneutics* (Grand Rapids: Baker Book House, 1988), 193.

8. John Mbiti, "Christianity and East African Culture and Religion," *Dini na Mila* 3 (May 1968): 4, quoted in Kwame Bediako, *Christianity in Africa: The Renewal of a Non-Western Religion* (Maryknoll, N.Y.: Orbis Books, 1995), 175.

9. This is not the first study to regard these categories of interpretation as the more appropriate ones to use in articulating an African theology. Fred Welbourn, in *East African Christian* (London: Oxford University Press, 1965), already drew a distinction between guilt and shame.

10. Ernest McFall, *Approaching the Nuer of Africa Through the Old Testament* (South Pasadena, Calif.: William B. Carey Library, 1970), 3. An awareness of the close resemblance shown by the two cultures should not preclude the fact that there are significant differences for which we must account.

11. Ibid., 4.

12. Ibid., 90.

13. Tiénou, *The Theological Task*, 24.

14. Kwame Bediako, *Theology and Identity: The Impact of Culture upon Christian Thought in the Second Century and in Modern Africa* (Oxford: Regnum Books, 1992), xvii (emphasis in original).

15. E. R. Dodds, *The Greeks and the Irrational* (Berkeley: University of California Press, 1951), esp. chapters 1–2.

16. D. Riesman, *The Lonely Crowd* (London: Oxford University Press, 1950).

17. Fred Welbourn, "Guilt and Shame," in *Christianity in Tropical Africa*, ed. Christian Beata (London: Oxford University Press, 1968), 183.

18. Gerhart Piers and Milton Singer, *Shame and Guilt* (Springfield, Ill.: Charles C. Thomas Publishers, 1953), 11.

19. M. Lynd, *On Shame and the Search for Identity* (New York: Harcourt Brace, 1958), 22.

20. A. Heller, *Power of Shame: A Rational Perspective* (London: Routledge and Kegan Paul, 1985), 3.

21. Ibid., 4.

22. Laurenti Magesa, *African Religion: The Moral Traditions of Abundant Life* (Maryknoll, N.Y.: Orbis Books, 1997), 170. But guilt for Magesa is merely "owning up" to wrongdoing. We cannot concur with this view, since we have defined shame as a public value as opposed to guilt, which tends to be internalized.

23. Harry Sawyerr, *Creative Evangelism: Towards a New Christian Encounter with Africa* (London: Lutterworth Press, 1968).

24. John S. Mbiti, *New Testament Eschatology in an African Background: A Study of the Encounter Between New Testament Theology and African Traditional Concepts* (London: Oxford University Press, 1971), 187.

25. Bediako, *Theology and Identity*.

26. Geerhardus Vos, *Biblical Theology* (Grand Rapids: Eerdmans, 1948), 52.

27. The human relationship to gods and God in ATR is characterized more by fear and awe than by shame. There was hardly any notion of fellowship associated with the gods in the ATR, apart from reverent worship and veneration. In fact, in the case of the Supreme Being, the common factor in African myths of creation seems to be that God distances himself from man because of something that man did (cf. Gen. 2–3).

28. See also Robert Jewett, "Babette's Feast and the Shaming of the Poor in Corinth," *Dialog* 36 (1997): 270–76; H. G. Link, "*aischunē*," *The New International Dic-*

tionary of New Testament Theology, 4 vols., ed. Colin Brown (Grand Rapids: Zondervan, 1986), 3:561–64.

29. Saul Olyan, "Honor, Shame and Covenant-Relations in Ancient Israel and Its Environment," *Journal of Biblical Literature* 115 (1966): 201–18.

30. Ibid., 213.

31. Lyn M. Betchel, "Shame as a Sanction of Social Control in Biblical Israel: Judicial, Political, and Social Shaming," *Journal for the Study of the Old Testament* 49 (1991): 63–64.

32. See also Judg. 3:25; 2 Kings 2:17.

33. S. Aalen, *"time"* and *"doxa,"* The New International Dictionary of New Testament *Theology*, 4 vols., ed. Colin Brown (Grand Rapids: Zondervan, 1986), 3:48–49.

34. Ibid., 49.

35. Wayne Meeks, *The Moral World of the First Christians* (Philadelphia: Westminster Press, 1986), 37.

36. Ibid., 37. Philip Esler, in *The First Christians in Their Social Worlds: Social-Scientific Approaches to New Testament Interpretation* (London: Routledge, 1994), 17–18, seems to agree when he states that the New Testament texts "are not literary works, disinterested by nature, and aimed at satisfying aesthetic instincts which are never easily understood but always involve the human love of imitation. . . . The New Testament texts are very interested indeed. . . . At the social level they may be interpreted as the vehicles for the construction of institutional and symbolic canopies within which the communities for which they were written might find meaning in the face of a hostile world."

37. Dodds, *The Greeks and the Irrational*, 26.

38. Meeks, *The Moral World*, 37.

39. B. Malina, "The Individual and the Community-Personality in the Social World of Early Christianity," *Biblical Theological Bulletin* 9 (1979): 128. *Dyadism* comes from the Greek word meaning "pair."

40. See Jerome Neyrey and B. Malina, *The Social World of Luke-Acts: Models for Interpretation* (Peabody, Mass.: Hendrickson Publishers, 1991), for a more detailed introduction to these characteristics.

41. R. A. Levine and B. B. Whiting, in *Six Cultures: Studies of Child Rearing*, ed. B. B. Whiting (London: John Wiley, 1963), quoted in Welbourn, "Guilt and Shame," 185.

42. Heller, *Power of Shame*, 4.

43. Welbourn, "Guilt and Shame," 186.

44. Polygamy may be a regrettable condition, but divorce destroys the very fabric of the culture of the people and is socially disruptive. Many Africans resented Christianity because of it. In fact, there is hardly any biblical ground for enforcing such a demand. Also destroyed was the male honor of the men who were forced to divorce their wives. They were the most honorable people in African society. Also female positive shame was imposed on the wives divorced. To be a polygamist in African societies was indicative of one's wealth and subsequently one's honor, for only a wealthy man could afford extra wives. For the women, it was better to be a second or third or fourth wife than not to be married at all, for marriage removed the shame of being unwed.

In Africa today, singleness is still looked upon suspiciously. In traditional African society, one was labeled with some form of evil practice (e.g., he or she was considered to be a witch or wizard, or to have an evil eye) if one did not get married. (It is no wonder that African Catholic priests are in the forefront of those demanding that priests be allowed to get married.) It is a most shameful thing never to marry or be married in African societies. One is regarded as a perpetual adolescent who never attains maturity. One never gets honor in such a society if he or she never marries. This is a negative stigma that the Scriptures have had to confront and with which they have had to deal. The clear response would be to show that honor is not a product of social status, but rather comes from God, while at the same time affirming strong family ties as something positive.

45. Mbiti, *New Testament Eschatology*, 7; also, Bnézét Bujo, *African Theology in Cultural Context* (Maryknoll, N.Y.: Orbis Books, 1991), 20.

46. John S. Mbiti, *African Religions and Philosophies* (Nairobi: Oxford University Press, 1968).

47. Vincent Mulago, "Traditional African Religions and Christianity," in *African Traditional Religions in Contemporary Society*, ed. Jacob Olupona (New York: Paragon House, 1991), 105.

48. John S. Mbiti, "Flowers in the Garden: The Role of Women in African Religion," in *Religious Plurality in Africa: Essays in Honour of John S. Mbiti*, ed. Jacob Olupona (Berlin: Mouton de Gruyter, 1993), 59–72.

49. Ibid., 68.

50. Kivuto Ndeti, in *Elements of Akamba Life* (Nairobi: East African Publishing House, 1972), 72, comments about the Akamba that one of the main functions of the *mbae* (clan) was "to make sure that its members adhere to the codes proclaimed by the founder. These codes include general good conduct, and disciplining any members who fail to fulfil their obligations of *mosie* (family)."

51. Magesa, *African Religion*, 264.

52. McFall, *Approaching the Nuer*, 91.

53. Jerome Neyrey, "Honor and Shame in the Johannine Passion Narrative," *Semeia* 68 (1996): 115.

54. Matthews Ojo, in "Charismatic Movements in Africa," in *Christianity in Africa in the 1990s*, ed. Christopher Fyfe and A. Walls (Edinburgh: University of Edinburgh Press, 1996), 106, notes that evangelism is partly defined as the "redemptive measure to loosen and to free human beings from the grip of evil spirits, from the forces of darkness and from bad luck." Thus it becomes an exercise of power and authority to challenge all the forces of evil.

55. Magesa, in *African Religion*, 211, shows that shame and guilt (though we do not agree with him that shame is private and guilt is public) play a major role in diagnosing most forms of affliction in African traditional religions. But even more importantly, he identifies the need for purification, to rehabilitate not only the individual, but also the community and the environment. This is accompanied by an admission of culpability, and a confession is demanded.

56. The biblical worldview, like the African worldview, has a three-level cosmos, consisting of the world (the dwelling of living men), heaven (the dwelling of God), and a spiritual world in between them (inhabited by good and evil spirits and ancestral spirits). The spirits in the intermediate world occasionally break into the world of men and affect them, either positively or negatively.

57. Bnézét Bujo, "Dangers de bourgeoisie dans le theologie africane: Un examen de conscience," *Euntes* 21 (November–December 1988): 315–27.

58. Ojo, "Charismatic Movements," 104.

59. Ibid., 106.

60. Bediako, *Christianity in Africa*, 243. Unfortunately, these concepts of the sacralized position persist not only in the political arena in Africa, where leaders, especially country presidents and prime ministers, are seen as the embodiment of sacred authority, but also have infiltrated the church. Bediako, then, calls for a desacralization of the positions of leadership from a biblical point of view that portrays ideal leadership as servant leadership, as exemplified by Christ in his life and symbolically when he washed the feet of his disciples. And, as Bediako contends, "the essential thrust of the New Testament is the continuation of this desacralizing impact."

61. Magesa, in *African Religion*, 264, discusses the importance of shame and guilt as social controls in the political organizations of African societies.

62. Bediako, *Christianity in Africa*, 182.

Chapter 16: The Power of the Gospel in Korea (1882–1912)

1. As a reflection of this growing interest, the Conference on Christianity in Korea was held September 26–27, 1997, in New York, sponsored by the Korea Society and Union Theological Seminary. A report summarizes: "It was an unprecedented gathering of scholars and experts on Korean Christianity from several nations, together with many from other fields who recognize the importance of this subject. During the conference invited respondents commented on sixteen presentations, while those in attendance contributed to lively and penetrating discussions" ("Conference Report," circulated by the Korea Society in 1998, p.1).

2. Sang-Kyu Yi, "Reformed Theology in Korea," in *Collected Essays on Historical Theology* (in Korean), ed. Kyung-Lim Kang and Sang-Oon Jung (Seoul: Yi-Rhe Suh-Won, 1999), 422. (In this chapter, translations into English are provided by author, Sung-Il Park.)

3. The Presbyterian missionaries in Korea decided to adopt the Twelve Creeds (a summary of the major Christian doctrines in twelve points) as the official confession of the newly organized Chosun (i.e., Korean) Presbyterian Church in 1907, rather than a major Reformed confession such as the Westminster Confession of Faith. This decision was based on the contextual needs of the Korean church at the time. To find the Twelve Creeds lacking in specific Reformed teaching, and thus to question how Reformed the Korean church is, is to misunderstand the historical context.

4. I believe that the late Harvie M. Conn's great contribution during his teaching career at Westminster Theological Seminary was his effort to encourage his students to go beyond the passive dependence on theological tradition and to pursue boldly, yet biblically, contextual gospel proclamation and praxis. His was an orthodoxy set in motion, a lively proclamation of grace and practice of mercy.

5. What I mean by "the Reformed worldview" here is a holistic application of the lordship of Christ to all areas of life. It is the realization of the spirituality of a marketplace and a public square, rather than that of a monastery.

6. Daniel J. Adams, "Church Growth in Korea: A Paradigm Shift from Ecclesiology to Nationalism," in *Perspectives on Christianity in Korea and Japan: The Gospel and Culture in East Asia*, ed. Mark R. Mullins and Richard Fox Young (Lewiston, N.Y.: Edwin Mellen Press, 1995), 13.

7. Ibid.

8. Ibid., 14.

9. Yung-Jae Kim, *A History of the Korean Church* (in Korean) (Seoul: Korea Society for Reformed Faith and Action, 1992), 49–51.

10. Ibid., 50.

11. Don Baker, "Unexpected Fruit: Catholicism and the Rise of Civil Society in Korea" (paper presented at a conference on Christianity in Korea, sponsored by the Korea Society, New York, September 26–27, 1997), 3.

12. Adams, "Church Growth in Korea," 27.

13. Yung-Jae Kim, *A History*, 58.

14. Ibid., 64.

15. Kyung-Bae Min, *The History of Christianity in Korea* (Seoul: Korean Christian Publishing House, 1992), 172. Min comments, "Sorae is the origin of church history in Korea."

16. Yung-Jae Kim, *A History*, 66.

17. Bruce F. Hunt, "Preface to the Fourth Edition," in John L. Nevius, *The Planting and Development of Missionary Churches* (Philadelphia: Presbyterian and Reformed Publishing Company, 1958), i.

18. Yung-Jae Kim, *A History*, 95.

19. *Dokleeb-Shinmoon* 4, no. 43 (1 March 1899), cited in Man-Yuol Yi, *Christian Nationalistic Movement in the late Yi-Dynasty* (Seoul: Pyong Min Sah, 1981), 20.

20. Man-Yuol Yi, *Christian Nationalistic Movement*, 21.

21. Samuel Hugh Moffett, "Rapid Church Growth in Korea: A Quick Survey" (paper presented at a conference on Christianity in Korea, sponsored by the Korea Society, New York, September 26–27, 1997), 5.

22. Yung-Jae Kim, *A History*, 94.

23. Ibid., 77.

24. Ibid., 78.

25. Ibid., 81. They included Park Yung-Hyo, Min Yung-Hwan, Yun Chi-Ho, Yi Sang-Jae, Yu Sung-Joon, Yi Won-Guk, Namgoong Uk, Kim Jung-Shik, Cho Jong-Man, and Shin Heung-Woo. Many of these names appeared earlier as the members of the Independence Club founded in 1896 by Suh Jae-Pil.

26. Byong-Suh Kim, "The Explosive Growth of the Korean Church Today: A Sociological Analysis," *International Review of Mission* 74, no. 293 (1985): 62.

27. Yung-Jae Kim, *A History*, 107. Kim notes that some missionaries voluntarily served on night patrols, and another served as a food taster for the king.

28. Ki-baik Lee, *A New History of Korea*, trans. Edward W. Wagner with Edward J. Shultz (Cambridge: Harvard University Press, 1984), 310.

29. Ibid., 313.

30. Yung-Jae Kim, *A History*, 109.

31. Chai-sik Chung, "Beyond Indigenization: Toward a Christian Transcendence in Korea" (paper presented at a conference on Christianity in Korea, sponsored by the Korea Society, New York, September 26–27, 1997), 6.

32. Yung-Jae Kim, *A History*, 109.

33. Yong-Kyu Park, *The Great Revivalism in Korea: Its History, Character, and Impact, 1901–1910* (in Korean) (Seoul: Word of Life Books, 2000), 15.

34. Ibid., 39.

35. Ibid., 44.

36. Ibid., 45.

37. Ibid., 207.

38. Ibid., 211.
39. Ibid., 216.
40. Ibid., 217.
41. Ibid., 219.
42. Samuel Hugh Moffet, "Rapid Church Growth," 4.
43. Yung-Jae Kim, *A History*, 128.

BIBLIOGRAPHY

Adams, Daniel J. "Church Growth in Korea: A Paradigm Shift from Ecclesiology to Nationalism." In *Perspectives on Christianity in Korea and Japan: The Gospel and Culture in East Asia,* edited by Mark R. Mullins and Richard Fox Young, 13–28. Lewiston, N.Y.: Edwin Mellen Press, 1995.

Alinsky, Saul David. *Rules for Radicals.* New York: Random House, 1971.

Allen, Roland. *Missionary Methods: St. Paul's or Ours?* Chicago: Moody Press, 1959.

Anderson, Allan. "A 'Failure to Love'? Western Missions and the Emergence of African Initiated Churches in the Twentieth Century." *Missiology* 29 (July 2001): 275–86.

Anderson, Gerald H. "Facing the Realities of the Contemporary World in Mission." In *Educating for Christian Missions,* edited by Arthur L. Walker Jr., 49–58. Nashville: Broadman Press, 1981.

Appiah, Anthony. "The Multi-Culturalist Misunderstanding." *The New York Review of Books,* 9 October 1997, 30–36.

Bakke, Raymond J. *The Urban Christian: Effective Ministry in Today's Urban World.* Downers Grove, Ill.: InterVarsity Press, 1987.

———. "Urban Evangelization: A Lausanne Strategy Since 1980." *International Bulletin of Missionary Research* 8 (4 December 1998): 149–54.

Barrett, C. K. *A Commentary on the Second Epistle to the Corinthians.* New York: Harper, 1973.

Barrett, David. *Schism and Renewal in Africa: An Analysis of Six Thousand Contemporary Religious Movements.* Nairobi: Oxford University Press, 1968.

———. "Silver and Gold Have I None: Church of the Poor or Church of the Rich?" *International Bulletin of Missionary Research* 7 (October 1983): 146–51.

———. "Annual Statistical Table on Global Mission: 1992." *International Bulletin of Missionary Research* 16 (January 1992): 26–27.

Bassham, Rodger C. "Mission Theology: 1948–1975." *Occasional Bulletin of Missionary Research* 4 (April 1980): 52–58.

Bauer, Walter, A. F. Arndt, and F. W. Gingrich. *A Greek-English Lexicon of the New Testament and Other Early Christian Literature.* Chicago: University of Chicago Press, 1958.

Baum, Alice, and Donald Burnes. *A Nation in Denial: The Truth about Homelessness.* Boulder, Colo.: Westview, 1993.

Beare, Francis Wright. *The Gospel According to Matthew.* Oxford: Blackwell, 1981.

Beaver, R. Pierce. "The American Protestant Theological Seminary and Missions." *Missiology* 4 (January 1976): 75–87.

Bediako, Kwame. *Theology and Identity: The Impact of Culture upon Christian Thought in the Second Century and in Modern Africa.* Oxford: Regnum Books, 1992.

———. *Christianity in Africa: The Renewal of a Non-Western Religion.* Maryknoll, N.Y.: Orbis Books, 1995.

Berger, Peter. *A Far Glory.* Toronto: Free Press, 1992.

Betchel, Lyn M. "Shame as a Sanction of Social Control in Biblical Israel: Judicial, Political, and Social Shaming." *Journal for the Study of the Old Testament* 49 (1991): 63–64.

Blowers, Paul M., ed. *The Bible in Greek Christian Antiquity.* South Bend, Ind.: University of Notre Dame Press, 1997.

Bonhoeffer, Dietrich. *Life Together.* Translated by John W. Doberstein. London: SCM, 1954.

———. *Christ the Center.* Translated by John Bowden. New York: Harper and Row, 1966.

———. "Prayerbook of the Bible: Introduction to the Psalms." In *Dietrich Bonhoeffer, Works.* Vol. 5, *Life Together and Prayerbook of the Bible.* Edited by Gerhard Ludwig Müller and Albrecht Schöner. Translated by Geffrey B. Kelly. Minneapolis: Fortress Press, 1996.

Bonk, Jonathan J. *Missions and Money.* Maryknoll, N.Y.: Orbis Books, 1991.

Bosch, David. *Witness to the World.* London: Marshall, Morgan and Scott, 1980.

———. *Transforming Mission: Paradigm Shifts in Theology of Mission.* Maryknoll, NY: Orbis Books, 1991.

Browning, Don. "Globalization and the Task of Theological Education in North America." *Theological Education* 23, no. 1 (autumn 1986): 43–59.

Bruce, F. F. *Paul: Apostle of the Free Spirit.* Exeter: Paternoster Press, 1977.

———. *The Hard Sayings of Jesus.* Downers Grove, Ill.: InterVarsity Press, 1983.

Brueggemann, Walter. *The Prophetic Imagination.* Philadelphia: Fortress Press, 1978.

Bruner, Frederick Dale. *Matthew, A Commentary*. Dallas: Word Publishers, 1990.

Brunner, Emil. *Justice and the Social Order*. London: Lutterworth Press, 1947.

Buckley, Michael. *At the Origins of Modern Atheism*. New Haven: Yale University Press, 1987.

Bujo, Bnézét. "Dangers de bourgeoisie dans le theologie africane: Un examen de conscience." *Euntes* 21(November–December 1988): 315–27.

———. *African Theology in Cultural Context*. Maryknoll, N.Y.: Orbis Books, 1991.

Capulong, Noriel C. "Globalization of Theological Education: From Whose Perspective?" *The Auburn News*, spring 1990, 1–4.

Carlston, C. E. "Proverbs, Maxims, and the Historical Jesus." *The Journal of Biblical Literature* 99 (1980): 87–105.

Carson, D. A. "'Worship the Lord Your God': The Perennial Challenge." In *Worship: Adoration and Action*, edited by D. A. Carson, 13–18. Grand Rapids: Baker Book House, 1993.

Cary, Phillip. *Augustine's Influence on the Inner Self: The Legacy of a Christian Platonist*. Oxford: Oxford University Press, 2000.

Case, Shirley Jackson. *The Social Origins of Christianity*. Chicago: University of Chicago Press, 1923.

———. *The Social Triumph of the Ancient Church*. New York: Harper and Row, 1933.

Casseus, Jules. *Pour une église authentiquement haïtien*. Limbí: Séminaire Théologique Baptiste d'Haïti, 1987.

Cerfaux, Lucien. "La section des pains: (Mc vi, 31–vii, 26; Mt xiv, 13–xvi,12)." In *Recueil Lucien Cerfaux I*, 471–85. Gembloux: Editions J. Duculot, 1954.

Clowney, Edmund P. *The Church*. Contours of Christian Theology. Downers Grove, Ill.: InterVarsity Press, 1995.

Coleman, James S. "Social Capital in the Creation of Human Capital." *American Journal of Sociology* 94 (supplement 1988): S95–S119.

COMLA. *Memorias del COMLA-4*. Lima: Ed. Paulinas, 1991.

Cone, James. *A Black Theology of Liberation*. Maryknoll, N.Y.: Orbis Books, 1986.

Conn, Harvie M. "Can I Be Spiritual and at the Same Time Human?" *The Other Side* 9, no. 5 (September–October 1973): 16–19, 42–47.

———. "Contextualization: Where Do We Begin?" In *Evangelicals and Liberation*, edited by Carl Armerding, 90–119. Phillipsburg, N.J.: Presbyterian and Reformed Publishing Company, 1979.

———. *Evangelism: Doing Justice and Preaching Grace*. Grand Rapids: Zondervan, 1982.

———. *Eternal Word and Changing Worlds: Theology, Anthropology, and Mission in Trialogue.* Grand Rapids: Zondervan, 1984.

———. "Any Faith Dies in the City." *Urban Mission* 3, no. 5 (May 1986): 6–19.

———. *A Clarified Vision for Urban Mission.* Grand Rapids: Zondervan, 1987.

———. "Normativity, Relevance, and Relativism." In *Inerrancy and Hermeneutic,* edited by Harvie M. Conn, 185–209. Grand Rapids: Baker Book House, 1988.

———. "Contextual Theologies: The Problem of Agendas." *Westminster Theological Journal* 52 (1990): 51–63.

———. "Genesis as Urban Prologue." In *Discipling the City: A Comprehensive Approach to Urban Ministry,* edited by Roger S. Greenway, 13–33. 2d ed. Grand Rapids: Baker Book House, 1992.

———. *The American City and the Evangelical Church: A Historical Overview.* Grand Rapids: Baker Books, 1994.

———, ed. *Planting and Growing Urban Churches.* Grand Rapids: Baker Book House, 1997.

Conn, Harvie M., and Manuel Ortiz. *Urban Ministry: The Kingdom, the City, and the People of God.* Downers Grove, Ill.: InterVarsity Press, 2001.

Cottle, Michelle. "Boomerang." *The New Republic,* 7 May 2001, 26–29.

Cox, Harvey. *The Secular City: Secularization and Urbanization in Theological Perspective.* London: SCM Press, 1966.

Damen, Franz. "Las sectas: ¿Avalancha o desafio?" *Cuarto intermedio, Cochabamba,* May 1987, 45–63.

Dickens, Charles. "The Frozen Out Poor Law." *All the Year Round: A Weekly Journal,* n.d., 446–49.

Dodds, E. R. *The Greeks and the Irrational.* Berkeley: University of California Press, 1951.

Doyle, B. Rod. "Matthew's Intention as Discerned by His Structure." *Revue biblique* 95 (1988): 34–54.

DuBose, Francis M. *How Churches Grow in an Urban World.* Nashville: Broadman Press, 1978.

Dulles, Avery. "Orthodoxy and Social Change." *America* 178, no. 21 (20–27 June 1998): 8–17.

Dumont, F. *Une foi partagée.* Montreal: Bellarmin, 1996.

Dupuy, A. *Haiti in the World Economy.* Boulder, Colo.: Westview Press, 1989.

Dyrness, William A. *How Does America Hear the Gospel?* Grand Rapids: Eerdmans, 1989.

———. *The Earth Is God's: A Theology of American Culture.* Maryknoll, N.Y.: Orbis Books, 1997.

Ebeling, G. *Word and Faith.* 1st Eng. ed. London: SCM, 1963.

Elliston, Edgar J., and J. Timothy Kauffman. *Developing Leaders for Urban Ministries.* New York: Peter Lang Publishing Co., 1993.

Erickson, Millard J. *Christian Theology.* Grand Rapids: Baker Book House, 1986.

Escobar, Samuel. "Biblical Basis for Intercultural Ministries: A Latino Perspective." In *Missions Within Reach,* edited by Enoch Wan, 10–20. Kowloon, Hong Kong: China Alliance Press, 1995.

Esler, Philip. *The First Christians in Their Social Worlds: Social-Scientific Approaches to New Testament Interpretation.* London: Routledge, 1994.

Étienne, Sauveur Pierre. *Haïti: L'invasion des ONG.* Montreal: Les Éditions du CIDIHCA, 1997.

Evans, G. R., A. E. McGrath, and A. D. Gallway. *The Science of Theology.* Grand Rapids: Eerdmans, 1986.

Farley, Edward. *Theologia.* Philadelphia: Fortress Press, 1983.

———. *The Fragility of Knowledge.* Philadelphia: Fortress Press, 1988.

Ferguson, Ronald F., and William T. Dickens, eds. *Urban Problems and Community Development.* Washington: Brookings Institute, 1999.

Finger, Thomas N. *Christian Theology: An Eschatological Approach.* 2 vols. Scottdale, Pa.: Herald Press, 1985–1989.

Ford, David. *Self and Salvation: Being Transformed.* Cambridge: Cambridge University Press, 1999.

Frame, John M. "Proposals for a New North American Model." In *Missions and Theological Education in World Perspective,* edited by Harvie M. Conn and Samuel F. Rowen, 369–86. Farmington, Mich.: Associates of Urbanus, 1984.

Freire, Paulo. *Pedagogy of the Oppressed.* Translated by Myra Bergman Ramos. New York: Continuum, 1989.

Fuller, Daniel P. "Biblical Theology and the Analogy of Faith." *International Journal of Frontier Missions* 14 (1997): 65–74.

Fung, Raymond. "Évangeliser les victimes du péché." In *L'évangile et le monde urbanisé,* edited by Glenn Smith, 3–8. 4th ed. Montreal: Direction Chrétienne, 1994.

Gellner, E. *Postmodernism, Reason and Religion.* New York: Routledge, 1992.

Gibbs, Nancy. "Answers at Last." *Time,* 17 December 1990, 44–49.

Glazer, Nathan. *We Are All Multiculturalists Now.* Cambridge, Mass.: Harvard University Press, 1997.

Gleason, Philip. "Melting Pot Redux." *Books and Culture,* July–August, 1999, 10–12.

Gornik, Mark R. *To Live in Peace: Biblical Faith and the Changing Inner City.* Grand Rapids: Eerdmans, forthcoming.

Green, Joel. *The Gospel of Luke.* New International Commentary on the New Testament. Grand Rapids: Eerdmans, 1997.

Greenway, Roger S. *An Urban Strategy for Latin America.* Grand Rapids: Baker Book House, 1973.

———. *Together Again: Kinship of Word and Deed.* Monrovia, Calif.: MARC, 1998.

Grigg, Viv. *Companion to the Poor.* Monrovia, Calif.: MARC, 1990.

Grunbaum, A. "Complementarity in Quantum Physics and Its Philosophical Generalizations." *Journal of Philosophy* 54 (1957): 713–27.

Guinness, Os. *The Gravedigger File.* Downers Grove, Ill.: InterVarsity Press, 1983.

Gundry, Robert. *Matthew: A Commentary on His Literary and Theological Art.* Grand Rapids: Eerdmans, 1982.

Hansen, G. W. "Galatians, Letter To." In *Dictionary of Paul and His Letters,* edited by Gerald Hawthorne, Ralph Martin, and Daniel Reid, 323–34. Downers Grove, Ill.: InterVarsity Press, 1993.

Harrington, Daniel. J. *The Gospel of Matthew.* Collegeville, Minn.: Liturgical Press, 1991.

Harrison, Lawrence. "Voodoo Politics." *The Atlantic Monthly,* June 1993, 101–7.

Hasel, Gerhard. "The Relationship Between Biblical Theology and Systematic Theology." *Trinity Journal* 5 (August 1984): 113–27.

Hatch, Nathan. *The Democratization of American Religion.* New Haven: Yale University Press, 1989.

Hauerwas, Stanley. *A Better Hope: Resources for a Church Confronting Capitalism, Democracy, and Postmodernity.* Grand Rapids: Brazon, 2000.

Hauerwas, Stanley, and William H. Willimon. *Resident Aliens.* Nashville: Abingdon Press, 1989.

Heim, S. Mark. "Mapping Globalization for Theological Education." *Theological Education* 26, supp. 1 (spring 1990): 7–34.

Heller, A. *Power of Shame: A Rational Perspective.* London: Routledge and Kegan Paul, 1985.

Hessel, Dieter. *Social Ministry.* Louisville: Westminster/John Knox Press, 1992.

Hesselgrave, David J. *Communicating Christ Cross-Culturally.* Grand Rapids: Zondervan, 1978.

———. "Redefining Holism." *Evangelical Mission Quarterly* 35 (July 1999): 278–84.

Hesselgrave, David J., and Edward Rommen. *Contextualization: Meanings, Methods, and Models.* Grand Rapids: Baker Book House, 1989.

Hiebert, Paul G. *Cultural Anthropology.* 2d ed. Grand Rapids: Baker Book House, 1983.

———. *Anthropological Reflections on Missiological Issues.* Grand Rapids: Baker Book House, 1994.

Hiebert, Paul G., and Eloise Hiebert Meneses. *Incarnational Ministry: Planting Churches in Band, Tribal, Peasant, and Urban Societies.* Grand Rapids: Baker Book House, 1995.

Hill, David. *The Gospel of Matthew.* Grand Rapids: Eerdmans, 1972.

Hogarth, Henry. "The Garden and the Gods." *Spring: A Journal of Archetype and Culture* 61 (spring 1997): 61–82.

Hubron, Laënnec. *Dieu dans le vaudou haïtien.* Paris: Payot, 1972.

———. *Comprende Haïti: Essai sur l'état, la nation et la culture.* Paris: Éditions Karthala, 1987.

———. *Les mystères du vaudoo.* Paris: Gallimard, 1993.

Hughes, Philip E. *The Second Epistle to the Corinthians.* New International Commentary on the New Testament. Grand Rapids: Eerdmans, 1962.

Iannaccone, L. R. "Why Strict Churches Are Strong." *American Journal of Sociology* 99 (1994): 1180–211.

Jaeger, Werner. *Early Christianity and Greek Paideia.* London: Oxford University Press, 1961.

Jewett, Robert. "Babette's Feast and the Shaming of the Poor in Corinth." *Dialog* 36 (1997): 270–76.

Johnson, Susanne. *Christian Spiritual Formation in the Church and Classroom.* Reprint, Nashville: Partheon Press, 1997.

Kalu, Ogbu U. "The Third Response: Pentecostalism and the Reconstruction of Christian Experience in Africa, 1970–1995." *Journal of African Christian Thought* 1, no. 2 (December 1998): 3–16.

Kelley, Dean M. *Why Conservative Churches Are Growing: A Study in Sociology of Religion.* New York: Harper & Row, 1972.

Kim, Byong-Suh. "The Explosive Growth of the Korean Church Today: A Sociological Analysis." *International Review of Mission* 74, no. 293 (1985): 59–72.

Kim, Yung-Jae. *A History of the Korean Church* (in Korean). Seoul: Korea Society for Reformed Faith and Action, 1992.

Kingsbury, Jack Dean. *Matthew: Structure, Christology, Kingdom.* Minneapolis: Fortress Press, 1975.

Kirk, J. Andrew. *What Is Mission?* Philadelphia: Fortress Press, 2000.

Kittel, Gerhard, and Gerhard Friedrich, eds. *Theological Dictionary of the New Testament*. Translated by Geoffrey W. Bromily. Grand Rapids: Eerdmans, 1964–1976.

Kraft, Charles M. *Christianity in Culture*. Maryknoll, N.Y.: Orbis Books, 1979.

———. *Communication Theory for Christian Witness*. Rev. ed. Maryknoll, N.Y.: Orbis Books, 1991.

———. *Anthropology for Christian Witness*. Maryknoll, N.Y.: Orbis Books, 1996.

Kretzmann, John P., and John McKnight. *Building Communities from the Inside Out: A Path Toward Finding and Mobilizing a Community's Assets*. Evanston, Ill.: Center for Urban Affairs and Policy Research, Northwestern University, 1993.

Kuyper, Abraham. *The Problem of Poverty*. Edited by James W. Skillen. Grand Rapids: Baker Book House, 1991.

———. *Lectures on Calvinism*. Grand Rapids: Eerdmans, 1994.

Larkin, William J. Jr. *Culture and Biblical Hermeneutics*. Grand Rapids: Baker Book House, 1988.

Laudin, Larry. *Progress and Its Problems: Towards a Theory of Scientific Growth*. Berkeley: University of California Press, 1977.

Lee, Ki-baik. *A New History of Korea*. Translated by Edward W. Wagner with Edward J. Schultz. Cambridge: Harvard University Press, 1984.

Leenhardt, Franz J. *The Epistle to the Romans: A Commentary*. London: Lutterworth, 1961.

Lerner, Michael. *The Politics of Meaning*. Menlo Park, Calif.: Addison-Wesley, 1996.

L'état du monde, 1999. Montreal: Boréal, 1999.

Levine, Amy-Jill. *The Social and Ethnic Dimensions of Matthean Social History*. Lewiston, N.Y.: Edwin Mellen Press, 1988.

Limpic, Ted. *Catálogo de organizaciones misioneras iberoamericanas*. Miami: Comibam, 1997.

Linthicum, Robert C. *City of God, City of Satan: A Biblical Theology of the Urban Church*. Grand Rapids: Zondervan, 1991.

Lohfink, Gerhard. *Jesus and Community: The Social Dimension of the Christian Faith*. Philadelphia: Fortress Press, 1984.

Lonergan, Bernard. *Method in Theology*. Toronto: University of Toronto Press, 1994.

Luther, Martin. *On the Councils and the Church (1539)*. In *Luther's Works*, vol. 41. Edited by Eric W. Gritsch. Philadelphia: Fortress Press, 1966.

Luzbetak, Louis. *The Church and Cultures: New Perspectives in Missiological Anthropology*. Maryknoll, N.Y.: Orbis Books, 1988.

Lynd, M. *On Shame and the Search for Identity.* New York: Harcourt Brace, 1958.

Lyon, David. "Post-modern Canada." *Ecumenism,* June 1997, 12–14.

Lyotard, J. F. *Le postmodernisme expliqué aux enfants.* Paris: Les Éditions Galilée, 1988.

MacKay, D. M. "Complementarity in Scientific and Theological Studies." *Zygon* 9 (1974): 225–44.

Magesa, Laurenti. *African Religion: The Moral Traditions of Abundant Life.* Maryknoll, N.Y.: Orbis Books, 1997.

Malina, B. "The Individual and the Community-Personality in the Social World of Early Christianity." *Biblical Theological Bulletin* 9 (1979): 126–38.

Marsden, George M. *Fundamentalism and American Culture: The Shaping of Twentieth-Century Evangelicalism: 1870–1925.* New York: Oxford University Press, 1980.

Martin, David. *Tongues of Fire: The Explosion of Protestantism in Latin America.* Cambridge: Basil Blackwell, 1990.

Mbiti, John S. *African Religions and Philosophies.* Nairobi: Oxford University Press, 1968.

———. *New Testament Eschatology in an African Background: A Study of the Encounter Between New Testament Theology and African Traditional Concepts.* London: Oxford University Press, 1971.

———. "The Biblical Basis for Present Trends in African Theology." In *African Theology en Route,* edited by Kofi Appiah-Kubi and Sergio Torres, 83–94. Maryknoll, N.Y.: Orbis Books, 1979.

———. "Flowers in the Garden: The Role of Women in African Religion." In *Religious Plurality in Africa: Essays in Honour of John S. Mbiti,* edited by Jacob Olupona, 59–72. Berlin: Mouton de Gruyter, 1993.

McFall, Ernest. *Approaching the Nuer of Africa Through the Old Testament.* South Pasadena, Calif.: William B. Carey Library, 1970.

McKnight, John. "Professionalized Service as Disabling Help." In *Disabling Professions,* edited by John McKnight, Ivan Illich, Jonathan Caplan, and Harley Sharken, 707–21. London: Marion Boyers, 1978.

———. *The Careless Society: Community and Its Counterfeits.* New York: Basic Books, 1995.

Meeks, Wayne. *The First Urban Christians: The Social World of the Apostle Paul.* New Haven: Yale University Press, 1983.

———. *The Moral World of the First Christians.* Philadelphia: Westminster Press, 1986.

Meier, John P. *Matthew.* New Testament Message. Dublin: Veritas, 1980.

Melchert, C. F. *Wise Teaching: Biblical Wisdom and Educational Ministry*. Harrisburg, Pa.: Trinity Press International, 1998.

Meyer, Ben. *Critical Realism and the New Testament*. Allison Park, Pa.: Pickwick Publications, 1989.

———. *Reality and Illusion in New Testament Scholarship: A Primer in Critical Realist Hermeneutics*. Collegeville, Minn.: Liturgical Press, 1994.

Miguez-Bonino, Jose. "Global Solidarity and the Theological Curriculum." In *Theological Education: Report of the U.S./Canadian Consultation Held at Trinity College, University of Toronto, Canada, 12–15 July, 1981*, ed. U.S./Canadian Consultation on Global Solidarity in Theological Education, 22–25. Geneva: Programme on Theological Education, WCC, 1981.

Mills, C. Wright. *The Sociological Imagination*. New York: Grove Press, 1959.

Min, Kyung-Bae. *The History of Christianity in Korea*. Seoul: Korean Christian Publishing House, 1992.

Minear, Paul. *The Obedience of Faith: The Purposes of Paul in the Epistle to the Romans*. London: SCM Press, 1971.

Mitchell, Rudy. *Studying Urban Communities*. Boston: Emmanuel Gospel Chapel, 1994.

Moltmann, Jürgen. *The Way of Jesus Christ: Christology in Messianic Dimensions*. Translated by Margaret Kohl. Minneapolis: Fortress Press, 1993.

Moody, J. *Rechristianization of Religion in Modern European History*. New York: Macmillan, 1964.

Morris, Leon. *The Epistle to the Romans*. Leicester: InterVarsity Press, 1988.

Mulago, Vincent. "Traditional African Religions and Christianity." In *African Traditional Religions in Contemporary Society*, edited by Jacob Olupona, 119–34. New York: Paragon House, 1991.

Myers, Bryant L. "Another Look at 'Holistic Mission.'" *Evangelical Missions Quarterly* 35 (July 1999): 285–87.

Ndeti, Kivuto. *Elements of Akamba Life*. Nairobi: East African Publishing House, 1972.

Nevius, John L. *The Planting and Development of Missionary Churches*. 4th ed. Philadelphia: Presbyterian and Reformed Publishing Co., 1958.

Newbigin, Lesslie. *Foolishness to the Greeks*. Grand Rapids: Eerdmans, 1986.

———. *The Gospel in a Pluralist Society*. Grand Rapids: Eerdmans, 1989.

Neyrey, Jerome. "Honor and Shame in the Johannine Passion Narrative." *Semeia* 68 (1996): 113–37.

Neyrey, Jerome, and B. Malina. *The Social World of Luke-Acts: Models for Interpretation*. Peabody: Hendrickson Publishers, 1991.

Nickle, Keith F. *The Collection: A Study in Paul's Strategy.* Studies in Biblical Theology. Naperville: Alec R. Allenson, 1966.

Nida, Eugene A. *Customs and Cultures.* 1954. Reprint, Pasadena, Calif.: Wm. Carey Library, 1975.

Niebuhr, Reinhold. *Love and Justice: Selections from the Shorter Writings of Reinhold Niebuhr.* Louisville: Westminster/John Knox Press, 1978.

Niebuhr, Richard. *Christ and Culture.* New York: Harper & Row, 1951.

Norwood, Fredrick. *Strangers and Exiles: A History of Religious Refugees.* Nashville: Abingdon Press, 1969.

Nüesch-Olver, Delia. "Immigrant Clergy in the Promised Land." *Missiology* 29 (April 2001): 185–200.

Ojo, Matthews. "Charismatic Movements in Africa." In *Christianity in Africa in the 1990s,* edited by Christopher Fyfe and A. Walls, 92–110. Edinburgh: University of Edinburgh Press, 1996.

Oleksa, Michael, ed. *Alaskan Missionary Spirituality.* New York: Paulist Press, 1987.

Olyan, Saul. "Honor, Shame and Covenant-Relations in Ancient Israel and Its Environment." *The Journal of Biblical Literature* 115 (1996): 201–18.

Ortiz, Manuel. "Who Are They Talking About?" *The Banner,* 28 August 2000: 27–28.

Packer, J. I. "What Is Evangelism?" In *Theological Perspectives on Church Growth,* edited by Harvie Conn, 91–105. Nutley, N.J.: Presbyterian and Reformed Publishing Company, 1977.

Park, Yong-Kyu. *The Great Revivalism in Korea: Its History, Character and Impact, 1901–1910* (in Korean). Seoul: Word of Life Books, 2000.

Pastor, Robert. "The Impact of U.S. Immigrant Policy on Caribbean Emigration: Does It Matter?" In *The Caribbean Exodus,* ed. Barry B. Levine, 242–59. New York: Praeger, 1987.

Pate, Larry. *From Every People.* Monrovia, Calif.: MARC, 1989.

Perkins, John. *A Quiet Revolution: The Christian Response to Human Need. A Strategy for Today.* Waco: Word, 1976.

Perkinson, Jim. "A Canaanitic Word in the Logos of Christ; or the Difference the Syro-Phoenician Woman Makes to Jesus." *Semeia* 75 (1996): 61–85.

Peters, John Durham. *Speaking into the Air: A History of the Idea of Communication.* Chicago: University of Chicago Press, 1999.

Peterson, Eugene. *Leap over a Wall: Earthly Spirituality for Everyday Christians.* San Francisco: Harper San Francisco, 1997.

Piers, Gerhart, and Milton Singer. *Shame and Guilt.* Springfield, Ill.: Charles C. Thomas Publishers, 1953.

Putnam, Robert D. "Bowling Alone: America's Declining Social Capital." *Journal of Democracy* 6 (January 1995): 65–76.

Ridderbos, Herman. *The Coming of the Kingdom*. Philadelphia: Presbyterian and Reformed Publishing Company, 1962.

Riesman, D. *The Lonely Crowd*. London: Oxford University Press, 1950.

Romain, Charles-Poissant. "La religion et le développement paysan en Haiti." *La nouvelle revue de monde noir* 1 (1986): 149–61.

Rooy, Sidney H. "Theological Education for Urban Mission." In *Discipling the City: Theological Reflections on Urban Mission*, edited by Roger S. Greenway, 175–207. Grand Rapids: Baker Book House, 1979.

Samuel, Vinay, and Chris Sugden, eds. *Mission as Transformation: A Theology of the Whole Gospel*. Oxford: Regnum, 1999.

Sawyerr, Harry. *Creative Evangelism: Towards a New Christian Encounter with Africa*. London: Lutterworth Press, 1968.

Schreiter, Robert J. *Constructing Local Theologies*. Maryknoll, N.Y.: Orbis Books, 1985.

————. *The New Catholicity: Theology Between the Global and the Local*. Maryknoll, N.Y.: Orbis Books, 1997.

Schuller, David. "Globalization in Theological Education: Summary and Analysis of Survey Data." *Theological Education* 22, no. 2 (spring 1986): 19–56.

Schultz, F. LeRon. "'Holding On' to the Theology-Psychology Relationship: The Underlying Fiduciary Structures of Interdisciplinary Method." *Journal of Psychology and Theology* 25 (1997): 329–40.

Scott, C., and J. Martin. "Matthew 15:21–28: A Test-Case for Jesus' Manners." *Journal for the Study of the New Testament* 63 (1996): 21–44.

Shaw, R. Daniel. "Contextualizing the Power and the Glory." *International Journal of Frontier Missions* 12 (1995): 155–60.

Shenk, Wilbert R. "The Whole Is Greater Than the Sum of the Parts: Moving Beyond Word and Deed." *Missiology* 20 (January 1993): 65–75.

Sider, Ronald J. *Just Generosity*. Grand Rapids: Baker Book House, 2000.

Sloan, Robert B. Jr. *The Favorable Year of the Lord: A Study of Jubilary Theology in the Gospel of Luke*. Austin: Schola Press, 1978.

Smith, Christian. *American Evangelicalism: Embattled and Thriving*. Chicago: University of Chicago Press, 1998.

Smith, Glenn. "Reaching Canada's Cities for Christ." *Urban Mission* 8, no. 1 (September 1990): 27–36.

————. "How Unique Is Québec's Religious Climate Anyway?" Montreal: Christian Direction, 1997.

Smith, Jonathan Z., ed. *HarperCollins Dictionary of Religion*. San Francisco: HarperCollins, 1996.

Snyder, Howard A. *Signs of the Spirit*. Grand Rapids: Zondervan, 1989.

Stackhouse, Max. *Apologia: Contextualization, Globalization, and Mission in Theological Education*. Grand Rapids: Eerdmans, 1988.

Stark, Rodney. *Conversion to Christianity*. New York: Harper, 1994.

Stendahl, Krister. "The Apostle Paul and the Introspective Conscience of the West." *Harvard Theological Review* 56 (1963): 199–215.

Stock, Augustine. *The Method and Message of Matthew*. Collegeville, Minn.: Liturgical Press, 1994.

Stoll, David. *Is Latin America Turning Protestant?* Berkeley: University of California Press, 1990.

Stott, John, ed. *Making Christ Known: Historic Mission Documents from the Lausanne Movement, 1974–1989*. Grand Rapids: Eerdmans, 1996.

Stott, John R. W., and Robert T. Coote. *Down to Earth: Studies in Christianity and Culture*. Grand Rapids: Eerdmans, 1980.

Stotts, Jack L. *Shalom: The Search for a Peaceable City*. Nashville: Abingdon Press, 1972.

Stranke, Marilyn. *Christians Supporting Community Organizing: A New Voice for Change Among Evangelical, Holiness and Pentecostal Christians*. Los Angeles: Center for Religion and Civic Culture, University of Southern California, 1999.

Stringfellow, William. "Traits of the Principalities." In *A Keeper of the Word: Selected Writings of William Stringfellow,* edited by Bill Wylie Kellerman, 209–13. Grand Rapids: Eerdmans, 1994.

Strom, Mark. *Reframing Paul: Conversations in Grace and Community*. Downers Grove, Ill.: InterVarsity Press, 2000.

Taylor, Charles. *Multiculturalism and the Politics of Recognition*. Princeton: Princeton University Press, 1992.

Taylor, John V. *The Primal Vision: Christian Presence amid African Religion*. London: SCM, 1963.

Thiessen, Elmer J. "Curriculum after Babel." In *Agenda for Education Change,* edited by John Short and Trevor Cooling, 220–45. Leicester: Apollos, 1997.

Theissen, Gerd. *The Social Setting of Pauline Christianity: Essays on Corinth*. Philadelphia: Fortress Press, 1982.

Thomas, Norman. "Globalization and the Teaching of Mission." *Missiology* 18 (January 1990): 12–23.

Tiénou, Tite. "Contextualization of Theology for Theological Education." In *Evangelical Theological Education Today: Agenda for Renewal,* edited by Paul Bowers, 42–52. Nairobi: Evangel Publishing House, 1982.

———. *The Theological Task of the Church in Africa.* 2nd rev. ed. Achimota, Ghana: African Christian Press, 1990.

Tillich, Paul. *Love, Power, and Justice.* New York: Oxford University Press, 1954.

Tippett, Alan R. *Introduction to Missiology.* Pasadena, Calif.: Wm. Carey Library, 1987.

Tizon, Albert. "Understanding Deeds as Proclamation in the Missional Task of the Church: A Luke-Acts Guide." *Phronésis* 7, no. 1 (2000): 35–51.

Trapp, Shel. In *Disclosure: The National Newspaper of Neighborhoods.* January 2000.

Turner, James. "Secular Justification of Christian Truth Claims: A Historical Sketch." In *American Apostasy: The Triumph of Another Gospel,* edited by R. J. Neuhaus, 15–28. Grand Rapids: Eerdmans, 1989.

Vos, Geerhardus. *Biblical Theology.* Grand Rapids: Eerdmans, 1948.

Wagner, C. Peter, and Pablo Deiros. *The Rising Revival: What the Spirit Is Saying Through the Argentine Revival.* Ventura, Calif.: Gospel Light, 1998.

Wainwright, Elaine Mary. *Towards a Feminist Critical Reading of the Gospel According to Matthew.* New York: Walter de Gruyter, 1991.

Wainwright, Geoffrey. *Doxology: The Praise of God in Worship, Doctrine and Life: A Systematic Theology.* New York: Oxford University Press, 1980.

Wallis, Jim. *The Soul of Politics.* Maryknoll, N.Y.: Orbis Books, 1993.

Walls, Andrew F. *The Missionary Movement in Christian History: Studies in the Transmission of Faith.* Maryknoll, N.Y.: Orbis Books, 1996.

Warfield, B. B. *The Right of Systematic Theology.* Edinburgh: T. and T. Clark, 1897.

Warner, R. Steven. "Work in Progress Toward a New Paradigm for the Sociological Study of Religion in the United States." *American Journal of Sociology* 98 (1993): 1044–93.

Webber, George W. *Today's Church: A Community of Exiles and Pilgrims.* Nashville: Abingdon Press, 1979.

Welbourn, Fred. *East African Christian.* London: Oxford University Press, 1965.

———. "Guilt and Shame." In *Christianity in Tropical Africa,* edited by Christian Beata, 182–96. London: Oxford University Press, 1968.

Wenk, Matthias. *Community-Forming Power: The Socio-Ethical Role of the Spirit in Luke-Acts.* Sheffield: Sheffield Academic Press, 2000.

Whiteman, Darrell L. "Contextualization, the Theory, the Gap, the Challenge." *Missiology* 25 (1997): 3–4.

Whiting, B. B., ed. *Six Cultures: Studies of Child Rearing.* London: John Wiley, 1963.

Williams, James G. *Those Who Ponder Proverbs.* Sheffield: Almond Press, 1981.

Wilson, William Julius. *When Work Disappears: The World of the New Urban Poor.* New York: Knopf, 1996.

Wink, Walter. *Naming the Powers: The Language of Power in the New Testament.* Philadelphia: Fortress Press, 1984.

Winter, Bruce W. *Seek the Welfare of the City: Christians as Benefactors and Citizens.* Grand Rapids: Eerdmans, 1994.

Witherington, Ben. *Jesus the Sage: The Pilgrimage of Wisdom.* Minneapolis: Fortress Press, 1994.

Witkower, Ann. "Latinos Bring New Flair to European Missions." *Christian Mission: A Journal of Foreign Missions,* summer 2001, 6–7.

Woodberry, Robert D., and Christian S. Smith. "Fundamentalism et al.: Conservative Protestants in America." *Annual Review of Sociology* 24 (1998): 25–56.

World Bank. *Haïti: Les défis de la lutte contre la pauvreté.* Washington: World Bank, 1998.

Wright, N. T. *The New Testament and the People of God.* Minneapolis: Fortress Press, 1991.

———. *Jesus and the Victory of God.* Minneapolis: Fortress Press, 1996.

Wuthnow, Robert, James Hunter, Albert Bergesen, and Edith Kurzweil. *Cultural Analysis in the Work of Peter L. Berger, Mary Douglass, Michel Foucault and Jürgen Habermas.* Boston: Routledge and Kegan Paul, 1984.

Yi, Man-Yuol. *Christian Nationalistic Movement in the Late Yi-Dynasty* (in Korean). Seoul: Pyong Min Sah, 1981.

Yi, Sang-Kyu. "Reformed Theology in Korea." In *Collected Essays on Historical Theology* (in Korean), edited by Kyung-Lim Kang and Sang-Oon Jung, 387–424. Seoul: Yi-Rhe Suh-Won, 1999.

Yoder, John Howard. *The Politics of Jesus.* Grand Rapids: Eerdmans, 1972.

———. *The Politics of Jesus: Vicit Agnus Noster.* 2d ed. Grand Rapids: Eerdmans, 1994.

Young, Mark. "Theological Approaches to Some Perpetual Problems in Theological Education." *Christian Education Journal,* n.s., 2, no. 1 (spring 1998): 75–87.

LIST OF CONTRIBUTORS

Susan S. Baker is assistant coordinator and adjunct professor of practical theology at Westminster Theological Seminary. She has served in cross-cultural inner-city ministries for more than thirty-seven years involving youth ministry, church planting, Christian schools, and indigenous leadership development. Baker has also written curriculum for the Center for Urban Theological Studies and has authored *Understanding Mainland Puerto Rican Poverty*.

Raymond J. Bakke is executive director of International Urban Associates and chancellor of Northwest Graduate School for the Ministry. For twenty years he pastored inner-city churches in Seattle and Chicago. Bakke co-founded the Seminary Consortium for Urban Pastoral Education and was professor of ministry at Northern Baptist Theological Seminary. He has been a resource leader for urban ministry consultations in more than two hundred large cities on six continents. Bakke's published works include *The Urban Christian, A Theology as Big as the City*, and *A Biblical Word for an Urban World*.

William S. Barker has taught church history for three decades, first at Covenant Theological Seminary, where he was president, and then at Westminster Theological Seminary, where he was vice president for academic affairs and professor of church history. He is author of *Puritan Profiles*, concerning influential contemporaries of the Westminster Assembly.

Harvie M. Conn (1933–1999) was professor of missions at Westminster Theological Seminary, Philadelphia, and director of its Urban Missions Program. Before that he served as a missionary in Korea for twelve years. His extensive writing and speaking reflected a life-long dedication to serving the needs of indigent people.

William A. Dyrness served for eight years as a missionary in the Philippines. He was dean of Fuller Seminary's School of Theology for ten years where he is now professor of theology and culture. He is author of several books, including *Changing the Mind of Missions: Where Have We Gone Wrong?* and *The Earth Is God's: A Theology of American Culture.*

Samuel Escobar is professor of missiology at Eastern Baptist Theological Seminary and a theological education consultant in Spain, under the International Ministries of American Baptist Churches. He is a founder and former president of the Latin American Theological Fraternity. Escobar has published extensively in Spanish and English.

Mark R. Gornik is the director of City Seminary of New York. Previously he was the founding pastor of New Song Community Church in Baltimore. He has written many essays and articles on urban ministry and community development and has authored *To Live in Peace: Biblical Faith and the Changing Inner City.*

Edna C. Greenway is professor emerita of Spanish at Calvin College. She is advisor for foreign language education, bilingual education, and English as a second language. Greenway has taught education classes in Korea, the Philippines, and Macao, as well as at Westminster Theological Seminary and Calvin Theological Seminary.

Roger S. Greenway is professor emeritus of world missiology at Calvin Theological Seminary. He served twenty years with Christian Reformed World Missions in Sri Lanka and Latin America. Greenway also was executive director of Christian Reformed World Ministries for four years. He is author or editor of more than a dozen books.

Paul G. Hiebert is associate dean of academic doctoral programs and professor of mission and anthropology at Trinity Evangelical Divinity School. He is also chairman of the mission and evangelism department. Hiebert was a missionary to India for six years, and has taught anthropology and missions at Fuller Theological Seminary. He has published several books and articles in those fields.

Charles H. Kraft has been on the faculty of the School of World Mission, Fuller Theological Seminary, for more than thirty years. He was a pioneer missionary to the Kamwe people of northern Nigeria and taught linguistics and African languages at UCLA and Michigan State University before coming to Fuller. Kraft has written more than twenty books and numerous articles on such topics as contextualization, anthropology, spiritual warfare, and African languages.

John S. Leonard is assistant professor of practical theology at Westminster Theological Seminary. He served ten years in France as a missionary with Mission to the World and Arab World Ministries. Leonard has written *Beyond Brazil: An Introduction to Missions* and *Great Faith.*

Samuel T. Logan Jr. is president of Westminster Theological Seminary, where he is also professor of church history. In connection with the Institute on the Religious Roots of America, which he founded, he leads study tours of Israel, France, and the British Isles. Logan has written numerous articles, and edited *The Preacher and Preaching.*

Andrew M. Mbuvi, born in Kenya, is a faculty member of Daystar University, a Christian liberal arts college in Nairobi. He was involved in urban youth ministry in Nairobi for eight years. He also serves as adjunct faculty in the Geneva College program at the Center for Urban Theological Studies in Philadelphia and is a Ph.D. candidate at Westminster Theological Seminary.

Manuel Ortiz, professor of ministry and mission and coordinator of the practical theology department at Westminster Theological Seminary, directs the seminary's urban program. His efforts have led to five church plants with indigenous Hispanic pastors, two elementary schools, and an extension school for theological education. Ortiz has written *The Hispanic Challenge* and *One New People,* and has co-authored *Urban Ministry* with Harvie M. Conn.

Sung-Il Steve Park is adjunct professor of apologetics and practical theology at Westminster Theological Seminary. With a keen interest in the development of Christianity in his homeland, he lectures at the seminary in the history and theology of the Korean church. He has been involved in various aspects of Korean-American ministries for the past sixteen years. Currently he is pasturing a bilingual church in Conshohocken, Pennsylvania. He has also been involved in numerous short-term mission projects in Asia and Central America.

Glenn B. Smith is executive director of Christian Direction, a ministry to cities of the francophone world. He is professor of urban theology and missiology at faculties in Canada and Haiti. Smith has co-authored a number of books on urban ministries and written numerous articles.

Clinton E. Stockwell is executive director of the Chicago Semester, an urban internship program sponsored by six Christian liberal arts schools of the Reformed tradition. He has written a number of articles, including "Abraham Kuyper and Welfare Reform: A Reformed Political Perspective" and "Standing on the Shoulders of Giants: The Protestant Legacy of Urban Social Justice in Chicago."

Tite Tiénou is academic dean and professor of theology of mission at Trinity Evangelical Divinity School. He has served as president and dean of the Faculté de Théologie Evangélique de l'Alliance Chretienne in Abidjan, Ivory Coast. He has written numerous books and articles, including *The Theological Task of the Church in Africa.*

INDEX OF SUBJECTS AND NAMES

INDEX OF SCRIPTURE